MW00476524

ghschol.com

Exploring Research
in **Music Education**
and **Music Therapy**

Exploring Research
in Music Education
and Music Therapy

Kenneth H. Phillips

Gordon College
The University of Iowa

New York   Oxford
OXFORD UNIVERSITY PRESS
2008

Oxford University Press, Inc., publishes works that further Oxford University's
objective of excellence in research, scholarship, and education.

Oxford New York
Auckland Cape Town Dar es Salaam Hong Kong Karachi
Kuala Lumpur Madrid Melbourne Mexico City Nairobi
New Delhi Shanghai Taipei Toronto

With offices in
Argentina Austria Brazil Chile Czech Republic France Greece
Guatemala Hungary Italy Japan Poland Portugal Singapore
South Korea Switzerland Thailand Turkey Ukraine Vietnam

Copyright © 2008 by Oxford University Press, Inc.

Published by Oxford University Press, Inc.
198 Madison Avenue, New York, New York 10016
http://www.oup.com

Oxford is a registered trademark of Oxford University Press

All rights reserved. No part of this publication may be reproduced,
stored in a retrieval system, or transmitted, in any form or by any means,
electronic, mechanical, photocopying, recording, or otherwise,
without the prior permission of Oxford University Press.

Library of Congress Cataloging-in-Publication Data

Phillips, Kenneth H. (Kenneth Harold)
  Exploring research in music education and music therapy / Kenneth H. Phillips.
    p. cm.
  Includes bibliographical references (p.) and index.
  ISBN 978-0-19-532122-7 (pbk.)—ISBN 978-0-19-533830-0 (hardcover) 1. Music—Instruction
and study—Research. 2. Music therapy—Research. I. Title.
  MT1.P5116 2008
  780.72—dc22   2007017266

9 8 7 6 5 4 3 2 1

Printed in the United States of America
on acid-free paper

To the students of the first graduating class in the master of
music education degree program at Gordon College

The Class of 2006

Jennifer Bowler

Carolyn Bray

Jennifer Garcia

Dale Jovin

Joshua Nannestad

Andrew Norton

Amanda Roeder

Jonathan Rosenthal

Alexa Vogelzang

These dedicated educators well represent the profession of
music education—teachers who serve students
through the power and beauty of music.

Contents

Preface

This text is written for students in music education degree programs and for those studying to be music therapists. It also may appeal to others who desire an introduction to the world of research in music.

Unlike traditional introductory research textbooks, this one does not attempt to teach students how to *do* research. Instead, it aims to help students *explore* research by deepening their understanding of and interest in professional journal articles. The focus of this text is to develop students' familiarity with research and technical terms and to show how findings can be applied to their own teaching and therapeutic situations.

ORGANIZATION

The contents are organized into five units of study: Research Basics, Historical and Philosophical Research, Qualitative Research, Quantitative Research, and Research and the Classroom. Each of these units comprises chapters that include full research articles that relate directly to music education or music therapy. Commentaries accompany a number of these articles to help guide students in comprehending the information presented. As students gain a greater understanding of how to read research and make sense of it, commentaries are omitted. The articles without commentaries are particularly useful for sparking class discussions.

Each chapter includes a section of Study and Discussion Questions. These can be used for directed reading and guided discussions. In addition, the Suggested Activities at the conclusion of each chapter will lead to thought-provoking experiences that help students engage more fully with the chapter contents.

KEY FEATURES

The text serves as a bridge between knowledge and real-life applications. It engages students in exploring synthesized research findings that can be applied in classrooms or therapeutic settings, and in so doing it gives students the tools to address challenges in their professions effectively.

A basic knowledge of statistics is necessary for understanding quantitative research. Students often approach the subject of statistics with dread, and indeed it is a difficult field of study. Rather than asking students to do statistical analyses before they have a grasp of what such analyses mean, this text teaches them to understand symbols and terms used throughout the literature in quantitative research.

The appendixes provide content from the two major handbooks in music teaching and learning research as well as a list of research journals in music education, music therapy, and the psychology of music. This list offers many avenues of exploration, including journals that are accessible online.

Exploring Research in Music Education and Music Therapy is for all students who may never be researchers (and also for those who may be) but who need to know and understand the literature. A strong foundation in reading research will advance the fields of music education and music therapy by turning knowledge into practice.

ACKNOWLEDGMENTS

I express gratitude to the following publishers for copyright permission to reprint articles and other materials cited in this text: Allyn & Bacon, American Music Therapy Association (*Journal of Music Therapy*), Council for Research in Music Education (*Bulletin of the Council for Research in Music Education*), Indiana University Press (*Philosophy of Music Education Review*), International Association for Research in Singing (*Journal of Research in Singing and Applied Vocal Pedagogy*), Lippincott Williams & Wilkins (*The Hearing Journal*), MENC: The National Association for Music Education (*Journal of Research in Music Education*, and *UPDATE: Applications of Research in Music Education*), the National Education Association (*NEA Today*), the Ohio Music Education Association (*Contributions to Music Education*), and Sage Publications, Inc.

I also express gratitude to those who provided reviews of the manuscript: Nancy Barry, University of Oklahoma; Jeff Bush, Arizona State University; Colleen Conway, University of Michigan; Bruce Gleason, University of St. Thomas; Diana Hollinger, San Jose State University; John Scheib, Ball State University; Robin Stein, Texas State University–San Marcos; and Peter Webster, Northwestern University.

Finally, I wish to thank the summer 2006 ("young and foolish") class in the master of music education program at Gordon College. These students helped pilot and proof this text and provided valuable feedback: Jennifer Brewer, Erin Cherry, Jim Donovan, Jonathan Eldridge, Jennifer Moros, Leeanne Porta, Cheryl Samiagio, Brian Spignese, Shannon Sullivan, and Lindsey Vaughan.

PART ONE

Research Basics

CHAPTER 1

Research in Music Education and Music Therapy

Welcome to the world of research. If you are like most music educators or music therapists, this is a rather unfamiliar area of study. Research may conjure up for you a certain amount of distrust, brought on by the popular media. This is unfortunate, for research in music can be very meaningful; it has advanced and continues to advance our understanding of music teaching and how music can be used to help others.

Why do music personnel not read or make use of research in general? The most obvious reason is lack of time. However, the inability to understand the many facets of a research article deters many readers. This book is an attempt to help you to understand how research can enhance music teaching and practice and how learning to read research will help you to differentiate between valid studies and those of questionable value. Reading research with understanding involves comprehending the jargon and knowing how to navigate through a research study. The application of research findings to the classroom or therapy setting is the ultimate goal of this text.

Before proceeding to the value of research, we must answer the question "What is research?" Heller and O'Connor (2006) relate the word *research* to the French, *rechercher*, implying a search for something. "Good research is that which provides as unbiased an answer as possible to a question supported by empirical evidence. 'Empirical' here is meant to be viewed as 'observations' " (p. 38). Research, therefore, can be defined as the search for solutions to problems via a systematic process of data collection. Heller and O'Connor note that research is not a panacea for the many problems faced in music education or therapy, but, rather, "one more human activity that strives to answer perplexing, interesting problems" (p. 42).

THE VALUE OF RESEARCH

Much of what is taught in schools has no research base. That is why materials and methods come and go so quickly. Someone has an idea for improving music reading, and before you know it another publication appears that has no research base. We buy

3

these publications hoping to help people become musically literate, only to find that many instructional approaches do not work.

One reason for using research is to learn to look for materials that have some research backing. Knowing whether or not materials have been investigated for effectiveness should be basic knowledge. The entire educational enterprise adopts textbook series that have not been studied for their effectiveness with learners. We are primed to fail. Choosing materials should begin with the question "Is there any research to support any of this?"

Another reason for exploring research is to understand how people learn music. Are there implications from research findings that will help us to learn more efficiently? Yes, there are. For example, students sing more accurately when asked to sing with patterns than with individual notes (Gordon, 1989), and students with disabilities have been shown to excel when mainstreamed (Lind, 2001). Also, primary school children are apt to sing more accurately alone than in a group (Goetze, 1986). Research in music learning has revealed important knowledge, and much remains to be discovered.

Learning what students and adults are thinking or know is a third reason to read research. Often we teach without considering whether successful learning is taking place. Research can help us understand whether we are succeeding and what differences exist in different learning environments. We know that students' attitudes toward singing often decline as they grow older (Phillips & Aitchison, 1999). If research could help find the answer to this problem, scores of general music teachers would be grateful.

Who are the important names in the history of music therapy and music education, and what contributions did they make? Historical research helps to answer these questions and provides the music educator and the music therapist with connections to their "roots," which may help to shed light on the future. Likewise, philosophical inquiry helps teachers to understand the *why* of what they do. Both history and philosophy contain important research that enlightens and directs the paths of today's music teachers and music therapists.

Music teacher preparation is another area in which music research has had an impact. How can college/university programs, along with school cooperating teachers, do a better job of helping the novitiate become a successful teacher? One study (Schleuter, 1991) found the cooperating teacher was integrating curricular goals so completely into the lesson that the student teacher could not identify the goals through observation alone. Cooperating teachers are urged by Schleuter to make goals explicit to student teachers apart from the instructional plan.

Music cognition is an important link to how people process music, and it helps us understand how the human brain organizes musical sounds into meaningful concepts. Edwin Gordon has been a leader in helping us understand how pattern sequencing enhances the area of music literacy instruction (Gordon, 1989).

Research into how the deaf respond to music when provided with cochlear implants (Turner, Gantz, Lowder, & Gfeller, 2005) is a fascinating topic, as is the relationship of music to health. Does deep breathing through singing help a person to be healthier? Who knows? There is no known research in this area, but claims do exist.

Social and cultural fields also have important research bases. These include areas such as community music, gender roles, the individual's role in a music setting, cultural reactions, and so forth. Understanding why different peoples have different values for music helps us to understand the social and cultural contexts of the workplace.

These reasons and others demonstrate that research is of value and is a useful tool for the music educator and the music therapist. The difficulty comes in (1) finding the research and (2) learning to read it with comprehension. Therefore, this introduction continues by looking at the various types of publications available for locating research studies in music education and music therapy.

RESEARCH PUBLICATIONS

Research in music education and music therapy are two rather young fields. The premiere research journal in music education, *The Journal of Research in Music Education,* is only a little over 50 years old. Its inception was in 1953, and for many years most articles in it were simple and unsophisticated. Therefore the knowledge base in music inquiry, while growing fast, contains many unanswered questions. However, the age of technology has helped spur on all research, and the same can be said for music. Research today is sophisticated and employs all manner of technology in designs and analyses.

Where do you find this research? Mainly in four places: (1) research handbooks, (2) research journals in hard copy, (3) online journals, and (4) dissertations and masters theses. We look first at two important handbooks.

Handbooks

MENC is responsible for producing two large handbooks that serve as primary sources for locating research in music: *Handbook of Research on Music Teaching and Learning* (1992) and *The New Handbook of Research on Music Teaching and Learning* (2002). Taken together, these two volumes are the best places to start when exploring the research base in music education and therapy. The handbook chapters, for the most part, present not individual research articles, but summaries or reviews of the literature. The reference sections are valuable places to find research studies.

Anyone attempting to begin a research project should make use of the handbooks for identifying what has been studied in the professions and what future directions are recommended. Prior to 1992 this valuable resource was unavailable. Now there are two such resources for exploring the scope of research on music teaching and learning.

Appendix A lists the contents of the first *Handbook of Research on Music Teaching and Learning* (Colwell, 1992), and Appendix B lists the contents of *The New Handbook of Research on Music Teaching and Learning* (Colwell & Richardson, 2002). Looking over the scope of these works you will see the breadth of research that has been accomplished in music education and music therapy.

The original *Handbook* contains 832 pages, while the *New Handbook* is 1222 pages long. There is very little duplication of research between the first volume and the second; the two stand independently and together present the fullest vision of research in music teaching and learning at the end of the twentieth century. Grateful recognition goes to the editors, Richard Colwell and Carol Richardson, for undertaking the huge and time-consuming task of preparing *The New Handbook*, and to Richard Colwell, for his vision as editor of the original *Handbook* (1992).

Research Journals in Hard Copy

Another place to look for research studies is in actual journals. Appendix C provides an exhaustive annotated listing of those journals in the field of music education and therapy. Some are published only once a year, while others appear two to six times annually. Represented are the major journals in music education, music therapy, and the psychology of music. The following are the premiere journals in each of these areas:

- *Journal of Research in Music Education*
- *Journal of Music Therapy*
- *Psychology of Music*

If a journal is refereed, or peer reviewed, it means that persons on the editorial board read, review, and approve or reject all articles submitted for publication. A refereed journal has far greater status than one not refereed. Journals lacking peer review as a requirement for publication are typically not publishing research.

Online Sources

The Internet has made it possible to communicate via electronic transmission. Search engines, such as Google Scholar, abound. The following are a few of the growing number of journals that may be found online:

- *Journal of Research in Music Education* (JRME)
- *UPDATE: Applications of Research in Music Education* (UPDATE)
- *Journal of Music Teacher Education* (JMTE)
- *Research Studies in Music Education* (RSME)

Additional information for online journals is available in Appendix C.

Professor Edward Asmus has produced a search engine for all music education journals through the University of Miami (http://www.music.miami.edu/mess/). Additional search materials can be located in the appendix content.

Dissertations and Theses

Doctoral dissertations are a major source of research in music education. Reading a dissertation is time consuming and can be quite challenging. Some dissertations appear later as articles in research journals, and they are easier to manage if only because the content is summarized and reduced in length. Someone doing a research project, however, should go to the primary source: the dissertation itself.

The main place where doctoral dissertations are abstracted is in the *Dissertation Abstracts International* (DAI), which is available online. A researcher can do a "topic search" and find those dissertations that are relevant to his or her subject area. A short abstract is included with each citation and usually provides enough information to determine whether or not the study is of interest. Dissertations can be ordered through

ProQuest Information and Learning (300 N. Zeeb Road, Ann Arbor, MI 48106), but the online version is overwhelmingly the popular choice for researchers and libraries. Beginning with Volume 30, the title of *Dissertation Abstracts* became *Dissertation Abstracts International*.

Masters theses are not so readily available as doctoral dissertations. Most colleges and universities do not require that theses be registered with a clearinghouse. Those that are registered can be found in the *Masters Abstracts International*. Prior to Volume 24, the title was *Masters Abstracts*.

The use of computer technology has made the job of locating research journals much easier. Finding good research, however, is not so easy. This requires the knowledge to make good, critical judgments. We move forward to this task.

RESEARCH GENRES

The following is a brief outline of genres, or classes, of research used for music education and music therapy. A general description of each is included in the next section of this chapter. By far the greater amount of research is found in the behavioral research genre.

I. Historical research—in search of the "elusive truth" about the past.

II. Philosophical research—in search of concepts or truths.

III. Behavioral/empirical research—in search of how people think and act.

    A. Quantitative—employs the scientific method of controlled experimentation for studying subjects; uses empirical data in quantifiable forms.

    1. Nonexperimental—no cause–effect relationships.
      a. Descriptive—describes *what is*.
      b. Correlational—describes relationships.

    2. Experimental—cause–effect relationships.
      a. True-experimental—implies cause–effect and randomization of subjects.
      b. Quasi-experimental—implies cause–effect; no randomization of subjects.
      c. Causal-comparative—*post hoc* study determining "cause" after the fact.
      d. Meta-analysis—analyzes results by combining numerous, similar studies.

    B. Qualitative—seeks "truth" as found in natural settings; uses narrative data collected in the form of observations.

    1. Narrative—studies peoples' lives through their stories.
    2. Phenomenology—studies the *essence* of human experience.
    3. Ethnography—studies intact cultural groups in natural settings.
    4. Grounded theory—studies theories grounded in views of participants.
    5. Case study—studies a single event, activity, or process over an extended time.
    6. Action—studies events without the constraint of formal research design.

    C. Mixed methods—employs both quantitative and qualitative modes.

    1. Sequential—quantitative and qualitative data collected in sequential order.
    2. Concurrent—both forms of data collected at the same time and integrated.
    3. Transformative—uses a lens technique as a framework for topics of interest.

UNDERSTANDING RESEARCH GENRES

The preceding genres of research need to be identified from the outset when learning to read research articles. Understanding the basic logic of each genre helps to guide the understanding of what research in each classification attempts to do and the problems it seeks to answer. For example, results of true-experimental research can be generalized to a population because of stringent controls used when selecting a representative group of subjects. However, caution must be used when generalizing from quasi-experimental research. Knowing this takes a certain degree of sophistication.

Historical Research

Historical research investigates the *elusive truth about the past*. It is elusive because we never can be quite sure that we have the whole *truth* on any issue; new and better sources continue to emerge. Only in recent years has it become known that Beethoven most likely died of lead poisoning received from his wine cup (Martin, 2000), which was made of lead. This was discovered through advanced testing techniques used on a lock of Beethoven's hair. The story makes for a great read (see the References section at the end of this book).

There is no great amount of historical research in music education or therapy. Nevertheless there is a journal in the field, *The Journal of Historical Research in Music Education* (Ithaca College), and historical articles appear occasionally in the *Journal of Research in Music Education*.

The process of historical research is not the same as might be done when writing a history report on a composer. In the latter case, you report basically what others have said and do not attempt to develop insights or themes. Real historical research is like other types of research, in that it attempts to identify a problem, formulate hypotheses, identify a method, collect data (with emphasis on primary sources), present the findings, interpret the findings in relation to the hypotheses, and present conclusions. A report using secondary sources is what most students do when assigned a *research* report. Real historical research involves using primary sources to investigate, discover, redefine, and give a new understanding to something old.

Study of the past can help us to understand the present and can help to predict the future. Historical research is the primary means by which we capture posterity, and it can help to fill in the gaps of our knowledge of past events and personages. Articles are rather easy to read, being free of most research jargon.

Michael Mark, a historical researcher, gives this insightful conclusion to an article on the nonmusical outcomes of music education.

> Beyond the benefits of good citizenship, it is likely that music will continue to be justified on the basis of nonmusical outcomes, just as it has been throughout Western history. The tension between aesthetic and nonmusical outcomes is healthy for the profession because it stimulates music educators to think deeply about their profession and it strengthens the bond between the music education profession and the social and physical sciences that continually explore and analyze the effects of music on humans. As science develops, new thinking on the subject is bound to evolve. As yet it has had little effect on the teaching of music; in the future, however, it is quite possible that

curricular developments will be based on the research of nonmusicians whose efforts illuminate the effects of music on humans. (Mark, 2002, p. 1051)

As someone who has championed the place of nonmusical outcomes in defending music education, I find it heartening to read of historical evidence supporting this position "throughout Western history." Nevertheless, I would never want to abandon our commitment to aesthetic outcomes. Philosophically, a balance between the intrinsic and the extrinsic is necessary (Phillips, 1993).

Philosophical Research

The study of philosophy in music education is one of the least developed areas of inquiry. Only of late has a research journal in this area emerged: *Philosophy of Music Education Review* (Indiana University Press). Perhaps the notion that philosophy is too esoteric has driven most researchers to shy away from the topic. Whatever the reason, the study of philosophy is important in helping to define why we do what we do.

The researcher in philosophical inquiry works to establish concepts or *truths* that are then used to form or modify beliefs, attitudes, and principles. "As a discipline, philosophy is concerned with the study of human knowledge; as an activity, philosophy stands for methods of logically correct reasoning" (Rainbow & Froehlich, 1987, p. 129).

Philosophical investigation tends to be viewed as a more nonstructured type of research. It is not. The researcher is just as interested as any other investigator in identifying a problem, formulating hypotheses, denoting a method, collecting data (most likely some type of written documentation), and presenting fundamental philosophical ideas, conclusions, implications, and recommendations. It is expected that the original outline of inquiry may be modified as the reasoning process continues.

Philosophical researcher Estelle Jorgensen (2002) links the study of philosophy to the school curriculum and discusses the very practical way in which philosophers can think about very practical issues:

> Curriculum is grounded on philosophical assumptions about the purposes and methods of education. As such, it relates fundamentally to educational values and is justified philosophically rather than verified or refuted scientifically (Scheffler, 1973). Many music curricula focus on instructional approaches and frameworks that are often presented with little justification, or justified on experiential and practical rather than systematic and logical grounds. (p. 49)

Jorgensen continues by stating that a broader and more inclusive school curriculum can create even more problems for music educators. "Rather than solving the problem of what values are to underlie it and how these are to be negotiated, a broader curriculum makes the work of music education even more difficult to justify and practice" (Jorgensen, 2002, p. 49). This is a philosophical statement sure to rankle many, and one worthy of philosophical inquiry. That is what good philosophical research does—it challenges us to think outside of ourselves in ways not previously considered. In doing so we may be led to discover new concepts or "truths" to guide future thinking.

Philosophical and historical research studies do not abound in music education. They are areas worthy of pursuit, and more music educators would do well to consider doing research in these fields.

Behavioral/Empirical Research

Research in music education and music therapy is largely behavioral in nature. Studies address how people think about music, how they perform under certain conditions, how they react at various ages, and so forth. In other words, this research investigates *behaviors* and the impact on music learning. Teachers and therapists want to know the best instructional approaches, the best materials to use, the best modes of instruction, the best ways to motivate persons, and the best assessment techniques. These and many more questions and answers are found in the realms of behavioral research.

The term *empirical inquiry* often is connected with behavioral research. Simply put, a researcher who collects empirical *observations* of human behavior and represents them in some form, numeric or descriptive (data), is involved in empirical research. For many years, only quantitative research was considered rigorous enough to be used in behavioral investigation. Today, qualitative inquiry also is accepted and valued.

Quantitative Research: Nonexperimental

The majority of behavioral research is quantitative; i.e., it involves the collection of data that are numeric in nature (scores on tests, ages, ranks, seconds, decibels, etc.). Anything that can be measured, quantified, or counted probably falls within the category of quantitative research. Quantitative study reflects a *positivist* approach; i.e., judgments are based on logic and reason rather than on intuition. The two most common forms of quantitative nonexperimental research are descriptive and correlational.

Descriptive Research A descriptive study is one that describes "what is" rather than what might or could be under certain conditions. It does not indicate cause and effect. Rather, it presents a current *picture* of a certain group or action. For example, studies have found that girls tend to be more accurate singers than boys in the elementary grades. This finding does not tell us why, only that more girls than boys sing accurately.

Another purpose of descriptive research is to determine needs, trends, or changes. State music educators' organizations survey their memberships to determine the types of services that would be beneficial to its members. Colleges track enrollment figures looking for trends in male and female populations, minorities, National Merit Scholars, and so forth. These types of data are presented in reports via bar graphs, pie charts, and other easy-to-grasp ways. Articles using only descriptive data are typically not as difficult to understand as those of the experimental genres, although mean-difference testing is frequently included, raising the level of sophistication.

Correlational Research Quantitative research also can be used to establish relationships among factors or conditions and is known as *correlational research*, which indicates the strength of relationship between two or more factors. This does not imply a cause-and-effect relationship. For example, Scott Phillips (2003) explored the music attitudes of middle school students in relation to home musical environment and self-concept. He found the correlation between home musical background and music attitude was stronger for boys than girls and that music attitude was more closely correlated with girls' self-concepts in music than their home musical environments (p. iii).

Another form of correlational inquiry is known as *predictive research*. "By examining the patterns of association between some set of variables and something that the investigator wishes to predict (usually called the *criterion variable*), it is possible to identify the best possible set of variables to use" (Locke, Silverman, & Spirduso, 2004, p. 138). Davis (1990) wanted to know what factors in instrumental students' back-grounds correlated strongly with their desire to be a music teacher. Using a question-naire the researcher found that encouragement from the high school band director yielded the strongest correlation. Music teachers have considerable influence over a student's choice of music teaching as a career, but probably few know it.

A third type of correlational study is *modeling research*, which includes both path analysis and structural equation. This genre "maps in graphic form . . . the relationships among a number of variables, displaying the degree to which any one of them can be used to predict one or more of the others" (Locke et al., 2004, p. 139).

Quantitative Research: Experimental

True-Experimental Research Studies of this genre investigate cause-and-effect relation-ships and are based on the scientific method. In its most classic form, two groups of sub-jects (experimental and control) are randomly chosen from a larger population. Both groups are pretested on what is called a *dependent* measure or variable. If the groups are randomly assigned, there should be little pretest differences between the two. Some type of treatment or instruction (the *independent* variable) is then administered to the exper-imental group. The control group can receive no instruction, but typically it receives some other type of instruction or a modified version of the treatment. (Something is typically better than nothing.) Following a treatment period defined in length by the researcher, both groups are posttested and the data are submitted to statistical analysis. If the study turns out as desired, the analysis will show that the treatment group performed significantly better than the control and that the treatment/instruction was successful.

Quasi-Experimental Research This type of research differs from a true experimental design in one major factor—it is not possible to randomize students into groups. This is a common condition in education, where classrooms exist as *intact* groups and stu-dents cannot be assigned to other subgroups. Not being able to randomize subjects indicates that the chance of having near-equal pretests between intact groups is com-promised. The researcher randomly assigns the intact classes to either of the research groups, and statistical adjustments can be made for initial differences.

Causal-Comparative Research This is a form of *ex post facto* study in which the data are collected after the treatment has occurred. The independent variable is categorical, not continuous, and two groups can be compared as to the incidence of factors or con-ditions influencing the dependent or measured variable. For example:

> The 1976 outbreak of "Legionnaires' Disease," when many people attending an American Legion convention in Philadelphia became deathly ill, is a classic example of causal comparative medical research. Medical teams, faced with a malady of unknown origin (effect), diligently searched for the cause. In such cases, the testing of possible causes proceeds through trial and error and inspired guesswork. (Busch & Sherbon, 1992, p. 126)

Meta-analysis Research This type of quantitative research allows researchers to combine the results of studies that have a common focus to derive a result that is more powerful than a single study. Original data are not collected, but the aggregate data from previous studies are. A special statistical formula is involved. The advance of computer technology has made this rather new form of research possible. "In some areas of inquiry, for example, a group of studies that has produced only modest results might be concealing the fact that the findings are substantial as well as persistent—a fact that can become apparent only through the magnifying power of meta-analysis" (Locke et al., 2004, p. 147).

Qualitative Research

Qualitative research does not subscribe to the scientific method and is more "holistic" or intuitive in nature. It is not concerned with comparing large groups of participants on some variable. Rather, qualitative study observes people in natural settings in the hopes of finding information that would be helpful to understanding the learner and their environment. A qualitative researcher might not be limited to research questions presented at the onset of a study, not wanting predetermined questions to mask other questions that could evolve in the course of the investigation. This is why qualitative researchers often *see* more in a research study than quantitative researchers, who are limited at the outset in what they are investigating.

> In the *qualitative paradigm* there is a range of positions, from the idealist belief that social and human reality are created, to the milder conviction that this reality is shaped by our minds. But, all the positions posit a degree of mind involvement with subject matter not acceptable to the quantitative, positivist, realist tradition. The idea that the process of investigation can be separated from what is being investigated is possible only within that realist perspective. In the realist view, an investigation is directed toward an external referent. In the ideal view, the process is external as well as internal, a part of the investigator's active participation in shaping the world. (Bresler & Stake, 2006, p. 277)

Therefore, while the quantitative researcher stands back and apart from his or her work to maintain objectivity, the qualitative researcher becomes part of the investigation to understand internally what is transpiring.

Qualitative research is empirical in nature—the data are collected in written form as observations of behavior. The nature of qualitative research is its subjectivity and how human beings in a particular context make meaning of something—to find out what a participant really thinks rather than what the subject might think a researcher wants to know. As well, the goal of quantitative research is to get at the truth, but qualitative research is getting at what the truth is to a person or several people, the full story.

To counter the subjectivity of this approach, qualitative researchers will often *triangulate* their data, i.e., confirm their observations in at least three ways, e.g., interviews, videotaping, and using another person to analyze the observations. In this manner, investigator bias is controlled. Triangulation is not universal in qualitative research, nor is the use of the term (see Bogdan & Biklen, 2003).

Qualitative inquiry is not about generalizing results to a population. Generalization is possible when a study is replicated with various other groups, but replication is not common in most forms of research. Nevertheless, the information presented from qualitative study can help music teachers and music therapists to think more deeply about how they are using music and how people learn best.

It was in the 1990s that qualitative research gained respect in music research. Prior to that time, qualitative study was viewed as unscientific and a poor substitute for quantitative study. As this bias began to diminish, qualitative articles began appearing in leading music journals, even the JRME. Today, qualitative investigation is a respected and accepted form of research in both music education and music therapy.

Narrative Research This is a form of qualitative inquiry in which the investigator studies the lives of people and asks one or more individuals to provide stories about their lives. The information is then retold or restoried into a narrative chronology that combines views from the participant's life with those of the researcher's life in a collaborate narrative (Creswell, 2003, p. 15).

Phenomenological Research The researcher identifies the essence of human experiences concerning a phenomenon, as described by participants in a study. The process involves studying a small number of participants through extensive engagement to develop patterns and relationships of meanings (Creswell, 2003, p. 15).

Ethnographic Research The researcher studies an intact cultural group in a natural setting over a prolonged period of time. Data are collected mainly through observation.

Grounded Theory The researcher attempts to derive a general, abstract theory of a process, action, or interaction grounded in the views of participants in a study. Multiple stages of data collection are involved as well as constant comparison of data with emerging categories (Creswell, 2003, p. 14).

Case Study The researcher explores in depth a single event, activity, process, or individual using a variety of data-collection procedures over an extended period of time. The case study is bounded by time and activity (Creswell, 2003, p. 15).

Action Research Some authorities would not consider action research a viable form of any type of research. In essence it does what people do all the time—trying out new ways of doing something in their own environment and accepting or rejecting the new ways based on the success of the outcomes. It is trial-and-error discovery.

There is in the educational community a growing respect for action research because it motivates teachers to try new ways of teaching. Such research typically focuses on three interventions: technical, practical, and emancipatory. Action research provides a framework for qualitative study by teachers and researchers in complex working classroom situations. It is not bound by the constraints of more formal research designs, but neither are the results considered highly reliable or generalizable.

Mixed Methods

This type of research has come of age and is appearing now in research journals. It includes both quantitative and qualitative procedures within the same study.

> The researcher bases the inquiry on the assumption that collecting diverse types of data best provides an understanding of a research problem. The study begins with a broad survey in order to generalize results to a population and then focuses, in a second phase, on detailed qualitative, open-ended interviews to collect detailed views from participants. (Creswell, 2003, p. 21)

Sequential Procedures. "The researcher seeks to elaborate on or expand the findings of one method with another method" (Creswell, 2003, p. 16). Quantitative and qualitative data are collected sequentially in either order, and the research can be generalized to a population when a large sample of participants is used.

Concurrent Procedures. "In this design, the investigator collects both forms of data at the same time during the study and then integrates the information in the interpretation of the overall results" (Creswell, 2003, p. 16).

Transformative Procedures. This design contains both quantitative and qualitative data. A theoretical lens "provides a framework for topics of interest, methods for collecting data, and outcomes or changes anticipated by the study. Within this lens could be a data-collection method that involves a sequential or a concurrent approach" (Creswell, 2003, p. 16).

Researchers from around the world are now developing and using procedures for mixed-methods designs. Though known by a number of other names (multimethod, convergence, integrated, and combined) *mixed methods* seems to be a recurring label.

This introduction to the values of research, sources for finding research, and categories of research genres can be slightly overwhelming. This is a complex topic, but familiarity will grow when you actually begin to read research. Being able to identify the various forms in which research exists, the intended use of each, and what the various genres can be used to *say* is an important first step in comprehending research.

STUDY AND DISCUSSION QUESTIONS

1. Why is it important for music educators and music therapists to read research?
2. What are the premiere journals of research in music education and music therapy?
3. What is the JMTE, and where can it be found?
4. What does DAI stand for, and what purpose does it serve?
5. What are the three main genres of research in music education and music therapy?
6. What genre of research is conducted most often in music education and music therapy?
7. What is the name of the new journal of research in philosophical studies in music education? From where does it originate?
8. What does philosophical research attempt to do?
9. Of what importance is historical research?
10. What are the three subgenres of behavioral research? Describe the focus of each.
11. What research genre indicates "what is"?
12. What type of study would involve using scores on a music aptitude test to predict success in playing a musical instrument?
13. What is the difference between true-experimental and quasi-experimental research?
14. What are the components of a true-experimental research design?

15. Why is randomization so important in research design?
16. What type of study is involved in causal comparative research?
17. How does qualitative research differ from quantitative research?
18. How do quantitative data differ from qualitative data?
19. How does the qualitative researcher often control for investigator bias? *triangulation*
20. What is mixed methods research, and why is it employed? *sequent concurrent or transfer*

SUGGESTED ACTIVITIES

1. Peruse Appendix C and locate the journals that appear online. Using a computer, try to locate one of the journals listed, e.g., *UPDATE: Applications of Research in Music Education* (www.menc.org), and print out an article.

2. Review the contents of each *Handbook* as presented in Appendix A and Appendix B. Note areas that particularly interest you. When possible, peruse each *Handbook* in the library.

CHAPTER 2

The Research Study

Most research studies are reported in some form for public dissemination. Research would be of little value to any profession if the results were not published. Those journals that present research in music education and music therapy are given in Chapter 1 and Appendix C of this text.

Research articles appearing in journals are typically summaries of studies and are not exhaustive presentations of investigations. Doctoral dissertations and masters theses often are in excess of 100 pages, but most studies appearing in journals are no more than 10–15 pages. Publications are expensive to produce, and most journals set a limit on the number of pages of manuscript that are permissible for submission. For example, the *Journal of Research in Music Education* accepts manuscripts no longer than 20 pages.

A journal article has the advantage of brevity. However, in summarizing a study, much of the narrative has to be omitted. This can produce "holes" in the writing, which leave the reader confused or unable to make a proper value judgment about the study. Theses and dissertations, however, are exhaustive reports—lengthy and time consuming to read. Replication of a study is easier from these genres than from summary articles.

It is best to begin reading research with research articles. While these are typically summaries, you are not as likely to become bogged down in the reading as with dissertations or theses. Articles that appear in refereed journals must receive the approval of the editorial committee and, therefore, should be void of gaps and writing that may confuse the reader. In this text the reading of research is limited to that of articles; but if you are interested in doing your own research project, you must, at some point, begin to read entire studies that can be found in libraries, mostly as theses or dissertations.

Guidance in locating dissertations to read can be found in the *Bulletin of the Council of Research in Music Education* (University of Illinois). The *Bulletin* regularly includes reviews of dissertations, and these can be very helpful in determining whether or not a study is worth time pursuing. This journal is one of the most respected in the field.

WHO DOES RESEARCH?

It is important to know the source of any research investigation. An article that summarizes a person's doctoral dissertation is a sign that the study is most likely his or her initial investigation. The research may have weaknesses often found early in a person's career. A study by a seasoned investigator is apt to command more respect.

College and University Professors

A majority of the research in music education and therapy is done by college and university professors. For the doctoral degree and some masters degrees, the terminal project is a research investigation. This is typically the first major research study that the student will have done, and it often serves to launch the person's career in higher education.

The Ph.D. degree is a research degree—it prepares the student to pursue a career that involves a research component. While other doctoral degrees (e.g., D.M.A.; Ed.D.; D.M.) may have a research component, the Ph.D. focus is on research. Unfortunately, many persons who receive the Ph.D. do not pursue further research (for various reasons). Therefore the number of active researchers in music education and music therapy is relatively small. For those who acquire professorial positions at research universities, research and publication are a major expectation. In fact, it has become so important that it is unlikely a professor could be tenured at such a school without an active and ongoing research agenda.

The pressure at research universities to "publish or perish" is very real. It forces some professors out of the profession or to choose positions at schools where such demands are minimal. For those who thrive in a research environment, there is always the problem of balancing the commitment to teaching with the expectation of publishing. It is not an easy task, but those who succeed serve the profession in two ways: (1) preparation of future professionals, and (2) discovery of new knowledge to help better understand how people function musically in society.

The "publish or perish" syndrome has a downside for which it is often criticized: Some research is carried out that is of little value—it merely creates another line on the professor's vita. This is bound to happen when schools are known to value quantity over quality. The frequently asked question of the junior faculty member is "How many articles does it take to receive tenure?" Rarely is an answer given, but someone (usually a dean) has something in mind. This creates more pressure for the untenured professor, a pressure that can cause sleepless nights.

Receiving tenure at a major research university is a real feat. The new professor wants and needs to prepare course content and establish a reputation as a good teacher. At the same time the tenure clock is ticking, and research demands are looming. Professors are expected to be involved in service to the university and community. This means committee work and making presentations at conferences or in the schools. Many education professors are involved in supervising student teachers, a task taking much time. The many demands outside of the classroom seem endless, and yet the professor is to establish a research agenda and become a specialist in some focused area. It is not an easy life, and those who continue to think of those lovely "halls of ivy" as some sort of panacea do not understand contemporary academia, with its multiplicity of demands. Those who succeed as professors juggle many roles, as do all teachers in general!

What does this mean to you, the research consumer? It means that you must understand that a considerable amount of research is "churned out" of academia because of the pressure to do research. The following question must always be in your mind: Was this study done because the question is legitimate, or does it just represent more fodder? It is not easy to make this determination, especially when you know little of the research field. However, this question should always be in the back of your mind as you read research. Understanding the motivating factor for a research study often is tantamount to determining whether the investigation had a legitimate purpose in the beginning. It is the job of the researcher to provide you with some evidence as to why the research topic in any article is of importance to him or her and a significant area of study.

Jellison (2002) presents an excellent example of explaining the significance of her research study in the following.

> The purpose of the present study was to assess the on-task participation of individual typical children in an inclusive elementary classroom and to describe their participation when they are in a classroom location that is physically close to or away from their peers with disabilities. Although results of research studies cited in the present study suggest that there is no negative impact of inclusion on instructional opportunities for typical students as a group, these findings also suggest that environmental factors may influence attentiveness and academic performance of individual students. If this is true, it then follows that a typical child's location in the classroom can create a specific environment that may influence that child's performance. (p. 345)

There is no doubt that what Jellison is proposing is of importance to music educators and music therapists alike and that the study could have serious implications for the music classroom setting.

Research in music education and music therapy is full of "one-shot" studies; i.e., no line of investigation is ongoing. One study in any area rarely provides definitive answers to any research question. When a researcher spends a career investigating a narrowly defined topic, it is probable that valuable answers may evolve over time. A researcher who jumps from topic to topic most likely will provide little in-depth knowledge on any topic. A focused research agenda is required in order that a researcher become an expert in a given area. The article by Jellision (2002) previously cited references three others research articles by her of studies she has done in the area of children with disabilities. This is a good sign that the author has had an ongoing research agenda.

A few larger universities have established centers for research in music education. Florida State University is a prime example. The purpose of this action is to focus the faculty's energies on research, sometimes collaboratively, and to focus on scholarly research as an ongoing commitment. A center for research that is funded by the university is able to provide greater resources for the faculty and sometimes is funded by grants sought for by the faculty as a whole. Such centers bring a certain status to music programs that stress research.

Teachers and Therapists

Teachers and therapists do research in their environments all the time. While it usually does not follow strict research protocol and typically is not published, it often leads to changes in the way things are done in the classroom or in the therapy setting. This type of investigation, termed *action research*, is discussed in Chapter 15. The main difference between well-controlled research and action research is the ability to generalize the results to a population. The main purpose of a well-controlled study is to find out something about a smaller sample of people that can be generalized to a larger population of the same persons. While this cannot be done from action research, you can improve your own way of doing things or understanding people in your own little world. Sometimes, findings from these types of investigations appear in newsletters or other informal venues.

Large, urban school districts sometimes employ research specialists for purposes of carrying out research specific to the achievement of the teachers and students within the prescribed district. These people are often specialists in statistics who can "number crunch" and present statistics vital to the understanding of educational objectives. They are less likely to carry out behavioral research in the traditional sense.

Clinical Researchers

There are also clinical researchers whose only job it is to explore the unknown. Drug manufacturers have large numbers of scientists who do nothing but experiment with developing new medications. Research in education rarely has groups of researchers who do nothing but investigate how people think and act. People who do this type of study typically are associated with large research universities, and often they are expected to teach as well. Their research is often supported by grants that permit them released time from a normal teaching load. Because there is little grant money available to researchers in music education and music therapy (in relation to that available to those in the "hard" sciences), the quantity of research in these areas is far less. The federal government of the United States awards research grants in the millions of dollars to those seeking cures for various diseases and mental disorders. It is natural, therefore, to expect that publications in these areas would far outnumber those found in music education or music therapy. Rarely is it possible for a music educator or music therapist to devote her or his career entirely to research investigation.

THE RESEARCH ARTICLE

A research article, in general, presents the particulars of a research study, from beginning to end. While this is a very simple description, it is impossible to define research studies with descriptions that would fit all types of investigation. Nevertheless, there are similarities that will be helpful to address.

Title and Author(s)

The title is an important indication of what any study involves. The *Publication Manual of the American Psychological Association* states:

> A title should summarize the main idea of the paper simply and, if possible, with style. It should be a concise statement of the main topic and should identify the actual

variables or theoretical issues under investigation and the relationship between them. (2001, pp. 10–11)

Another important part of the title is to identify the participants in the study. If you are looking for studies concerning the effects of improvisational instruction with early childhood students, a title that states the generic *children* will be of little help. Much time can be saved if the title accurately reflects what was studied and with whom. In addition it is helpful to know what measures were used to collect the data. For example, the title "Individual Differences in Music Listening Responses of Kindergarten Children" (Sims & Nolker, 2002) tells you what was studied (music listening responses), with whom (kindergarten children), and what was measured (individual differences).

Titles should clarify what, who, and types of data collection (where space permits) and must be rather short. The American Psychological Association recommends that titles be 10–12 words. Journal editors do not want to waste space on long and rambling titles.

Following the title will be the author's name and place of affiliation. When there is more than one author, the main or lead author's name will appear first. Titles, such as Dr. and Professor, are omitted. Some journals (e.g., the JRME) will include a footnote giving the address of the author(s), email address(es), and copyright notice.

A running head on each page is used by journals to identify that all pages belong to a specific article. Often this is an abbreviated form of the title; with the JRME, it is the author's or authors' name(s).

Abstract

Most refereed articles contain an abstract at the beginning of a report. This gives the reader an opportunity to read a brief summary of the study and to decide whether or not to read the entire article. The *Publication Manual of the American Psychological Association* states:

> An abstract is a brief, comprehensive summary of the contents of the article; it allows readers to survey the contents of an article quickly and, like a title, it enables abstracting and information services to index and retrieve articles. All APA journals except *Contemporary Psychology: APA Review of Books* require an abstract. (2001, p. 12)

In music education and music therapy, dissertations are abstracted in *Dissertation Abstracts International* (DAI). This service is available online, and copies of dissertations can be ordered for purchase by individuals, or copies can be borrowed through interlibrary loan (see specific information in Chapter 1).

The following is an abstract of an article titled "Connections Between the Musical Life Experiences of Young Composers and Their Compositions" by Sandra L. Stauffer (2002).

> The case-study records of six sixth-grade composers were examined for evidence of connections between the music and life experiences of the students and compositions they wrote. Analysis revealed rich and varied connections between the students' contexts and their music. Idiomatic writing related to instrumental and ensemble experiences was present in their works, and links between instrumental fluency and fluency in composing became evident. Familiar melodies from instrumental experiences, films,

and television served as starting points for compositions. Social and cultural cues related to other media as well as to school and home life were also evident in compositions. Findings suggest that young composers draw on their sociocultural milieu and personal experiences to create music that is relevant and meaningful to them. (p. 301)

Can you tell what genre of research is represented by this abstract? The following statement may help: "Observations of these sixth-grade composers and analysis of their works indicate that..." (p. 317). Another hint: No quantitative data are presented. The answer: It is qualitative research (case study).

Introduction

The article opens with an Introduction that presents the specific problem(s) of the study. Because the Introduction appears first, it is not labeled as such. The Introduction ought to answer the following questions:

- What is the study about?
- What is the theoretical basis underlying the study?
- Does the study relate to previous work or literature?
- Is the need for the research presented clearly?
- Are the research questions clear?

Theses and dissertations are expected to have exhaustive reviews of literature that consume many pages. In an article, however, the *review of literature* is typically short and is focused only on the most related literature in the field. However, *the Publication Manual of the American Psychological Association* advises:

> Demonstrate the logical continuity between previous and present work. Develop the problem with enough breadth and clarity to make it generally understood by as wide a professional audience as possible. Do not let the goal of brevity mislead you into writing a statement intelligible only to the specialist. (2001, p. 16)

The review of related literature is a valuable part of any research article and often provides references for the reader who wants to pursue other studies related to the one being read.

In larger works (e.g., dissertations) the Introduction typically concludes with subsections, such as *need for the study*, *purpose of the study*, *research questions*, and so forth. In an article these sections tend to appear but are not labeled, for lack of space. Quantitative investigations will typically present the variables being studied and the research questions. You should know from reading a quantitative study what variables the investigator manipulated (independent) and what variables were measured (dependent).

Method

The Method part of any article must describe in detail how the study was conducted. It is impossible to evaluate the validity and reliability of a study without clear information. Sometimes, in the need for brevity, an author will compress this part of the article so much as to leave the reader bewildered. Reviewers are likely to catch this problem, but some mistakes get by them.

It is common to have this section of the report divided into subsections, such as *subjects* (or participants in qualitative research), *materials, procedures*, and so forth. If the *design of the study* is rather complicated, a separate section for it is appropriate. It is up to the author to determine the necessary subsections for the Method. Research articles must present detailed evidence that the observations and recordings of the data were done with accuracy and that the level of accuracy was appropriate to address the demands of the research questions.

Subjects or Participants

An author must clearly identify the research *subjects* (*participants* in qualitative research). It is important to know such factors as age, gender, grade level (if appropriate), SES (socioeconomic status), school environment (e.g., a college town), ethnicity (when appropriate), whether any grouping factors might be involved (e.g., advanced-ability students or students with disabilities), and other factors that could influence the outcome of the study (people with certain diseases, e.g., emphysema). Without a clear description of the sample of subjects it is impossible to generalize results to a similar population.

It is also important to know how the subjects/participants were chosen. Sometimes, researchers choose people only because of their availability; i.e., access to students makes the job of finding subjects/participants easier. In an article by Ebie (2002) in which he analyzed the contents of the JRME from 1953 to 2002, he found that 34% of the samples were drawn from college/university settings, 21% from elementary settings, and only 19% from secondary settings (p. 280). What would this tell you about the access of professors to college and university students? Nevertheless, legitimate research has been done with college students. It is good to realize, however, that easy access to any sample of the population may result in research that was driven more by the participants' availability than by the research questions.

The number of subjects or participants chosen for the study is another important consideration. In educational research, experimental studies with fewer than 40 subjects are suspect. Statistical measures can be used to adjust for the small number of subjects. Some mention by the author should be made as to this statistical adjustment if the participant number is small (n is less than 40). Such a consideration is not important in a qualitative study where only a few participants may be involved. (The statistics N and n often appear in quantitative research when referring to subjects. N refers to the number in the population; n refers to the number in the sample.)

It is important to know how the subjects were assigned to the experimental and control groups in an experimental study. If intact classes were used, were the classes assigned at random to either group? Was it possible to assign the entire sample (n) at random to either group? If so, the study has a higher level of credibility. It is difficult to assign subjects at random in behavioral research because most groups of students exist as intact classes.

The use of human subjects/participants in a study, especially minors, introduces the concept of ethics in research. It is unethical (and often illegal) to use people in research studies without their knowledge and written consent. Every institution of higher learning has an Institutional Review Board (IRB) that reviews all research prior to its inception. Part of this review is to determine if those who serve as subjects or participants may in any manner be placed in danger by being part of the research and if all necessary precautions have been taken by the researcher to protect the rights of those in the study (anonymity, nonreversal of effects, etc.). This includes the right to withdraw from the study at any time. Minors must have the written consent of parents or guardians to participate. Without IRB approval, the study cannot go forward. In research articles, evidence of permission to use people as subjects/participants is often lacking, because of space limitations. It is always included in theses and dissertations.

A final factor when reading about subjects is to determine how many may have dropped out of the study, why they did so, and how many were remaining for the final data analyses. An imbalance of subjects in groups being compared may jeopardize the results of a study, especially when the sample number is small. Even in qualitative research, where groups are not typically compared, it is important to know who started and who ended the study.

Materials or Apparatus

When special materials or apparatus are used in a study it is appropriate to describe them and their function in the investigation. If commercial products were used it is good to look for model numbers and manufacturers' names. "Complex or custom-made equipment may be illustrated by a drawing or photograph. A detailed description of complex equipment may be included in an appendix" (*Publication Manual of the American Psychological Association*, 2001, p. 20).

Sometimes music educators or music therapists use in studies sophisticated equipment about which they are not very knowledgeable. In these cases, it is good to look for some evidence that the researchers were well trained in the use of the instrumentation or that they had help from those knowledgeable about such instruments. Even when this is the case, the researcher might show evidence of doing a pilot study or trial run where use of the instrumentation was tested before being employed in the actual study.

Procedures

Once the researcher has described the subjects/participants, how they were chosen and assigned (when appropriate), and what materials/apparatus were used, it is time for the researcher to describe as much as possible how the study was carried out. Such information can include: instructions to the participants, specific forms of instruction or observation, how long a period of time was involved, efforts made to protect the validity of the process (e.g., guarding against experimenter bias), how the data were collected, and how the data were analyzed. This is the *design* of the study.

The quality of the data collected is of utmost importance in any research study, quantitative, qualitative, or mixed. Sloppy or lost data entries cannot be tolerated. The researcher should provide evidence that every precaution was taken to protect the accuracy of the data, i.e., that the data were a *real* reflection of the participants.

A researcher once gave the *Intermediate Measures of Music Audiation* (IMMA) test (Gordon, 1989) to a class of fifth-grade students as a means of collecting data on musical aptitude. Because the test was being given via a cassette tape, she noticed that one of the students was looking out the window and not actively participating. Walking slowly around the room and coming to his desk, she noticed that the student had already circled all of the answers on the test when the test had just begun. Clearly his answers were not a clear indication of anything but hostility or something else, and the researcher eliminated his data from the study. Researchers must take precaution that data collected are an accurate representation of the sample.

The *data analysis* is sometimes set off as a subsection or is included as the final part of the Procedures section. This is typically the most difficult section of the article for the novice reader to understand. A statement such as "The data were analyzed using a two-way analysis of variance (ANOVA) with two levels of each factor (treatment–control, male–female)" is going to go right over most peoples' heads. While it is not necessary to completely understand such a statement in order to read research, an attempt is made later in this book to present you with a general understanding of such writing.

Most data today are analyzed using some type of computer program. Computers have greatly streamlined the job of processing data, and sophisticated research analyses are possible today that would not have been possible just a few years ago. The problem with computers is that we tend to believe everything they present. Computers only do what humans tell them to do, and that is the problem. If the input of data is not correct, the study is no longer viable. The researcher must show a "feel" for the data, i.e., look at the computer printouts and be able to surmise if the data make sense based on what was observed during the study. For example, if the researcher does not consider whether or not the data may be skewed, the results of the data analysis cannot accurately reflect reality. Readers of research must be aware that numbers can lie; this can happen intentionally and unintentionally. When in doubt, common sense must prevail.

One final factor in data analysis is something called *rater reliability*. This is found when human raters (e.g., teachers) have been used to judge responses on some type of standardized or investigator-designed measure. Using more than one judge to determine a participant's score is preferable, but the agreement between or among the judges is necessary to know. This, again, can be done by a computer program. The results are reported, typically, as a reliability coefficient. For example, $r = .92$ would indicate a rather high agreement among the judges, but $r = .34$ would not.

Results

The Results section of a quantitative research article presents the findings of the data analyses in an objective and straightforward manner. Data are summarized as averages and not as raw scores. The results are presented according to the research questions posed in the introduction. In qualitative research, the results will typically include the themes or findings, presented in narrative format.

Tables and figures in quantitative research are often used to enhance the presentation of the results. Tables report data; figures present graphs, pictures, and drawings. In order to save space, some journals now request that authors eliminate tables of data in favor of presenting a summary of statistical outcomes directly within the text. A sentence reading as follows gives in parentheses just the data necessary to support the stated result: "The difference was significant (F (4, 132) = 13.62; $p < .01$) in favor of the treatment group."[1] At this point you need not worry about what the data in the parentheses mean. Just know that statistics are commonly reported in this manner.

Tables of data presented in a study come in basically two forms: (1) *descriptive*, in which means and standard deviations are most commonly given, and (2), *results of analyses*, in which results of statistical analyses, including *t* tests, *F* tests, and chi-square, are displayed. When a researcher finds a significant difference between two groups on some measure, it is reported in the analysis table. Looking at the means in the descriptive table will then help to determine which of the groups had the higher mean score. This will all make more sense when we deal with these tables later in this text.

The Results section of a qualitative study typically does not contain numerical data (unless of a mixed design). Findings are grouped into observations of commonality, e.g., a set of observations that would suggest that the subjects were thinking or doing something alike on a particular factor. Many times the results in a qualitative study are *a priori*, i.e., not predicated on specific questions set forth in the Introduction.

In a large work, e.g., a dissertation, the Results section often comes to a conclusion with a subsection called Conclusions. Here the findings of the study are presented concisely and not elaborated on. Research articles typically do not include a separate Conclusions section.

Discussion

The Discussion section of a research article is the place where the researcher is permitted to "wax eloquent" as to what he or she thinks the results of the study indicate. When a quantitative study generates nonsignificant results, it may behoove the author to speculate as to what happened and why. Results that were unexpected in a positive direction also may need some explaining. In general, the Discussion section tries to make sense out of what happened in the study and relates it all to the real world. This is the only place in the study where the author is permitted to be somewhat subjective. It is not the place, however, for alibis and trying to hide the hard facts that something did not happen as planned.

In my own dissertation (Phillips, 1985), I found that students in the treatment group (vocal instruction) did better on a posttest measure singing louder but not longer than those in the control group (song approach). This did not seem logical. Then it dawned on me: I had used the same vocal measure for both decibel level and duration. That was not a good idea, because singing louder uses more air. It stands to reason that students in the treatment group who sang louder did not sing longer because they were consuming their air at a faster rate. With some humiliation I had to bring that to light in the Discussion section (pp. 182–183).

The Discussion should end with some type of *implications of the results* and/or *recommendations for future research*. Attaching the results to the education or therapy setting is an important outcome of many behavioral studies. However, beware of

---

[1]The term *significant* has special meaning for quantitative research. In this case it means a "true" or statistical difference exists between groups, as opposed to a result that only appears different. This is discussed further in Chapter 10.

authors who want you to believe that they have discovered the ultimate truth on any issue. Behavioral research does not definitively *prove* anything, and statements to that end are always suspect. Because human behavior is so hard to control, there is always the possibility that the results have occurred by chance. Also, a study that uses fifth-grade students as subjects and then generalizes to *all* students is very questionable.

Finally, the author most likely will recommend some course of future research, e.g., replicating the study with more subjects or with another grade level and so forth. Sometimes recommendations include correcting mistakes that the investigator found in doing the study or improving on procedures or measures used. This is of great benefit to future researchers, who can be helped from making similar mistakes.

References

A journal article most typically concludes with a References section. While larger works often contain an Appendix section, articles rarely do, given space constraints.

Most references are in the format found in the *Publication Manual of the American Psychological Association* (APA). Rather than using footnotes or endnotes, the APA has each reference cited within the text (as is done throughout this text) and a master list of references presented at the end of the article. References are listed in alphabetical order by the main author's name, followed by the year of publication. The title of the article is given next (using mostly small letters instead of caps. for most words), followed by the name of the journal, the volume number, and the page numbers. A perusal of the References section at the end of this book will make this clear.

The APA system has many "quirks" that seem difficult for beginning researchers to master. However, good examples are given in the *Manual* and need to be studied closely when preparing a references list. Many scholars believe the APA style to be easier and less time consuming than the *Chicago* style, which is mainly for philosophical and historical writing. Researchers using *Chicago* feel that it is more exact and detailed than APA. The References section of this book is in APA style and provides a good place to become acquainted with this format.

QUALITY OF PRESENTATION

The authors of the APA *Manual* recommend the following directives to evaluate a research study. These directives make for a handy checklist and have been slightly modified to include a broader spectrum of research than just quantitative.

- Is the topic appropriate for the journal in which it appears?
- Is the introduction clear and complete?
- Does the statement of purpose adequately and logically orient the reader?
- Is the literature adequately reviewed and related to the research topic?
- Are the citations appropriate and complete?
- Is the research question clearly identified?
- Are the conceptualization and rationale perfectly clear?

- Is the method clearly and adequately described? In other words, can the study be replicated from the description provided in the article?
- If observers were used to assess variables or behaviors, is the interobserver reliability reported? In qualitative research, are the data triangulated?
- Are the techniques of data analysis appropriate, and is the analysis clear?
- Are the assumptions underlying the statistical procedures clearly met by the data to which they are applied?
- Are the results and conclusions unambiguous, valid, and meaningful?
- Is the discussion thorough? Does it stick to the point and confine itself to what can be concluded from the findings of the study?
- Is the article concise?
- Does the article follow the proper writing style (e.g., Chicago or APA)?

Regarding a quality research presentation, Locke, Silverman, and Spirduso (2004) remind us that much that is in print purports to be research but does not qualify as research. "Included among those materials are most articles in newspapers and popular magazines, the majority of articles in professional journals, and even the contents of most researched-based college textbooks" (p. 26).

> We make this point not to disparage any of these forms of communication. They can be serious, accurate, insightful, and even important contributions to discourse about particular scientific issues. They are not, however, research reports, and that is not a trivial distinction. (p. 26)

The authors go on to note that even research reviews that appear in journals such as the *Bulletin of the Council for Research in Music Education*, although of enormous value, are not research reports. Similarly, incomplete or partial reports, state the authors, "do not allow us to judge the adequacy of the methods used in the study and, thereby, the credibility of any conclusions derived" (p. 27). Truly, identifying a quality piece of research is not an easy task. There is much to know.

THE TRUST FACTOR

There is a certain amount of trust the reader can place in a journal article when it appears in a refereed journal. Members of an editorial board are chosen for their competence in doing research as well as for their knowledge about research. Nevertheless, all of the decisions as to what constitutes a valid and believable investigation cannot be left to others. Subjective biases surface, and articles are printed that lack depth of scrutiny. At some point you have to know for yourself whether you are reading quality work.

Locke et al. (2004) provide a number of warning signals of which you should be aware when reading research. The following is a summary of their points on this topic (pp. 46–56).

- *Technical problems.* Pay attention to the details. When items are glossed over, the fabric of the presentation begins to sag.

- *Sampling.* Pay attention to how the sample was chosen, its size, and what population it is supposed to represent.
- *Lack of replication.* Pay attention to one-time studies that lack replication. Don't put a lot of faith in them.
- *Conflicts.* Pay attention to someone or sponsors supporting the research financially. Do they have a vested interest?
- *Carelessness.* Pay attention to sloppy work. Sloppiness may not condemn the entire study, but it is an indication that the researcher may have not been careful with detail.
- *Errors and poor scholarship.* Pay attention to honest errors. If they result in poor scholarship, abandon ship!

Can you trust this research article? That is the ultimate question you must ask of any study you read. Most of the general public is gullible on this point. If it is research and in print, it must be true. Others do not believe anything reported by researchers. The best approach is to maintain a healthy skepticism. Research has produced knowledge that has advanced our understanding of many areas, including how people learn and react to music. However, research in music education and music therapy remains a relatively young field. We know a lot, but there is so much more we do not know. The only way you are going to find out what we know and need to know is to read research.

STUDY AND DISCUSSION QUESTIONS

1. The JRME limits manuscript submission to how many pages? Why is this?
2. Who does the majority of research among music educators and music therapists? Why?
3. What is the emphasis of the Ph.D. degree?
4. What are the pluses and minuses of the "publish or perish" syndrome?
5. Why are one-shot studies not entirely reliable? What helps this problem?
6. What type of research do teachers and therapists often do "in the field"?
7. What important elements should the title of an article identify?
8. What is an abstract, and what purpose does it serve?
9. How does the Introduction of an article differ from that of a dissertation?
10. What occurs at the end of the Introduction?
11. What are the basic subparts of the Method? Describe each briefly.
12. What is contained in the Procedures part of a research article?
13. How do the Results and Discussion sections of an article differ?
14. In what two forms do tables of data appear in quantitative articles?
15. What writing style is typically used for quantitative studies? Qualitative?
16. How does research found in journals differ from that found in newspapers?
17. How is quality research distinguished from mediocre studies?

18. What characteristics of sampling should be observed in a quantitative study?

19. Why should you be cautious of research sponsored by instrument manufacturers?

20. What is the best answer to the question "Can you trust this research article"?

SUGGESTED ACTIVITIES

1. Determine what is wrong with the following research article title: "A study of listening habits among students in general music."

2. Peruse the References list at the conclusion of this text. What is the order of elements cited for a book by one author? An article that appears in an edited book? A dissertation study?

CHAPTER 3

Reading Research

A Commentary

Learning to read research requires patience and endurance on the part of the student. This type of reading is often very technical, and it is easy to become "lost" in the verbiage. Pages of small print can become discouraging, and sometimes the outcome hardly seems worth the effort. However, as one of my professors once said, "Each research project adds only a grain of sand to our knowledge, but after a while, the sand pile begins to take on real meaning" (loosely paraphrased).

RESEARCH WITH TYPICAL AND DISABLED CHILDREN

The first full article in this book is a case study by Judith A. Jellison, the Mark D. Bold Regent's Professor of Music in the School of Music, The University of Texas at Austin. The abstract for the article appears earlier, in Chapter 2.

On-task Participation of Typical Students Close to and Away from Classmates with Disabilities in an Elementary Music Classroom

Judith A. Jellison, *The University of Texas at Austin* (2002)
Journal of Research in Music Education, 50(4), 343–355.

Reprinted by permission of MENC: The National Association for Music Education.
Copyright © 2002 by MENC.

Since the passage of The Education of All Handicapped Children Act of 1975 (Federal Register, 1977) there have been continuous efforts to include students with disabilities in regular education classrooms. With each reauthorization of this law, now known as IDEA (Individuals with Disabilities Education Act of 1990), amendments and revisions have been put forward to improve inclusive school practices. The field of special education is dedicated to providing services and support for children with disabilities so that they can benefit from participation in a free and appropriate public education, and many of the practices and research efforts have focused on children in inclusive classroom settings. Although earlier research was focused on the process of children with disabilities in inclusive classrooms, within the past decade, there is increasing research in which investigators have examined the social and academic success of typical children in inclusive classrooms.

Empirical studies in special education show increases in positive social outcomes among typical students and students with disabilities as a result of inclusion (e.g., Cole & Meyer, 1991; Fryxell & Kennedy, 1995), although increases are greatest when teachers structure specific situations and opportunities for interactions (e.g., Hunt, Alwell, Farron-Davis, & Goetze, 1996; Hunt & Goetze, 1997; Jolly, Test, & Spooner, 1993). Studies concerning the academic progress of students with disabilities are less common, although an emerging body of literature suggests that full-time membership in a general education classroom offers a more optimal learning and social environment than does placement in a special class (Hunt & Farron-Davis, 1992; Schnoor, 1990) and that instructional groupings is an advantageous strategy for students with disabilities and typical students (e.g., Dugan, Kamps, Watkins, Rehinberger, & Stackhaus, 1995; Hunt, Staub, Alwell, & Goetze, 1994; Johnson & Johnson, 1991; Logan, Bachman, & Keefer, 1997).

Commentary

The introduction to any research article strives to present a more global background before becoming too specific. In this case, Jellison refers to the federal legislation of 1977 and 1990 when introducing the topic of classroom inclusion for individuals with disabilities. She hints at her particular study's focus in the statement "there is increasing research in which investigators have examined the social and academic success of typical children in inclusive classrooms" (p. 344).

Next Jellison begins to build a foundation of research studies for her investigation. This "review of related literature" is important because it presents to the reader what already has been done in this research area. Unlike a dissertation, where the review of literature is exhaustive, a literature review in an article is far shorter, concentrating only on the most important research related to the topic. Often a number of research studies support the same finding, and a string of authors' names will appear in parentheses. This is sometimes known as a "dit-dit-dit" citation.

The reference system found in this article is that of the American Psychological Association (APA). Instead of using traditional footnotes for citations, the APA system includes the name of the author and the date of the article referenced directly in the narrative. When there is a direct quote, the page number is also given.

The Article *(continued)*

The impact of the presence of children with disabilities on typical students' learning in general education settings continues to receive attention in special education. Several studies show that the development of typical children does not decelerate as a result of the presence of children with disabilities in regular classrooms (e.g., Bricker, Bruder, & Bailey, 1982; Monset & Semmel, 1997; Sharpe, York, & Knoght, 1994). In comparative studies of classrooms with and without children with   disabilities, no significant difference has been observed in teachers' engagement rates, suggesting that there is no negative impact on instructional opportunities for children with and without disabilities (e.g., Hollowood, Salisbury, Rainforth, & Palombaro, 1995; McDonnel, Thorson, McQuivey, & Keifer-O'Donnel, 1997).

Although systematic study of inclusive music settings is scant (Darrow, 1996); Jellison, 2000), several studies show findings that parallel those in special education research. When social relationships and social behaviors are examined, findings show that social interactions between preschool children with and without disabilities increase as a result of specially designed music activities (Gunsberg, 1988; Humpal, 1991); positive attitudes of typical elementary-age children toward peers with disabilities and positive interactions increase as a result of structuring small groups or small groups combined with a music-listening contingency (Jellison, Brooks, & Huck, 1984); levels of on-task behavior of students with and without disabilities are similar in general music education classrooms (Thompson, 1986); and stereotypic behaviors associated with autism (e.g., hand-flapping) decrease in regular music classes compared to special music classes (Kostka, 1993).

When performance of music and nonmusic academic tasks is examined in inclusive music classrooms, social behavior (i.e., on-task) is usually assessed. Force (1983) found no significant differences for on-task and off-task behavior and music test performance between two music classrooms, one inclusive (four children with retardation) and one not inclusive. Other studies indicate benefits for students with disabilities and typical students as a result of specially designed or adapted curricula. In studies with preschool children in an inclusive music therapy setting, children with disabilities and typical children were on-task and learned facts, concepts, and prewriting skills (Standley & Huges, 1997) when adapted or specially designed curricula were used. Similar findings are evident for the general music classroom, where students with disabilities are successful at music tasks and are on-task when adapted music instruction is used (Colwell, 1995). In a year-long case study of a child with disabilities who attended both music education and music therapy classes, Jellison and Gainer (1995) observed several differences in the child's on-task participation and correct task performance as a result of the two settings. The authors concluded that a child's familiarity with tasks and environmental factors (e.g., number of students, adults, and opportunities to respond) will affect a child's success in an inclusive music setting and that appropriate actions must be taken to ensure successful transition from specialized to regular music settings.

Commentary

The review of literature continues and becomes far more specific in nature. First, Jellison cites studies of inclusion done in general educational settings. Research in music often finds a base in the general education literature. Then she turns specifically to music, noting that "systematic study of inclusive music settings is scant" (p. 344). However, she reports that "positive attitudes of typical elementary-age children toward peers with disabilities and positive interactions increase" (p. 344). Here, the author cites her own previous work, which is important; it helps the reader to know that Jellison has established a research base in this field of investigation.

The Article (*continued*)

The purpose of the present study was to assess the on-task participation of individual typical children in an inclusive elementary classroom and to describe their participation when they are in a classroom location that is physically close to or away from their peers with disabilities. Although results of research studies cited in the present study suggest that there is no negative impact of inclusion on instructional opportunities for typical students as a group, these findings also suggest that environmental factors may influence attentiveness and academic performance of individual students. If this is true, it then follows that a typical child's location in the classroom can create a specific environment that may influence that child's performance.

The present investigation was a year-long case study of 10 children in the context of their inclusive elementary music classroom. Research questions included the following: How does location of typical students, either close to or away from peers with disabilities, affect students' levels of participation? Do typical students participate similarly in different locations and with different peers with disabilities?

Commentary

The conclusion of the introduction/review of literature presents the reader with the "purpose of the study." In a dissertation this section would be labeled as such, but in an article the segue from introduction to review to purpose is uninterrupted, for space purposes.

From the purpose of the study, the reader learns the investigation is to:

1. assess on-task participation of individual (10) typical children.

2. describe their participation when their classroom is physically close or away from their peers with disabilities.

3. determine if a typical child's location within an inclusive classroom can influence that child's performance.

The last paragraph of the introduction states that this was a year-long case study of 10 [typical] children within the context of their inclusive elementary classroom. Two research questions are then given that reflect the statements of purpose. These questions have greater specificity than the more general statements of purpose.

The Article (continued)

Method

Ten typical fourth-grade children who attended an inclusive music class in a public elementary school in Texas were selected for observation. The 10 students were members of a music class of 24 and were selected for observation because of their seating placements in the classroom—on some occasions they were seated close to one of two peers with disabilities, and on other occasions they were seated away from the same peers. In this paper, I identify the two students with disabilities as Ann and Thomas.

Ann and Thomas attended music class with their fourth-grade peers every third day. Both received special education services and music therapy. Music class was Ann's only inclusive placement, and Thomas participated in a full-inclusion program. For most classes, the music teacher assigned typical students as partners for Ann and Thomas, although no specific training was given to any of the partners. Each day, Ann arrived at music class unassisted; Thomas arrived with a paraprofessional who sat close to Thomas and his partner.

Since Ann was observed for an entire school year in both her inclusive music education class and music therapy as part of another study (Jellison & Gainer, 1995), there are extensive descriptions available regarding her class participation. Observations show Ann as an enthusiastic participant in activities with her classmates. She smiled frequently, and seemed to enjoy music class. Ann was a student with mild retardation and minor problems with coordination. Her speech was limited. Rarely did she initiate spoken communication with her peers. Ann did not show a high rate of success for music tasks in her music class; she attempted many of the tasks; she was more on-task than off-task; and she was compliant.

Thomas was a student with severe intellectual and physical disabilities. He did not speak but relied on vocalizations and arm movements to make requests for attention or to protest. He vocalized from time- to time during class, although his vocalizations were usually brief. Thomas had visual and hearing impairments and walked with the aid of a metal walker and his paraprofessional. When positioned properly in his bean-bag chair, he was able to grasp and hold small instruments and materials placed in his hands, although he would usually release them quickly. He usually sat in his chair between students, with his paraprofessional close by.

I collected all of the data from observations of videotapes that we made for the year-long case study of Ann (Jellison & Gainer, 1995). After reviewing all of the tapes, I identified all the typical students who were observed participating in class lessons while seated close to (within arm's length of) either Ann or Thomas. Ten students were identified, and several of these same students were also observed participating in a location away from Ann and Thomas. The typical students are identified by letter names (A–J) throughout the present study.

There were a total of 22 observations: 15 of the 22 observations of students close to their classmates with disabilities, and 7 observations of students away from their classmates with disabilities. Students A–D (two girls and two boys) were observed close to Thomas and students E–J (three girls and three boys) were observed close to Ann. Students A, B, E, F, G, H, and I were also observed as they participated away from both Ann and Thomas, and these data were used as a control or baseline for each of the individual students.

Observation of each of the 10 students' on-task participation was conducted using computerized software developed by Duke and Farra (2001). For purposes of this study, four behavior codes for observations were: (1) On-Task (looking at the teacher when the teacher is speaking or modeling, and/or following the teacher's directives during ongoing instructions; on-task may include teacher-directed interactions among students, with and without disabilities); (2) Off-Task Looking (off-task as a result of looking at a classmate with disabilities during ongoing instruction and when there was no teacher instruction to do so); (3) Off-Task Active (off-task as a result of touching or prompting a classmate with disabilities during ongoing instruction and when there was no teacher instruction to do so); and (4) Off-Task Other (any behavior that was not on-task and did not involve classmates with disabilities). Behaviors of typical students dur-ing "downtime" (before and after class, activity transitions, interruptions such as phone calls, announcements, etc.) were not recorded. On-task and off-task categories were directly related to ongoing instruction.

Commentary

The Method for this study tells the reader four important things: (1) the genre of research, (2) who the subjects are, (3) the design of the study, and (4) how the study was carried out. Often these areas are implied rather than specifically labeled, which is common in journal articles, where space is limited.

This is descriptive research, i.e., the investigator observes, collects data, and reports her findings. There is no attempt here to manipulate any type of instruction or to set up an experiment. Descriptive research reports "what is," not "what could be" under given circumstances. It is also quantitative research in that Jellison *counted* students' on-task and off-task behaviors. She did not make a written data narrative of what was happening, as might be found in qualitative or mixed research. This, then, is quantitative research of a descriptive nature.

The subjects are 10 typical fourth-grade children ($n = 10$) attending an inclusive music class ($N = 24$). (The capital-N statistic of 24 represents the total "population" of the class, while the lowercase-n statistic represents the 10 students in the study, or the "sample.") Participants were chosen because of their seating placements in the classroom—close to or away from two peers with disabilities (Ann and Thomas).

The research design is that of a case study (more commonly found in qualitative research). This design is common in the investigation of applied behaviors. A series of observations are made under differing conditions, in this case, when the typical students are close to or away from their peers with disabilities, and the results reported.

It is important to realize in this study that data are not being gathered on the two students with disabilities. They are used to create the situation (close by or away from) when collecting data observations of the 10 typical students. There are 22 observations (15 close and 7 away from); these observations were conducted using some type of computerized software, which Jellison does not describe. She does detail, however, the four behavior codes involving on-task and off-task behaviors.

The Article (continued)

Frequencies and percentages for on-task and off-task categories for each observation of the 10 typical students are presented in Figure 1 (Students A-D, proximity to Thomas) and Figure 2 (Students E-I, proximity to Ann). Students were observed for the entire time they were visible on the videotapes. The total observation time across 15 observations for the category Close was approximately 4 hours, with approximately 2 hours total for students close to Ann and 2 hours for students close to Thomas. Total observation time across 7 observations for the category Away was approximately 1 hour. Twenty percent of the 22 observations were randomly selected for purposes of intrareliability observation. Reliability across all categories was 89.4%, with On-Task = 88.7%, Off-Task Active = 81.5%, Off-Task Looking = 100%, and Off-Task Other = 87.5%.

Overall, students were more on-task (78%) than off-task (21.5%), although percentages for on-task were higher when they were located away from their peers with disabilities than when they were close (Close On-Task = 68.9%; Away On-Task = 87.2%). A difference was found for students who were close to Thomas (Close On-Task = 55.9%; Away On-Task = 83%) compared to students who were close to Ann (Close On-Task = 81.8%; Away On-Task = 91.4%).

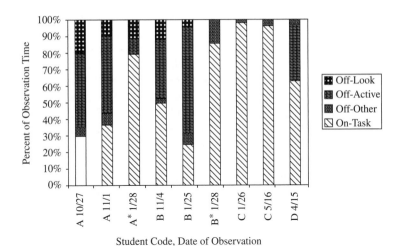

Figure 1 Percentage on-task and off-task for typical students (A–D) close to and away from (*) Thomas, their classmate with disabilities in an elementary music classroom.

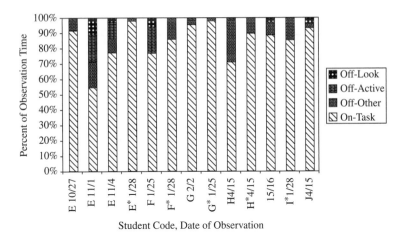

Figure 2 Percentage on-task and off-task for typical students (E–J) close to and away from (*) Ann, their classmate with disabilities in an elementary music classroom.

There was also a higher overall percentage for the category Off-Task (19.3%) compared to Off-Task Looking (5.1%), with the greater difference for students who were close to Thomas (Off-Task Active = 32%; Off-Task Looking = 6.9%) compared to students who were close to Ann (Off-Task Active = 6.6%; Off-Task Active Looking = 3.2%). As expected, the overall percentages for Off-Task Active were low (less than 1%) when students were in locations away from their peers with disabilities. Percentages for the category

Off-Task Other were 10% or less for students close to and away from either of their classmates with disabilities.

When percentages for individual observations for each student (Figures 1 and 2) were examined, differences are shown among students close to Thomas (Figure 1) and close to Ann (Figure 2). Figure 1 shows that Student C remained on-task during the two times he was observed close to Thomas (98% and 95%), although percentages for on-task were 64% or lower for Students A, B, and D when they were close to Thomas. On-task was 30% and 37% when Student A was close to Thomas and 80% when she was in a location away from Thomas. A similar pattern was found for Student B, who was on-task 50% and 25% of the time when close to Thomas and 86% of the time when he was away from Thomas.

All students had higher percentages for on-task when they are in locations away from their peers with disabilities, although the differences for individual students who are close to or away from Ann (Figure 2) are not as great as those for Thomas (Figure 1). Student E showed variability across four observations, with on-task close to Ann at 55% for one observation and 94% for another. Student G was on-task whether she was close to (96%) or away from (98%) Ann. Percentages for on-task for all other students close to Ann were above 70%. Student H showed the greatest difference for percentages close to (71%) and away from (89%) Ann.

Commentary

The results section of the article presents the findings without much comment. It is full of numbers and not easy to interpret at this point. That is why Figures 1 and 2 are so important. Much can be understood by studying theses figures, the first for students observed reacting to Thomas and the second for those observed reacting to Ann.

Each figure presents the percentage of observation time spent on each of the four observation categories: Off-Look, Off-Active, Off-Other, and On-Task. Also shown, across the bottom, is the letter code for each student observed, date of observation, and whether each subject is close to or away from (marked by an *) Thomas or Ann.

For example, in Figure 1, subject C on 1/26 and 5/16 is showing almost total on-task behavior while close to Thomas, whereas subjects A and B are closer to 60% off-task behavior when close to Thomas. On-task behaviors are higher for subjects when close to Ann. "All students had higher percentages for on-task when they are in locations away from their peers with disabilities" (Jellison, 2002, p. 348).

The results section of this study is somewhat ambiguous. The reader is given a lot of numbers to digest, and many seem contradictory. This is quite common in research; how nice it would if all results were neat and easily understood. This is rarely the case, and is why the final section of the article, Discussion, is so important. It presents the author the opportunity to "interpret" and make sense of it all.

The Article *(continued)*

Discussion

Results of this study show differences in typical students' on-task and off-task behavior when they are in different locations either close to or away from their classmates with disabilities. When group means for the behaviors of typical students are examined, the results are not unexpected; however, when individual data are examined, we find several students with unique patterns of behavior. Results show that during music instruction in an inclusive elementary setting: (1) there are observable differences in the on-task and off-task behavior of typical students depending on their proximity to peers with disabilities; (2) on-task is highest when typical students are in a location away from peers with disabilities; (3) there are observable differences in the on-task and off-task behavior of typical students related to which classmate with disabilities they are close to; and (4) there are differences in on-task and off-task among typical students; not all typical students respond similarly in relation to classmates with disabilities.

Data show that most of the typical students were more on-task when they were located away from either of their two peers with disabilities and that individual students were more on-task when seated close to Ann (the student with mild disabilities) than when seated close to Thomas (the student with severe disabilities). Importantly, some students showed an ability to remain on-task irrespective of their placement (close to or away from Ann or Thomas). One student seated close to Thomas remained on-task for over 95% of the time.

Many teachers identify a priori the environmental events (activities and classmates) that will cue and maintain a particular student's on-task or off-task behavior. Variations among the abilities of children to stay on-task in different situations in this study confirm what most teachers know—that some students come to a classroom having learned to remain on-task without close monitoring or intervention and others do not. For example, when Student A was close to Thomas, her on-task was as low as 30%. Even though she was more on-task away from Thomas, her highest percentage for on-task (80%) was still lower than most students in either location. Although Student A's interaction with Thomas may be interpreted as kind and affectionate, these interactions preclude learning the skills and knowledge designated by the teacher. The positive and somewhat reciprocal social relationship between Student A and Thomas should be continued and nurtured, but closeness and interactions should first occur outside formal class instructional time (e.g., before and after class as appropriate). As Student A learns to remain attentive to the teacher's instructions in different classroom locations, the teacher may choose to gradually move her closer to Thomas.

In contrast, high percentages of on-task (95% and 98%) were observed for Student C for each of the occasions when he was seated close to Thomas. During classroom instruction, Student C appears to be a better "partner" for Thomas than Student A.

Few typical students remained on-task when located close to Thomas, although many had high percentages of on-task, irrespective of their placement close to or away from Ann. The mean percentage for on-task for typical students close to Ann was 83%, and away from Ann it was 91%.

Teachers regularly use placement and "changing seats" as a strategy for classroom management. The results of this study suggest that teachers should give careful attention to the placement of students in inclusive classrooms to improve the learning environment and academic success of students with and without disabilities. Separating good friends seated next to each other who talk too much or socialize and moving them to placements that bring out their academic best is a consequence that is natural and even expected of the teacher in a regular classroom. As children with high percentages of off-task behavior learn to remain on-task as the school year progresses, they should also be given opportunities to demonstrate this ability close to their classmates with disabilities.

In addition to differences in individual students' abilities to remain on-task, it is possible that Thomas and Ann elicited different types of off-task responses. Students were generally more off-task with Thomas, a student with severe disabilities who would occasionally vocalize. Since children received no particular instruction on how to help, typical students may have viewed Thomas as needing more help than Ann. Each of Thomas's partners may have acted in a manner they saw as responsible and just did their best to assist their classmate; Thomas's vocalizations were often followed by his partner's touch to soothe and comfort. On some occasions, Thomas would reach out and touch his partner who was on-task; his partner would reciprocate and subsequently stop attending to classroom instruction or participating in the activity (e.g., singing, playing recorder).

York and Tundidor (1995) report that typical students are willing to do far more in helping peers with severe disabilities in general education classes than they are asked to do by adults. In the present study, typical students demonstrated positive behaviors toward their classmates with disabilities, although efforts to assist their classmates interfered with their own opportunities to participate in class activities. Teachers can direct the good efforts of typical students toward appropriate actions and interactions with classmates with disabilities.

Different types of activities may also cue higher frequencies of off-task behavior. Although data were not recorded in relation to specific activities, off-task seemed to be higher when activities involved materials (e.g., playing classroom instruments, pointing to and holding cards when listening to music). Informal observations of this type of lesson show that many typical students do not know how to assist their peers appropriately, particularly when materials are involved. Typical students repeatedly tried physical prompts that were unsuccessful (e.g., holding Ann's fingers on the recorder, placing cards in Thomas's hands, and physically holding his hand and lifting his arm to show sections of music).

Throughout all of the observations, although there was much kindness on the part of the typical students who were close to Ann and Thomas, students were often excessive and inappropriate in their helping. Inappropriate helping and prompting results in a high percentage of off-task for typical students and few systematic learning opportunities for Ann or Thomas. Although a paraprofessional was frequently uninvolved, on some occasions the paraprofessional contributed to typical students' inappropriate helping and off-task behavior.

Paraprofessional were not formally observed in this study, although there were occasions when the paraprofessional directly and indirectly affected the behavior of the typical students and their classmates with disabilities. The role of paraprofessionals in inclusive classrooms has received increased attention in the special education literature (Giangreco, 1997; U.S. Department of Education, 1999). Some professionals argue that as more students with disabilities are placed in inclusive settings, they will need fewer of the services provided by paraprofessionals, and that only in the most extreme circumstance should a paraprofessional be assigned to a student (Brown, Farrington, Knights, Ross, & Ziegler, 1999). Informal observations from this study highlight the importance of providing guidelines for the roles and duties of paraprofessionals in inclusive music classrooms.

Since individual differences exist in levels of participation among typical children in inclusive music placements, teachers will need to give specific attention to placement in their lesson planning. Teachers often tend to think in terms of the group, not the individual, as they plan content and activities (Clark & Yinger, 1979; Janney & Schnell, 1997), and teachers tend to first plan daily lessons for their typical students and then plan adaptations for students with disabilities (e.g., Potter, 1992). To help identify placements for students, busy teachers may want to request observational assistance early in the school year from music therapists, special educators, paraprofessionals, and others. Based on several observations of on-task participation of typical students in various locations early and throughout the year, teachers are better prepared to plan classroom environments that will be more conducive to individual and group learning.

There is a solid body of research that documents beneficial outcomes for students with and without disabilities in inclusive classroom settings (U. S. Department of Education, 1999) and the practice of inclusion will undoubtedly continue. With increasing attention given to the general education of students with disabilities, the educational progress of typical students should continue to be monitored. In many situations, goodwill and positive social outcomes occur in inclusive classroom settings, but it is critical that no child's academic development be hindered as a result of inclusion. Every child in an inclusive classroom must be taught to remain on-task to academic instruction and must be taught when, how, and under what conditions their social interactions and good intentions to help their classmates will be both appropriate and beneficial.

Commentary

Jellison states, "When group means for the behaviors of typical students are examined, the results are not unexpected; however, when individual data are examined, we find several students with unique patterns of behavior" (p. 349). The author does not present the reader with any statistical means by which to reach that conclusion. The reader must rely solely on the percentages in the two figures.

Following two paragraphs in which Jellison states again the findings of the study, she begins a discussion of the implications for the classroom music teacher. While a number of these points are not substantiated in the present study, this is the place where the researcher is permitted some freedom when "interpreting" the results of the study.

What follows in the discussion is something most teachers know: Students vary in their abilities to stay on-task when in the proximity of students with disabilities. However, Jellison's point is a good one: "Teachers should give careful attention to the placement of students in inclusive classrooms to improve the learning environment and academic success of students with and without disabilities" (p. 350). In other words, the seating chart should reflect this concern.

Jellison makes the point that typical students often do not know how to interact or positively help students with disabilities. She notes the actions of typical students sometimes end up interfering with their own academic achievement. "Teachers can direct the good efforts of typical students toward appropriate actions and interactions with classmates with disabilities" (p. 351).

Many times observations are made in studies that are not part of the research design. Such is the case when Jellison remarks about the effectiveness of paraprofessionals in the music classroom. "Informal observations from this study highlight the importance of providing guidelines for the roles and duties of paraprofessionals in inclusive music classrooms" (p. 352). "Providing guidelines" means that the music teacher must help the paraprofessional know what his or her role is in the music class and how he or she can help in a positive manner.

Jellison is clearly concerned that so much attention is now being given in education to students with disabilities that typical students' needs are ignored. Her final statement says it all: "Every child in an inclusive classroom must be taught to remain on-task to academic instruction and must be taught when, how, and under what conditions their social interactions and good intentions to help their classmates will be both appropriate and beneficial" (p. 352).

The Article (continued)

REFERENCES

Bricker, D. D., Bruder, M. B., & Bailey, E. (1982). Development integration of preschool children. *Analysis and Intervention in Developmental Disabilities, 2,* 207–222.

Brown, L., Farrington, K., Knight, T., Ross, C., & Zigler, M. (1999). Fewer paraprofessionals and more teachers and therapists in educational programs for students with significant disabilities. *The Journal of the Association for Persons with Severe Handicaps, 24,* 250–253.

Clark, C. M., & Yinger, R. J. (1979). Research on teacher thinking. *Curriculum Inquiry, 7,* 279–394.

Cole, D. A., & Meyer, L. H. (1991). Social integration and severe disabilities: A longitudinal analysis of child outcomes. *Journal of Social Education, 25*, 340–351.

Colwell, C. M. (1995). Adapting music instruction for elementary students with special needs: A pilot. *Music Therapy Perspectives, 13*(2), 97–103.

Darrow, A. A. (1996). Research on mainstreaming: Implications for music therapists. In B. L. Wilson (Ed.), *Models of music therapy intervention in school settings: From institution to inclusion* (pp. 27–47). Silver Springs, MD: The National Association for Music Therapy.

Dugan, E., Kamps, D., Leonard, B., Watkins, N., Rehinberger, A., & Stackhaus, J. (1995). Effects of cooperative learning groups during social studies for students with autism and fourth-grade peers. *Journal of Applied Behavior Analysis, 28*, 175–188.

Duke, R. A., & Farra, Y. (2001). *SCRIBE: Simple Computer Interface for Behavioral Evaluation.* Austin, TX: Learning and Behavior Associates.

Federal Register. (1977). Education of Handicapped Children. Implementation of Part B of the Education of the Handicapped Act, *42* (163), pp. 42474–42518.

Force, B. (1983). The effects of mainstreaming on the learning of nonretarded children in an elementary classroom. *Journal of Music Therapy, 25*, 2–16.

Fryxell, D., & Kennedy, C. (1995). Placement along the continuum of services and its impact on students' social relationships. *The Journal of the Association for Persons with Severe Handicaps, 20*, 259–269.

Giangreco, M. F. (Ed.). (1999). Special series on paraprofessionals (Special issue). *The Journal of the Association of Persons with Severe Handicaps, 24*, 250–281.

Gunsberg, A. (1988). Improvised musical play: A strategy for fostering social play between developmentally and delayed and nondelayed preschool children. *Journal of Music Therapy, 25*, 178–191.

Hollowood, T. M., Salisbury, C. L., Rainforth, B., & Palombaro, M. M. (1995). Use of instructional time in classrooms serving students with and without severe disabilities. *Exceptional Children, 61*, 242–253.

Hunt, P., Allwell, M., Farron-Davis, F., & Goetz, L. (1996). Creating socially supportive environments for fully included students who experience multiple disabilities. *The Journal of the Association for Persons with Severe Handicaps, 21*, 53–71.

Hunt, P., & Farron-Davis, F. (1992). A preliminary investigation of IEP quality and content associated with placement in general education versus special education classes. *The Journal of the Association for Persons with Severe Handicaps, 17*, 247–253.

Hunt, P., & Goetz, L. (1997). Research on inclusive educational programs, practices, and outcomes for students with severe disabilities. *The Journal of Special Education, 31*(1), 3–29.

Hunt, P., Staug, D., Alwell, M., Goetz, L. (1994). Achievement by all students within the context of cooperative learning groups. *The Journal of the Association for Persons with Severe Handicaps, 19*, 290–301.

Humpal, M. (1991). The effects of an integrated early childhood music program on social interaction among children with handicaps and their typical peers. *Journal of Music Therapy, 28*, 161–177.

Individuals with Disabilities Education Act of 1996 (IDEA). PL 101–457. (October 30, 1990). Title 20, U.S.C. 1400 et seq.: U.S. Statues at Large, 104 (Part 2), 1103–1151.

Janney, R. E., & Schnell, M. E. (1996). How teachers use peer interactions to include students with moderate and severe disabilities in elementary general education classes. *The Journal of the Association for Persons with Severe Handicaps, 21*, 72–80.

Janney, R. E., & Schnell, M. E. (1997). How teachers include students with moderate and severe disabilities in elementary classes: The means and meaning of inclusion. *The Journal of the Association for Persons with Severe Handicaps, 22*, 159–169.

Jellison, J. A. (2000). A content analysis of music research with disabled children (1975–1999): Applications in special education. In American Music Therapy Association (Ed.). *Effectiveness of music therapy procedures: Documentation of research and clinical practice* (pp. 199–264 (3rd ed.). Silver Spring, MD: The American Music Therapy Association.

Jellison, J. A., Brooks, B., & Huck, A. M. (1984). Structuring small groups and music reinforcement to facilitate positive interactions and acceptance of severely handicapped students in the regular music classroom. *Journal of Research in Music Education, 32*, 228–247.

Jellison, J. A., & Gainer, E. W. (1995). Into the mainstream: A case-study of a child's participation in music education and music therapy. *Journal of Music Therapy, 32*(4), 228–247.

Johnson, D. W., & Johnson, R. T. (1991). *Learning together and alone: Cooperative, competitive, and individualistic learning* (3rd ed.). Englewood Cliffs: NJ: Prentice Hall.

Jolly, A. C., Test, D. W., & Spooner, F. (1993). Using badges to increase initiations of children with severe disabilities in play settings. *The Journal of the Association for Persons with Severe Handicaps, 21*, 53–71.

Kostka, M. J. (1993). A comparison of selected behaviors of a student with autism in special education and regular music classes. *Music Therapy Perspectives, 11*, 57–60.

Logan, K. R., Bachman, R., & Keefer, E. B. (1997). Effects of instructional variables on engaged behavior of students with disabilities in general education classrooms. *Exceptional Children, 63*, 481–498.

Manset, G., & Semmel, M. I. (1997). Are inclusive programs for students with mild disabilities effective? A comparison of model programs. *Journal of Special Education, 31*, 155–180.

McDonnell, J., Thorson, N., McQuivey, C., & Keifer-O'Donnell, R. (1997). Variables associated with in-school and after-school integration of secondary students with severe disabilities. *Education and Training in Mental Retardation, 26*, 243–257.

Potter, M. L. (1992). Research on teacher thinking: Implications for mainstreaming students with multiple handicaps. *Journal of Developmental and Physical Disabilities, 4*(2), 115–127.

Sharpe, M. N., York, J. L., & Knight, J. (1994). Effects of inclusion on the academic performance of classmates without disabilities. *Remedial and Special Education, 15*, 281–287.

Schnoor, R. F. (1990). "Peter? He comes and goes..." First graders' perceptions of a part-time mainstream student. *The Journal of the Association for Persons with Severe Handicaps, 21*, 53–71.

Standley, J. M., & Hughes, J. E. (1996). Documenting developmentally appropriate objectives and benefits of a music therapy program for early intervention: A behavioral analysis. *Music Therapy Perspectives, 14*, 87–94.

Standley, J. M., & Hughes, J. E. (1997). Evaluation of an early intervention music curriculum for enhancing prereading/writing skills. *Music Therapy Perspectives, 15*, 79–85.

Thompson, K. P. (1986). The general music class as experienced by mainstreamed handicapped students. *Journal of the International Association of Music for the Handicapped (formerly MEH Bulletin), 1*(3), 16–23.

U.S. Department of Education (1999). To assure the appropriate public education of all children with disabilities. *Twenty-first annual report to Congress on the implementation of the Individuals with Disabilities Education Act.* Washington, DC: Author.

York, J., & Tundidor, H. (1995). Issues raised in the name of inclusion: Perspectives of educator, parents, and students. *Journal of the Association for Persons with Severe Handicaps, 20*, 31–44.

STUDY AND DISCUSSION QUESTIONS[1]

1. In what two years were federal laws passed regarding children with disabilities?
2. Why has Jellison focused on "typical" children rather than children with disabilities?
3. Who were the subjects in this study, and why were they chosen?
4. What was the design of the study, and what did it involve?
5. How were the data collected and analyzed?
6. In Figure 2, what percentage of subject F's time on 1/28 was spent "on-task" when close to Ann?
7. Why does it appear that subjects were more distracted when closer to Thomas than to Ann? Is this a research finding?
8. What is the genre and subcategory of this research study?
9. Did the results surprise you? Did you learn anything new about the interaction of typical students and children with disabilities?
10. What does the research of York and Tundidor (1995) show?
11. Much of what is presented in the Discussion section was not part of the actual investigation. Why?
12. What has been your experience working with paraprofessionals?

SUGGESTED ACTIVITIES

1. Reflect upon how "students with disabilities" laws have affected the music education class and the role of the music teacher.
2. Study Figure 1 and determine which of the subjects, overall, was more off-task when close to Thomas.

---

[1] The Study and Discussion Questions in this and subsequent chapters where articles are presented contain references to both the content of the chapters and the content of the articles. The articles were chosen not only as representative examples of the research genres, but also for their interest value to music educators and therapists. The questions that refer to the articles are an attempt to ensure that readers understand the content and its implications for the classroom or therapy setting. Reading research of little content value would be a waste of time.

PART TWO

Historical and Philosophical Research

CHAPTER 4

Historical Research

In the book *1776*, Pulitzer Prize–winning author, David McCullough (2005) presents a very real and down-to-earth picture of George Washington. Gone are all the pretty accolades and Romantic notions that often surround this Revolutionary War hero. Instead, McCullough concludes:

> He was not a brilliant strategist or tactician, not a gifted orator, not an intellectual. At several crucial moments he had shown marked indecisiveness. He had made serious mistakes in judgment. But experience had been his great teacher from boyhood, and in this greatest test, he learned steadily from experience. Above all, Washington never forgot what was at stake and he never gave up. (p. 293)

This is what historical research does—it presents a real picture of the past, not some sentimental portrait. McCullough, in digesting a large number of documents regarding the Revolutionary War, found "the father of the nation" not to be some "larger than life" character, but, rather, a regular human being with many weaknesses. Fortunately for the fledgling country of America, his strengths of "leadership and unrelenting perseverance" produced an outcome "little short of a miracle" (McCullough, 2005, p. 294).

PURPOSES AND PROCEDURES

The role of historical research has evolved in music education and therapy as a means by which practitioners discover their "roots" and chart their futures. For example, Lowell Mason firmly believed that all children could learn to sing, and singing was taught as a "method" in America's public schools for a hundred years following Mason's example. However, with the advent of progressive education and the child study movement, early twentieth-century educators turned from the "song method" to the "song approach," in which children were taught to sing through the singing of songs, without specific pedagogical instruction. The results of this shift became evident in an adult population that lacked singing confidence. Today, music teachers recognize that learning to sing involves a developmental sequence of psychomotor skills along with quality song literature (Phillips, 1992). It is unfortunate that it took the profession so long to see the damage that the "song approach" had caused. Fortunately, history served as the basis for change, and music teachers are once again teaching singing as a psychomotor skill.

Historical Research Genres

Research genres for historical research are not as well defined as those for empirical research. However, Volk (2003), in an article appearing in the *Journal of Historical Research in Music Educations*, hypothesizes that such classifications, while not always apparent, do exist; she attempts to demonstrate specific genres in relation to music education research. The first four approaches she models after those of Charles Tilly (1990), who describes various types of research modes available to the historical researcher. These four are as follows.

- **Small-scale humanistic:** This genre focuses on the historical impact of one or two persons, e.g., Carol Pemberton's (1985) *Lowell Mason: His Life and Times*.
- **Large-scale humanistic:** This is another genre that focuses on the historical impact of entire classes of people, e.g., Eileen Southern's (1971) *The Music of Black Americans: A History*.
- **Large-scale social-scientific:** This genre is quantitative and focuses on the historical impact of large-scale demographic figures, e.g., Jere Humphrey's (1998) "Membership of the Music Educators National Conference from 1912–1938: A Demographic and Economic Analysis."
- **Small-scale social-scientific:** Another quantitative genre, it focuses on the historical impact of small-scale demographic figures, e.g., Michael Roske's (1987) article, "The Professionalism of Private Music Teaching in the 19th Century: A Study with Social Statistics."

Methodologies

Volk (2003) relates that each of Tilly's genres employs different methods for collecting data, which are used independently and in combination. She describes the following.

- **Immersion or saturation** "refers to the act of simply gathering and reading everything possible on the topic, preferably from primary sources." An example is Edward B. Birge's (1928) *History of Public School Music in the United States* (p. 55).
- **Content analysis** "looks over a long period of time seeking evidence of trends, changing philosophies, or development of terminology." An example is Maureen Hooper's (1969) dissertation "Major concerns of Music Education: Content Analysis of the *Music Educators Journal*, 1957–1967" (p. 55).
- **Oral history** "involves interviews. This means actually talking with people who were present at a time in history, who knew the people being studied, or who played a role in the specific event being explored." An example is Daniel Steele's dissertation (1988), "An Investigation into the Background and Implications of the Yale Seminar on Music Education" (p. 56).

- **Collective biography,** in which "The researcher reads biographical information available on an entire group of people and searches for commonalities. This is most frequently used for finding distinctions between two groups." An example is Volk's article (1993) "Factors Influencing Music Educators in the 'Rote-Note' Controversy, 1865–1900" (pp. 56–57).
- **Genealogical sources,** "ranging from information found in family bibles to the Internet, can be used as part of the saturation method, or as statistical studies of their own, and most often they use a descriptive research model" (p. 58).
- **Government sources** "include laws passed, speeches given, court decisions, and records from government agencies. Some of these have direct impact on music education." An example is Mark's article (1999) "The Public Policy Roots of Music Education History" (p. 57).

Procedures

As with all types of investigation, historical research has become more analytical and more exacting. Techniques commonly found in the social and natural sciences are being employed, e.g., quantitative measures. Added to the "traditional" approach (i.e., use of primary sources/documents) and the chronological approach, the use of oral history, psychohistory (study of human psychology to explain why certain events or changes occurred), and quantitative history (employing empirical data gathering as an aid to understanding history) have made for an ever-expanding field of historical research.

The procedures for a historical study are basically as follows.

- Identify the event or topic (narrowly defined).
- Formulate the hypothesis(es) in relation to the event/topic.
- Gather data and verify.
- Determine usefulness of data (i.e., what to use or eliminate).
- Interpret and present the data.

Identifying a topic is a problem in all types of research. Beginning researchers often focus on areas that are too large in scope. However, prescribing a narrow focus typically requires extensive knowledge of a subject, which translates to much reading of the literature by the researcher. Working with someone who has in-depth knowledge in an area of study (e.g., a thesis director) is highly advisable for a novice researcher. Once the topic is narrowly defined, the real research can begin.

Hypotheses (declarative statements) are similar to research questions. David McCullough (2005), in *1776*, wanted to know: "What type of person was George Washington?" "Was he a natural leader?" "Did he have weaknesses?" The hypothesis suggests a picture of a Washington whom few had seen before.

Research questions often are formulated following a pilot study, and other research questions can emerge as the study progresses. However, if a study is too "open" from the beginning, it is apt to wander, looking for focus. "Only after a certain number of sources have been located and inspected by the researcher, and only after the feasibility of the research topic has been ascertained, should the research purpose be stated in final form" (Rainbow & Froelich, 1987, p. 109).

GATHERING AND VERIFYING THE EVIDENCE

Historical research involves the collection of two kinds of data: primary and secondary. A primary source, considered "firsthand" information, is most valued. Such sources are commonly found in libraries, archives, newspapers, periodicals, professional publications, government documents, theses, personal letters, diaries, wills, photographs, and accounts by witnesses. (The archive for music education is located in the music library of the University of Maryland, College Park, and is a valued resource for the profession. It contains such things as audiotapes of sessions from regional and national conferences, interviews with past presidents of MENC, and tapes from the Tanglewood Symposium.)

Primary sources are not "hearsay," or the report of someone who "heard about" something. A primary source places the researcher about as close to an event without having been there, and every effort must be made to obtain original sources. When reading a historical study, the individual should be aware of how important primary sources are to the validity of the investigation.

Secondary sources should only be used when primary ones are unavailable. Even so, they must be trustworthy and well documented. Most history books are secondary sources, as are encyclopedias and most Internet information. Quotations taken from primary sources when published by another then become secondary sources.

Many historical researchers today take notes using some form of personal computer. No matter what the form of data collection, they must take care to document all sources accurately. It is terribly frustrating for a reader to try to find a source incorrectly referenced in an article. It is equally frustrating for the researcher to try to track down a reference for which incomplete information was taken.

Interviews are a main form of data collection in oral history research. This is not the same as conducting informal interviews. An approach to an oral history interview requires a well-thought-out structure of questions in keeping with the topic of the research. Not to have such an outline may lead people to ramble and get off the subject. The use of a portable tape recorder is common because it is too difficult to write everything down as the interview progresses. Also, a verbatim transcript can be made from the tape, protecting parties from any legal action that might ensue.

On occasion, the *Choral Journal*, presents interviews of conductors who have had distinguished careers in the field. The following is an excerpt from an article by Alan Raines (2005), in an interview with Donald Neuen, director of choral activities at UCLA, the Angeles Chorale, and conductor of the Crystal Cathedral Choir.

> *Raines:* Are choirs better today than they were fifty years ago?
> *Neuen:* Yes. Because of the conducting of Robert Shaw and the teaching of Julius Herford. Choral conductors started learning from them in the late 1940s and early '50s by their examples set forth in workshops, recordings, and performances. This was the first time that the choral sound was neither to the right, with overly dramatic singing, [n]or to the left, with a nonvibrato, more conservative style of singing. Shaw brought singing to the center. He taught us that choral singing could be based on musicality and

a nonmanipulated beautiful tone. Choirs began to improve throughout the nation and quality graduate choral conducting programs began to spring up.

I must add an incredible debt of gratitude to those pioneers who developed choral singing before Shaw, and before ACDA and MENC choral workshops were available. The great conductors who worked alone, paving the way: Olaf Christiansen, John Finley Williamson, Elaine Brown, Fred Waring, Howard Swan, and many others. They laid the foundation on which Robert Shaw and the rest of us were able to flourish. (p. 34)

This excerpt demonstrates what a valuable resource oral history is and how the past, through the eyes of those who were there, is illuminated. Few people know the name Julius Herford like they know the name Robert Shaw. Herford had a long and distinguished career as professor of musicology at Indiana University, and it is Herford whom Shaw credits for teaching him how to analyze and understand a score structurally. Neuen was a firsthand witness of both these men, and choral conductors are indebted to his insights for a picture of their "roots."

External Criticism

Once the data are collected in a historical study, it is important to verify the data as truthful. Also known as *external criticism*, this process allows the investigator to determine if the data are authentic. Phelps (1980, pp. 138–139) notes that the process includes at least seven questions.

- Where was the item originally located? Where is it now?
- Is this document an original version or a copy? If a copy, where is the original?
- What is the estimated age of the item? Does it appear to be as old as it should be to be authentic?
- Are there autographs or other identifications that will make the process of verification easier?
- Is the handwriting (in the case of manuscripts) consistent with other items by the reputed writer?
- Are there any indications (diaries, newspaper accounts, etc.) that such an item may have existed?
- Is there any reason to suspect that this item may be a hoax?

Internal Criticism

Once external criticism has been established, the investigator looks at the *internal criticism* of the data. This process seeks to determine if the data are what they appear to be and mean what they say. Again, Phelps (1980, p. 144) gives a number of questions that need to be considered.

- Is the document consistent stylistically with others by the writer? Are there major inconsistencies?
- Are there any indications that the writer's reporting was inaccurate?
- Does the writer actually mean what he or she says?

• Could this work have been written by someone else in the style of the individual?

• Is there any evidence that the writer is biased or prejudiced?

The question regarding bias needs to be addressed in all research settings but especially in the historical genre, where subjectivism is a more common criticism. Although it is difficult to be completely unbiased, the individual needs to keep the possibility of bias in mind while reading historical research. There is truth in the notion that researchers can make words and numbers say anything they want. The educated reader must, at the least, know the possibility exists.

INTERPRETING THE EVIDENCE AND DRAWING CONCLUSIONS

Three basic approaches are used by historians to organize historical data: (1) topically, (2) chronologically, and (3) in combination. In all cases the data should be presented logically in relation to the research problem(s). Also, the writing style must be clear so as to advance the report in an easy and understandable manner.

When a study lacks flow and clarity, it can be due to the author's inability to couch the writing within a frame of reference, i.e., the times and cultural backgrounds of the people or events being presented (context). Lacking this information, it becomes difficult to interpret the data meaningfully. Knowing what came before and after an event helps the reader to understand continuity and importance. Relationships among the data also need to be stressed, especially those involving cause and effect.

The use of primary sources in historical research has been stressed previously. However, the importance of such sources is not always apparent to the reader. It is the job of the author to report all sources and the significance of each. A little-known diary that reflects the personal thoughts of some personage can be vastly more important than some personal letters written to friends. However, if the diary presents only musings that are unrelated to the research topic, the contents may be of scant importance, no matter how significant the diary may be historically.

The topic of bias has been addressed, and so must the problem of fact versus fiction. It is easy for a researcher to read beyond the objective data to reach a wrong conclusion. Sometimes the data are scant and provide little information from which to work. The temptation, then, is to draw inferences that may or may not be there. Better that the investigator abandon the subject than to draw spurious conclusions.

It is beneficial if a historical study in music education or therapy helps the reader to understand current practices. This, after all, is the reason for any research—to help advance current understanding of a particular area. Knowing what has happened in the past can help direct future events and makes historical research of significant importance.

READING HISTORICAL RESEARCH

Reading historical research is unlike reading a music history text in which historical knowledge is summarized and set forth in overarching historical eras. Valid historical research tends to be narrowly focused and based on a presentation of primary sources.

The following article by Martha Chrisman Riley (1990) looks at the music education program in Louisville, Kentucky, during its formative years. The picture it presents is typical of so many schools, then and now: a music program that is up and down, depending on those in charge who do or do not support music education. It makes for interesting reading.

Portrait of a Nineteenth-Century School Music Program

Martha Chrisman Riley, *Purdue University*
Journal of Research in Music Education, 38(2), 79–89.

Reprinted by permission of MENC: The National Association for Music Education.
Copyright ©1990 by MENC.

Each sketch of music education activities in a particular time or place contributes to the overall picture of American music education. This portrait of early school music education in Louisville, Kentucky, is particularly important since Louisville was one of the first cities to include music in the public school curriculum. One of the most influential American music educators of nineteenth century, Luther Whiting Mason, began his career there. This article describes the beginning of public school music in Louisville, the subsequent struggles and strengths of the program, the debate over "note" versus "rote" teaching methods, and the music books and song repertoire chosen for instruction and performance. Was Louisville's early school music program unique, or was it typical of music education in other American cities during the same period? A study of this question provides insight into nineteenth-century music education in America.

Historical Setting

In the early 1800s, Louisville was a bustling and prosperous city. The town had grown rapidly since its establishment in the 1770s due to its accessible location on the southern bank of the Ohio River. River trade was brisk, and Louisville benefited greatly from the fact that all passengers and merchandise going between New England and New Orleans had to pass through the town. By 1820, the city had a population of 10,000 and had become a cultural center of the West.

Music activities in Louisville reflected cultural trends of New England cities. In 1820, only five years after the founding of the Boston Handel and Haydn Society, a musical society was founded in Louisville (Casseday, 1852). By the 1860s, there were at least seven musical societies, including the hundred-member Mozart Society, which presented monthly choral concerts and the forty-member Musical

Fund Society, which performed large instrumental works (Campbell, 1864). Before railroads were in operation, concert artists made their way down the Ohio River to Louisville by steamboat. The arrival of railroads in the 1840s made the city even more accessible, and touring opera companies, minstrel troupes, and family singing groups performed there annually.

The public enthusiasm for parlor music that swept across the country around the middle of the century was evident in Louisville as well. In 1850, there were at least three music stores that sold sheet music and pianos, three music publishers, and one piano and organ manufacturer (Casseday, 1852). Private music instruction was a booming business. Music lessons were fashionable, and many people considered them a necessary part of a nineteenth-century genteel education. Young ladies or gentlemen could receive music instruction from one of Louisville's thirty private teachers (Casseday, 1852) or at any of the exclusive male or female seminaries. The decision to offer music in the public schools was, in part, an attempt by the school board to make the public school curriculum more like that of the private seminaries and thus more attractive to the general public.

Introduction of Music into the Louisville Schools

Music became an official part of the Louisville public school curriculum in 1844 (Louisville Board of Education, 1844), just six years after Boston had established its public music program. Boston's lead had been followed by Chicago, Baltimore, and a few small northern cities, but Louisville was the first southern city officially to include music.

The first music teacher was William C. Van Meter, who was paid a modest salary of $350 for the 1844–45 school year. Unfortunately, funding for the music position decreased the following year; in fact, Van Meter taught without pay for half the year (Louisville Board of Education, 1845). He resigned his post in 1846 and was not immediately replaced.[i]

In 1852 the school board employed Luther Whiting Mason and William Fallin to teach in the city's six grammar schools. The original plan was to give each teacher three of the schools on a trial basis, hold an examination after three months to determine which teacher had made the most progress with his pupils, then hire the better of the two to instruct all six schools. The examination consisted of a public performance by each teacher's pupils, judged by five school board members and four "musical gentlemen" from the community (Louisville Board of Education, 1853). The conclusion of the judges and the enthusiastic audience was that both teachers were equally competent, and so both were retained.

Mason and Fallin taught in the Louisville schools for several years. The primary schools were added to their schedules in 1853. This was a progressive action on the part of Louisville; even in Boston, music was not taught in primary schools until 1864. School board members heartily supported the music program, praising the physical, intellectual, social, and religious benefits gained from the study of music (Louisville Board of Education, 1853). The superintendent felt music instruction was responsible for an increased interest of Louisville citizens in the schools as well (Board of Trustees, 1853).[ii] The importance of music instruction in the eyes of the school board is evident in the fact that Mason and Fallin were paid the highest salaries of any teachers in the school system (Board of Trustees, 1853).

In June 1855, Fallin resigned for unexplained reasons. In the middle of the 1855–56 school year, Mason also resigned. Mason's resignation may have been due, in part, to his unpopularity in some of the schools. He had been reprimanded by the school board for losing his temper and speaking in a disrespectful manner, for pinching and pulling students' ears, and for hitting students on the head and hands with his violin bow (Louisville Board of Education, 1854). On one occasion, the board had received a petition signed by forty-three people complaining of the "conduct of Mr. L. W. Mason, singing teacher for the Western district, and requesting his discontinuance" (Louisville Board of Education, 1854, Vol. B, 264).[iii] Mason and Fallin's positions were filled by several different music teachers over the next few years.[iv]

In 1857, the Louisville music program was abruptly suspended. Although there is nothing in the school board minutes that states the reason for its suspension, it was no doubt related to the retirement of the president of the board, Reverend John H. Heywood, in 1856. Heywood had been the music program's most ardent supporter. It was he who had urged the board to hire Mason and Fallin in 1852, and who, the following year, had successfully introduced music into the primary schools as well. It was his influence that had obtained the high salaries for the music teachers. After Heywood's retirement, enthusiasm for the music program diminished, and it was nearly ten years before music regained a solid position in the curriculum.

Reestablishment of the Music Program

During the Civil War years, 1861–65, Louisville's primary and grammar schools were used as military hospitals. Classes continued to be held in church basements and rented buildings, but the financial situation made it impossible for any but the most basic subjects to be taught. Music was offered in the Female High School, however. For several years, Professor H. G. S. Whipple had taught music lessons independently at the high school, being paid directly by his students. In 1861, the school board officially hired him to teach three classes a week to all the young ladies.

Near the end of the war a demand arose for the reintroduction of music in the primary and grammar schools. Parents went so far as to collect enough money to rent pianos and employ teachers in several schools. Over $300 was collected in the Sixth Ward school alone, and there were five pianos in that building during the 1864–65 school year (Board of Trustees, 1865).[v] The strong interest of parents in the matter forced the school board to reestablish the music program, and, in 1866, music was again made part of the curriculum. School board members justified music instruction on the basis of its moral, religious, and patriotic values. In addition, they felt music instruction would help children of lower social classes fit into the mainstream of Louisville's cultural society by enabling "the child of the humblest citizens [to] read the printed pages of music by the side of the child of wealth." (Board of Trustees, 1865, 59).

During the fall of 1866, Professor Whipple and his assistant attempted to teach music twice a week to every class in grades 1–8 and the Female High School, but the large number of schools made this schedule impossible to maintain. To ease the load, they dropped the primary grades from the schedules and offered methods courses to the primary teachers instead. In 1868, a third music teacher was employed. As the number of schools continued to increase, the music teachers cut the number of lessons from two to one per week. The board also hired a fourth teacher, Florence Hull, to teach music in the primary schools, the normal school's laboratory, and, for the first time, in the black schools (Louisville Board of Education, 1872).

During the years immediately following the Civil War, the music program received strong support from the school board and the superintendent. The board defended music with references to improved discipline, physical health, class morale, and speech. The superintendent stressed the importance of music's aesthetic value. The strong Romantic influence of the nineteenth century is evident in his statement about the value of developing children's affective responses to music:

> Its study is the culture and embellishment of that portion of the human faculties usually included in the comprehensive term, the heart. Its tendencies are all refining, elevating, humanizing.... By the knowledge of music thus acquired, the child is made susceptible to the melting influences of songs sung round the fireside and the home, and the memory of which, in after years, when he has wandered far away from the parental roof, may bring back to him all the subtle influences linked therewith, tending to awaken in him the affections, soften the stubborn heart, and reclaim the wanderer. (Board of Trustees, 1870, 110–111)

With the changing of school board members in 1872, interest in the program began to wane. The new president of the board felt that music instruction was a waste of time and that more attention should be paid to academic studies (Board of Trustees, 1872). In 1876, there were four music teachers; in 1877, there were two; and in 1879, the music department was eliminated entirely.[vi]

Thus, the first era of public music education in Louisville came to an end. Although the program had known periods of considerable strength, its stability was always dependent on the attitudes of the current school board members. Its strongest years were the 1852–56 period, when Reverend Heywood was president of the board and worked energetically to develop the program, and the ten-year period following the Civil War, when parents, board members, and the superintendent were outspoken advocates of the value of music instruction. Although music was taught by classroom teachers during the 1880s, it was not until 1892 that a unified course of music instruction began to be rebuilt.

Teaching Methods

Almost immediately after music was introduced into the Boston schools, the controversy over "note" teaching versus "rote" teaching commenced. Beginning with Joseph Bird's 1850 pamphlet, in which he voiced objections to Lowell Mason's rote song methods, advocates of both sides vigorously expressed their opinions through speeches and papers (John, 1953). The debate was carried on in Louisville as well. In the 1850s, Luther Whiting Mason used a rote teaching approach while William Fallin stressed note reading. Fallin's approach, which followed the singing-school tradition, was the more generally accepted method. He drilled the children on the principles and symbols of music before allowing them to sing. When his students were finally given a piece of music, they were able to sing it at once at sight. In a letter to the *Louisville Journal* in 1854, one concerned citizen highly praised Fallin's teaching method while criticizing Mason's rote approach as unscientific and totally in error (McConathy, 1922).

In spite of such skepticism, Mason's method was also quite successful. Mason had his students imitate intervals and tunes before presenting the notation. His students were able to sing scales by each of the intervals and to take difficult dictation exercises with complete accuracy. Members of the Boston Germania Band, while on a concert tour in 1854, observed Mason's classes and commended him for making his pupils "thoroughly acquainted with the rudiments of music without stuffing their heads with far-sought and, to children, incomprehensible expressions" (McConathy, 1922, 161). The school board was unconcerned about the variance in teaching methods of the two music professors, allowing each to proceed in his own manner.

In the 1860s, the school board adopted a curriculum that all three music teachers were supposed to follow. The course of instruction was a combination of rote and note methods. The youngest children learned songs by imitation, but they also practiced drawing notes and reading simple scale exercises. Children in the middle grades learned songs by note as well as by rote, studied more advanced theory, and took dictation. Junior high and high school students were expected to be proficient sight-readers (Board of Trustees, 1868). Although the instruction books adopted for the music classes changed every few years, the general course of instruction remained the same from that time until the 1880s. Students were required to purchase the music book assigned to their class.

Music Books and Song Repertoire

Eleven vocal instruction books were adopted by the Louisville school board during the first period of the music program. The first two were chosen by Mason and Fallin: William Bradbury's *The Singing Bird* (1852) and George F. Root's *The Academy Vocalist* (1852). *The Singing Bird* contained folk songs and composed songs for young children, with exercises interspersed among the songs. *The Academy Vocalist* began with a treatise on music theory followed by a large section of exercises. The repertoire was geared toward older students and included arrangements of songs by Donizetti, Rossini, Handel, Mendelssohn, and Bellini, as well as many songs by Root himself.

Following the Civil War, the board adopted Lowell Mason's three-volume *Song Garden* (1864). This was the first set of instruction books to be called a music "series," and the books were used by many school systems, including those of Washington, D.C., and St. Louis (John, 1953). The repertoire of these volumes included a large number of German folk songs.

Three new instruction books were adopted in 1870. George Loomis' *First Steps in Music, Second Book*, whose first edition was published in 1868, was chosen for the youngest pupils. (Since no 1868 edition was available for study, the author examined the second edition [Loomis, 1875] for analysis of contents.) Loomis' series enjoyed popularity as the first graded series that attempted to teach music reading in a child-developmental way, beginning with a one-line staff, then two lines, and so forth (John, 1953). W. O. Perkins's *Golden Robin* (1868) was assigned to the intermediate grades, and Perkins's *The Laurel Wreath* (1870) was selected for the Female High School. Each of Perkins's books was divided into sections that included a theoretical introduction, exercises, a large number of part songs, and sacred songs. Perkins wrote many of the songs.

The last set of books to be adopted before the music program was suspended was the 1870–71 version of Luther Whiting Mason's *National Music Course* (Mason, 1870, 1871a, 1871b). Complete sets of books and accompanying charts were donated to each school by a Louisville citizen "of high musical taste" (Board of Trustees, 1871, 33). This series was widely used, not only in America but also in Germany and Japan (John, 1953). The books contained no treatises on the elements of music; Mason advocated rote teaching in the beginning. The repertoire in these three relatively small books included folk songs and songs by European, particularly German, composers.

The music in all eleven books used in Louisville was simple with respect to rhythm, melody, harmony, and form. The songs were written for one to four voices, with rounds and three-part songs predominating. The standard form was the rounded binary (AABA), though bar form (AAB) was frequently found in the German folk songs. Rhythms were straightforward and repetitious. Melodies were nearly all major in tonality. Harmonies consisted of tonic and dominant chords, with some subdominants and secondary dominants. Texts were set syllabically. In general, the songs were quite tuneful and singable, though many had wide ranges and frequent large leaps.

Over one-fifth of the songs had religious or moral texts. These included hymns to open and close the school day and songs of praise to God. Though religious instruction was prohibited in the Louisville schools (*History of the Ohio Falls Cities*, 1882), members of the school board approved of and encouraged the singing of religious songs. Their opinion was:

> If our children cannot all join in a common confession and prayer, they can all
> unite in a song of praise to the Creator. (Board of Trustees, 1868, 31)

Songs of philosophy and advice were also common. Children were instructed to manage their time wisely, honor their elders, and stay out of trouble. Songs about nature were the most frequent type in the books for younger children. Each season was depicted romantically in song: spring songs feature birds and flowers, tinkling brooks, and gentle showers; summer songs described bright sun, blue skies, and warm breezes; autumn songs portrayed colorful forests and harvesttime. Other songs focused on specific aspects of nature, such as rainbows, mountains, or snow. Animal songs were also common in young children's books. The most popular creatures were lambs, foxes, ponies, dogs and cats, rabbits, fish, bees, butterflies, and many types of birds.

All the books contained songs about home and family. Images of the family sitting together around the fire, children playing, and babies sleeping were common. These happy songs portrayed in a romantic and rosy light such everyday activities as kissing mother good morning or waiting for papa to come home from work.

Songs of school were also found in all the books. Though some of these were intended for instructional purposes, such as to help memorize multiplication tables, most had texts of love and devotion to school, teachers, and classmates. Other categories included patriotic songs, songs about occupations or recreation, and songs in praise of music.

In general, a sentimental and genteel tone ran through all the song texts. Childhood was portrayed as a happy time, although children's songs were refined and polite, never silly, and rarely even humorous. Reverence for God, love of home and family, and loyalty to friends and country were set forth as important values. In addition, children were encouraged to study hard, avoid temptation, and follow the Golden Rule.

Public Performance

Music performances given by Louisville children were well received by parents, the school board, and the general public. Concerts of Professor Whipple's students were publicized in local newspapers. In 1863, the annual performance of a popular touring group, "The Continental Old Folks," generated a "Little Folks Old Folks Concert." Professor Whipple conducted this imitation of the adult concert, which included popular and patriotic songs, solos, and duets by such "artists" as Little Red Riding Hood, Goody Two Shoes, The First Bride of Huntsville, and Queen Elizabeth ([Louisville] *Daily Democrat*, 1863). The program was such a success that the citizens demanded a repeat performance, which was cheerfully given. The following year, Whipple conducted his young ladies in a staged production of a children's operetta by George F. Root, *The Flower Queen, or The Coronation of the Rose* (1853).[vii] This also was repeated a few years later.

Louisville citizens could also hear Whipple's students during the annual commencement exercises of the Female High School. These performances included opera arias, duets, and choruses, and were similar to the programs presented by touring concert artists of the mid-nineteenth century. Some of the composers represented in the programs were Mozart, Donizetti, Weber, Rossini, Meyerbeer, Bellini, Verdi, Mendelssohn, and Gounod.

Conclusions

Louisville was pioneering in that it was the first southern city to include music in the school curriculum and the first city in the country to include music instruction in its primary schools. With respect to school board support, teaching methods, and choices of curricula, however, Louisville's music education program was typical of music programs in other major American cities during the same period.

The Louisville school board endorsed music instruction because of its perceived moral, intellectual, physical, patriotic, social, and religious benefits to the students. In addition, the superintendent stressed the importance of developing children's aesthetic responses to music. These arguments were similar to those used by the Boston School Committee and other school boards of the day. Additional reasons were the board's desire to make the public school curriculum more attractive to the general population, the need to satisfy parents who demanded music instruction, and the attempt to provide children of lower social classes with music opportunities in order to help them fit into the genteel social and cultural life of the city.

Problems encountered by the Louisville music program were similar to difficulties faced by other nineteenth-century schools: (1) financial problems, resulting in the paring down of the curriculum and the maintenance of the "basics" at the expense of music; and (2) disinterest of school board members in the subject. In Louisville, the attitude of the school board determined the quality of the program. A respected, outspoken, and persuasive member was able to effect tremendous change. It is interesting to note that these same issues continue to challenge today's music educators.

The rote-versus-note question that emerged in Louisville was not unique, though it was perhaps unusual to have teachers with such distinctly opposing viewpoints teaching in the same school system at such an early date. Music teachers everywhere debated the same issue, however, and the argument continues in American schools today. Louisville's resolve to combine the two approaches in a unified curriculum proved to be a successful solution there.

The music books chosen for instruction in the Louisville schools are representative of music books of the time; in fact, many of the books were used in other cities. The songs in these books were European folk songs, songs by the authors of the books in the popular style of the day, and adaptations of songs by European masters. They were uniformly simple in rhythm, melody, harmony, and form. Nearly all were major in tonality. Texts ranged from serious subjects, such as God and morality, to lighter themes of music and recreation, but all were polite and sentimental in tone. Louisville children's performances also reflected national trends. Root's Flower Queen was one of the most popular children's operettas in the country, and the Female High School's renditions of European opera selections were an echo of concerts of the time.

Though Louisville's early school music program had unique aspects, its development for the most part paralleled that of other programs. Thus, this portrait of music education in Louisville provides not only a glimpse of the events in that colorful and lively city, but a clearer view of music education in nineteenth-century America.

REFERENCES

Annual Report for the Year Ending July 1, 1853. 1853. Louisville, KY: Board of Trustees of the Public Schools of Louisville.

Annual Report of the Board of Trustees of the Male High School, Female High School, and Public Schools of Louisville to the General Council of the City of Louisville for the Scholastic Year of 1864–65. 1865. Louisville, KY: Bradley and Gilbert.

Annual Report of the Board of Trustees of the Male High School, Female High School, and Public Schools of Louisville to the General Council of the City of Louisville for the Scholastic Year of 1866–67. 1866. Louisville, KY: Hull and Brother.

Annual Report of the Board of Trustees of the Male High School, Female High School, and Public Schools of Louisville to the General Council of the City of Louisville for the Year Ending June 30, 1868. 1867. Louisville, KY: Bradley and Gilbert.

Annual Report of the Board of Trustees of the Male High School, Female High School, and Public Schools of Louisville to the General Council of the City of Louisville for the Year Ending June 30, 1870. 1870. Louisville, KY: Bradley and Gilbert.

Annual Report of the Board of Trustees of the Male High School, Female High School, and Public Schools of Louisville to the General Council of the City of Louisville for the Year Ending June 30, 1871. 1871. Louisville, KY: Bradley and Gilbert.

Annual Report of the Board of Trustees of the Male High School, Female High School, and Public Schools of Louisville to the General Council of the City of Louisville for the Year Ending June 30, 1872. 1872. Louisville, KY: Bradley and Gilbert.

Bradbury, W. B. 1852. *The Singing Bird or Progressive Music Reader.* Chicago: S. C. Griggs and Co.

Campbell, J. D. 1864. *Louisville Business Directory for 1864.* Louisville, KY: L. A. Civill.

Casseday, B. 1852. *The History of Louisville from Its Earliest Settlement till the Year 1852.* Louisville: KY: Hull and Brother.

Chrisman, M. C. 1985. "Popular Songs of the Genteel Tradition: Their Influence on Music Education in Public Schools of Louisville, Kentucky, from 1850 to 1880." Ph.D. diss., University of Minnesota, Minneapolis.

History of the Ohio Falls Cities and Their Counties, Vol. I. 1882. Cleveland: L. A. Williams.

John, R. W. 1953. "History of Vocal Instruction Books in the United States." Ph.D. diss., Indiana University, Bloomington.

Kapfer, M. B. 1964. "Music Instruction and Supervision in the Public Schools of Columbus, Ohio, from 1845 to 1900." Ph.D. diss., Indiana University, Bloomington.

Keen, J. A. 1982. *A History of Music Education in the United States.* Hanover, NH: United Press of New England.

Loomis, G. B. 1875. *Loomis's Progressive Music Lessons, Book Two.* New York: Ivison Blakeman.

Louisville Board of Education. 1844–1880. Minutes of the Board of Education of Louisville, Vols. A–D. Unpublished journals in the Louisville Board of Education Archives, Louisville, KY.

The [Louisville] *Daily Democrat*, June 9, 1863. University of Kentucky Library, Lexington, p. 2

Mason, L. 1864–1866. *The Song Garden* (Vols. 1–3). New York: Mason Brothers.

Mason, L. W. 1870. *Second Music Reader.* Boston: Ginn, Heath.

———, 1871a. *First Music Reader.* Boston: New England Conservatory of Music.

———, 1871b. *Third Music Reader.* Boston: Ginn, Heath.

McConathy, O. 1922. "Evolution of Public School Music in the United States," in *Volume of Proceedings of the Music Teachers National Association.* Vol. 55, 163–74.

Perkins, W. O. 1868. *The Golden Robin.* Boston: Oliver Ditson.

———, 1870. *The Laurel Wreath.* Boston: G. D. Russell.

Podrovsky, R. 1978. "A History of Music Education in the Chicago Public Schools." Ph.D. diss., Northwestern University.

Root, D. L. 1981. *American Popular Stage Music, 1860–1880.* Ann Arbor, MI: UMI Research Press.

Root, G. F. 1852. *The Academy Vocalist.* Boston: Oliver Ditson.

———, 1853. *The Flower Queen, or the Coronation of the Rose.* New York: Mason Brothers.

———, 1891. *The Story of a Musical Life.* Cincinnati, OH: John Church.

Troiano, A. B. 1984. "A History of the Development and Determinants of Milwaukee Public School Arts. Policy from 1870 to 1930." Ph.D. diss., University of Wisconsin—Milwaukee.

NOTES

i. William C. Van Meter subsequently moved to New York, where he developed a reputation as a distinguished music teacher. In 1855, along with George F. Root, he led the first musical convention held in Virginia. Root described Van Meter as "a preacher, exhorter, singing-master...eloquent and magnetic as a speaker in his strange western way.... Let Mr. Van Meter get an audience together and there was no resisting him. He could make people laugh or cry at will and paint in more glowing colors whatever he described than any man I ever knew. He always induced a large number of people to attend conventions" (G. F. Root, 1891, 102).

ii. In the 1840s, teachers and administrators in the public schools of Columbus, Ohio, also used music as a means of drawing public attention to the schools and increasing public interest and acceptance (Kapfer, 1964).

iii. After leaving Louisville, Mason took the position of superintendent of music in the Cincinnati schools, where he developed a strong and positive reputation as a successful music teacher. In 1864, he went to Boston, where he introduced music into the primary schools and published his *National Music Course* (1870–75), one of the first graded music series. Mason later led music training institutes in Boston and served as governmental music supervisor for Japan, where his influence was so great that school music there was known as "Mason Song" (Keene, 1982).

iv. Louisville public school music teachers from 1855 to 1857 were Louis Tripp, who subsequently went into the music sales and publishing business, Nelson Hyatt, and John Harvey. Charles Godfrey taught music from 1858 to 1860.

v. Parental involvement in school music instruction was not unique to Louisville. In Chicago, money was collected to pay a public school music teacher as early as 1847 (Podrovsky, 1978). Music lessons were also funded by parents in Milwaukee public schools in the 1860s, eventually forcing the school board there to hire a music teacher in order to control the instruction (Troiano, 1984).

vi. Music teachers between 1866 and 1879 were H. G. S. Whipple, M. F. Price, Herman Glagan, Joseph Clark, J. W. Lurton (who taught for only four months in 1869), Green H. Anderson, and Florence Hull.

vii. *The Flower Queen* is the story of a gathering of flowers in the forest to choose a queen. A depressed recluse happens by and is drafted by the flowers to make the selection. As each flower sings a solo, the recluse is warmed by their teachings of love, goodwill, piety, kindness, and beauty. He chooses the rose to receive the crown while he, himself, is rescued from despair and solitude and returns to the world rejuvenated.

STUDY AND DISCUSSION QUESTIONS

1. What is the major purpose of historical research?
2. How has historical research changed over the years?
3. What is the small-scale humanistic genre of historical research?

4. What is the content analysis method of historical research?

5. What is the difference between primary and secondary sources?

6. In the Riley study, is Keen's *A History of Music Education in the United States* a primary or a secondary source of information?

7. What is external criticism? Give an example from the Riley study.

8. What is internal criticism? Give an example from the Riley study.

9. How can personal bias influence a report?

10. In what ways can the researcher clarify the data?

11. What is the main research question of Riley's study?

12. Why does Riley present a "historical setting" for her study?

13. Why does Riley feel that music was most important "in the eyes of the school board" (1853)?

14. Why was support for music in Louisville withdrawn in 1857?

15. Outside the schools, who raised money for the music program?

16. What philosophy of music was espoused by the superintendent of schools in 1870?

17. What was the "rote versus note" controversy, and who was on each side?

18. Who wrote the *Song Garden*? The *National Music Course*?

19. How could the school song literature of the times be characterized?

20. How does Riley answer the main research question of her study?

SUGGESTED ACTIVITIES

1. Try to locate copies of nineteenth-century music books. In what ways do these early music books differ from today's basal series?

2. Debate this topic: "A knowledge of the past, in reality, does not change the future. People keep on making the same mistakes."

CHAPTER 5

Philosophical Research

Whereas historical research tells the reader "what was," philosophical research is concerned with discovering "what should be." The study of metaphysics is the basis for this mode of inquiry. Metaphysics involves investigating the *truth* that characterizes and underlies all things. While no one can have complete knowledge of truth, the knowledge of numerous persons on a particular topic often yields greater understanding of the idea. That is what researchers in philosophy do—they compare and reflect on the ideas of others (and their own) in an attempt to analyze, synthesize, and reach a "truthful" conclusion.

This is not an easy process, and the dialogue is often difficult to follow. The narrative is argumentative as the researcher attempts to shed light on the issue. Pros and cons are typically addressed, and you can often become lost in the bevy of ideas that are set forth. In truth, philosophical research is sometimes the most difficult of genres to understand. Reading such research, however, is often revealing of truths that could be hidden. Enduring the process can be worthwhile.

THE PURPOSE OF PHILOSOPHICAL RESEARCH

Estelle Jorgensen (2006a) characterizes the "doing of philosophy" in terms of certain functions she calls "symptoms of the philosophical." These "symptoms" include (1) clarifying its terms, (2) exposing and evaluating underlying assumptions, (3) relating its parts as a systematized theory that connects with other ideas and systems of thought, and (4) addressing questions that are characteristically philosophical (p. 176).

The following are brief summaries of how Jorgensen (2006a) describes each of the four "symptoms" of philosophical purpose. For a more complete presentation of each, you are encouraged to read the entire article, "On Philosophical Method," as cited in the References at the end of this book.

Symptoms of the Philosophical

Clarifies Terms

Words are the basis of communication, but word meaning is often ambiguous. The philosopher is concerned with clarifying meaning and refining ideas. "For example, if two studies of musical appreciation are compared, unless one has a basis for believing that the expression *musical appreciation* means the same in each case, the comparison does not make sense; the two studies may be about different things" (p. 177).

Clarifying terms also enables philosophers to critique ideas and permits them to compare their ideas with those of others. Jorgensen notes that the clarification of terms "enables studies to be devised that utilize these ideas in research and apply them in practice" (p. 178).

Exposes and Evaluates Underlying Assumptions

Assumptions underlie actions; e.g., we assume that we are going to be paid for the work we do. Not all assumptions are clear, and the philosopher often seeks to expose and evaluate these assumptions so as to make them clear. This involves critical and analytical thinking.

> Suppose that a school district plans to adopt a particular course in musical appreciation for children.... Beyond considerations of the material's age-appropriateness...are basic questions about the course's underlying assumptions. What is the author's concept of musical appreciation? On what philosophical grounds is its author's concept defensible? What does the course assume about the ways in which its author believes musical appreciation can be taught and learned? On what grounds can one justify the author's chosen methods? These, among other questions, go beyond an analysis of course content...to look at the factors prior to and behind it, and in so doing reveal the central issues of causation and motivation, offering the tools to answer such questions as "Why is this position being taken? Should it be endorsed? (pp. 180–181)

Relates Parts as a Systematized Theory That Connects with Other Ideas and Systems of Thought

Philosophers in this mode create a systematized theory of thought that connects various ways of knowing. These connections help to create a broader perspective of the world. This pattern of knowing also helps to explain why things are the way they are.

> Music education would benefit from the development of paradigms that reflect the variety of world musics, the international pervasiveness of music education, its multidisciplinary nature, its relevance to the entire life cycle, under the auspices of the various social institutions that carry it forward. (p. 184)

Addresses Questions That Are Characteristically Philosophical

Philosophy addresses questions that differ from other ways of knowing. These include: *ontological* (the nature of being and reality); *epistemological* (the nature of knowing and understanding); *axiological* (matters of valuation); *ethical* (underlying social mores and rules of a society or social group); *logical* (rules of reasoning); *political* (issues of governance and social order); and *aesthetic* (artistic questions).

> These philosophical question sets address a wide range of issues in music education. Their common point of reference is their challenge to the validity of extant ideas and practices: They systematically ask whether these ideas and practices are well grounded. They bypass the peripheral and trivial issues, going to the core of why things are as they

seem to be and where they seem to be going. As such, they address central questions relating to music education and challenge its very reason for being. (pp. 187–188)

PHILOSOPHICAL PERSPECTIVES AND ANALYSES

Philosophical inquiry involves a number of philosophical perspectives that serve as the basis for investigative purposes. Since philosophers are constantly looking for truth in relationship to life, these are presented with a brief explanation of what constitutes truth:

- *Absolutism*: Truth is objective and unquestioned.
- *Empiricism*: Truth is in experience and is collectable as data.
- *Existentialism*: Truth is subjective and based on individual experience.
- *Formalism*: Truth is in a system based on law and rules.
- *Idealism*: Truth is in the mind, the vision of the ideal form.
- *Materialism*: Truth is found only in physical matter.
- *Naturalism*: Truth is derived from nature and natural causes.
- *Pragmatism*: Truth is based on practical value and application.
- *Rationalism*: Truth is reflected in reasoning and abstract thinking.
- *Referentialism*: Truth is found in references to things beyond itself.
- *Relativism*: Truth is relative to each person for each time and place that person acts.

It is important to have some understanding of the "ism" that is guiding the philosophical article being read. Regarding these "isms", or schools of philosophical thought, Rainbow and Froelich (1987) state:

> Because of the large number of extant philosophical positions, it is unlikely that schol-ars will ever agree on any one system for the categorization of philosophical perspec-tives. Therefore, it is wise to be less concerned about the label one attaches to a set of beliefs and more concerned with describing the content of that set of beliefs. This is to say that a concise statement about a philosopher's general perspective may be more valuable than how that perspective is categorized and made to fit the existing labels of schools of thought. (p. 135)

Analysis

Philosophical analysis involves the processing of human knowledge as expressed in language so as to derive meaning. The analysis typically involves the use of logic in order to get at the truth. This process can be *propositional*, i.e., a statement that reflects a belief/opinion about a philosophical issue, *dialectical*, in which a dialogue or debate occurs between opposing ideas, or *critical*, where objectives, practices, or concepts are evaluated.

Propositional Reasoning

Propositional analysis or reasoning is linear in nature; it requires a beginning print and an endpoint in the drawing of inferences. There are two types of propositions: *analytic* and *synthetic*. Analytic statements express a definition, whereas synthetic do not. The truth of the analytic proposition can be determined by analyzing the words alone. No investigation outside the sentence is necessary to determine if the proposition is true. For example, "Music is a universal phenomenon" is an analytic statement.

A synthetic proposition often hides the truth through its choice of words or use of unclear logic. For example, the statement "Music is a universal language" is synthetic because what may be uplifting music in one culture may be an example of melancholy in another. In a synthetic proposition, truth can be initially hidden and later discovered *a posteriori* because experience is necessary to determine whether or not it is true. Synthetic propositions are often highly speculative.

Dialectical Reasoning

Dialectical reasoning draws inferences by discussing or debating opposite ideas (thesis and antithesis). Truth, which is often illusive, emerges from the contrast of tension and release of these opposing theses. Some philosophers consider dialectical analysis as a truly scientific method of inquiry, in that finding truth is a never-ending process.

The article by Jorgensen (2006b) found later in this chapter is an example of dialectical reasoning. When searching for a worldview philosophy of music education, Jorgensen contrasts the "theory-of-everything-in-the-world-of-music-education" approach with that of the "figurative/metaphor." In her conclusions she recognizes both approaches, that opposites have contributions to make, and the "truth" lies somewhere in a successful combination. Keep this in mind as you read the article—dialectical reasoning weaves in and out of the argument—it is not linear.

Critical Reasoning

A third mode of analysis used by the researcher in music education/therapy is the "critical" analysis approach. Here the writer determines whether objectives, practices, or views are desirable or should be revised. Some predetermined standard must be adopted for comparison purposes. "In music education the process of critical inquiry might serve to point out the most desirable ideas in teaching music reading" (Phelps, 1980, p. 250).

Curricular issues are at the heart of this type of analysis. Jorgensen (2002) addresses "Philosophical Issues in Curriculum" in *The New Handbook of Research on Music Teaching and Learning*, where she presents a list of "images" of curriculum, all of which, she notes, are limited or flawed in one way or another. These include "curriculum as instructional content, system, process, realm of meaning, and discourse" (p. 48). This type of research "necessitates teachers and students being actively involved in the educational enterprise, thinking critically about the things that they are teaching and learning, and working to improve the human situation" (p. 56). Critical reasoning ought to be employed more frequently when writing curriculum.

THE METHOD OF PHILOSOPHICAL RESEARCH

The method used in philosophical investigation involves the process of logical inquiry. Inquiry follows the standard outline of all research: (1) presentation of the purpose of the study, (2) statement of the problem, (3) formulation of research question(s), (4) collection of data, and (5) presentation of conclusions. When reading a philosophical study it is important that the narrative continue to reflect the problem and the research question(s). It is easy for a writer to get into an area that is not the focus of the investigation.

Purpose of the Study

The purpose of the study should reflect the researcher's philosophical perspective ("ism") and how it relates to his or her profession. For example, the writer might be an idealist who believes that all students have some aptitude for music. Given this background you are better able to understand the framework of the research.

Statement of the Problem

The statement of the problem identifies the specific nature of the research. It involves the presentation of a *thesis*, i.e., a statement that reflects a belief/opinion about a philosophical issue. This is not an "out on a limb" belief, but a statement the person feels strongly about, one involving in-depth exploration, observation, and investigation. In the article by Estelle Jorgensen (2006b) the problem is identified as a belief in transcending nationalistic discourse for a broader view of philosophy in music education.

Research Question(s)

A research question naturally flows from any stated problem/thesis. In the Jorgensen article cited in this chapter appears this question: "How shall we address philosophically the multiplicities and pluralities, commonalities and differences in music education internationally" (p. 16)?

Collection of Data

Depending on the type of study, the investigator looks for evidence to support the thesis. In some cases quantitative measures may be collected. More often philosophers look to other writers to provide statements for or against the thesis.

Statements (e.g., propositions) that lead to a logical conclusion form the basis of the *argument*.

> The stronger the proof that the evidence is valid, the more trustworthy the conclusions become. The validity of that evidence is determined, however, by the validity of the line of argumentation employed in the discourse and by the precision with which all terms in the argumentation are being defined. (Rainbow & Froehlich, 1987, p. 1)

In the presentation of the evidence, the writer should present the argument in a logical and sequential manner. It is important that all terms related to the argument be defined. Then all of the evidence (data) relevant to the argument are set forth. As noted earlier, this may be in propositional, dialectical, or critical forms. Such evidence may or may not strengthen the argument. If too much evidence is found in the negative, the thesis must be abandoned or revised.

Presentation of Conclusions

Naturally the writer wants to conclude in favor of his or her belief/thesis and to provide a clear and lucid answer to the research question. When the evidence permits, this is the logical conclusion. However, when the evidence is weak or negative, a revision of the argument should take place. As with all research, the philosopher must be careful not to permit bias to enter the conclusions. Because philosophical inquiry can be highly subjective, the writer must take precautions to let the "argument" speak.

PROBLEMS WITH PHILOSOPHICAL RESEARCH

Two basic fallacies are common to philosophical argument: the *fallacy of relevance* and the *fallacy of ambiguity*. Fallacies of relevance include appeal to force, abusive argument, circumstantial argument, arguing from ignorance, appeal to pity, appeal to the public, appeal to authority, hasty generalizations, false cause, and begging the question. Regarding begging the question, Rainbow & Froehlich (1987) state:

> [B]egging the question is a fallacy of argumentation in which the strength of one's beliefs is cited as the evidence in support of that belief. This kind of fallacy may occur, for example, when music educators are asked to justify the place of music in the school curriculum. In that case it will not be enough to refer to the importance of music simply because of one's own belief in it. Instead, music teachers are expected to provide concrete evidence in support of their belief. That, however, is hard to do, and often causes music educators to find themselves at a loss for a well-founded line of argumentation that is based on documented evidence. (p. 153)

Fallacies of ambiguity concern terminology or propositions that are vague and easily misinterpreted. These include terms that have a double meaning (equivocation), propositions relative to the "part" leading to conclusions about the "whole" (composition), and conclusions about the whole yielding propositions relative to the part (division). These often occur when the researcher fails to define the terms in an argument and when stepwise reasoning is lacking.

> In summary, the application of disciplined inquiry to philosophical discourse in music education is a necessary and much-needed dimension of research. The results of such inquiry, however, can be of benefit to the field only if the truth of each statement in an argument is asserted before any conclusion is drawn. Also, the more the assertions are based on principles of verification of evidence, the closer the researcher may come to finding valid answers to a given question. (Rainbow & Froehlich, 1987, p. 155)

READING PHILOSOPHICAL RESEARCH: A COMMENTARY

The following article by Estelle Jorgensen (2006b) appears in the *Philosophy of Music Education Review*. This is a brief example of rationalistic perspective with which to begin reading philosophical writing. Commentary is provided to aid the process of digesting the contents.

Reflections on Futures for Music Education Philosophy

Estelle Jorgensen, *Indiana University*

Philosophy of Music Education Review, 14(1), 15–21.

Reprinted by permission of Indiana University Press, Copyright © 2006.

In 1990, when I convened the first International Symposium for the Philosophy of Music Education at Bloomington, Indiana, there was one dominant philosophy of music education in the United States and another was about to make its appearance. The five succeeding symposia (Toronto, Canada, in 1994, led by David Elliott; Los Angeles, United States, in 1997, led by Anthony Palmer and Frank Heuser; Birmingham, United Kingdom, in 2000, led by Mary Reichling and Forest Hansen; Lake Forest, Illinois, United States, in 2003, led by Iris Yob, Frank Heuser, and Forest Hansen; and Hamburg, Germany, in 2005, led by Charlene Morton, Paul Woodford, Frede Nielsen, and Jürgen Vogt) have promoted other philosophies. And this burgeoning of different voices and perspectives has greatly enriched the philosophical underpinning of music education and moved us from relying on a narrow range of philosophical views towards a plethora of them.

In our infant society, the International Society for Philosophy of Music Education (ISPME), we are creating and institutionalizing a forum that can nurture and critique ideas and practices and sustain the work of philosophical reflection in music education over the longer term. We have also benefited from long-term commitments by the Indiana University School of Music and Indiana University Press in publishing the *Philosophy of Music Education Review*, now in its fourteenth volume (building on three years of publication of the *Philosophy of Music Education Newsletter*), and the *Counterpoints: Music and Education* series that provides an important venue for publishing cutting-edge scholarship in our field. And over the past two years, we have begun to build an international team of philosophers committed to establishing a strong philosophical society in music education.

Beyond institutionalizing philosophical scholarship in music education, our society is committed to creating a genuinely international community that offers a global perspective. In the past, music education grew up within national borders and its work was often nationalistic in emphasis. Now, we face new challenges of thinking beyond those national commitments to a world of music education. This world might be seen as what Maxine Greene aptly terms "multiplicities and pluralities,"[1] the many differing groups forged within language groups, religious perspectives, political ideologies, economic strictures, and familial obligations. And as philosophers, we work especially within our various linguistic and cultural traditions as we also seek to transcend these traditions in a common discourse.

Commentary

The introduction to this article focuses on a philosophy of music education from an international perspective. Jorgensen outlines the emergence of ISPME, which makes, among other things, this dialogue possible. A philosophy of music education journal (PMER) exists to disseminate ideas reflective of a worldview. The last sentence of the preceding excerpt presents the research problem: transcending nationalistic discourse for a broader view of philosophy in music education.

The Article *(continued)*

How shall we address philosophically the multiplicities and pluralities, commonalities and differences in music education internationally? Radical relativism and pluralism offer contrasting perspectives.[2] Radical relativism sees the host of different music education beliefs and practices around the world as incommensurable and focuses on differences between them. For example, viewing Japanese and British music education within this stance would suggest that since Japanese and British music education reflect Japanese and British society and culture, respectively, each cannot be understood in terms of the other, they are different and incommensurate with the other, and it is important to understand each in its own terms. Pluralism, however, sees differences as commensurable and focuses on shared attributes. Since human beings are the creators of culture and society, common threads amidst the differences emerge from this common humanity. For example, as a reflection of their different societies and cultures, although we expect to encounter differences between British and Japanese music education, we may also observe commonalities since they both bear the imprint of a shared humanity.

Commentary

The main research question of this article is stated in the first sentence: "How shall we address philosophically the multiplicities and pluralities, commonalities, and differences in music education internationally?" Jorgensen contrasts radical relativism and pluralism and sides with pluralism. Her argument follows.

The Article *(continued)*

Notwithstanding the musics and educational systems seem, upon first glance and when considered specifically, to be incommensurable, a deeper and more general examination turns up evidence supporting a pluralist perspective.[3] Historically, cultures regularly borrow from different others as if there were common human threads. Maurice Ravel, Carl Orff, and Paul Simon are among twentieth-century composers to draw on cultures from the Far East and Africa. In music education, Masafumi Ogawa's study of the introduction of Luther Whiting Mason's ideas into Japan in the nineteenth century,[4] the dissemination of Shinichi Suzuki's ideas into the United States, the spread of Zoltán Kodály's, Émile Jaques-Dalcroze's, and Carl Orff's and Gunild Keetman's ideas into other part of Europe, Asia, Africa, Oceania, and the Americas, and the influence of African ideas on Europe and North America (especially those forwarded by Christopher Small[5]) exemplify these borrowings. And these intersections confirm that musicians and teachers regularly act as if there are commonalities with different others.

Psychological evidence of musical ability also provides grounds for believing that people share psychological and musical similarities around the world. Rosamund Shuter-Dyson's inclusion of cross-cultural attributes of music ability[6] and Anthony Palmer's studies of human consciousness and musical ability[7] are cases in point. And it is reasonable to expect musical commonalities because of this common humanity.

Humanistic arguments for education are predicated on the assumptions that all people are of worth and while flawed nevertheless have widely shared aspirations, namely, to be loved, to be safe, to be able to make choices freely, and to exercise their creative powers.[8] Although specific manifestations differ, the arts religions, myths, and rituals express these aspirations and it is not surprising that they are pervasive in human societies and educational systems. If education is to be humane and if it is to place human beings and their development at the center of the enterprise, these evident specific differences may be expected to be commensurable and common in certain respects.

Commonalities need to be distinguished from universals. Although pluralism focuses on shared characteristics it does not insist on viewing music education within the frame of one over-arching music educational perspective that subordinates others. Views are inevitably disparate and subjective; commonalities are not value-neutral but are impacted by observer biases. When I look into another's society, I cannot divorce myself from the framework of my own experience and upbringing. I see what I am disposed to see and find common themes that reflect m own values, judgments, attitudes, and perspectives. While I might hope and even expect, as does Immanuel Kant,[9] that others might agree with me, the likelihood is that they may disagree. Greene's "multiplicities and pluralities" aptly describes the groups that coalesce from time to time around particular beliefs and practices and the dynamic processes that shape individual and collective thinking. Politically and practically, pluralism evidences dissonances, cracks, fissures, and tensions that are dialectical in the sense, as Hans-Georg Gamader might see things, that players play upon the stage or, as Susanne Langer might envision, dancers dance up it.[10] We might wish for them to coexist peacefully, as does Randall Allsup,[11] but the reality is often more complex and problematic. To embrace pluralism, then, is to act on behalf of our common humanity in a world in which forces both enhance and subvert it.

Commentary

Jorgensen presents her argument for a pluralistic philosophy of music education from three perspectives: historical/cultural, psychological evidence of musical ability, and humanistic arguments for education. She points out the need for commonalities but not universals: "To embrace pluralism, then, is to act on behalf of our common humanity in a world in which forces both enhance and subvert it" (p. 18). The author supports her argument by references to scholarly writers whose ideas reflect her own, e.g., Ogawa, Rosamund Shuter-Dyson, and Anthony Palmer. These citations are, in effect, the research data.

The Article (continued)

What needs to be the response of philosophers of music educators to these commonalities and differences? As philosophers, we are responsible for clarifying and articulating distinctions and conceptualizations of the realities we see through the lenses of our various cultural heritages and languages. Since philosophy is accomplished linguistically, we need to work in our various languages as well as communicate across them. Language privileges the powerful and it is difficult to escape the present political order of things. Out international conversation benefits from a common working language and it is also important to stress the contributions that philosophers around the world make to education and find ways to share these contributions among us all across the barriers of our languages.

There are at least two philosophical strategies to address the commonalities and differences in music education worldwide. First, there is the "theory-of-everything-in-the-world-of-music-education" approach exemplified in Bennett Reimer's "music education as aesthetic education" philosophy,[12] David Elliott's "praxial" philosophy,[13] and Frede Nielsen's "*musikdidaktik*."[14] I want to take Nielsen's theory because it attempts to map the world of music education systematically. Nielsen's purpose, as I understand it, is to show the common threads of music education that transcend specific differences. This theory provides a "road map" or guide for music teachers. How is a music teacher to apply Nielsen's theory to his or her practical situation? Here, we need the benefit of the German philosophical understanding of what I want to follow Max van Manen[15] to call "tact"—from *takt*, to touch, and musically, to beat time. Tact refers to what Gadamer, among others, signifies as the intuitive and imaginative way in which a body of theory is applied to particular phenomenal situations. This application of theory to practice is not a mechanical process but a deeply reflective one as the teacher senses where a theory might apply and uses it sensitively in the phenomenal world. Since practice also generates theory, Nielsen's view takes account of practice. Still, Nielsen privileges theory since theory is the normative body of wisdom and knowledge that is then applied to specific practical situations to which it is taken to more or less apply. This theory is then subject to empirical and logical test. Although applied intuitively and subjectively, it seeks rationality and objectivity. It also attend principally to common threads rather than differences (although it may take differences into account). Since it aspires to objectivity, universality, and systematic description, as "the-theory-of-everything-in-the-world-of-music-education" and although it includes art and science as components, it seems more suited to rational testing as a science with the obligation of refuting its hypotheses by objective means.

A contrasting philosophical strategy of perceiving commonalities and differences is to see music education figuratively, among other things, as metaphor. This view-point differs in emphasis from the "theory-of-everything-in-the-world-of-music-education" in that it is more figurative than literal, subjective than objective, artistic than scientific, and particularistic than universal in addressing how music eduction ought to be. I came to this approach in my current writing on *Pictures of Music Education* by way of my study of myth and music education. This study was prompted by an international conference David Carr and his colleagues organized at the University of Edinburgh in September 2004 entitled "Reasons of the Heart: Myth, Meaning and Education." I came to see how rich are the possibilities of think-ing about the work of music education figuratively. Such a strategy employs what Mary Reichling describes as analogical reasoning[16] and treats the subject of study (itself figurative) in a way that is sympathetic to it (that is, figuratively) such that the "message" is embodied in the "medium" as the "medium" expresses the "message."

Such a figurative approach to music education is artistic in terms of Nelson Goodman's symptoms of the aesthetic—syntactic and semantic density and syntac-tic repleteness[17]—that directly appeal to imagination (with its aspects of intuition, perception, reason, and feeling).[18] Rather than offer a theoretical basis for rational testing, its purpose is to illumine music education and inspire those who undertake its work. As I began to think about possible metaphors that ground music education, a plethora of pictures emerged that appeal mythically and spiritually. These pictures, I thought, might prompt music teachers to think imaginatively about their situations, focus almost instinctually on particular situations prodded by these pictures and the insights of stories, pictures, and music that spring to mind, and alter the ways teach-ers think and transform their actions.

This is not the time for a full-blown critique of both of these philosophical strate-gies. Still, the more I think about them, the more it seems that either approach taken alone does not suffice. The "theories-of-everything-in-the-world-of-music-educa-tion" pay insufficient attention to the figurative ways in which teachers are and work, are static rather than dynamic, see teachers dipping into stocks of knowledge rather than constructing their ideas and practices, and focus on truth claims that are not as transforming of heart, mind, and behavior as I would like to see. On the other hand, a figurative or metaphoric approach may pay less attention to literal, objec-tive, and scientific aspects of music education, underlying commonalities rather than particularities, and reason rather than intuition, perception, and feeling, than may be desirable. In short, I found myself in the dilemma of wanting to keep aspects of both approaches—to think in terms of theories and metaphors with the rigorous testing of theories. In this ground between metaphor and model, I was interested in Iris Yob's suggestion of "metaphoric models,"[19] and following Aristotle's lead, the logical possibilities of their counterpoint in "modular metaphors." Whatever the logical possibilities, whether closer to model or metaphor, the conjunction of elements that are particularistic and universal, rhapsodic and systematic, literal and figurative intrigue me. Also, thinking about theories figuratively reminds us that whenever conceptual entities are applied in the phenomenal world, there is already a metaphor since the worlds of abstract theory and phenomenal practice are often disjunct. Friederich Schiller's admonition to the artist to think of people "as they ought to be when called upon to influence them" but "think of them as they are, when tempted to act on their behalf"[20] rings true in its evocation of the differences between the theoretical and the practical. Thinking about metaphors literally also reminds us of our obligations as music educators to the phenomenal world, of the impact of our work on the circumstances that affect people's lives, and of our responsibilities as philosophers to articulate these realities and make a difference for good in this world. And so, as you can imagine, this sort of dialectical thinking is shaping my present study of *Pictures in Music Education.*

Commentary

The argument continues. Jorgensen presents two philosophical strategies that address music education worldwide: "theory-of-everything-in-the-world-of-music-education" (Reimer) and the figurative/metaphorical approach (Reichling). She appears to lean toward the latter because of the possible "pictures" that could ultimately "alter the ways teachers think and transform their actions" (p. 19). However, she sees positive aspects of both for theory and practice. She seeks truth through rationalism—argument based on reasoning and abstract thinking.

The Article *(continued)*

As we examine the commonalities and differences in music education around the world, we may call upon these and other strategies for doing our work. Each has its limitations and strengths. As we knit our own philosophical garments, together we may be a metaphor for the multiplicities and pluralities that constitute music education internationally, learning from each other as also put ideas to the test. Given the inevitable divergences in the manner and ends of our work and implications for music education practice, it is essential that we ensure the space and freedom to engage in this conversation, locally, regionally, and internationally from our differing philosophical perspectives while also insisting on the highest standards of philosophical rigor and discourse. As an international society, we can create openings for developing philosophical thought in music education worldwide and reflect on how people ought to come to know and do music. Notwithstanding the inevitable flaws and tensions along the way, it is important to foster this diversity of perspectives and acknowledge the common human ties that bind us together, and to think literally in ways that provide testable assumptions and figuratively in ways that inspire those involved in music education. And since each person sees only a part of a wider truth, we shall need each other as fellow philosophers of music education as we constitute "the one and the many" in search of truth in our field.

Commentary

Jorgensen answers the main research question of this article by stating that a number of strategies can be called on to address philosophically the multiplicities and pluralities, commonalities, and differences in music education internationally. She notes that each has limitations and strengths. Jorgensen recommends that she and her colleagues "foster this diversity of perspectives and acknowledge the common human ties that bind us together, and to think literally in ways that provide testable assumptions and figuratively in ways that inspire those involved in music education" (p. 20). This philosopher has begun a dialogue that she hopes will motivate others to continue in this line of inquiry from both literal and figurative viewpoints. She believes that a world-wide philosophy of music education is possible and challenges the profession to explore more deeply the common threads that could result in such a philosophy.

NOTES

1. Maxine Greene, *The Dialectic of Freedom* (New York: Teachers College Press, 1988), especially chap. 4.
2. Isaiah Berlin, *The Crooked Timber of Humanity: Chapters in the History of Ideas* (New York: Vintage Books, 1992), especially 11–12, 79–83.
3. Here I think of Alastair Taylor's ("Systems Approach to the Political Question of Space," *Social Information*, International Social Science Council 14 [1975]: 7–40) concept of "integrative levels of analysis" or generality at which an analysis may be cast. Commonalities may be observed, for example, in the common uses to which music is put around the world as ways of celebrating, mourning, worshipping, and entertaining.
4. Masafumi Ogawa, "Japanese Traditional Music and School Music Education," *Philosophy of Music Education Review 2* no. 1 (Spring 1994): 25–36.
5. Christopher Small, *Music-Society Education*, 2nd rev. ed. (London: John Calder, 1980).
6. Rosamind Shuter-Dyson and Clive Gabriel, *The Psychology of Musical Ability*, 2nd rev. ed. (London; New York: Methuen, 1981).
7. Anthony J. Palmer, "Consciousness Studies and a Pilosophy of Music Education," *Philosophy of Music Education Review 8* no. 2 (Fall 2000): 99–110.
8. Among those to advocate a humane approach to education are Seyla Benhabib, *The Claims of Culture: Equality and Diversity in the Global Era* (Princeton, NJ: Princeton University Press, 2002); Raymonda Gaita, *A Common Humanity;*

Thinking about Love and Truth and Justice (New York: Routledge, 2000): Martha C. Nussbaum, *Cultivating Humanity: A Classical Defense of Reform in Liberal Education* (Cambridge, MA: Harvard University Press, 1997).

9. Immanuel Kant, *Critique of Judgment*, transl., James Creed Meredith (Oxford: Clarndom Press, 1952), §8 56; §19, 82.

10. Sophie Haroutunian-Gordon, "Estelle Jorgensen's Vision of 'Transformation,' " *Philosophy of Music Education, 2000*, ed., Lynda Stone (Urbana, IL: Philosophy of Education Society, 2001), 256, quotes Hans-Georg Gadamer's *Truth and Method*, 2nd ed., transl., Sheed and Ward, Ltd. (New York: The Crossword Publishing Company, 1985), 101–102 use of the metaphor; Susanne K. Langer, *Problems of Art: Ten Philosophical Lectures* (New York: Charles Scribner's Sons, 1957), chap. 1.

11. Randall Everett Allsup, "A Response to Estelle R. Jorgensen's, 'Four Philosophical Models of the Relationship Between Theory and Practice,' " *Philosophy of Music Education Review*, 13 no. 1 (Spring 2005): 104–108.

12. Bennett Reimer, *A Philosophy of Music Education: Advancing the Vision*, 3rd ed. (Upper Saddle River, NJ: Prentice-Hall, 2003).

13. David J. Elliott, *Music Matters: A New Philosophy of Music Education* (New York: Oxford University Press, 1995).

14. Frede V. Nielsen, *Almen Musikdidaktik* (København, Denmark: Akademisk Forlag, 1998). For a summary of Nielsen's ideas in English see his essay, "Didactology as a Field of Theory and Research in Music Education," *Philosophy of Music Education Review* 13 no. 1 (Spring 2005): 5–19.

15. Max van Manen, *The Tact of Teaching: The Meaning of Pedagogical Thoughtfulness* (Albany, NY: State University of New York Press, 1991), 1.

16. Mary J. Reichling, "On the Question of Method in Philosophical Research," *Philosophy of Music Education Review*, 4 no. 2 (Fall 1996): 117–127, distinguishes deductive, inductive, and analogical reasoning.

17. Nelson Goodman, *Languages of Art: An Approach to a Theory of Symbols* (Indianapolis, IN: Hackett, 1976), 252–255.

18. Mary J. Reichling, "Images of Imagination," *Journal of Research in Music Education*, 38 no. 4 (Winter 1990): 284–293.

19. Iris M. Yob, "Religious Metaphor and Scientific Model: Grounds for Comparison," *Religious Studies* 28 (1992): 475–485.

20. Friederich Schiller, *On the Aesthetic Education of Man in a Series of Letters*, eds., Elizabeth M. Wilkinson and L. A. Willoughby (Oxford: Clarendon Press, 1967), 61.

STUDY AND DISCUSSION QUESTIONS

1. Why is the study of metaphysics the basis of philosophical research?

2. Why is it important for philosophical research to "clarify terms"?

3. How does philosophical research "expose and evaluate assumptions"?

4. What purpose does philosophical research serve in "relating parts as a systemized theory that connects with other ideas and systems of thought"?

5. What types of question "characteristically philosophical" does philosophical research investigate?

6. What is the nature of "truth" in each of the following? Absolutism, Existentialism, Idealism, Naturalism, Rationalism.

7. What is a philosophical thesis?

8. What type of statement is "Music is a universal phenomenon"?

9. What type of statement is "Music is a universal language"?

10. How are data presented in most philosophical research?

11. What is an "argument" in philosophical research?

12. What are the differences among propositional, dialectic, and critical reasoning?

13. What is the fallacy of relevance?

14. What is the fallacy of ambiguity?

15. What is the research problem in Jorgensen's article?

16. What is the main research question of Jorgensen's article?

17. What are the three perspectives from which Jorgensen develops her argument?

18. Does Jorgenson's article represent propositional, dialectical, or critical inquiry?

19. What are the two strategies that Jorgensen develops in addressing a worldwide philosophy of music education?

20. What conclusion does Jorgensen present?

SUGGESTED ACTIVITIES

1. Topic for class discussion: "Is philosophical research really research?" Does it fit the definition as presented in Chapter 1?

2. Write an analytic proposition and a synthetic proposition for the belief that all students of Western cultures should be exposed to music of non-Western cultures.

PART THREE

Qualitative Research

CHAPTER 6

Principles of Qualitative Research

Qualitative research is one of three main forms of behavioral research used in music education and music therapy (the others being quantitative and mixed). Bresler and Stake (2006) describe the various types of research within the qualitative genre as sharing four basic characteristics:

> (1) *noninterventionist* observation in natural settings, (2) emphasis on *interpretation* of both emic issues (those of the participants) and etic issues (those of the writer), (3) highly *contextual description* of people and events, and (4) validation of information through triangulation. (p. 271)

These researchers note that qualitative research has great value in studying the personal and political nature of education.

While qualitative researchers can collect quantitative data (at least to some limited degree), the typical qualitative study is recognized by its reliance on *words* for data and for the *narrative* to tell the story. The main outcome of qualitative research is not to look at the big picture but, rather, to present a close-up picture of one participant or a small group of participants in relation to some criterion. It does not adhere to the scientific method, but neither does it pose questions that need to be asked following the strict guidelines of quantitative research. This is a way of doing research where the quality of the experience is more important than the quantity.

CHARACTERISTICS OF QUALITATIVE RESEARCH

Rossman and Rallis (1998) summarize the characteristics of qualitative inquiry from the traditional viewpoint, but they also incorporate some of the newer thinking in this area. The following is a distillation of their thoughts (Creswell, 2003, pp. 181–183). The following eight characteristics involve wide variability as research procedures are quite flexible.

Natural Setting

Qualitative research involves a natural setting (home, office, etc.). In this way the researcher can interact with the individual or place and be highly involved in the actual experiences of the participant.

Multiple Methods of Data Collection

Qualitative research uses multiple and interactive methods for observing human actions. The methods of data-collection are growing, and qualitative researchers often involve their participants in the data collection process and seek to build rapport and credibility with the individuals. The researcher does not disturb the setting any more than necessary. Traditional methods of data collection, e.g., open-ended observations, interviews, and documents, now include such materials as sound, emails, and scrapbooks in text and picture forms.

An Emerging Process

Qualitative research emerges as the study continues. Questions can change as the researcher finds out more about the participant(s). The data-collection process also can change as the researcher learns more about the phenomenon of interest. The theory or general pattern of understanding emerges as it develops into broad themes and coalesces into a grounded theory or broad interpretation. This unfolding research model makes it difficult to prefigure qualitative research tightly at the proposal stage.

Multiple Strategies of Inquiry

Qualitative research uses one or more strategies of investigation as a guide for the process of the study (e.g., observation, interview, videotaping). Beginning researchers typically use only one strategy until comfortable with this mode of research.

Fundamentally Interpretive

Qualitative research is, at its core, interpretive; i.e., the researcher interprets the data. This includes developing a description of a participant or setting, analyzing data for themes, and drawing conclusions about their meaning both personally and theoretically. The researcher thus filters the data through his or her personal lens, which is influenced by social, political, and historical cultures. The personal interpretation of qualitative data is another of this genre's fundamental characteristics.

Holistic View

Qualitative research is viewed holistically. This is why qualitative research appears as reflecting a broad view. In addition, the more complex, interactive, and encompassing the narrative, the better the qualitative study. Visual models often are used in establishing this holistic picture.

Reflexivity of the Researcher

Qualitative research reflects on who the researcher is and is sensitive to their personal background and how it shapes the study. The personal self is inseparable from the researcher self. It also represents honesty, acknowledging that all inquiry is laden with personal values. Statements of personal reflection are included and considered a basic part of the research.

Complex, Cyclic Reasoning Process

Qualitative research employs complex reasoning This reasoning is largely inductive, but inductive and deductive processes are at work. The thinking process is cyclic, moving back and forth from data collection and analysis to reforming the problem. In addition are the simultaneous activities of collecting, analyzing, and writing up data.

MODES OF INQUIRY

As many as 28 approaches have been identified as modes of inquiry for qualitative research (Tesch, 1990, in Creswell, 2003). Creswell states, however, that most current qualitative investigations fall into one of five genres: narrative, phenomenology, ethnography, case study, and grounded theory (p. 183). A sixth genre, action research, also can be considered a form of qualitative study. A definition of each of these six modes of inquiry is found in Chapter 1.

Qualitative research approaches also are grouped into two broader genres: *Interpretive* and *Critical Theory* (Locke, Silvermen, & Spirduso, 2004). Interpretive studies seek "to understand a situation from the perspective of the participant," whereas critical theory studies seek "to understand and critique power within society" (p. 149).

Interpretive Studies

The six modes of inquiry for qualitative research just given fall under the heading of *interpretive* research.

> In this kind of study, by acting as the primary instrument for data collection, the investigator builds an extensive collection of *thick description* (detailed records concerning context, people, action, and the perceptions of participants) as the basis for inductive generation of an understanding of what is going on or how things work (an *explanatory theory*). Often, the purpose of interpretive research is to understand the setting for social action from the perspective of the participants.
>
> Reports can contain richly detailed narratives that are grounded in the data of the participants' own words, as selectively extracted from transcriptions or interviews. Descriptions of context and events are often developed directly from notes (commonly called *field notes*) made in the course of observations at the actual site of interest in the study (a research strategy generally referred to as *fieldwork*). Questions that might be asked in an interpretive study include "How do Native Americans view the criminal-justice system?" "How do teachers implement a new state-mandated curriculum in the classroom?" and "What is the experience of teenage runaways when they become homeless?"
>
> Among the methods commonly used by interpretive researchers are interviews, systematic observation of the setting or events under investigation, and analysis of documentary materials (lesson plans, police reports, hospital records, new stories, and diaries). Typically, collection and analysis of data take place concurrently, with preliminary insights and new questions being used to inform and guide subsequent data collection. (Locke et al., 2004, pp. 150–151)

The researchers note that trustworthiness of data is as important in qualitative research as it is in other research. Threats to validity and reliability can and do occur. Qualitative research is not based on the scientific method, but this does not free it from the demands of proper investigative procedures and reporting.

Critical Theory

Critical theory inquiry is concerned with empowering human beings to transcend the constraints placed on them by race, class, and gender (Fay, 1987). Examples of such studies include: feminist, deconstruction, postmodern, popular culture, and critical ethnography.

> Investigators doing critical research begin with a number of assumptions that differ sharply from those made by people working with the qualitative research traditions (or within the quantitative paradigm). Most scholars who work from the perspective of what is commonly called critical theory value the production of new knowledge through research (although they would insist on defining *knowledge* in their own terms), but only when it is conducted in a socially responsible manner—as they (individually) understand that moral imperative. Again, most of them would regard it as incumbent on the investigator to be concerned with how knowledge is used and, particularly, how that use relates to inequities in the distribution of power and material resources in our society....
>
> [C]ritical research does not require the investigator to maintain complete objectivity about the study. Indeed, most critical theorists regard objectivity in social science as no more than a polite fiction. That, however, does not indicate a disregard for care and close attention to detail in the planning and execution of a study. Nor does it suggest that critical researchers are not concerned about the quality of data obtained, the systematic use of analytic techniques, or a full accounting of both method and results in the report. They simply believe that all research is value bound and see it as appropriate that they make their subjectivity (personal values about the question and commitments about their role as researchers) explicit and public, for both participants and readers. (Locke et al., 2004, pp. 160–161)

The authors also note that critical theory is concerned primarily with making a better society through (1) improved understanding of social mechanisms and (2) empowerment of people.

DATA COLLECTION, ANALYSIS, AND INTERPRETATION

The process of qualitative investigation follows the previously presented protocol for each of the genres. What is central to all of these genres is the interpretive nature that researchers bring to the process. Biases, values, and personal interests must be addressed up-front because these can affect all or any parts of the study. The reader should consciously look for statements that reveal the author's experience in the topic area, any connections between the researcher and the participants, steps taken to obtain permission from a review board, and permission to study the participants themselves.

Ethical issues that can arise also must be addressed. For example, if the p████
from a school identified as having some negative characteristic, it would be ████
to identify that institution by name. The characteristic, however, should be r████
because it could, undoubtedly, affect the results of the study.

Data Collection

Creswell (2003, pp. 185, 188) describes the following characteristics of the data-collection process in a qualitative investigation:

- Identifies the *purposefully selected* sites or individuals for the proposed study. The idea behind qualitative research is to *purposefully* select participants or sites... that will best help the researcher understand the problem....

- Indicates the type or types of data to be collected. In many qualitative studies, inquirers collect multiple forms of data and spend a considerable time in the natural setting gathering information. The collection procedures... involve four types....

  1. *Observations*, in which the researcher takes field notes on the behavior and activities of individuals at the research site.

  2. *Interviews*, in which the researcher conducts face-to-face interviews with participants, interviews participants by telephone, or engages in focus group interviews....

  3. *Documents*, which are collected during the process of the research. These may be public documents (e.g., newspapers, minutes of meetings, official reports) or private documents (e.g., personal journals and diaries, letters and emails).

  4. *Audio and visual materials*, which may take the form of photographs, art objects, videotapes, or any forms of sound.

- In the discussion about data-collection forms, the author is specific about the types and includes arguments concerning the strengths and weaknesses of each type....

- Includes data-collection types that go beyond typical observations and interviews. These unusual forms create reader interest in a proposal and can capture useful information that observations and interviews may miss.

Analysis and Interpretation

Analyzing the data of a qualitative study involves understanding both text and image. The message is rarely superficial and requires in-depth interpretation. Creswell (2003, pp. 190–191) combines his ideas with Rossman and Rallis (1998) when characterizing the data-analysis process:

- It is an ongoing process involving continual reflection about the data, asking analytic questions, and writing memos throughout the study. It is not sharply divided from the other activities in the process, such as collecting data or formulating research questions.

- It involves using open-ended data, for the most part. This requires asking general questions and developing an analysis from the information supplied by participants.

- Researchers... tailor the data analysis beyond the more generic approaches to specific types of qualitative research strategies.

g of the data. Coding helps to produce a description of
or themes for analysis. Themes are often interconnected,
ophisticated interpretation. Computer-assisted qualitative
w available, e.g., NUD*IST and HyperResearch.
roach to presenting the data analysis is to use a narrative
ironology of events along with the presentation of themes,
examples, quotations, and so forth. This narrative is often
n a quantitative study.

Validity is an impor...it concept in qualitative research. This refers to the internal trustworthiness of how the data were collected and analyzed. It does not refer to the external generalizability of the results, which is of little importance in a qualitative study.

Numerous techniques are used to validate the data collection and analysis. Creswell (2003, pp. 196–197) identifies eight approaches.

1. Triangulation: three concurrent analyses used to verify any given set of data.
2. Member-checking: accuracy of data checked using feedback from participants.
3. Thick description: conveys the findings in such a rich format that readers can experience the setting.
4. Bias clarification: clears possible misconceptions about the researcher's bias.
5. Differing perspectives: presenting information that runs counter to the themes.
6. Prolonged time: researcher spends in-depth time understanding the topic by spending a greater amount of time in the field.
7. Peer briefing: involves another person (a peer debriefer) to review and ask questions about the data.
8. External auditor: someone new to the researcher who can review the project throughout the research process.

The reader of qualitative research should look for evidence that the author has addressed the validity issue in a forthright manner. Given the nature of qualitative data, this issue is extremely important to the value of any qualitative study.

Interpretation of the data is the final segment of the study. The results can take many forms, e.g., the researcher's personal views, findings derived when comparing results to other studies, and the suggesting of new questions. The formulation of new theories is also common.

READING QUALITATIVE RESEARCH: AN ETHNOGRAPHY

The following article is an example of ethnography, an interpretive genre of qualitative research. Derived from the field of anthropology, ethnographic research presents a picture of participants in their own cultural environment(s). It attempts to discover how people act and react in cultural settings. In the following study, music education students in Hong Kong and the United States are interviewed in order to understand their ideas about music teaching, how these differ, and how they are alike. The article appears in *Contributions to Music Education,* a publication of the Ohio Music Educators Association. Few states produce a research journal.

An Ethnographic Study of Hong Kong and American Music Education Students

Manny Brand, *Hong Kong Baptist University*

Contributions to Music Education, 29(2), 47–65.

Reprinted by permission of OMEA: Ohio Music Educators Association. Copyright © 2002 by OMEA.

In the belief that by studying and comparing music education students from distant lands one gains an important sense of perspective, the purpose of this study is to identify, describe, and compare Hong Kong and American university music education students by focusing on style of communication, self-concept, and selected music teaching issues.

Cultural and Educational Context for This Study

A long stick horizontally rests on the shoulders of an old Chinese man, wearing a straw broad-rim hat, in tattered clothes, with hunched shoulders, living in squalor. This picture typifies many Americans' image of (traditional) Asia. Contrast this stereotype with a more realistic image familiar to travelers to any large Asian city, such as Beijing, Tokyo, Hong Kong, Taipei, Manila, Kuala Lumpur, or Jakarta. Hordes of uniformed school children are carrying heavy book bags, often with piano music or a violin or *erhu* in tow, hurrying to or from school, usually during peak hours.

Modern Asia has always taken pride in the education of its children. Probably due to the explicit expectations of their parents, Asian children score the highest in science and math in worldwide comparisons (Elliott, 1999). Scholars often refer to Asians' "quest for excellence", while the popular press call Asian children "whiz kids" (Brand, 1987).

Asians' educational achievement (as a group) is certainly not a result of natural superiority (see Sui, 1992). Rather, Asians' educational or for that matter musical achievements are, at least in part, a result in some combination of cultural and family values and can be traced to: (1) a cultural tradition that places a high value on education for self-esteem, self-improvement, and family honor; and (2) a sense of determination reflected in willingness to delay gratification and invest in education (Schneider & Lee, 1990). Hartman and Askounis (1989) assert that the Chinese culture emphasizes achievement in school to a greater extent than the American culture, and others (e.g., Lee, 1984; Hess et al., 1987; Holloway, 1988; Reglin & Adams, 1990; Schneider and Lee, 1990; Stevenson et al., 1991; and Feng, 1994) have found that Asian parents have higher educational expectations and standards for their children than do Anglo parents.

Therefore, since family orientation, cultural and family values, and other societal factors account for the differences among Asians and non-Asians, what are those differences and how might they be relevant to music teacher education in America? What can we learn by examining music education students from an entirely different cultural tradition? How might this knowledge impact our perceptions and understandings about the professional preparation of music teachers? Perhaps, if our beliefs about music education majors are ethnocentric, music teacher educators could benefit from exposure to and careful assessment of Asian music education majors' outlook, style of interaction, attitudes, and perceptions.

Chinese Proverb: "When we all contribute wood, the fire is the biggest."

Common notion supports the view that Asian cultures tend to be "collectivistic" while Western culture is "individualistic." That is, Asian ethnic identity is often based on the relationship of the group, while the American culture emphasizes independence, individualism, and competition. Triandis (1990) associates collectivist cultures with cardinal values such as reciprocity, obligation, duty, security, tradition, dependence, harmony, obedience to authority, and equilibrium. Maoist ideology emphasizes that the needs of society take precedence over the needs of the individual. In contrast, individualistic cultures seem to embrace creativity, bravery, self-reliance, solitude. Stevenson and Lee (1990) assert that in the American culture, the individual is responsible for his or her accomplishments and difficulties, while in the Chinese culture, members of the family, teachers, or a larger group are expected to hold some responsibility for the success or failure of the individual.

The defining force for Chinese social behavior is Chung-ni K'ung (or Confucius, as he is known in the West). Bond (1986) states that Chinese people are "enmeshed in the Confucian tradition" (p. 215). Confucian philosophy, which encourages restraint over one's desires and equal distribution of the limited resources among members of a group, became tantamount to an official philosophy of the state, which later was congruent with the communist ideology, in place during the last 50 years in China (Fairbank and Reischauer, 1973).

These Confucian ideals (which include respect for elders, delayed gratification, and discipline), are also a strong influence. The natural order of the Universe was based on a straightforward hierarchy: children respected their parents, students deferred to their teacher, and the people obeyed the benevolent, authoritarian emperor. Moreover, the Asian family views intergenerational obligations as paramount to those of the nuclear family. Article 15 of China's family law states that: "Children have the duty to support and assist their parents, their parents have the right to demand that their children pay for their support" (Bond, 1991, p. 6). Children are taught to respect their elders, and the task of caring for grandparents and other elderly relations often supersedes the nuclear family relationships. It is this emphasis on lineage that distinguishes many Asian cultures. It is not surprising that Baruth & Manning (1992) conclude that teachers (viewed as surrogate parents) in Asian culture are accorded a higher status than teachers in the United States. Folk songs along with other cultural transmitters advocate Confucian philosophy as a way of institutionalizing a narrowly defined political and social order. Siu (1992) characterizes this "Confucian work dynamism" as a focus on persistence, a sense of shame, protecting "face," and respect for tradition—all collectivist values and motivating factors that characterize the Confucian approach to education.

Purposes and Methodology

The purposes of this study were to examine the following questions:

1. How do present-day Asian music education majors reflect these collectivist attitudes?
2. In what ways are Confucian philosophies shaping and driving Asian music education students? That is, what are Asian music students' expressed concerns about music teaching?
3. How do these attitudes contrast with American music education majors?
4. What are the similarities and differences in styles of interacting for Asian and American music education students?
5. To what extent do American music education majors reflect the Western emphasis on individualism, critical thinking, and self-reliance?
6. Do their Asian counterparts share the same ideals, goals, and attitudes toward teaching music to young people?

Ethnographic Approach to Studying Music Education Students

This study attempts to examine many of these issues by utilizing ethnographic interviewing methodology. Ethnographic research involves drawing out the meanings that life in a particular setting has for individuals, what Van Maanen (1988) calls the "practice of representing the social reality of others" (ix). The ethnographic interview captures and preserves the insights and understandings of an individual.

Spradley (1979) sees ethnography as a fundamental tool for understanding ourselves and the multicultural societies of the modern world. Ethnography provides the opportunity to step outside our narrow cultural backgrounds and begin to understand the world from the viewpoint of others who live by different meaning systems. Indeed, this study is based on the assumption that ethnography offers an invaluable mirror for both American and Hong Kong music education majors and their music education faculty in obtaining a more informed assessment of themselves.

To provide a comparative music education context for this ethnographic study, a brief portrait of Hong Kong school music education is appropriate. A more thorough description of Hong Kong's music education system is offered by Wong, (1990) and Ng & Morris (1998). More recently, Brand & Ho (1999) examined the changes in Hong Kong music education following the 1997 reunification of Hong Kong with the People's Republic of China.

For the nearly one million children attending over 1,000 elementary and secondary schools (Education Department, 1997), Hong Kong school music programs strongly reflect the 150 years of British Colonial rule in terms of music education practices, policies, and materials. In contrast to American school music education, general music (called classroom music lessons) holds a dominate position (in both elementary and secondary schools), and performing groups, such as Western bands, choirs, and orchestras and Chinese instrumental music ensembles, are extracurricular, meeting after school hours and sometimes on Saturday.

With large class sizes, classroom music lessons consist of singing, music reading, and music listening/appreciation, with some recent attempts to incorporate creative composition. Taught by music specialists as well as nonmusic teachers, classroom music in elementary schools generally contains 35 minutes of instruction, two times per week. Interestingly, in Hong Kong secondary schools, classroom music is required of all students, ages 12 to 15, and includes 35 to 80 minutes of instruction held twice a week throughout the school year.

Ethnographic Interviews of Hong Kong and American Music Education Students

Six undergraduate music majors, three Americans and three Hong Kong citizens, were selected to participate in this study. The American music education majors were in their third year of studies at a large state university music department in Texas. The Hong Kong students were also in their third year of studies in music education at a Hong Kong government–funded university. Each student was interviewed for approximately ten hours over a six-week period at their respective institutions.

The six interviewees used in the present study were selected based on their abilities to articulate their perceptions, views, and feelings. Since the interviews represented a significant time commitment for these music students, their willingness and availability were practical factors in the selection of the interviewees.

Ethnography was used to describe these music education students' style of communication, self-concept, and attitudes toward music teaching space. Instead of studying these music education majors, ethnography (see Spradley, 1979) means learning from them, as revealed through speech, both in casual comments and in lengthy interviews. Therefore, the ethnographic interview, described by Bogdan and Biklen (1982), Emerson et al. (1995), and Ely et al. (1997), was the dominant strategy for data collection. The specific interview approach employed with these music education students was adapted from Spradley (1979) and mirrored two distinct but complementary ethnographic interviewing processes: developing rapport and eliciting information. Therefore, each interview generally incorporated the following elements, strategies, and routines:

1. Welcoming/greeting/establishing rapport
2. Providing ethnographic explanations
   explaining the project
   explaining the nature of the questions
3. Asking ethnographic questions
   asking descriptive questions
   asking structural questions
   asking contract questions
4. Expressing interest
5. Expressing cultural ignorance
6. Restating informant's terms
7. Incorporating informant's terms
8. Creating hypothetical situations
9. Asking friendly questions
10. Closure

For the purposes of developing insights and understandings on how American and Hong Kong students interpret dimensions of their music education world, the interviews captured descriptive data in these six music education majors' own words. Bodgan and Biklen (1982) portray the ethnographic researcher's role as being a detective, "fitting bits and pieces of conversation, personal histories, and experiences together in order to develop an understanding of the subject's perspective" (p. 139).

Analysis of Data

During these ethnographic interviews, data were collected based on asking descriptive questions, making general observations, and recording the interview (field) notes. Subsequently, data were analyzed by means of reviewing field notes in a search for meaning, identifying cultural issues, and searching for relationships among these themes. The last stage is the actual writing of the ethnography. This consists of describing these six American and Hong Kong music education students by portraying their music education-related perspectives, and focusing on the students' style of communication, self-concept, and attitudes about selected music teaching issues.

This systematic collection of data and written ethnography attempts to uncover selected Asian and American music education students' perceptions and feelings as revealed in the researcher's interview notes, observations, feelings about dialogues with these music education students, memos to self about what was being learned, and images that come to mind during and following the interviews (see Spradley, 1979). Cultural meanings and concepts are presented based on the perspectives held by music education students. Finally, their insights, the words they used, their style of interacting, use of personal space, self-image, reference to family, attitudes, concerns about teaching, aspirations as prospective music teachers, and roles they hope to play in their respective societies are revealed.

Results

Extended conversations and interviews with these six interviewees does not provide the basis for offering unequivocal generalizations concerning American and Hong Kong music education students. However, a number of specific themes were observed during the interviews, detected in the interview notes, and identified as a result of the analyses of the interview data. These featured thematic issues also served to categorize the data and provide a structural function for reporting the results of the 60 hours of interviews. In capturing and presenting the thoughts and perspectives of the interviewees, I have combined and integrated materials that may have been taken from several different interviews with these music education students. In order to maintain confidentially and protect personal privacy, I have changed the names and altered details so as to prevent identification of particular individuals.

Getting Started: Initial Impressions

I approached each interview with the mind set that these dialogues with Hong Kong and America music education majors held the potential of revealing their ways of viewing the world. Since I was not acquainted with these six students prior to beginning the interview, I looked forward to our first meetings.

The initial impression is that the American music majors generally appeared more outgoing, even extroverted, when compared to these Hong Kong music education students. Possibly the Hong Kong students felt less comfortable being interviewed by a Westerner in English, their second language. On the other hand, the Hong Kong music education students all attend a (Hong Kong) university in which English is the dominant language of instruction, and many of the faculty are Westerners—particularly in the music department. The Hong Kong students appeared cheerier and in better moods than did the American music students. Maybe being good natured is more useful than extroversion in a collectivistic culture in which maintenance of group strength is an important consideration.

My immediate impression was that the Hong Kong music education students appeared younger—not necessarily by age, but by persona. While American music students sought a more sophisticated image, the Hong Kong music students projected a certain childlike, even naïve, image. All of the Hong Kong music students prominently carried cell phones, usually in little plastic holders decorated with cartoon figures and with "Snoopy" key chains or other small, stuffed animal figures dangling from their backpacks.

Use of Personal Space

During each interview, I was struck by the differences in use of personal space between the American and Hong Kong music education students. The American music students always plopped their possessions, backpacks, music bags, purse, and instrument down on the floor and on the seat next to them. In other words, they filled the available space with the "stuff" associated with being a music student. The Hong Kong students conserved the use of space. First, they carried fewer possessions, and they always kept their backpack, music, and even instrument on their laps unless I repeatedly invited them to place their possessions elsewhere. Hong Kong students always kept their coats or jackets on, while the America music students always took their jackets off before sitting down for the interview.

Initially, I felt more at ease while interviewing the American music education students. "Am I more comfortable around Americans?" I wondered. Would a degree of unconscious ethnocentrism make it more difficult for me to effectively interview and analyze the Hong Kong students? After several interviews I realized what was making me uncomfortable during the Hong Kong interviews; it was space. The office I used for the Hong Kong interviews was tiny, as nearly all (public and housing) space in Hong Kong is, while the interview office for the Americans was "Texas size." During the second interview with Ming Wa, I noticed I kept moving my chair back away from her. Soon the back of my chair was against the wall and she was still moving toward me. "Gee, I wish I could move the wall back," I thought to myself as I still felt like I did not have enough personal space. I thought about this issue of the distance we keep between each other. Sometimes referred to as "conversational distances," we use distance to control our privacy and level of intimacy. Each of the three Hong Kong music students would attempt to narrow the space between us. Yuen Keung would lean forward, eventually appearing to nearly fall out of the chair. Hing Kee would move the chair four to five inches closer to me before even sitting down. Ming Wai, Hing Kee, and Yuen Keung felt more comfortable narrowing the conversation space, and I felt more comfortable widening the space. Studies (e.g., Argle, 1975) show that cultural groups vary in the distances they keep from one another.

Conversations and Compliments

The American Interviewees were at ease in using conversation as a means of initially establishing a relationship. Sue would start chatting about the weather. Robert would talk about traffic, and MaryBeth would comment about the heavy workload for music students. Ming Wai, Hing Kee, and Yuen Keung were at ease with silence. None of the Americans were. These Hong Kong music students were more cautious in their assertions. I kept thinking of the Chinese saying "A word once uttered cannot be drawn back, even by a team of four horses." These American students' verbal style was more direct and pointed, whereas the Hong Kong music education students had an indirect, more subtle, verbal style. Yuen Keung, Ming Wai, and Hing Kee were more at ease in asking questions, whereas Sue, Robert, and MaryBeth were more comfortable in asserting their positions by making statements. The Hong Kong students were calmer and showed emotional restraint, while the American music students were more confident, self-revealing, and assertive during the interviews.

Interestingly, these Hong Kong and American music education majors responded to compliments in different ways. For instance, during the third interview I deliberately complimented each music education student (e.g., "Your answer shows insight into the importance of music education.") Sue, Robert, and MaryBeth acknowledged the compliment and proceeded to expound, in greater detail and with increased confidence, on the importance of music education.

In contrast, Yuen Keung, Ming Wai, and Hing Kee found compliments disturbing. My compliment had the effect of interrupting the conversation, and usually resulted in the Hong Kong students' refuting the compliment by countering that they really did not have enough insight into the importance of music education. In fact, there was a strong tendency for Yuen Keung, Ming Wai, and Hing Kee to play down their skills or competencies. They were much more at ease in talking about group accomplishments rather than individual accomplishments. I kept thinking of I Ching's advice that "haughtiness invites ruin; humility receives benefits." In contrast, the American music students showed greater use of first-person form (e.g., "I," "my," and "mine") in answering questions and discussing their concerns. Bond (1986) reports on the tendency for the Chinese culture to view an alliance between self and individualism as "unhealthy." The issue of the self is particularly interesting in a collectivist culture; maybe concern with the self is minimized in favor of group considerations.

Concerns About Teaching

All six interviewees were individually asked to name their biggest concerns about teaching music. Interestingly, the Hong Kong and the American music education majors approached this question from entirely different perspectives. The Hong Kong students were concerned with issues of self-worth, while the American students were external in their perspectives. For example, MaryBeth, an earnest voice student from Elgin, Texas, said:

> My main concern is the quality of school. Because I really don't want to teach in a music program that is inadequately funded. My high school band program was heavily supported by the community and we had the equipment and instruments that are necessary to build a successful band program.

In contrast, Yuen Keung's response is focused on issues of self-worth. She said:

> I worry about not knowing enough and having the personality to be successful in teaching music. For example, what if I am working with a choir and they don't make adequate progress. It is my responsibility to make sure the children can sing musically and with good tone.

The Hong Kong students' concerns about music teaching were usually focused on their capacity to please others—principals, parents, children. While the American interviewees expressed concerns about student learning, their comments were often centered on external issues connected with school and societal conditions that a first-year teacher has little control over, such as funding, school discipline, school violence, and parental support.

Each of the American music education students mentioned "student discipline" or "behavior problems" as a worry. Sue, Robert, and MaryBeth acknowledged that schooling in America is, at times, associated with drugs, violence, vandalism, and tragic school shootings; an environment very different from the Hong Kong schools in which Mng Wai, Hing Kee, and Yuen Keung will find themselves teaching. In contrast, none of the Hong Kong music education majors mentioned student behavior except for Yuen Keung, who stressed the importance of "encouraging the children so they won't be naughty."

Ho (1986) asserts that traditionally Chinese parents have been more concerned with impulse control and less tolerant of misbehavior in their children than Western parents. His research shows that Asian children tend to be discouraged from being independent, active, and exploratory and there is more of an emphasis in the West on children's self-expression, mastery, and creativity.

One's Place in the Family

All three of the Hong Kong college students lived at home, generally with not only both parents and one or two siblings, but also with a grandparent. All three American music students lived with roommates in their own apartments. Whereas the American students rarely mentioned their families of origin, the Hong Kong students tended to talk about their nuclear families at least once during each interview, thus reminding me of the Chinese proverb "When a family is united, everything succeeds."

Interestingly, this reference to family was a major difference between these music education students when each of the interviewees was asked to describe themselves during the very first interview. The Hong Kong music students all made some reference to their family. "Tell me about yourself," I asked. Hing Kee began, "I am the son of a piano teacher and a junior high school science teacher." Another student, Ming Wai, said, "I am the granddaughter of a very famous Cantonese opera singer."

Instead of describing themselves in terms of their place in the family, the American students described themselves in terms of personal qualities, using words such as "determined," "caring," "impatient," "emotional," "fair," "cautious," or "musical." These self-descriptors reflected strikingly different vantage points during one afternoon as Yuen Keung began talking about the joys of teaching music to primary-age children.

> My mother was a primary music teacher, and my father was a principal so I know that the early years are so important in the overall development of a child and a society. I want to be part of building a child's musical, social, and language skills. Most importantly though is teaching children to relate to other children. Hong Kong children need to be taught that getting along and fitting in is the most important attribute. The immediate needs of one come behind the needs of the group. It is not good for Hong Kong children to be so self-centered like I think of children in the West.

Another time, Ming Wai commented that "In my family there was a great deal of importance placed on obedience, appropriate conduct, and fulfilling obligations. Maybe this is one reason I want to teach music—to serve others." In contrast, Sue said:

> My Dad and Mom raised us to become independent. We moved a lot so we had an adventuresome upbringing. It was music that was a constant no matter where we lived, and my music teachers assisted me in adjusting to these different places we lived.

Interesting themes emerge in contrasting Ming Wai's with Sue's statements. Ming Wai uses words such as "obedience" and "obligations," concepts that lie at the heart of Confucian thinking, whereas Sue reflects Western values when she speaks of being "independent" and "adventuresome."

Yuen Keung said that it was important for the sake of her parents to do well in her studies. "I always feel the pressure. Sometimes it is stated and other times I just feel it in the air at our flat." One noted researcher (Ho, 1986) refers to the parental pressure on students to study hard and to do well in examinations as being notorious in Hong Kong" (p. 30).

"Advocacy Sounding Like Arguing"

Advocacy on behalf of music education was another issue differentiating these Hong Kong and American music education students. All three American students spoke of the importance of a music teacher advocating music and music education. Robert said, "What good is a strong school music program, one that teaches musical skills, understanding, and creativity, but not valued by the community, or recognized by the taxpayers?"

Along with Robert, Sue and MaryBeth were particularly passionate and articulate in defending the place of music in the school curriculum. In comparison, Ming Wai, Hing Kee, and Yuen Keung never mentioned advocacy as an important professional dimension for music teachers. Even when the interviewer deliberately raised the topic, Ming Wai said that "advocacy sounded like arguing." "A good person should not argue," noted Ming Wai. Challenging or questioning government or educational policy was an uncomfortable notion to these Hong Kong students. Even when presented with a typical (music education methods class discussion) scenario about their music program receiving a budget cut and music teacher jobs being in jeopardy, these prospective Hong Kong music educators felt that saving the music program was not more important than maintaining the quality of relationship with the principal, government educational authorities, or with other teachers. "Music teachers need to be modest and need to understand balance in society," said Hing Kee.

Discussion

"Within the four seas, all men are brothers."

This study represents a cross-cultural exploration of six undergraduate music education majors. Utilizing an ethnographic interview approach, the purpose of this study was to compare Hong Kong and American music education majors by focusing on style of communication, self-concept, and selected music teaching issues. Persons of Chinese ethnicity constitute over one-fifth of the world's population. Data which considers the Chinese culture is nearly absent within American music education research, and the few cross-cultural studies within music education narrowly explore differences in music preferences (see, for example, Morrison & Cheung, 1999, and Geisler, 1990).

Given the complexities of preparing prospective music teachers, there is a need for understanding how music education students see their experience. And the ethnographic interview provides a means of understanding through the eyes of music education students from both our culture and from another culture. The chance to walk outside our own narrow cultural backgrounds and limited music education traditions and comprehend the world—in this case, the education world—from other viewpoints leads to an understanding of the cultural differences that characterize human beings. Thus, this study's potential contribution is in assisting in more fully comprehending the nature of that cultural diversity within the perspective of music teacher education.

Certainly this study does not allow unequivocal generalizations to be made about a single Hong Kong or American music education way of perceiving the world. However, focusing on styles of communication, self-concept, and selected music teaching issues, this study finds that for the participants in this particular study, striking differences exists between Hong Kong and American music education majors in a number of areas, including style of interacting, use of personal space, self-image, concerns about teaching, reference to family, and attitudes toward advocacy on behalf of music education.

While the emphasis in this study has generally been on the differences between American and Hong Kong music education students, there are, however, several fundamental similarities between the two cultures, such as the desire to communicate, exchange ideas, and share experiences among individuals interested in and dedicated to teaching music. Thus, while acknowledging differences due to diverse backgrounds, different social forces, and disparate cultural perspectives, the overall impression [sic] is that there is much held in common among these music education students who live nearly 10,000 miles apart.

Abdu'l-Baha asserted long ago that "the East and the West must unite to provide one another with what is lacking" (Bond, 1991, p. vii). Thus, the value of this cross-cultural exploration for music teacher education is not just the uncovering of differences. It is also the celebration of common ideals, such as the desire on the part of both these Hong Kong and American music education majors for a life in music—sharing music study with others, and seeking a sense of accomplishment and joy in teaching and guiding others. Also, these students share a common desire to achieve a sense of fulfillment and become more confident and competent in preparation for starting a career in music teaching. Therefore, this study's emphasis on the differences should not detract from the obvious sense of commonality among all music education students, whether living and studying in Hong Kong, Houston, or Hanover.

Future research should extend this bicultural study of music education majors by exploring a multicultural approach utilizing music education subjects from many cultures. Adler & Adler (1995) specifically call for more research that uses in-depth interviewing as an essential research tool for understanding significant educational and cultural issues. Ethnographic research is not the answer to all questions, but it can address some issues better than any other approach. This approach encompasses a much broader and more complex paradigm, incorporating these students' nuances, and better capturing the richness and complexities of their lives. Technology and computerization have increased music education researchers' reliance on sophisticated statistical packages. Thus, there is even a greater need for systematically collecting ethnographic data that relies on the perspicacity of researchers in uncovering and interpreting wide-ranging patterns of musical and educational thoughts as a means of more fully comprehending and appreciating the great cultural diversity bestowed on the human species.

REFERENCES

Adler, P. A. & Adler, P. (1995). The demography of ethnography. *Journal of Contemporary Ethnography, 24*(1), 3–29.

Argyle, M. (1975). *Bodily communication*. Portland: Book News.

Ballard, B. & Clanchy, J. (1984). *Study abroad: A manual for Asian students*. Kuala Lumpur: Longmans.

Baruth, L. G. & Manning, M. L. (1992). *Multicultural education of children and adolescents*. Needham Heights, MA: Allyn and Bacon.

Bogdan, R. C. & Biklen, S. K. (1982). *Qualitative research for education*. Boston: Allyn and Bacon.

Bond, M. H. (1986). *The psychology of the Chinese people*. New York: Oxford University Press.

Bond, M. H. (1991). *Beyond the Chinese face*. Hong Kong: Oxford University Press.

Brand, M. & Ho, W. C. (1999). China recaptures Hong Kong: A study of change for music education. *British Journal of Music Education, 16*(3), 227–236.

Brand, D. (1987). The new whiz kids. *Time*, (9, Aug. 31), 42–51.

Education Department, Hong Kong (1997). *Teacher survey 1996*. Hong Kong: Government Printer.

Elliott, D. (1999). Learning to think. *Newsweek*, (6, September), 38–41.

Ely, M., Vinz, R., Downing, J. & Anzu, M. (1997). *On writing qualitative research*. London: Falmer.

Emerson, M. R., Fretz, R. I. & Shaw, L. L. (1995). *Writing ethnographic field notes*. Chicago: The University of Chicago Press.

Fairbank, J. K. & Reischauer, E. O. (1973). *China: tradition and transformation*. New York: Houghton Mifflin.

Feng, J. (1994). *Asian-American children: What teachers should know* (Final Report). (ERIC Document Reproduction Service No. EDO-PS-94-4).

Geislere, H. G. (1990). A cross-cultural exploration of musical preference among Chinese and Western adolescents in Hong Kong. *Dissertation Abstracts International, 51*, 1151.

Hall, E. T. (1966). *The hidden dimension*. Garden City, NY: Doubleday.

Hartman, J. S. & Askounis, A. C. (1989). Asian-American students: Are they really a model minority? *The School Counselor, 37*, 109–112.

Hess, R. D., Chang, C. & McDevitt, T. M. (1987). Cultural variations in family beliefs about children's performance in mathematics: Comparisons among Peoples Republic of China, Chinese-American, and Caucasian-American families. *Journal of Educational Psychology, 79*, 179–188.

Ho, D. Y. F. (1986). Chinese patterns of socialization: A critical review. In M. H. Bond (Ed.), *The psychology of the Chinese people*. Hong Kong: Oxford University Press.

Holloway, S. D. (1988). Concepts of ability and effort in Japan and the United States. *Review of Educational Research, 58*, 327–345.

Kahn, H. (1979). *World development: 1979 and beyond*. London: Croom Helm.

Lee, Y. (1984). A comparative study of East Asian and Anglo-American academic achievement: An ethnographic study. *Dissertation Abstracts International, 45*, 322.

Morrison, S. & Cheung, S. Y. (1999). Preference responses and use of written descriptors among music and nonmusic majors in the United States, Hong Kong, and the People's Republic of China. *Journal of Research in Music Education, 46*, 5–17.

Ng, F. Y. F. & Morris, P. (1998). The music curriculum in Hong Kong secondary schools— intentions and constraints. *International Journal of Music Education, 31*, 3–58.

Reglin, G. L. & Adams, D. R. (1990). Why Asian American high school students have higher grade point averages and SAT scores than other high school students. *The High School Journal, 45*, 143–149.

Samuelowicz, K. (1987). Learning problems of overseas students: Two sides of a story. *Higher Education Research and Development, 6*, 121–134.

Schneider, B. & Lee, Y. (1990). A model for academic success: The school and home environment of East Asian students. *Anthropology and Education Quarterly, 21*, 358–366.

Spradley, J. (1979). *The ethnographic interview*. New York: Holt, Rinehart and Winston.

Stevenson, H. W., Lee, S., Chen, C., Lummis, J., Stigler, J., Fan, L. & Ge, F. (1991). Mathematics achievement of children in China and the United States. *Child Development, 56*, 1259–1270.

Stevenson, H. W. & Lee, S. Y. (1990). Contexts of achievement: A study of American, Chinese, and Japanese children. *Monograph of the Society for Research in Child Development, 55*, (1–2, Serial No. 221).

Sui, S. F. (1992). How do family and community characteristics affect children's educational achievement? The Chinese-American experience. *Equity and Choice, 8*(2), 46–49.

Triandis, H. C. (1990). Cross-cultural studies of individualism and collectivism. In *Nebraska symposium on motivation*. Lincoln, NE: University of Nebraska Press.

Van Maanen, J. (1988). *Tales of the field: On writing ethnography.* Chicago: University of Chicago Press.

Vernon, P. E. (1982). *The abilities and achievements of Orientals in North America.* New York: Academic Press.

Wong, M. (1990). *The music curriculum in the primary and secondary schools of Hong Kong.* Unpublished doctoral dissertation, Columbia University Teachers College, New York City.

STUDY AND DISCUSSION QUESTIONS

1. What is the general focus of qualitative research?
2. What are eight characteristics of qualitative research identified by Creswell (2003)?
3. State and define the six modes of inquiry for qualitative research.
4. How does interpretive inquiry differ from critical inquiry?
5. Is objectivity less important in interpretive or critical research?
6. What is the meaning of "The data collection occurs in *purposefully select* sites"?
7. How do field notes differ from any other type of note taking?
8. Why do qualitative researchers often use open-ended questions?
9. Explain the process of "triangulation of the data." Why is this done?
10. In what ways can the interpretation of the data be done in qualitative research?
11. Describe ethnography and why it is a valuable form of qualitative research.
12. What did the review of literature in Brand's study say about Asian parents' expectations of children?
13. By what method did Brand collect the data for his study?
14. Why does Brand include a brief portrait of Hong Kong's music education system?
15. Describe the participants in Brand's study.
16. How did Brand validate his data analysis?
17. What does Brand state about the generalization of the results?
18. What are the results for each of the six original research questions that appear earlier in Brand's study?
19. What meaning is attached to the statement "Advocacy sounds like arguing"?
20. What did you learn from Brand's research that could impact your understanding of future student teachers under your direction?

SUGGESTED ACTIVITIES

1. Identify a topic that would be suitable for a qualitative study, and state (1) the participants, (2) the site, (3) the mode of inquiry, (4) theme(s), (5) data collection, (6) analysis, and (7) why the topic would be of value to your profession.

2. Identify the genre/research classification for each of the following qualitative studies:

   a. Performance Anxiety Among Beginning Piano Students

   b. My Family's Influence on My Becoming a Music Educator

   c. Shape-Note Singers as They Exist Today in Appalachia

   d. Growing Up with Musical Parents: A Collaborative Study

   e. Classroom Observations of Teaching Improvisation with an Orff Approach

   f. Developing a Theory of Why Adult Nonsingers Think They Cannot Sing

CHAPTER 7

Critical Reading of Qualitative Research

Reading a qualitative research article is much like reading a novel. The setting is established, the characters introduced, the plot developed, and the story-line resolved. The report is typically free of jargon and is easier to follow than most quantitative articles. However, because the narrative is more typical of regular prose, it is easy to overlook the fact that standards do exist for qualitative writing. Therefore, you need to read critically to determine whether or not a study has value.

Perhaps the most fundamental characteristic of qualitative research is its flexibility. While it is common to speak of the research *design* in quantitative study, it is less common to do so in qualitative writing. Rather, the format of qualitative research often is evolving as questions and responses dictate the flow of the investigation.

Qualitative research has advanced rather quickly in the music education and music therapy fields. Investigations are now more diverse and more complicated, making the job of the reader all the more difficult. Basic assumptions are not always commonplace and the logic sometimes not apparent. Learning to read critically takes time, but an understanding of general and more specific standards can help in this process. However, qualitative research cannot be evaluated according to a strict set of rules. For example, in quantitative studies it is common to find at least a brief review of related literature near the beginning of an article. Qualitative studies, however, may or may not include such a review, depending on whether or not the researcher determines that it is needed. Additionally, quantitative researchers are careful to report reliability coefficients for tests and judges' ratings, whereas qualitative researchers tend to be more interested in such things as credibility, dependability, and confirmability, to name a few. Expect a great deal of variability as you read qualitative research.

GENERAL CONTENT STANDARDS

The following are six generic forms of content that you might find in any qualitative report. These address broad-based concerns as summarized by Locke, Silverman, and Spirduso (2004, pp. 214–216).

- *You should find a description of the provenance of the study and what it is about.*
  Somewhere, and better early than late, the report should describe what the study

is about. This description should include an account of what provided the impulse for the investigation, the origin of the researcher's interest or concern, what shaped the initial question(s), what facts might make the findings significant, and why a qualitative format for study was selected. The information might be offered in a single section or be scattered throughout a discursive introduction.

- *You should find a description of the context in which the data were collected.* This might include social, economic, physical, and, when relevant, historical aspects of the locale. This description will answer the question "where?"—although much more than geography and physical circumstance are likely to be involved.

- *You should find an account of what was done in that context.* Ordinarily, this should include answers to the standard questions: "Who?" "What?" "When?" "How?" and, particularly, "Why?" The topics circumscribed by these questions cover the unfolding story of design, method for data collection, and procedures for analysis of the data. Because many qualitative studies involve responses and adjustments to the data while they are being collected (and to the analysis that often runs concurrently with data collection), the account might describe an evolving process rather than a series of fixed and predetermined steps.

- *You should find presentation of actual data and its analysis.* The data are usually embedded in the description of what was done and how conclusions were drawn. For reasons of economy, data must be presented in compact and often abbreviated forms, such as selected quotations, short vignettes, diagrams of relationships, or even photographs. Such data displays should be (a) selected to highlight salient features of the data, (b) designed to give vivid color to the setting and participants, and (c) laid out in a manner that allows the reader to consider some of the same evidence that confronted the investigator. In that way, the reader gains insight into how the interpretations were developed and the subsequent conclusions formed—and how well supported by the data they all seem to be.

- *You should find an explicit effort to summarize, as well as to articulate, one or several conclusions.* The summary might be formal and segregated under a single heading or be woven into the discussion in a closing section. It might include attention to data, analysis, or salient events encountered during the course of the study. The process of asserting conclusions involves a return to the purposes of the study and explicit questions raised. That task requires two distinct activities: (a) explaining what has been learned from the study by stating what has been concluded from analysis of the data, and (b) describing how what has been learned can be fitted into the world of ideas—a world sometimes represented by existing (or proposed) research literature but in other instances by our common notions about how things work.

- *You may find a component that relates to the world of practice.* This might consist of something as explicit as a list of directions for policy or professional action, or it can be as oblique (and modest) as the noting of possible implications derived from the study. Although such a component is not a generally accepted requirement for a complete report, there is no doubt that many researchers find it offers a satisfying kind of closure for the story of the study.

SPECIFIC CONTENT STANDARDS

The following are four forms of specific content standards that you might find in any qualitative report. These are more specific to particular problems encountered in reading reports, and they are summarized by Locke et al. (2004, pp. 217–220). The authors are quick to point out that detecting a flaw in a study does not mean that the report should be automatically discarded. Also, they note that not all of the following points can be found in all qualitative studies, given the great diversity of research in this genre.

- *How much do you learn about the investigator(s) as a person?* If a researcher is the principal "instrument" for inquiry in a qualitative study, to assess the capabilities, dependability, and potential biases of that instrument, we believe that you need to know at least the essentials of its history with the topic, the context, the participants, and that methodology. It is essential here to remember that in qualitative research, objectivity can't be achieved by maintaining distance between researcher and participant. Although a degree of neutrality toward the data is what qualitative researchers struggle to sustain, they will be present as human entities throughout every step of the study. It is *absolutely essential* that they recognize their own subjectivity and monitor how that is functioning in the research context. It also is at least desirable that salient parts of that information be shared with the reader.

- *How often does the report substitute a word or phrase label for an actual description of something done during the study?* This question deals with the sin of *nominalism* ... instances where the author of a qualitative report announces use of a procedure by naming (labeling) the procedure—and then gives no hint about what actually happened in its application. The implication is that you are familiar with the procedure named, you will know (more or less) what was done and don't need to read about the messy details. In some cases, that is perfectly legitimate, either because the operation is simple and purely routine ("The list of volunteers was stratified by both gender and marital status."), or because the operation indeed was of such length and complexity that the author is forced to depend, in some measure, on the reader's prior knowledge ("The use of grounded theory determined both the strategy of the study and the primary mode of analysis.").

- *How carefully and openly does the author discuss alternatives to the decisions about design and method taken before and during the study, alternatives to his or her interpretations of the data, and alternatives to the conclusions derived from the findings?* It is an axiom among scholars that thoughtful discussion of rival hypotheses (a collective term covering alternative courses of action as well as other interpretations of data) is a sign of scientific maturity, self-confidence, and a strong sense of ethical responsibility. That description might go a bit too far, but openly in a qualitative report—along with assertion of the argument(s) favoring the decision or interpretation selected—readers are left with far more than an enhanced respect for the author's person. They have in hand information that allows them to audit the trail of process in the questions about "why?" as well. This form of detail is usually the most reassuring when reading the conclusion that this is a careful study, likely to accurately represent the participants, and likely to deserve your trust.

- *How vivid are the representations of the context, the participants, the researcher(s), and the events of the study?* Clear, forceful, uncomplicated writing produces the power of research reports—quantitative or qualitative. There are, however, some insufficiently appreciated differences between what constitutes effective writing for telling the study's story in the two types of research.

  For quantitative reports, it is highly desirable to employ writing that is vivid in description and interesting in style, as well as just plain transparently clear. For qualitative reports, these characteristics are absolutely essential. Colorful descriptions, portrayals of intense affect, flashes of humor, and vivid sketches of context are at the h of the investigator's purpose—to make the familiar seem strange and exotic, and the strange seem comfortably familiar. For that to be accomplished requires that the people seem alive, that the story of what is happening to them seem worth hearing, and that the insights gained into the human condition seem sharply defined and fully believable.

No, that is not an appeal for flashy writing to take the place of rigor, or for personal journalism to displace thorough descriptions in qualitative reports. If you find the people and places of the study uninteresting and lifeless, if the study has no power over your thoughts and imagination (even if only for time it takes to read the report), then we think the report has failed in one vital respect. And how will you make that evaluative judgment about a report? Read it, and you will know! The quick and the dead will always be with us, but nothing is so deadly as a boring research report.

BEHIND THE SCENES

Locke et al. (2004, pp. 221–225) take a look behind the scenes of qualitative reporting and suggest five pieces of the research "machinery" that lurk behind the pages of qualitative research reports.

- **Time:** Some qualitative researchers do not spend enough time in the contexts and with the participants that they purport to examine. There is no rule about this, not even a useful rule of thumb. In the end, however, the believability of a qualitative study depends upon our senses that the investigator got close enough to the data sources to be really familiar with what was going on. The reader needs to be reassured that he or she was unlikely to be taken in by devious participants, was unlikely to distort descriptions because important aspects simply were overlooked, and was unlikely to have fastened onto the first interpretation that popped into mind, without listening and watching until something beyond the merely facile come into focus. All that takes time, repeated opportunities, and long contemplation of data.

- **Subjectivity:** Understandably, all researchers bring to the work of an investigation the freight of who they are, what they know, where they have lived, how they think, and why they are doing the study. What is less well understood is how important it is for them to (a) be aware of the content of that freight, (b) be watchful about how their unique subjectivity interacts with decisions about questions, data collection, analysis and interpretation, (c) be firm and creative in devising ways to step back and allow the data to be what they are, (d) be diligent about keeping a careful record of subjective encounters within the study, and (e) be open and artful about sharing that record in the report.

  After all, the researcher is the one who, with all of his or her humanity, serves as the primary instrument in all that transpires. How subjectivity is managed really matters (it can never be eliminated, nor should it be)—it must be dealt with by deliberate actions, not by confessional contrition, and it has consequences for both the ꞏꞏty of data and the believability of the story told in the report. Always look for ꞏe that researchers are concerned about their biases and that they have strug-ꞏware of where those dispositions lie and how they might be at work. Too ꞏic is ignored, or it is briskly pushed aside with brief references to reli-ꞏs for coding and categorizing of data.

  The search for negative data, the analysis of outliers and extreme ꞏplanations for the incongruent products of triangulation, and .visive fallout from peer debriefing sessions (all of which are common requirements in a qualitative study) should involve *actually doing things*. It is here that the sins of nominalism run amok! The researcher should think about why exceptions in the data did occur and what they might mean, and then actually decide what to do about them. Simply ignoring what does not fit, or just taking cursory notice and moving on without response, represents dangerously inadequate use of qualitative methodology.

When something does not fit with the investigator's preferred understanding, the researcher has to take action, even if (in all honesty and after every effort has been made to find an alternative) that action is simply to recognize that, when people are studied, there are likely to be exceptions to any generally useful rule about their behavior. If the investigator does not respond to contrary data or to clearly visible alternative interpretations, those unexamined loose ends just hang around the study like uninvited ghosts—haunting the party and spoiling everyone's appetite.

To avoid that unhappy condition, the reader should be more concerned about evidence that shows what happened in a study after a search for disconfirming cases was undertaken than by being impressed by mere assertions that it was done. When you finish reading a qualitative research report, ask yourself, "Am I persuaded that the author did not sweep anything under the rug (either data itself or alternative interpretations of the data) but gave everything encountered in the course of the study full and honest consideration?"

- **Relationships:** Everyone knows that what people say to you and how they behave in your company is conditioned in large part by the nature of your relationship. Close friends and casual acquaintances do not exchange the same opinions, stories, jokes, or personal feelings. How you behave with clients or visitors in a professional setting is not how you behave with colleagues. And what happens between a researcher and a participant reflects how each presents himself or herself to the other and how the perception of mutual roles is progressively defined by subsequent interactions. It makes an important difference whether researchers elect to present themselves (and then act) as interested visitors, genuine friends, professional colleagues, needy supplicants (common with doctoral students), omniscient scholars (occasional with professorial types), political allies, dispassionate observers, the biological equivalents of a tape recorder, or warmly sympathetic listeners. The list of possibilities goes on, but, make no mistake, each relationship has an effect on what will be collected as data. That puts the interpersonal, and the nature of perceived relationship, at the heart of qualitative inquiry.

- **Context:** Descriptions of context (physical, social, economic, historical) are given in the report and (among other functions) serve to allow the reader to decide about the appropriateness of transferring findings from the study to the reader's own environment. That process is made possible, however, by actions taken before and during the study. A sufficient body of facts and descriptive detail has to be collected if it is to support a thorough and vivid description of context. If there is any place that effort is well expended to develop what it is now trendy to call *thick description*, it is in the area of capturing the surroundings where the action takes place.

So much is explained about the participants by knowing their location—in culture, in social class, in economic strata, in regional geography, and in the very places where they live. All of this information can provide for the rich contextualization that (at the first level) helps the investigator interpret what is seen and heard, subsequently (at the second level) helps the reader more fully understand what is asserted in the findings and conclusions, and, finally (at the third level), allows assessment of the study's relevance to other contexts.

What is found in journal reports, however, too often looks like something clipped out of the real estate section of our hometown newspaper ("Well-maintained contemporary home in nice locality, near public transportation, and suitable for large family.") Charitably, the reader would like to assume that the researcher knew (and used) a great deal more information than is offered in that sketch—but how can it be sure?

The paragraph or two devoted to contextualization in some reports might read like thin stuff because what the researcher actually had bothered to find out was itself thin stuff. Something of the order produced by Margaret Mead for the islands of the South Pacific is not expected, but some return to the respect awarded to the centrality of "place" in classical ethnography would not itself be out of place. When you finish reading a qualitative research report, ask yourself, "Did I learn enough from reading this report to have a picture in my mind of where the study took place, and does the picture have enough color and detail to let me sense how it might be both like and unlike other places that I know?"

It was mentioned in the first chapter of this text that space constraints in most journals produce serious limitations when a researcher tries to present all the details needed to fully comprehend or replicate a study. This is especially true for writers of qualitative research. Because the writing is dependent on a narrative format, much "rich" detail must often be omitted. A qualitative researcher learns effectively to summarize large amounts of data, but summaries often do not present the best "picture." As you read qualitative research you must keep in mind that space limitations can impact the full scope of what is presented.

READING QUALITATIVE RESEARCH: A COMMENTARY

Case studies typically appear as a report on one person in a given setting. The following study, however, represents a collective case study in which data from four music teachers in a midwestern school were collected and examined together in relation to six role stressors. The results should interest both music teachers and music therapists.

Role Stress in the Professional Life of the School Music Teacher: A Collective Case Study

John W. Scheib, *Ball State University*
Journal of Research in Music Education, 51(2), 124–136.

Reprinted by permission of MENC: The National Association for Music Education. Copyright © 2003 by MENC.

People often perceive the expectations of their jobs based on what others communicate to them (Kahn, Wolfe, Quinn, & Snoek, 1964). These are the expectations that people within organizational systems communicate to each other about the definitions of jobs and roles. Job descriptions are formed by these interactions. A lack of congruence between expectations can create conflict and tension. Occupational stress researchers have categorized this as a conflict between expectations, or a role conflict (Kahn et al., 1964). Role stress can create job dissatisfaction and occupational stress (e.g., Jenkins & Calhoun, 1991; Thompson, McNamara, & Hoyle, 1997), anxiety (e.g., Capel, 1992), lack of commitment (e.g., Billingsley & Cross, 1992), insecurities and feelings of futility (e.g., Amey, 1990), emotional exhaustion and depersonalization (e.g., Crane & Iwanicki, 1986), and a propensity to leave the profession of teaching (e.g., Billingsley & Cross, 1992; Gonzalez, 1995).

Occupations in which people hold positions between organizations or systems, called "boundary positions" (Kahn et al., 1964), are more susceptible to role conflicts (e.g., Fisher & Gitelson, 1983; Jackson & Shuler, 1985). For example, teachers who also coach competitive athletic teams often struggle with role conflicts due, in part, to their boundary positioning between the academic and athletic world, (e.g., Figone, 1994). Like the teacher-coach, the school music teacher also teeters between different worlds. There are those who believe the school music teacher is first and foremost a director of performing ensembles, while others believe the school music teacher should be most concerned with the academic pursuit of music education in the classroom.

Investigators in several studies have looked at the occupational stress–related issues of the school music teacher, but few specifically address role stress as a contributing factor. Results of these studies reveal that school music teachers who are dissatisfied with their professional life report feeling undervalued as teachers (e.g., Nimmo, 1986), due to a perceived lack of support from their administration (e.g., Krueger, 20000), students (e.g., Heston et al., 1986), or parents and other teachers (e.g., Gordon, 2000). This lack of support often results in insufficient salary and resources to accomplish the overwhelming amount of work required of the music teacher (see Nimmo, 1986; Krueger, 20000; Gordon, 2000).

The findings from these studies more than adequately describe the "what" of stress in the school music teacher's work life, but what remains is the question of "why?" For example, although association with uncooperative or negative people might be stressful, the statement needs further explanation to truly understand what is at issue. Why is it stressful? Obviously the informants perceive the negative attitudes and behaviors, but is their perception clouded by the incongruence of their beliefs to the realities of the position? Role theory provides us with another lens to view these sources of discontent in order to better understand why they are stressful for the school music teacher, and to investigate the underlying elements and sources of the stress.

This study focuses on six role stressors that, according to researchers, affect job satisfaction: role conflict, role ambiguity, role overload, underutilization of skills, resource inadequacy, and nonparticipation. Role conflict occurs when two or more contradictory role messages (expectations) are sent to the focal person that result in psychological conflict. Role ambiguity stress is a result of both information deficiency and unpredictability. Role overload happens when the quantity and wide variety of different roles expected of the focal person is overwhelming to the point that no one role can be performed satisfactorily. Underutilization-of-skills-related tension occurs when the expectations of the focal person do not allow him/her to use his/her unique skills and abilities—a type of role underload. Resource inadequacy stress occurs when the focal person is forced to try to "make things work" without the necessary tools and resources. Nonparticipation role stress occurs due to the focal person's not being included in decisions affecting his/her role expectations. The purpose of this study was to shed light on school music teacher role stress, on the complicated lives of school music teachers, and to help practitioners, as well as policymakers and school administrators better understand the role-related issues that can lead to teacher attrition, dissatisfaction with career, ineffectiveness, and stress in the workplace.

Commentary

The introduction to this article cites a number of research studies that have found role stress to be an important characteristic of the music teaching profession. From this review of literature the author chooses six role stressors to study that are prominent in previous research. Scheib indicates that he is using the technique of "role theory" as a "lens" to view these sources of stress among music teachers in order to investigate the underlying elements and sources of the stress.

The Article (continued)

Method

A collective case study of one high school's music department in the midwestern United States, consisting of four music teachers, served as the focus. The collective case study is a study consisting of several cases in order to examine a "phenomenon, population, or general condition" (Stake, 2000, p. 437). In this study, the researcher looked both at the individual professional lives of four music teachers and the combined experience they all share.

Site selection was primarily based on three criteria: (1) access to the site and subjects; (2) a high school music department that offered band, choir, and orchestra; and (3) a site that had well-established programs. Observations took place throughout the school's fall academic semester (August 2001–January 2002) in both formal and informal situations. In addition to carrying out these daily observations, I interviewed each focal subject twice. School policy publications (e.g., student handbooks, teacher handbooks, job descriptions, mission statement), documents sent to students and parents, and concert programs were also collected for analysis.

All transcripts from recorded interviews, field notes from observations, and documents were analyzed using various coding techniques. Internal codes for this study included the six role stressors. Data were used to generate detailed descriptions of the site, the individuals, and the context. For clarity and accuracy, interview transcripts and field notes were made available to the individual subjects for their review. A balance was gained by the use of multiple subjects, observations, and document analysis. Triangulation of this data was essential to finding this balance.

Commentary

Scheib identifies the genre of this research as a collective case study involving four music teachers. His three reasons for choosing the site of the investigation are clearly presented as well as the dates of observations. In addition to observations, Scheib interviewed each participant twice and reviewed school publications. Transcripts were analyzed and coded according to the six role stressors and were made available to the participants for their review. Triangulation of the data was accomplished by the use of observation transcripts, document analysis, and feedback from the participants as to the accuracy of the investigator's observations.

The Article (*continued*)

Profiles

Site: Lakeview Glen High School

Lakeview Glen High School (LGHS) is in the city of Lakeview, a small urban community of approximately 8,000 people in the midwestern United States.[i] It is surrounded on all sides by the state's capital city, which has a population of over 208,000. LGHS has a student enrollment of about 800 students. The school operates on an eight-period day: four periods in the morning, lunch, then four periods in the afternoon. Each period lasts 47 minutes. Although located within a larger city, LGHS more closely resembles a typical upper-middle-class suburban school.

Case 1: Lisa Nevoga (Choir): "Striving for Excellence"

In 11 years, Lisa's program has grown quite noticeably. Lisa's philosophy has shaped what is now a large performance-based operation. Lisa believes that her primary goal as vocal music teacher at LGHS is to provide experiences for her students to be the "best that they can be." She has an unrelenting desire for excellence in herself, her students, and her program. Lisa has more than 200 students involved in her program, split among four traditional concert-repertoire choirs that meet during the school day. In addition, Lisa offers two show choirs and two madrigal ensembles that meet either before or after school. Lisa is also responsible for the annual spring musical production. Of the four music teachers at LGHS, she is the only one who is completely fulltime at the high school only. The remaining three periods of the day are spent either fulfilling administrative responsibilities, planning, or teaching lessons.

Lisa expects her students to give their best efforts at all times. At the core of Lisa's own professional and educational philosophy is a drive for what she calls "excellence." When speaking to her students during rehearsal, she occasionally mentions previous "star" students, choirs, and performances for the students to work to try to equal or excel.

This drive for excellence, combined with trying to give her students a wide variety of choral music, propelled Lisa to expand her program by adding additional groups and significantly raising the expectations for performance. For example, the show-choir program grew from having only a few local community performances to being a highly competitive organization that participates in numerous show-choir competitions. As a result, members of the show choir attend mandatory camps, need to participate in several fund-raising opportunities, rehearse several hours each week outside the school day, and perform at numerous competitions around the state. Lisa uses competition as a motivation for her students to excel. She believes that through competition her students are better motivated to strive for "excellence."

Lisa's main tension as a teacher is the struggle between her drive for success and excellence in her choir program and her role as mother to her three young children. Her increasingly busy schedule at school often results in her children being either baby-sat or with her and her husband during late evening and weekend rehearsals. Lisa seems to be coming to a crossroads in her professional life in balancing the needs of her family and the needs of her choir program. However, she refuses to settle for less with her choir program in fear of diminishing the experience she desires for her students. She claims that she is overworked and understaffed in her position, but she states that it is mostly her own fault. Due to the success of her program, she has increased the choir membership from 120 to nearly 200 students over the past 11 years and has also greatly expanded the extracurricular offerings. This has resulted in work being much more demanding of her time.

Case 2: Don Turner (Band): "Ex-Workaholic"

Don Turner has been teaching in the Lakeview Glen school district for 30 years. Don shares the high school's instrumental music program with another director, Pete Dunn. It is a unique situation in that both Don and Pete team-teach at the middle school and high school, but each has his own primary responsibilities. Don helps out at the middle school by teaching some lessons, but spends most of his time at the high school either teaching or managing the instrumental music program. While Pete is primarily responsible for the 8th- and 9th-grade bands, Don heads the 10th- and 11th–12th-grade bands. There are roughly 60 students in each high school band. The three high school bands rehearse in the afternoon during the back-to-back periods. This allows both Don and Pete to be available at the middle school in the morning. In addition to directing the concert bands during the school day, Don and Pete are also both responsible for an extracurricular jazz program, consisting of three jazz ensembles that meet before and after school.

Like most high school band programs, service functions can be a significant part of the curriculum. Don and Pete share these responsibilities. In the fall, all three high school bands combine into one noncompetitive marching band that primarily performs at home varsity football games and local parades. The band is able to rehearse as a whole only on the day of a performance. Although Don accepts this situation, it presents a unique set of challenges. Whenever he needs to assemble all the bands for a rehearsal, Don has to take students out of their regularly scheduled classes, which puts a strain on relations with teachers in other subjects.

Maintaining a balance between professional and personal roles is something that Don has struggled with throughout his career. Don discloses that he was once a "workaholic." Like many young directors, he pushed himself and the program to see how far it could go. Through the years, this unrelenting drive eventually gave way to a feeling of futility. The demands of an active band program that was straining his personal life resulted in him "stepping back" a bit in his professional life. Don's wife, keenly aware of his compulsion to stay at work through the evening, registered Don for tennis lessons in order to force him to leave work at a reasonable time each day. This gradually helped Don develop more of a balance between his personal and professional life. Don states that he is "burned out" and that he "doesn't care anymore," but I observed him repeatedly working nearly nonstop from the minute he arrived at school (well before the contracted time) to the minute he left (typically well after the contracted time). In addition, he spends time at home on department chair duties so he does not have to spend school time doing them. While at school, Don spends most of his time teaching, preparing for the next class, or fulfilling administrative functions. Since he spends no more than 9 hours working at school each day, Don says that he feels he is not giving as much as he should.

Case 3: Pete Dunn (Band): "Putting out Fires"

Pete's educational philosophy somewhat mirrors Don's in that he believes his primary responsibility as a teacher is to help students become socially responsible adults. In addition, Pete feels an important aspect of his teaching is to try to maximize his students' potential and give them everything they need to be independent musicians.

Pete and Don's philosophy differs from Lisa's in that they do not want to specifically focus on the high-achieving students. Pete states that the high-achieving student does not need his attention as much as the less-talented student because the talented student usually has additional opportunities outside school (e.g., private teachers, youth orchestras, etc.). Pete chooses to focus on the extrinsic goals of helping all his students become responsible adults through the lessons they learn by negotiating the responsibilities of membership in a musical ensemble. In contrast, Lisa seems to focus her energies on creating the "star" performer and the "excellent" performance.

Pete's philanthropic educational philosophy is evident through his self-imposed role as music education advocate within the school. Pete was very active in thwarting an effort by the administration at LGHS to implement a four-period schedule that he believed would negatively affect the music program. Pete calls this type of activity "putting out fires." From talking with parents and students who are having problems to the ongoing role of music advocate within the school district, Pete spends much of his time trying to keep the music program from being negatively affected by outside influences. A significant stressor for Pete is that the time he must devote to "putting out fires" interrupts and conflicts with his planning and teaching time.

Pete, like his colleagues, has difficulty at times juggling the demands of his role as a school music teacher and his role as a husband and father to three young children.

Pete seems to care deeply about his students and what is best for their future, even at the expense of his music program or his family life. Some of his greatest joys in teaching are the connections that he makes with his students.

Case 4: Chris Davis (Orchestra): "Building a Program"

At Lakeview Glen, Chris is responsible for one high school orchestra of about 60 students that meets first period, and three orchestras at the middle school (grades 6–8). Although he has a desk in the high school music office, he is rarely seen there. Most of his teaching responsibilities are in the middle school. Like Lisa, Chris has greatly developed the orchestra program throughout his time at LG, and is now lob-bying the school board to add more staffing. Chris focused much of his effort over the past 8 years in trying to build the program, and is now beginning to reap the rewards. He looks forward to when he no longer needs to be as preoccupied with recruiting efforts. Chris's main goal is to provide a learning experience for his stu-dents to grow not only as musicians, but also as intelligent consumers of music and life-long supporters of the arts.

Chris is now in his ninth year at Lakeview Glen and very much enjoys his job. Out of all four of the subjects for this study, Chris seems to exhibit and report the least amount of tension and stress. Chris does, however, have a very busy schedule, since he is a parent, husband, teacher, and performer. Chris feels tension in his life juggling the different responsibilities and time commitments each role demands. Chris also feels frustrated when he senses being disconnected with his students and colleagues. He says that he feels this when he is too busy to meet with them informally, when having to rush from one functions to another, and when he does not have enough time to meet their demands.

Commentary

Each of the four participant's profiles is presented in narrative form as a summary of the data. The six role stressors serve to organize the presentations. The overall picture that Scheib presents is one common to most music educators—overworked, too little time, and conflicts between personal and professional roles.

The Article (continued)

Findings

Role Ambiguity

Role ambiguity was not a significant stressor for the subjects. This is inconsistent with other role ambiguity occupational stress studies. One subject's answer to a role ambiguity–related question points to one reason why all four teachers did not exhibit tension from role ambiguity: "That sounds like a young teacher to me" (Lisa, 12/4/01, p. 7).

Role Conflicts

All four teachers exhibited varying (and significant) levels of stress from interrole conflicts (two or more incompatible roles) between personal and professional roles—specifically that of parent/spouse versus music director. In particular, Lisa suffers greatly from a conflict between what she perceives as the traditional expectations of motherhood and the expectations of being a director of a very active choir program. This conflict most often finds Lisa neglecting her family responsibilities for the needs of her program. It also results in Lisa feeling she is shortchanging her career's expectations by not being able to attend conferences and workshops. Lisa, who says that she already feels guilty for not being home enough with her family, finds it very difficult to make time for these events because it will take more time away from her family and choir program.

Lisa also says that she feels interrole conflicts as she deals with the administrative tasks of her very active performance-based curriculum. Whether the task is organizing fund-raising for her program or handling ticket orders for performances, Lisa says that these administrative expectations conflict with teaching. In addition, the program's active performance schedule does not allow her to address individual needs during the full choir rehearsals. This creates another interrole conflict for Lisa: To meet the expectations of her performance curriculum, she often has to shortchange the individual needs of students.

Pete's main role conflict lies between his roles as an educator and a director of bands. As a director, it is expected that he will demand high levels of performance from the ensembles—the product is the goal. The expectations of being an educator direct Pete to care for each of the students and to use the group experience as an educational vehicle. In the latter case, the process is as important as (if not more important than) the product.

Like Pete, Don also exhibits tension at times between his roles as director and educator. On one hand, he would like to produce performing ensembles of a high caliber to build a program of stature. On the other hand, his educational philosophy tugs at this drive and questions the overall effect that building such a program would have on those involved. Is the effort worth the price? Rather than just producing a high-performance band program, Don believes his role as an educator is, in part, to make sure his students are able to have many different experiences without being overcommitted to just one area.

Although Don's core philosophical belief is that teachers should produce well-rounded students who have a variety of experiences, he believes that teaching a theory class (something that contributes to this well-roundedness) conflicts with his role as a band director. However, instead of Don feeling tension from his role as a director of bands dominating his role as a music teacher, he says that he feels tension from his role as a music teacher dominating his role as director of bands (or band teacher). It seems, for Don, that tension is reduced when a balance is achieved between the two roles—a balance specified by Don's beliefs.

Chris's main stressor is an interrole conflict over his need to increase student involvement in orchestra. To increase student enrollment (and activity) in the orchestra program, Chris believes that he needs to continually maintain a "fun" experience for his students while also working to present high-quality performances to the public so he can attract new students to the program. To do this, he needs to rehearse effectively and efficiently. Chris feels frustration because he would like to rehearse more effectively by isolating smaller sections of the music during rehearsal. However, because of students' immaturity and their need for a "fun" experience, Chris senses that he must keep the whole group playing whenever possible. This results in tension for Chris: While he wants to provide a positive experience for his students, he realizes that he needs to rehearse the ensemble for concerts. Sometimes fulfilling one role makes it very difficult to fulfill the other—at least with younger students who are more interested in the social aspect of orchestra than in preparing a work for performance.

Meeting the demands of teaching, directing performing ensembles, and maintaining a personal life apart from the responsibilities of work proves quite challenging for these teachers. Sometimes this tension does not come necessarily from a conflict of roles, but from the sheer number of different responsibilities that creates a sense of being overwhelmed. It is not a conflict between roles, but a sense that no role can be fulfilled satisfactorily due to being "spread too thin." This is called role overload.

Role Overload

Beyond various role conflicts and an overall sense of inadequate resources, role overload was the next most significant stressor for all four subjects. The sense of role overload, for these teachers, had a great deal to do with resource inadequacy issues, particularly inadequate staffing.

Lisa's situation is complicated by the fact that she is a parent of three children, something that often conflicts with the demands of her teaching position. Lisa feels that she is at a greater risk of role overload stress due, in part, to being a working parent. Lisa's overall occupational stress seems to be intimately linked to this role overload. Lisa blames herself for her misery due to her insatiable drive to produce "excellent" music experiences for her students. She would, in fact, rather resign her position at Lakeview Glen than do less with her program.

Like Pete, Chris also says that he feels more role overload tension than anything else, but Chris's tension is more similar to Lisa's experience of personal and professional roles combined making an almost intolerable existence at times. In addition to having children and a spouse, Chris is also a professional musician and performs with several different groups. This additional role rather complicates his life. However, his colleague Don is not affected as much from role overload as he is from having to fulfill unwanted roles—something more associated with tension due to underutilization of skills.

Underutilization of Skills

The subjects of this study experienced tension often when having to fulfill unwanted, unimportant, or tedious tasks that took time away from their desired activities—especially performing tasks that in their view should be under the responsibility of other nonteaching personnel (e.g., administrative staff, custodians).

In fact, performing tasks they felt were not best using their skills as professional educators greatly contributed to their role-overload tensions. Time spent on low-skill tasks interfered with carrying out more professional roles, such as teaching, planning, and student assessment.

As an example, Lisa found herself having to spend a significant amount of time fund-raising. This contributed to a sense of role-overload stress. She not only felt stress from spending precious time performing the role of fund-raising manager (something she felt was not a good use of her time) but she also felt a residual stress from not being able to use that time on other more meaningful tasks.

Don spends much of his time fulfilling administrative roles—something he would rather not have to do (even though he is the department chair). During marching band season, Don often spends his time preparing the practice field for rehearsal—something he thinks the custodial/grounds maintenance staff should do. Much of Don's time is also spent making sure schedules do not conflict between his after-school programs and other school activities. Don often takes the initiative to resolve potential problems.

Pete describes his underutilization-of-skills tension coming from a lack of adequate planning time. Pete feels that because he is not able to adequately plan for a rehearsal, he is not using his skills as a teacher to the fullest—simply because he has not had time to plan. Pete's underutilization-of-skills tension seems to come from not being able to adequately plan for a rehearsal (due to role overload). Pete feels that he is underutilizing his skills in rehearsal because he does not have adequate time to prepare.

Of the four subjects, Chris exhibited the least amount of tension in this area. He attributes this to his lack of cocurricular ensembles to manage and administer, unlike his colleagues. Chris spends most of his time at the middle school, which might account for more time teaching and less administration. Chris feels most of his tension comes from being understaffed and having to split his time between two schools—issues more related to role overload and inadequate resources.

Resource Inadequacy

When we think of an inadequacy of resources, we often think of a lack of funding-related resources—such as facilities, supplies, equipment, or staffing. I was surprised to find that the subjects of this study believed (for the most part) that they have adequate resources—or at least have what resources they expect as public-school employees; they realize and accept the limitations of funding that comes with working in a publicly financed system. However, they say that they feel tension related to the resource inadequacies of appropriate staffing in their programs (which significantly relates to their sense of role overload), and in dealing with the most important resource for their success: students. All four subjects experience tension in their professional lives from their need to maintain and build student enrollment in their programs, schedule rehearsals and performances that take place outside of the school day, and juggle the expectations of their program with what their students can offer in time, abilities, talents, and commitment.

Chris is concerned with maintaining and increasing student enrollment in orchestra. He would like to eventually provide a full symphony orchestra experience (with an ensemble that includes strings, winds, brass) for his students, but he is not able to offer it because there are not enough qualified students.

Much of Pete and Don's stress comes from having to be active advocates for their program and lobbyists for the music department. Pete was an active participant in opposing a change to a block schedule at LGHS. He felt that such a schedule would decrease student enrollment in band. He feared that his most important resource—students—would be significantly affected.

Lisa is the least affect by a resource inadequacy relating to students. Because the choir program is the most active in the music department, the other programs schedule activities around Lisa's schedule. Also, Lisa can be more selective with students for these groups due to the numbers of students they attract—there are more students than spots available. Although Lisa does not seem to experience student-resource-inadequacy tension, she does, however, feel that her program is understaffed.

Lisa and Chris both report feeling understaffed in their programs. Both have lobbied the administration and school board repeatedly to add teaching positions to alleviate the problems associated with increased student load. All four teachers report that adding a secretarial position solely dedicated to the music department would greatly help them be less overworked.

Nonparticipation

Like role ambiguity, another area where all four subjects report low stress is in the area of nonparticipation. Although the participants believe they control their own program's destiny, they also show concern about not having enough power over appropriate funding allocations for their programs. Quite possibly one of the reasons that these teachers do not experience tension over nonparticipation is that they are all active advocates for their programs. Because of their seniority, they have political clout within the school culture. As is true with many successful music programs, they also have significant support from parents.

Commentary

The findings are clearly set forth. "Role ambiguity was not a significant stressor for the subjects." (The terms *significant* and *subjects* are more commonly found in quantitative research.) "All four teachers exhibited varying (and significant) levels of stress from interrole conflicts...between personal and professional roles—specifically that of parent/spouse versus music director." Here again Scheib uses the term *significant*, which may indicate to the experienced reader that some type of statistical analysis was used in analyzing the data. It was not. This is clearly Scheib's personal interpretation of the data. Interrole conflict is reported as creating the highest level of stress among the four participants.

Role overload is reported by Scheib as creating the second-highest level of stress, while underutilization of skills also was found to create tension. Resource inadequacy was reported as a mixed bag of reactions, although inadequate staffing problems emerged as a common complaint. Low stress was reported by all participants for nonparticipation.

The Article (*continued*)

Discussion

Many of the different role stressors are closely related and often seem to overlap. For example, much of the reported role overload the subjects report experiencing is related to resource inadequacy (e.g., a lack of adequate staffing). If more staff were available in each music program, the overload for each teacher would be lessened. Another overlap is between role overload and underutilization of skills. The findings suggest similarities and connections between the stress associated with too many responsibilities and stress caused from responsibilities that are unwanted or tedious.

The subjects of this study seem to be more influenced by their own musical and educational experiences and other music teachers whom they respect and admire than by people outside the music field (e.g., administration, community members, parents). The subjects report that they themselves are to blame for any tension or stress they endure, since they are the sole determiners of the expectations and roles of their position. This could account for tensions they experience when their view of what their music program should look like (based on influence from outside the culture of their community and school) collides with the system that their community and school provide in which to operate their programs.

The experiences that these teachers want for their students are based largely on the experiences that they once had as students. Conflict and tension can result from the teachers' trying to transplant these curricular ideas (from an external system) into the LGHS school culture without first considering the fit of the two different systems. Often, stress comes from the incongruence of the teacher's expectations and beliefs versus what the system allows. These teachers try to operate programs that are not necessarily designed to reach the level of involvement their expectations demand. This results in teachers who feel overwhelmed when they try to meet their expectations, or unworthy if they "pull back" and try to reside within the confines of the system. "Pulling back" is not an option for Lisa; she does not want to lessen the experience for her students by scaling back her program. Don, Pete, and Chris want to provide high-quality experiences for their students, but not at the price of both the teacher and students being overwhelmed.

Findings from this study suggest further research is needed to explore significant issues for these subjects. Praxis-oriented research should be conducted to help circumvent music teacher role stress created by fulfilling the role of music educator. Communication is the best weapon in the battle of incompatible role expectations. Teachers need to understand that each music program is, to some extent, confined by the system that surrounds it. Each program has its own limitations and possibilities based in no small part on the culture of the school and community in which it operates. Practitioners need to be involved in research that seeks to define that culture.

Commentary

Scheib interprets his study in broad terms. Stressors tend to overlap, and clear distinctions are difficult. He acknowledges that participants took the blame for much of their stress because they were sole determiners of the expectations and roles of their positions.

Scheib concludes by noting that programs are limited by the culture of the school and community; i.e., the program that music teachers want can be more than their particular school administrations want or expect. This is an unexpected observation that emerges because of the qualitative nature of the study. This is a benefit of qualitative research—identifying problems "after the fact."

The Article (continued)

NOTE

i. All names are pseudonyms to protect the privacy of the teachers surveyed.

REFERENCES

Amey, M. J. (1990). Bridging the gap between expectations and realities. *New directions for Higher Education, 18*(4), 79–88.

Beehr, T. A. (1987). The themes of social psychological stress in work organizations: From roles to goals. In A. W. Riley & S. J. Zaccara (Eds.), *Occupational stress and organizational effectiveness* (pp. 71–101). New York: Praeger.

Billingsley, B. S., & Cross, L. H. (1992). Predictors of commitment, job satisfaction, and intent to stay in teaching: A comparison of general and special educators. *Journal of Special Education, 25*(4), 453–471.

Capel, S. A. (1992). Stress and burnout in teachers. *European Journal of Teacher Education, 15*(3), 197–211.

Crane, S. J., & Iwanicki, E. F. (1986). Perceived role conflict, role ambiguity, and burnout among special education teachers. *Remedial and Special Education (RASE), 7*(2), 24–31.

Figone, A. J. (1994). Teacher-coach role conflict: Its impact on students and student-athletes. *Physical Educator, 51*(1), 29–34.

Fisher, C. D., & Gitelson, R. (1983). A meta-analysis of the correlates of role conflict and ambiguity. *Journal of Applied Psychology, 68*(2) 320–333.

Gonzalez, P. A. (1995). *Causes and cures of teacher attrition: A selected bibliography focusing on special educators.* Alexandria, VA: National Association of State Directors of Special Education.

Gordon, D. (2000). Sources of stress for the public school music teacher: Four case studies. *Contributions to Music Education, 27*(1), 27–40.

Heston, M. L., Dedrick, C., Raschke, D., & Whitehead, J. (1996). Job satisfaction and stress among band directors. *Journal of Research in Music Education, 44,* 319–327.

Jackson, S. E., & Schuler, R. S. (1985). A meta-analysis and conceptual critique of research on role ambiguity and role conflict in work settings. *Organization Behavior and Human Decision Processes 36*, 16–78.

Jenkins, S., & Calhoun, J. (1991). Teacher stress: Issue and intervention. *Psychology in the Schools, 28*, 60–70.

Kahn, R. L., Wolfe, D. M., Quinn, R. P., & Snoek, J. D. (1964). *Organization stress: Studies in role conflict and ambiguity*. New York: Wiley.

Krueger, P. J. (2000). Beginning music teachers: Will they leave the profession? *Update: Applications of Research in Music Education* (Fall/Winter 2000).

Nimmo, D. J. (1986). *Factors of attrition among high school band directors*. Unpublished doctoral dissertation, Arizona State University, Phoenix, AZ.

Stake, R. E. (2000). Case studies. In N. K. Denzin & Y. S. Lincoln (Eds.), *Handbook of qualitative research* (2nd ed., pp. 435–454). Thousand Oaks, CA: Sage Publications.

Thompson, D. P., McNamara, J. F., & Hoyle, J. R. (1997). Job satisfaction in educational organizations: A synthesis of research findings. *Educational Administration Quarterly, 33*(1), 7–37.

STUDY AND DISCUSSION QUESTIONS

1. What is the fundamental characteristic of qualitative research, and how is this reflected in the research report?

2. What are the six generic forms of content in a qualitative study? What does each of these address?

3. What are the four forms of specific content standards found in qualitative reports, and what does each of these address?

4. What are the five pieces of research machinery found in qualitative research, and what does each address?

5. How does a single case study differ from a collective case study?

6. What is the basic hypothesis of the study by Scheib?

7. What are the six role stressors that are investigated in the Scheib study, and what does each involve?

8. What types of data were collected by Scheib?

9. How were the data triangulated by Scheib?

10. Who were the subjects in the study, and what labels did Scheib provide for each?

11. Do you identify with the profile of any of the subjects? Explain.

12. What was the finding for role ambiguity?

13. What were the findings for role conflicts?

14. What were the findings for role overload?

15. What were the findings for resource inadequacy?

16. What was the finding for nonparticipation?

17. Whom do the subjects blame the most for their stress?

18. What observation is made "after the fact" by Scheib?

19. What is probably going to happen to Lisa as her career progresses?

20. How would you evaluate the importance of this study using 1 (poor) to 5 (excellent)?

SUGGESTED ACTIVITIES

1. Consider your own career in teaching and what stressors you might be experiencing. Are there parallels between the findings of the study by Scheib and your own stress sources/levels?

2. Discuss what a music teacher or music therapist must do in order to avoid professional burnout.

CHAPTER 8

Reflecting On Qualitative Research

The following article by Lois Schleuter (1994/1995), which is not a research study *per se* (the actual study appears in Chapter 14), delves into the thought process behind doing qualitative research and leads us into a greater understanding of how and where qualitative research is beneficial. Schleuter reflects on the presentation of qualitative dialogue and on the problem of writing objectively while discussing data that are predominantly observations of subjective behaviors. Clarity of writing is always a primary factor in the presentation of any research study.

THE THOUGHT PROCESS

Qualitative Study of Dialogue: A Thought Process

Lois Schleuter, *University of Toledo, Toledo, Ohio*
Bulletin of the Council for Research in Music Education, No. 123, 58–62.

Reprinted by permission of CRME: Bulletin of the Council for Research in Music Education.
Copyright ©1994 by the Council for Research in Music Education.

Supervision of student teachers has been part of my university teaching responsibility for over 20 years. Many questions about the process have emerged as I have fulfilled my role as supervisor. I was particularly curious about how student teachers' academic knowledge and skill came together with the existing practices of cooperating teachers to result in music instruction for elementary school children. The study I conducted, "Cooperating Teachers' Sharing of Curricular Thinking," focused on the conferences between two student teacher/cooperating teacher dyads during simultaneous 10-week student teaching experiences. Cassette tapes were provided to each dyad to record all their conferences on site. These tapes were then transcribed to facilitate detailed analysis of curricular content.

Data analysis focused on two main questions. First, what topics were addressed in the conferences and in what manner. Data provided insight into differences between a preconference approach and a postconference approach. Differences in the amount of cooperating teacher curricular directives and control also were found. A second analytical process determined the amount of conference dialogue devoted to various curricular topics within each week and then across the entire experience. This process provided insight into the situational import of each field placement and how context-specific each student teaching experience should be.

Several factors entered into the formulation of the study and analysis of data. First and foremost was a long-term interest and intensive involvement with student teaching experiences. At various times, I have been a student teacher, cooperating teacher, and university supervisor. Doing qualitative research requires sufficient interest in a topic to be able to devote considerable time to the study of it; it also requires a feeling for the settings to aid in understanding the data collected. Other factors contributed to formalizing the study topic and conducting the research.

Research Base

Formulation of the research questions came after an extensive literature review in the areas of teacher thinking and student teaching. The focus of the study was aided most by the limitations on research found in the teacher thinking studies. These studies had established the validity of investigating the thought processes occurring before and after the actual teaching process and data collection procedures such as thinking aloud and dialogue taping. My time to be on site for data collection was limited; therefore, the opportunity to study naturally occurring on-site activities such as student teacher/ cooperating teacher conferences at my own schedule was a critical factor.

The teacher thinking studies also confirmed that teachers do think about things already categorized into aspects of goals, activities, evaluation, and so forth. These existing categories were important in guiding the data analysis. I looked for patterns that were already found in previous studies and for deviations or additions to these patterns.

Studies of preservice teachers provided insight into differences in thinking between experienced and inexperienced teachers. These studies were also a guide to the various stages of student teacher development, another factor that had to come under consideration when analyzing the transcripts.

Data Analysis

The majority of data analysis was devoted to flow of dialogue, who initiated topics, and in what way. One of the research questions, however, required quantitative analysis. I was concerned that making such statements as "They spend a lot of time talking about..." would be too subjective; therefore, I derived percentages of dialogue devoted to each curricular category during the conferences each week and across the entire time. Readers could then determine for themselves whether or not to agree with my assessment of 2% of dialogue devoted to goals and objectives as about right, too little, or too much.

The detailed analysis required to derive percentages unexpectedly turned out to be one of the keys to understanding how the curricular thought process worked. A sentence such as

> I didn't know if the kids would be able to control their hands well enough to do that one rhythm (taps the rhythm on desk) on tambourine, but they could and they even liked it a lot, so I decided that we'd try it again when the form lesson comes up next week.

moves among curricular categories. Sorting became much like diagramming sentences in sophomore English but without the branching system as a guide. I finally settled on using a different colored highlighting pen for each category. I could then determine percentages and visually perceive the flow of curricular thought among categories without becoming bogged down in content detail and without considerable rereading. Both the detail of conversation and the broad flow could be analyzed. Both types of analysis were crucial to understanding the data and answering the research questions.

I also enlisted the aid of a coreader who went over large portions of the data. She was to agree or disagree with the curricular categories I had color-coded. Her input reduced my concerns about subjectivity in sentence content analysis.

Reliance on transcription data was sometimes insufficient. On occasion, I found it necessary to refer to the tapes for nuance and to confirm occasional use of sarcasm. "They really did well with that" was not necessarily a positive evaluation of student achievement! Also, transcripts cannot do justice to the devastated tone of voice a student teacher would use when describing an unpleasant classroom experience, nor does the compassion of the cooperating teacher leap off the page. The same could be said of the jubilant expressions heard in discussions of a truly outstanding triumph in the classroom. All of this information is of great import when developing the description needed to make a case study come alive to the reader.

Drawing Conclusions

As mentioned in the opening paragraphs, I felt that conducting qualitative research in an area with which I'd had years of experience was an advantage. In drawing this conclusion, I was keenly aware that the years of experience worked positively for me. I was also aware that previous experiences can contribute to subjective interpretation, so every effort was made to be alert.

As I read through the data, I recognized patterns that I had heard and seen across the years. The conclusions I drew that were included in the final draft were ones supported within the study and also across the previous student teaching situations in which I had been involved. I felt this would be the most helpful information to persons who decided the study findings and conclusions were transferable to situations in their own experience.

Conducting qualitative research requires involvement in the world of the participants. My unobtrusive entry into their world was as a person well acquainted with student teaching experiences but one who looked very closely at the experiences of the persons in the dyads for their particular idiosyncrasies. My concerns about subjectivity led me to be extremely careful about formulating conclusions that could be supported from within the data gathered for the study.

Final Thoughts

Overall, I feel that one of the advantages of qualitative research is that it can account for and include information that comes to light during the process of data collection. However, I find it crucial to have clearly defined limits, clear research questions that focus the study, and be grounded in existing research. These three factors guide the process and help with anticipating some aspects of the situation to be encountered.

Because qualitative research is wordy by nature, opposed to presentation of data through numerical data, it is important to write in a concise manner. I find that it is necessary to formulate clear research questions that may be pursued in as direct a method as possible. Clear questions make it possible to select a workable design and write clearly about what was found. Any extraneous information is then more easily identified. The researcher may then determine what it is and how important the data may or may not be to the study. "Outside" data may expand and amplify; however it is possible for the "outside" data to overtake and muddy the original study. In my case, I find it better to construct a separate study rather than to expand the present one.

If I anticipate publication, I need to go over the data several times to become aware of the main points, because length of the document becomes more important than when I do research for my own information. Qualitative research dialogue can become too detail oriented. Many conversations are very intriguing and the intricacies become well known to the researcher. This can lead to overinclusion of quotes and details in the final document.

Readers come to the article with a desire to learn what was done and what was found. Sufficient quotes are needed to support findings and to provide flavor for the reader, but their fascination with the subjects will never equal your own that has developed through deep and lengthy involvement. Provide descriptions and share insights in a substantive but interesting manner to help maintain reader interest and keep the document manageable.

READING QUALITATIVE RESEARCH

The following is a phenomenological study published in 2002 in the *Journal of Music Therapy*. Creswell (2003) describes this genre of qualitative research as one in which "the researcher identifies the 'essence' of human experiences concerning a phenomenon, as described by the participants in a study" (p. 15). The process typically involves a small number of participants who are observed over a prolonged time for the purpose of detecting patterns and relationships of behaviors. In this study by Wheeler (2002), experiences and concerns of music therapy students were studied during the preclinical or practicum experience. "Interviews with students were intended to lead to an understanding of these experiences as the students perceived them" (p. 274). Implications for education and clinical training are presented.

Experiences and Concerns of Students During Music Therapy Practica

Barbara L. Wheeler, *Montclair State University*
Journal of Music Therapy, 39(4), 274–304.

Reprinted by permission of JMT: Journal of Music Therapy. Copyright © 2002 by American Music Therapy Association.

There has been considerable research and writing on various aspects of music therapy clinical training, including both preclinical or practicum experiences and the music therapy internship. This literature, which has been summarized by McClain (2001), deals with the structure and content of the practica, ways of helping students achieve necessary competencies, evaluation of practicum experiences and skills, improving the effectiveness of supervision, and various other issues, including practica, internships, and supervision. A recent book on music therapy supervision (Forinash, 2001) contains chapters on general supervision issues (Dileo, 2001; Estrella, 2001) and preprofessional supervision, including supervision of practicum students and interns (Farnan, 2001; Feiner, 2001; Hanser, 2001; Shulman-Fagen, 2001; Stige, 2001; Summer, 2001; Thomas, 2001).

There is no question that music therapy educators and supervisors, in general, are sensitive to the feelings and perceptions of their students and interns, and that they receive ongoing input as to the students' experiences. Hearing the student's or intern's perceptions is key to the music therapy supervision process. Many of the chapters in the Forinash (2001) book, as well as other materials on music therapy supervision (Stephens, 1984, 1987), stress the need for supervisees to communicate their concerns, including their feelings and perceptions, and suggest strategies to assist them in doing this. It is clear that the authors of these materials on supervision are sensitive to their students' concerns and work to help them to share these concerns.

Music therapy supervisors often receive feedback from students as to students' experiences in the practicum or internship. Indeed, one of the requirements for National Roster Internships through the American Music Therapy Association is an evaluation that the intern must complete, including evaluation of the provisions for supervision (AMTA, 2001). How much interns use this opportunity to evaluate and provide feedback on the supervision and supervisor, and, if they do, how much this reflects their experience of the internship is not clear, but it does provide an opportunity to hear from the student.

Some, or perhaps most, supervisors make special efforts to hear from the student. Feiner (2001) says:

> Help your intern understand how much you value communication and need feedback, for understanding each other is a two-way street. An intern must feel comfortable bringing up whatever s/he feels is relevant to the internship and supervisory relationship. Communicate this with your words and actions. Structure a space for this type of communication from the beginning: checking in on feelings, being matter-of-fact in assuming that there will be feelings (i.e., about starting, about being in a new role, about clients that are elicited during observations and interactions, about supervision). Really listen. Read you intern's written journals or logs and give them back promptly with feedback that values their perspective while expanding their knowledge. Make sure a section on personal reactions is included, conveying how important it is for you to know how they react to things and what is on their mind. Explore when this is resisted.
>
> I always tell my intern that I will try to do my best, but at times I will get things wrong or unintentionally say something hurtful. I say that the student knows him or herself best, so s/he should tell me when this happens. I want them to know that I want feedback too. (pp. 109–111).

In spite of this sensitivity to the needs and feelings of practicum students and interns, the majority of the literature on practica and internships does not specifically address the concerns of students, nor is most of it based upon student input gained in a systematic fashion. Several studies do investigate students' concerns and experiences.

McClain (1993) sought out students' perceptions of the content, structure, and supervision of practicum training, and their self-perceptions of the process. She surveyed 138 music therapy majors from 12 colleges and universities and also interviewed 20 of those surveyed. She found that students desired

> more on-site music therapy supervisors who can observe students and be observed by them; greater input into their practicum placements; more diversity of practicum settings; more orientation before beginning a new practicum; more of a gradual sequence from less difficult to more difficult clients, and from individuals or small groups to larger ones; an earlier start in practicum training; and opportunities to assist or colead before conducting sessions independently. (p. iv).

In terms of students' self-perceptions, she found that students felt most competent "first, as a person, second, as a musician, and third, as a therapist" (1993, p. iv), and that they were most concerned as therapists about their clinical skills, especially those that involved understanding and meeting clients' needs and establishing rapport with them.

Grant and McCary (1990) studied emotional stages in the music therapy internship. They had 59 music therapy interns use a Likert scale to rate their feelings on 20 pairs of words describing feeling states. Both personal and professional feelings were included. This was done at the beginning and the end of the internship. Interns also had the opportunity to write narrative statements about their feelings. These researchers found patterns of feelings which varied from month to month throughout the internship.

Madsen and Kaiser (1999) studied preinternship fears of music therapy majors. Students listed the three greatest fears that they had concerning their internships and these fears were then classified based on a taxonomy developed in an earlier study. They found "general preparation/being prepared" to be the primary fear, followed by issues relating to "failure/not cut out for therapy"; concerns about he "internship placement," and the "physical environment," including money, moving, house, and so forth (p. 17).

Although music therapy supervisors receive verbal and written input from students in narrative form, this input has not been studied systematically. The present phenomenological research study was intended to investigate various concerns and experiences that music therapy students have during their preclinical or practicum experiences. By interviewing students about their experience of the music therapy practicum over the course of an academic year, I hoped to gain an understanding of these experiences as the students perceived them.

Method

Stance of the Researcher

The study was conducted based on the perception that students have thoughts and feelings about the practica that faculty never suspect, and that these thoughts and feelings influence both their experience of the practica and their work in them. The ontological view that guided the inquiry was that one can understand another's experience enough to be meaningful. This was connected to the epistemological stance that this understanding can be obtained through what people say about their experiences.

The impetus to investigate this area came when a student, as a topic for a hypothetical research study, said that he would like to focus on practicum students' experiences in dealing with criticism from their supervisor.* His use of "dealing with criticism" was very different from my perception of the supervisory experience, which I would have phrased as "receiving feedback." This added to my previous impressions that students may perceive the practicum differently than do faculty, and I felt that I could learn from their perceptions. Therefore, I structured the interviews in order to hear as much as possible of the students' experiences and approached them as openly as possible.

Initial Questions

Questions as I began the study included:

1. What issues do students find pertinent in their practica?
2. What makes students anxious?
3. What strategies do they use to ease their anxiety?
4. What makes them comfortable?
5. What is useful in the supervision process, both by on-site and university faculty supervisors?

---

* The wording that I relay here is my memory of what the student said. While he remembers the conversation and the general focus, his memory of the exact wording is somewhat different from mine.

6. What are the challenges in doing practica?

7. How can the experience best be structured?

I intended to gather as much information as possible about the students' practicum experiences from a range of students, then see if there were common experiences. If common experiences were found, I would examine whether they followed any patterns. My intent in this study was to: (a) enable the students to talk about their experiences in such a manner that they could convey their actual experiences; (b) determine the types of experiences that they have, and the categories and patterns into which they fall; and (c) look at implications of these findings for the music therapy practicum.

Procedures

Interviews

All students were enrolled in the undergraduate music therapy program of the university in which I taught. Four students in sophomore practica and four in the upper level practica were interviewed, three females and one male at each level. The students in the sophomore practicum were all traditional undergraduate students. One of the sophomore students changed his major at the end of the semester, and another student was thus added for only the second semester. One student in the upper-level practicum was a traditional undergraduate student who had transferred after having been out of school for a period of time, and one was an equivalency student who had returned to school after a career in another field.

Informed Consent

Students volunteered to participate in the study after being informed verbally and in writing of the purpose and expectations of the study. They had an opportunity to ask questions or discuss the research and then signed consent forms.

Interview Procedures

The interviews were open-ended and designed to elicit as much of the students' experiences and as many of their feelings as possible. The specific focus of the questions and thus the direction of the interviews changed somewhat over time, as did the nature of the students' experiences. Questions and the questioning style suggested by Spradley (1979) in *The Ethnographic Interview* were used as guidelines. All interviews were tape-recorded and transcribed.

Spradley's (1979) perspective guided me in thinking of the interviews in an ethnographic manner: I was attempting to understand the culture of the practicum student and it is a culture that is not mine. I assumed that my status as a faculty member affected what was revealed to me and the content of the interviews (although I had made it clear that these interviews would not affect their grades and would be kept confidential from anyone involved with their practica), so I made provisions to minimize this influence as much as possible.

The first interview took place midway through the first semester of the practicum. This interview had some guiding questions, although the direction that the interview took was determined largely by the student's responses. In this interview, as in all of the interviews, the purpose of the study was first explained to the interviewee, generally in the words "I am trying to get as good an understanding as possible of your experience of the music therapy practicum, including the clinical experience itself, the supervision by both the on-site supervisor and the faculty supervisor, and the practicum class. As you know, I will be tape-recording our interview and will transcribe the tape for analysis. Everything that you say will be confidential and nothing that you say will influence your grade." Students were then asked to talk about their practicum experience, starting with whatever came to their mind. At some point in the interview, they were asked to think of a situation with a client which they felt was important and to describe it, and their description of and reactions to the experience were discussed. They were asked at another point if they felt that they were the same person in practicum that they were in the rest of their lives. If they did not bring it up on their own, they were asked at some point to talk about the on-site supervision and the supervision by the university supervisor, and about how they found the class that accompanied the practicum experience. As stated earlier, any of these or other responses could be expanded upon by the student. Thus, each interview was quite different.

In the second interview, near the end of the first semester, the purpose and confidentiality were again reviewed. Students were then asked to talk about their current experience of the practicum and questioned about various aspects if they did not speak of them spontaneously. At some point, they were asked if they remembered what they had shared in the first interview, particularly any issues that were of concern to them, and to speak of their current experience in those areas. (As interviewer, I had reviewed the transcripts so could remind them of the earlier issues.)

Students were only interviewed once during the second semester, near the end of the semester. They were contacted early in the semester and told that this was the plan and that if they felt that it would be helpful to meet earlier in the semester, that would be arranged. No student requested this. In this interview, students were asked to talk about the experience of the practicum in that semester and to compare this experience with what had occurred in the first semester. I was aware of and influenced by the content of the interviews when I did the next interviews, but for logistical reasons transcriptions of the interviews were not completed until all of the interviews had been finished.

The student who changed his major at the end of the first semester had only two interviews. The student who was added in the second semester had two interviews during that semester. Both were in the sophomore practica.

After the interviews were transcribed, I divided them into segments that conveyed a single idea or concerned a particular topic. I then formulated summary statements of the segments. These were brief statements summarizing the thought or feeling described in the segment. The transcription and summary statements were sent to the students for their input to insure that they accurately reflected their experiences, and so that their feedback could be included in the final data analysis. At the time that they were asked for this feedback, they were asked to share any reflections that they had at that time, during the academic year which followed the interviews. They were also asked to share any thoughts that they had as to how the interviewer being a faculty member, including at times their supervisor and/or practicum class teacher, had influenced their responses.

Structure of Practica

The early practica were normally taken in a student's sophomore year and were done in conjunction with beginning music therapy courses, the first of which was Therapy and Observation Skills for Music Therapy and the second, Methods and Materials in Music Therapy. The upper-level practica were taken when students were juniors or seniors, in conjunction with the courses Music Therapy with Children and Psychology of Music.

The practicum was structured so that students did weekly clinical work with a group of clients. All students worked under the supervision of an on-site music therapist. The sophomore students worked with elderly people while the upper-level students worked with children. Some worked with the same group for both semesters.

Most of the fall semester of the sophomore practicum was spent observing and assisting the music therapist, with the suggestion that they could begin conducting a portion of the session when they and their supervisor felt that they were ready. In the second semester of the sophomore practicum and both semesters of the upper-level practicum, students were responsible for conducting the group, although occasionally they did a portion of this with the music therapist as cotherapist.

Students who were conducting groups were observed twice in the semester by a supervisor from the university. This was either a full-time faculty member (including me, the researcher) or a part-time faculty member. In these settings, the student would have formal observations with the supervisor in the role of faculty observer in addition to the regular weekly supervision. Faculty observations were graded.

Students in both practica met 1 hour a week in a class, with a separate class for each level of practicum. One full-time faculty member taught the sophomore practicum while another taught the upper-level practicum. This time was spent discussing the clinical work and various aspects of conducting music therapy sessions, sharing resources, and role-playing.

Roles of Researcher

I had several roles with these students in addition to being the researcher, and possible influences on the research of these roles must be considered. As researcher, I interviewed the students, then analyzed the responses and shared the results of the research. I was also a faculty member in the program in which all of the students were enrolled and, in that position, had various contacts with them throughout their education. I taught the practicum course in which some of students were enrolled as well as the course that they took concurrently with the practicum. I was also the faculty observer for some of the students.

Because of these multiple roles, I took extra precaution in the research. First, I was careful to avoid using my position to influence the students' willingness to participate in the research. I distributed a written description of the research and told them that I would welcome their participation, but, in general, did not seek out students for the research but rather let them volunteer. I made it clear in the initial invitation that participation would not influence grades, recommendations, or anything else.

Second, throughout the research I stressed that, while I appreciated the students' assistance, their participation in the research was separate from any grades, recommendations, or other aspects of their education. I also made it clear throughout that the information that I received as a result of the interviews was confidential and would not be conveyed to anyone else, would not be brought into class by me, and would be presented in the final report in a way that would protect confidentiality.

Finally, in follow-up communication with the students after the interviews had been completed, when I was working at a different university, I wrote:

> I am trying to do whatever possible so that the research will reflect your truthful feelings and thoughts. Since I had several roles in addition to interviewer, including teacher, supervisor, advisor, etc., it is possible that you did not feel free to be completely honest. Perhaps with the time that has elapsed... you may have some thought or insights that you would share differently. Please, for each interview, would you take a minute to write a brief addition that reflects any updated perspective that you have, particularly where you feel that you could share something that you did not share at the time or in some other way make the interview more creditable. If you have no further thoughts, just make a note of that.

While I know that I am not always totally aware of everything that students (or anyone else) are thinking, I am under the impression that my efforts to get honest and accurate information were successful. This is based on several things: (a) Students seemed to be frank and honest in the interviews, (b) All indications were that they understood the boundaries and limits of this as well as other facets of our relationship, (c) We seemed to have good and open relationships, and (d) Only one student's feedback to the follow-up letter that was sent related to the multiple roles to which I referred, giving me the impression that the students had not considered my various roles to be an issue.

Data Analysis

The data analysis involved the following steps:

1. Interviews were transcribed.
2. Summary statements of segments of the interviews were made.
3. Transcriptions and summary statements were sent to the students for their input; at the same time, students were asked to share any reflections that they had at that time, during the academic year following the interviews, and were also asked to share any thoughts that they had as to how the interviewer being a faculty member, including at times their supervisor and/or practicum class teacher, influenced their responses.
4. Changes in summary statements were made based on students' feedback.
5. Summary statements were divided into categories and subcategories.
6. After reviewing the data analysis and its usefulness, subcategories were placed under the initial questions that had guided the research.
7. Comments were regrouped under areas of interest and explanatory from the transcripts added.

A principle that guided the data analysis was that the presentation of the results in qualitative research is part of the data analysis (Aigen, 1995). Therefore, until the presentation of the results was clear, the search for ways to make it clear and thus the continuation of the data analysis continued.

Results

Students' suggestions for changes in the summary statements were minor and generally included adding information. The revised summary statements, alongside the initial transcriptions, were used when formulating categories.

Only one student indicated, in response to my follow-up letter, that she felt that she had stated anything differently because of my multiple roles. She felt that this had led her to understate a problem during the interview.

Categories that emerged from the initial analysis included: supervision, practicum class, reactions to clients, personal awareness and observations, anxiety and concerns about sessions, easing of anxiety and concerns, structure of practicum or setting, and musical skills. Each category contained numerous subcategories.

After the categories and subcategories had been formed, it became clear that they did not completely convey the students' experiences of the music therapy practica, primarily because the categories were based largely on the questions that had guided the interviews rather than around types of experiences that emerged from what the students had said. While the reasons for this were clear, it decreased the usefulness of the categories in understanding the students' experiences. In working to find a way to convey the experiences that the students had during their clinical work, the idea of organizing them under areas of interest emerged. These areas of interest seem to serve a more useful means of categorizing the experiences and presenting them in written form.

The areas of interest are presented below as they evolved and in a form that seems to adequately convey the students' experiences. They are organized under six main areas: challenges encountered by students, means of dealing with challenges, involvement with clients, areas of learning, supervision issues, and structure of practicum. Comments are taken from the transcripts of the sessions and are the words that the students used, with some exceptions. My questions or comments, intended to help the students look more deeply into their experiences or share more about them, have been eliminated or incorporated into the students' words. Supervisors' names have been changed to "supervisor" and clients' names have been eliminated. Other minor modifications of their actual words have been made but in no case do I think that their meaning or style of speaking was altered. Students are not called by their real names but gender-appropriate names are used.

Challenges Encountered by Students

Fear of new experiences. Fears of a new practicum placement were described by students in the early, or beginning, practicum. This is conveyed vividly by Rebecca as she describes her initial visit to her clinical facility:

> Before I went, I wasn't nervous, I was excited. Until I got to the door, and then
> I realized, I don't know where I'm going, I don't know what I'm doing, I don't

know who these people are, I don't know anything. I knocked on the door and, you know, hi, I'm here for music therapy. I didn't even know who I was talking to. So not knowing makes it easy to come up with, oh no, what if I go to the wrong place or what if I ask the wrong person? It makes you think of wild things that probably wouldn't even happen.

This part of the experience changed as students became familiar with the setting and the work. But Melanie, another student in the early practicum, had a similar concern in an interview early in her second semester of clinical work:

I'm afraid I'm going to be just as nervous next semester when it's a whole new population and a whole new setting. I'd like to think that I'll be OK, I've done this before and I've been the new girl before and I did fine and I was successful at the last place. Hopefully I can just do that again, but it's going to be scary all over again, at least for the first few weeks, especially with a new therapist.

Session planning. Students had many concerns about planning sessions. The primary one was what to do in the sessions—what activities to use. Patricia, a student in the upper-level practicum (but only beginning her clinical experience with children/adolescents), said:

My biggest anxiety at this point is that I don't know enough activities to do, and I don't know any resources where I can find activities for adolescents. We seem to have a lot of things for young children, but I don't see anything for adolescents.

This theme, the difficulty of planning what to do, occurred repeatedly with several students. With other students, it came up in a different form. For Melanie, in the early practicum, it was a concern over what to do when things did not go as planned. In an interview early in the second semester of this work, she said:

The unpredictability is definitely the biggest challenge. And trying to always have a back-up plan, and being flexible to what they want to do. I've been working with this group for a few weeks now, and it never goes as I've planned.

Needs of clients. Several students in the upper-level practicum were concerned about working with children because they did not have experience with children, particularly children with multiple disabilities. These fears were shared by Megan:

I don't know anything about children. I mean, I was a child but I don't remember anything about it, at the level that these children are at. I don't remember how it was to be 2 or 3 years old. I'm trying to become familiar with the different levels, getting more comfortable in working with them.

Another concern was how to deal with clients who functioned at different levels. Kyle, a student in the upper-level practicum, said, "I'm having a hard time with how to get four or five kids who are all at different cognitive levels to respond to me."

Music skills. Feeling the need for better music skills was an issue for two of the students, both voice majors who had begun their training with minimal music skills outside of singing. One of these students, Megan, said:

I think that when we come into this field we are not as prepared as we should be—not everyone, but myself. Musically, I don't have the background that some of the other students have and I think that's the hardest part in the practicum, getting the music to sound the way I want it to so that I can work with the children and have the music sound the way that I want it to sound.

Concerns about grades. Several students expressed concerns over the grading aspects of the practicum. One concern was about the struggles of deciding whether to work on the practicum, for which she received only one credit, or another class for which she received more credit. Megan said:

It's a lot of work with the other classes and this class. And also that it's one credit. I have these three-credit classes which will mean a lot more if I get an "A." I want to do well, but do I get an "A" in my practicum or do I get an "A" in my other classes? It's stressful. If there were no grades it would be wonderful, you'd just do what you want.

Means of Dealing with Challenges

Self-devised strategies to ease discomfort. One student in the early practicum, Rebecca, was creative about finding strategies to help ease her discomfort. Looking ahead to the second semester, she said:

Next semester, I plan on trying to go to the facility ahead of time and just get a feel for the place and maybe, if possible, get introduced to a couple of people, go observe an extra session just for my own comfort.

Relating her experience of the second semester, at a new facility, she said, "When I started, I asked my supervisor for a few songs that they were familiar with, so I could start out with something that they knew instead of jumping in and changing everything."

Involvement. The level of involvement was an issue for students in the early practicum, since their first semester was set up to be primarily observing and assisting. While they were encouraged to conduct a portion of the session at some point in the semester, the point at which that would occur and the amount of the session for which they would be responsible was left open, with the decision to be made by them and their supervisor, with feedback from the instructor or class if they sought it out. Rebecca describes her initial contacts with group members:

And then the patients started coming in and all the interns and the therapist were busy. Basically, the patient got wheeled in and was sitting there. I was already sitting there, and we were kind of just staring at each other. If you're in a room with anybody and you're just staring at them, you feel very uncomfortable. So I said, "Hello," explained that I was a music therapy student, and then the client explained that he really enjoyed it and that he thought it was great that that's what I wanted to do. So before I knew it, the time has passed quickly and it didn't feel so uncomfortable.

Lara spoke of how being included as part of the group, rather than observing from the outside, eased her discomfort.

[In the third week the therapist that we worked with] said our names at the beginning of the session. "This is xxx and this is xxx," and everyone was saying their names and it felt better. We were included in the group. The other thing with the third week is that we didn't start off the session as an outsider, outside the circle. We started off immediately in the circle, and that made a lot of difference.

Knowledge of clients. Students all felt more comfortable as they spent time in the practicum and with the population. Lara, a student in the early practicum, said at the end of the semester:

> I think it's easier this semester, in the sense that it's a lot easier to deal with the people, it's a lot easier for me being around older people. It's not my favorite thing to do, but I'm adjusted to it more, I know what to expect.

At the end of the second semester, Patricia said:

> The second semester was certainly better than the first because I felt more comfortable. I worked with the same children, so I knew them and I knew what to expect and I had some ideas of what I could do with them.

Musical progress. All of the students in the upper-level practicum spoke of their musical progress. While it had not been planned, all four of the upper-level students who took part in this study had voice as their primary instrument and did not play piano or guitar until learning them as part of their music therapy training. Jenny spoke of her improved musical skills when she was first interviewed in the second month of her practicum:

> Well since it is my last year, I'm a senior, and I'm finishing, this year I feel a lot more in control; I feel a lot more prepared musically, and I think that's impacting how I work or how I feel about doing the practicum.

Megan said at the end of the first year:

> I feel more comfortable with my music because I can see that I can do things, like improvise, which I never tried before. I can do that in the session and it's really helpful. My supervisor has asked me to write a couple of songs in the sessions, on the classroom themes, and that's challenged me to do something different.

Kyle found himself able to try new things and be more comfortable using the piano, and expressed this at the end of the second semester:

> I tried a lot more things out the last couple of sessions. I've been doing stuff with the piano, and tomorrow my supervisor's going to let me do it by myself, but she's going to work really closely with me next to the piano, to help me pick up on cues. I think that one of my biggest problems when I go from using my voice to using another instrument—at least I found this with the piano—is that I'm not quite sure if I'm using the piano in a way that's picking up on what the kids are doing. I felt more comfortable doing it with my voice. A lot of it has to do with I'm not so familiar with the piano, although I am getting more confident in my piano playing. I think the proximity to the kids is different, too, when I go to the piano.

Applications of experiential learning. One student, Rebecca, was at a placement in which interns and practicum students were part of an experienced music therapy group. This was a special experience to have, and must have been personally challenging in her very first practicum. She appeared to benefit from the experience, and spoke of applying the knowledge:

> In the student group, I'm learning a lot about myself and I'm learning a lot about music therapy at the same time. I like going to it, even though I'm a little apprehensive because I don't know what we're going to do. It's OK. I like the fact that I'm pushed to jump in and try and learn things. I think it's a good experience.
>
> The student group, which was just myself and the other interns, got me to realize that different people have different perspectives, and then once I got into the patient group, I was able to apply it, see how they dealt with it.... That brings up a lot of questions. Was this spur of the moment or was this planned, what the music therapist decides to do? When a client yells something out, do you go with it, or do you ignore it? It was pretty interesting since they each have their own interpretation.

Involvement with Clients

Meeting clients' needs. Throughout the practica, meeting the needs of the clients was a primary concern of the students. Rebecca, from the early practica, spoke of the changes from the first semester of practicum, when she was primarily observing, to the second semester, when she was actually responsible for the clients.

> Well, in the session this semester there's a lot more going on. Now it's beyond, I have to learn this song, it's that I have to remember to speak in so and so's left ear, and I have to remember that I need to directly face someone else because they're also hard of hearing and they won't see that I'm addressing them. This semester, I know what to work for, and I'm trying to work on how I can help that. Last semester I was very worried about what to look for, and now I think I've got a pretty good handle on that, so it's, well, what can I do? I see one patient slumping over. What should I do? Should I get up? Should I grab him? Should I speak louder? Now it's basically things that I need to work on.

Changes in clients. One of the most consistent and gratifying parts of the students' experience was when they saw positive changes in the clients and could attribute part of those changes to their work with them. Joshua, a student in the early practicum, spoke several times in his second interview, near the end of the first semester, of how he felt when he saw changes in the elderly clients whom he had observed and assisted:

> I had a good idea of what we were working toward, and I knew it would take some time, but I wasn't noticing any improvement in the patients. And being new to the major, not having much experience with music therapy sessions as a whole, I've never seen it over a period of time. I started thinking, I'm not seeing any change in anybody, and it let me down.
>
> I started seeing improvements in the clients that I had not seen earlier towards the end of our sessions. All of a sudden everybody's behavior started changing towards the goals that we were working on. I was like, yeah, we did do something, all right!

Kyle, in the upper-level practicum, shared his sense of progress over the year:

> It's different this semester than last semester because I'm getting more from the kids, so there's more for me to watch out for. Or maybe I'm aware of it more

this semester than I was last semester. But I'm starting to see little nuances, smaller increments than I was either looking for or seeing last semester. I look back at the kids from the very beginning when I started and where they are right now, and there's a sense of pride that maybe I helped get them to where they are, even just a little bit, so that's exciting to see.

Positive responses and interactions. The positive responses from and interactions with clients were very gratifying for students at both levels. Melanie, working with elderly people in the second semester of the early practicum, said:

> One patient gave me a hug and a kiss before we left. Normally she touches me a lot, but she stood up and put her arms around me and gave me a kiss on the cheek. That's just the sweetest thing ever, that she's happy right now, and I contributed to that in some form.

Jenny, near the end of her work in the upper-level practicum, said:

> There's one student in my group who is ambulatory and there's another student who is not, and the student who is not is also nonverbal. We were doing movement, a dancing kind of thing, one day, and the student who is ambulatory and verbal was trying to get the other involved. She came over to her and took her hand and was dancing with her, and she picked up this towel and wiped the drool off of her face and kept dancing with her. It really moved me.

Concerns about clients. Students had concerns about their clients, ranging from the clients' lives or conditions to their ability to reach them to other aspects of their treatment. Melanie, in the early practicum, shared her sadness about a client's loneliness and isolation:

> She has the most depressing life history that I've come across. The woman has had two husbands and six children and they've all died. She was an only child, her parents are dead, and she's the highest-functioning one of the eight that we originally had. And the only reason she's there is that she just had nowhere else to go. And she's so depressed all the time, and it's so sad. And it's discouraging because, even if you can get her to participate, which she does, and even when she appears to be happy for the 30 minutes that she's in there, as soon as you stop singing or the music stops, she's back into her little cocoon. And it's sad because you just wish that someone could pay attention to her all the time.

Joshua, early in the first practicum, had many concerns about the clients and described his own reactions vividly:

> Sometimes with the dementia you just can't get feedback, and sometimes you get feedback but it's really nothing that makes any sense whatsoever. One person in practicum dozes off, and when he wakes up he's talking about something. He knows what he's talking about, and I know what it's related to because I know his history based on the charts. But from where we are at that point in time it has no bearing. You kind of sit there and say, OK, and just bring him back into the group.... I feel really emotionally upset. I feel that right now there is not much I can do because I haven't had the training. Physiologically, my stomach churns a little bit. I get a little upset, my mind starts jumping around a lot trying to think of ways that I could help him. My heart goes out to him. I wish I knew what was

going on in his head. Sometimes I think it's because I haven't had the training, or sometimes I think that's just how it is.

Megan, in the upper-level practicum, shared concerns about whether she was doing what the children needed: "I think that's my biggest problem when I'm working with the children, am I really reaching them? Am I really getting them to do what they need to do so they reach their IEP goals?

Students had some concerns about the treatment of clients by others involved in the treatment. Rebecca said:

> There's a lack of compassion from the other staff members. There's more sympathy and empathy and participation going on between the members of the group than there is from the staff to the patients. I think that is a really significant problem. They don't get the patients up out of bed when they know they have somewhere to be. They sit there and they wait in line forever, they don't get dressed right away in the morning. The one client was up, he was ready, he had his haircut, he was shaven and I was so surprised, and then it ends up being his birthday. It shouldn't have to take being somebody's birthday to do your job.

Areas of Learning

Personal issues. Students shared a variety of personal revelations that came about as part of their clinical work. Lara spoke of an experience early in the practicum that forced her to think of mortality in a way that had not previously occurred to her:

> They were taking somebody out in a body bag and we were like, Oh, my God, I hope everyone's in our session today. At the beginning of the weeks I was like, yeah, these people are pretty old, they could probably die, but I wasn't thinking that Maggie, the woman that sits next to me that gets really agitated that loves to sing that was smiling at me last week, might be dead this week. That didn't occur to me.

Lara also spoke of how she managed to get through new experiences:

> I always try to be assertive, and I usually do always go through new experiences, but in the back of my mind I'm so scared if I fail. I don't show it, but it's always in the back of my mind. I put up a really good front. I go in like I know what I'm doing and I haven't a clue.

Jenny, early in the upper-level practicum, shared insights and a tool that she had developed from feedback in an earlier practicum:

> Their progress does weigh on what I do and the way I do things. I'm trying, because in the adult psych practicum, I learned to separate myself and not be, I must save everybody. I must make everybody better and it all lies on me—it's all my responsibility. I learned that I did that and that it's really not acceptable or healthy and it doesn't help anybody. So if something doesn't go in a session, I'm OK with that. But I would want to see some sort of progress or one of my objectives get met every time I'm there, just to feel like something is going right.
>
> I write in a journal and say, "I felt really upset about this today. I wonder what it was. Do I feel a need to control the situation? Maybe I should just let that go." And it helps me to move through it. It really helps you to lay out what it is internally—what's going on with you that made you react that way.

Miscellaneous personal observations. Lara reflected on how it felt to actually be doing music therapy.

> I'm surprised that I'm only 19 and I'm doing stuff outside of the school in my major because a lot of my friend's majors—they're not doing that. They don't end up doing stuff with education until their junior or senior year or something, but I'm already doing it. Also, when I see the therapist dong it, I think, in a few years I'm going to be doing that. I'm happy about it, I get a good feeling about it.

Jenny spoke of how she felt when she was with the children:

> I wasn't sure how I personally was going to act. Was I going to act strange? Was I going to fear them or something I didn't understand, like the way they were positioned or some way that they looked that made me uncomfortable just because I didn't understand it? And I got there and, when I first walked in, I saw all these weird carts and stands. But then, after I watched and interacted with the children in my group, maybe they gave me that sense of comfort, they themselves as people gave me what I needed to feel OK about.

Kyle had trouble getting himself to work on his own with the children, rather than assist the supervising music therapist, in his second semester of practicum, and reflected on this:

> When I came back after the break, the kids had progressed from the last time that I had seen them. I guess it must have been 5 or 6 weeks. I wasn't confident in what was going on, and after the first session I began to get nervous again. I guess I didn't think that I was progressing with the kids, and it was like me reevaluating again where they were. I guess most of it was probably having that break and then coming back and seeing some of the things that I didn't see. I was a little uncomfortable about how to approach it again. So it took a little more time in getting back into doing it by myself again.

Supervision Issues

On-site supervision. Students were supervised regularly by an on-site music therapist. They were quite clear about what they liked and did not like as far as supervision. In the first interview, while she was observing, Rebecca spoke of what was useful:

> The last time I was there, she explained a little bit more because I had said that I had a lot of questions, and she gave me some specific things to look for, like how many times a patient participated, if he only participated when he made the suggestion, the contributions of the patients and the therapists musically, the interns' contribution musically, Just different ways of looking at the things. Without those kind of guidelines I was just looking all over the place and didn't really have a focus of what to look at.
>
> She's great. She always gives us extra articles and things to supplement questions or discussion that we've had which have been very helpful. For example, we had a discussion about countertransference, then she gave us an article. When things like that happen, she'll make a comment—she sort of reinforces what we discuss. That's been very helpful also, because there's a big difference between reading something and having somebody explain it to you, then actually seeing it. You have a little light bulb go on—oh, that's what we were talking about!

Melanie, in the second semester of the early practicum, when she had begun conducting her own sessions, said:

> I really like the therapist that I work with. I guess the best part is, she offers so much feedback and she's very helpful. I was so nervous when I first started leading the sessions. I was so afraid I wasn't prepared enough because she's been through so many years of schooling and so many years of actually being a professional therapist, and how am I supposed to achieve what she does, but she makes you feel really comfortable and, once you actually get in there, I wasn't as nervous and felt more comfortable. If she likes something, she'll tell me, "That's a great idea. I'm going to use that. That was a very good idea." I like that, because then I know that she's not really feeling superior to me.

At the end of the year, Megan, from the upper-level practicum, reflected on her supervisor:

> She was really great with supervising because she gave me a different perspective and a different way to try some of my activities, whereas if my activity worked good this way, she'd say, "Why don't you try it next time that way and see if you can push them a little bit more", which was really helpful because sometimes I got stuck in my ways with the activities. She was really supportive.

Faculty supervision. In addition to the on-site supervisor, beginning with the time that they conducted their own sessions, students were observed twice a semester by a supervisor from the university. At the end of the year (and of the first semester in which the students in the early practicum had conducted their own sessions), Lara said:

> I think that it was significant getting observed and knowing I had to change what I'm doing. I can't just do what my supervisor is doing or what the other student does, 'cause it's not working with what I want to do, or it's not working with the clients.

And her reflection on a suggestion that had been made by the faculty supervisor was: "And then, the first time to actually do 'Beat the Drum Once,' I realized that it worked. It was like, wow that really worked!"

At the end of the first semester, Patricia said, "Concerning observations by the school, I think the observations are important and helpful. I would find them more helpful if the observer would make suggestions on activities based on the observation."

Megan had thoughts on how often the faculty supervisor should observe: "I think it's important for you to have the person see you work more than once or twice, because they get to see you develop and see what you really are doing."

Kyle found observations by the faculty supervisor to be pivotal in his work. The first observation, midway through his first semester, helped to bring together what he had perceived as a different way of working by his on-site supervisor from what he was being taught at the university. He said:

> I think most of it came after the first observation, having the validation from the supervision and again from talking with both supervisors together. And clarifying more of what exactly I was supposed to be looking for. I think that at the

beginning, I wasn't quite sure what my expectations were in the session, and because it was so unclear to me, it didn't get cleared up until after I did that session. Maybe the [university supervisor's] wording was a little clearer, but it was very similar. But the fact that this was my professor and this was the first time not only watching me and giving me suggestions for the future by grading me, and it was the person I was going to see at school. It all made a difference.

Rebecca, near the end of the first semester of the early practicum, said:

The practicum class is great because there's a lot of things that I need to say. Hearing everybody else's experiences is also comforting because it's just a reminder that we're all going through the same thing. Sometimes somebody else will have a better way of explaining what I want to say. They might have experienced it also, so sometimes I have the questions answered that I didn't even know to ask.

Lara found role playing in class to be helpful. She said, at the end of the year:

In some ways the class helps, like the activity that I tried to do. When I had them tap the drum, it helped me realize that I have to be incredibly elementary, and I wasn't thinking that way. I had to really stop and take time, let each individual person concentrate on tapping the drum. So, before I actually did it in my session, I thought beating a drum was going to be so boring, they would tap the drum and it's over in 2 seconds. But it took 15 minutes to do, so I saw in real life that this activity is something that these people need. So I just take a lot of time with each person.

Suggested changes. Students had numerous suggestions for changes that might make the practicum experience more useful or positive. Rebecca felt that an outline of what to look for when making the first contact, as an observer, would be useful:

If we had an outline, like what kind of patients are in the group, how many are in the group, what are your general goals for the group, just some guidelines, because if they say, "Do you have any questions?" we don't even know what questions to ask.

Joshua, at the end of the first semester of the early practicum, suggested more role playing:

I'm the kind of person who learns from actually doing and watching. I think had that occurred earlier in the semester a little more, I would have known a little better what I was trying to observe and what skills I needed to use in my actual sessions.

Near the end of the second semester of the early practicum, Rebecca spoke of what she learned from others in class buy also of how she wished that people were able to describe their clients more vividly:

I don't have much experience with the low-functioning aspects, so it's definitely helping. But I just think that some other students could be a little more articulate so we'd know exactly what they're facing. I try to explain a person's mannerisms and all the things that they're doing, but sometimes I don't have a sense of how the lower-functioning patients act.

Students in the upper-level practicum were sometimes frustrated because they felt that the discussions in the practicum class were not relevant to the children with whom they worked, who were either lower-functioning or older than the children on whom they felt that the class discussion focused. Kyle said:

> It was hard because a lot of the times in practicum we talk about what we've been doing and I guess in that sense I didn't feel like I was getting much because a lot of what the other students were doing, there was no way that I could do it in my session.... I felt like everybody else was relating on a different level. The kids were on a different level.

Jenny felt that sharing resources and how to adapt them for various populations and levels would be useful. She said at the end of the first semester:

> That would be something for beginning students to do in classhow...to adapt a song like that can be difficult if you haven't done it before. Like, next week we're going to do this holiday, so everybody bring in a piece for this holiday for everybody in the class. Then it would be some solid talking about things. We need to do this sort of thing every week in order to build up a reasonable number of resources.... Activities, and maybe ideas for music, instruments, how to deal with an aide that's always jumping in the way. (We did talk about that.) Just more practical things.

Seeing the same or different clients. Some of the students worked with the same clients for both Semesters, while others changed groups. There seemed to be advantages and disadvantages to both. Kyle said, at the end of the year: "I think it was good to stay with the same kids. I think that 10 or 12 weeks is just too short a time to move from one to the next group, for the kids and for the students."

Presenting the other view, Jenny said:

> This semester I'm working with a different group of students, and I think that's been extremely beneficial to me because I got a chance to experience a different level of functioning, not only cognitively but physically.... It's given me the experience of dealing with other classroom settings, different teachers, different staff, different students and ages, and that's been extremely important.

Several suggestions were also made of ways to increase students' experiences with varying clients. Melanie suggested, at the end of the second semester:

> I had this idea of perhaps having each person go to one of our other places and see what ideas they use, see what works. And that way we can give them feedback, as well. I could give her feedback and also get ideas for my session.

Jenny shared an addition that was made by her on-site supervisor: "As part of my experience, I'm watching another group, at a totally different level, and that's helpful in that I'm seeing another angle at which to do things or ways to adapt the same activities."

Discussion

My understanding, as interviewer and researcher, of students' experiences of music therapy practica has grown as a result of this study. As stated earlier, there are limitations in the extent to which this occurred because I am not a student. But I hope that my efforts were successful in entering into their world as they spoke with me about these experiences, and that I have adequately conveyed their experiences in this writing.

Of course, there are differences in how music therapy clinical experience is approached in various universities, and those differences may make some of the experiences relayed by these students less useful than others. But readers are urged to look for the commonalities and to apply them to their situations. For instance, some student concerns may seem specific to undergraduate students but may be applicable to graduate students in a different form. A graduate student might not express fears about a new situation as overtly as did the undergraduates, but reading this study might sensitize someone who teaches graduate students to students' wishes to know more about a facility before they begin their work and enable them to provide more information, even though the urgency of the need or the way that it is expressed may differ. As another example, at a different educational institution all students may not receive on-site supervision by a music therapist, but the educator in this situation could apply these students' feedback about the types of supervision that they appreciate to supervision by a nonmusic therapist in order to improve the level of supervision received. Similarly, a student reading this study might realize that his or her desire for ideas of strategies that are appropriate for use with adults is similar to the wish expressed by students in this study to learn activities appropriate for adolescents as well as younger children. Knowing that these needs are felt by other students, although in a different situation, may encourage the student reading the study to be assertive about asking for these ideas. There are numerous other potential applications, even when situations are not identical.

My understanding, as a faculty member, of students' experiences has also increased, and this will influence my approach to certain aspects of the students' clinical experience. One of those changes has to do with taking care to be sure that I do not make assumptions about what students are thinking or feeling. One of the things that struck me as I did these interviews was that there were times in which I simply did not think as the students did. Beyond that, I couldn't imagine why they thought the way that they did. One of these was in a situation in which Patricia, from the upper-level practicum, said that she did not feel that she had gotten enough assistance on what to do with the adolescents in her music therapy group from class discussions. I share this below, with my comments (which expressed far more of my own feelings than did my normal comments):

> *BW:* I'm curious. Why didn't you go in and say, "I need more help on activities for my kids, and they're older"?
> *Patricia:* Well, that was known, it's not something that wasn't known. (laughter). I didn't go in and say, OK, give me some activities, but it was known that I worked with older kids.
> *BW:* I don't mean to be provocative about this, but if people were bringing in questions that they had that they needed help with and that was what you needed help with, did it not feel like you could do that, or did you not feel that people would know the answers?

Patricia: I guess I didn't feel that I could be helped by it. A couple of times I think that I probably said something, but the answer didn't seem to fit me so I just....

BW: So you sort of gave up on it.

Patricia: Yeah.

This interaction was instructive and humbling. While I generally assume that I understand how students think, I obviously did not understand what led this student to not seek out assistance for the problem that she was having. Of course, the fact that this particular student handled this issue in this way does not mean that all students would do so, but it did illustrate for me the chasm that can exist between student and faculty perceptions. The realization that this separation can exist, as mentioned earlier in this paper, provided the initial motivation for this study.

The students' concerns included several of those that McClain (1993) had found in her survey of music therapy students, as summarized earlier in this paper. Both studies found that students desired more orientation prior to beginning the practicum. While McClain found that one of students' greatest concerns was about their clinical skills, students in this study were similarly found to be concerned about meeting the clients' needs and seeing changes in their clients. Other areas of concern were not as similar.

The increased understanding of students' experiences and concerns during their music therapy practica can be helpful in improving music therapy education and supervision. Students' greatest concerns are discussed below.

Students often want more guidance as to what to do in sessions. As a faculty member, I am aware of this, but the extent to which the students spoke of it as a concern reminded me of their sense that they need more help in knowing what to do. I often emphasize to students that they have access to many methods and materials but need to focus on learning to use them appropriately for the clients with whom they are working. Perhaps in my efforts to help them learn how to use their methods appropriately, I lose track of how important they feel that it is to know what to do. I am not willing to abandon my way of looking at this due to their input, but must take that feedback seriously as I continually work to meet students' needs in my teaching.

Another area about which students spoke that made me think about our different perceptions was in their wish for more guidelines or information before they begin their clinical work. This occurred particularly with the students in the early practicum, when, of course, they had less music therapy experience. I have felt that I give a reasonable amount of information and structure to these early clinical experiences, considering that students are going to a number of different facilities with different supervisors, and that each facility and supervisor is somewhat different and thus has its own set of thing to know. However, this student feedback has prompted me to reconsider the amount of information that I should provide and the need for guidelines for beginning students. It is clear that what I think is sufficient information does not feel adequate to a new student—thus, I need to rethink what I provide.

The students' perceptions of their supervisors and the supervisory experience were enlightening. It is not a surprise, but was good to be reminded, that they want a supervisor who supports them but also gives them feedback that helps them move forward in their clinical work. Students felt good when their supervisors respected them. Another point was their discomfort with being graded by the faculty supervisor, particularly when that person only observed them a few times.

Students' concerns about the impact of grading was also a surprise. This is another area in which I know that students perceive things differently than I do as a faculty member, but I tend to ignore these differences. I see grades as an indication of the quality of work but encourage students not to dwell on them. Their focus on grading and its importance reminds me that, whether or not I agree with their perceptions, grades are very important to students.

The importance that they placed on seeing improvements in their clients was heartening. The number of students who spoke of it (not all of whom were quoted in this article) and the variety of improvements that they described were more than I would have expected. This is a positive sign of the motivation of these future music therapists.

The final point is that the students had a wide range of perceptions. Not all of them focused on the same areas and they did not all agree on those on which they focused. This points to the need for flexibility in approaching clinical training, and for working with individual student needs just as we work with the needs of individual clients. The variety of students' needs and perceptions must be honored.

This research has allowed me to learn about my students' experiences in a manner that would not normally be available to me as a faculty member. This has been a real privilege. Although I know that I will never be able to totally understand things from a student's viewpoint, nor will I probably ever hear that viewpoint completely candidly, I believe that I approached this while doing this study. I hope that my sharing of it will help others to understand these experiences and use this increased understanding to improve them.

REFERENCES

Aigen, K. (1995). Principles of qualitative research. In B. I. Wheeler (Ed.), *Music therapy research: Quantitative and qualitative perspectives* (pp. 283–311). Gilsum, NH: Barcelona.

American Music Therapy Association (2001). *National roster internship guidelines* (Rev. 2001). Silver Spring, MD: Author.

Dileo, C. (2201). Ethical issues in supervision. In M. Forinash (Ed.), *Music therapy supervision* (pp. 19–38). Gilsum, NH: Barcelona.

Estrella, K. (2001). Multicultural approaches to music therapy supervision. In M. Forinash (Ed.), *Music therapy supervision* (pp. 39–66). Gilsum, NH: Barcelona.

Farnan, L. A. (2001). Competency-based approach to intern supervision. In M. Forinash (Ed.), *Music therapy supervision* (pp. 117–134). Gilsum, NH: Barcelona.

Feiner, S. (2001). A journey through internship supervision: Roles, dynamics, and phases of the supervisory relationship. In M. Forinash (Ed.), *Music therapy supervision* (pp. 99–115). Gilsum: NH, Barcelona.

Forinash, M. (2001). *Music therapy supervision.* Gilsum, NH: Barcelona.

Grant, R. E. & McCarty, B. (1990). Emotional stages in the music therapy internship. *Journal of Music Therapy, 27,* 102–118.

Hanser, S. B. (2001). A system analysis approach to music therapy practica. In M. Forinash (Ed.), *Music therapy supervision* (pp. 87–97). Gilsum, NH: Barcelona.

Madsen, C. K. & Kaiser, K. A. (1999). Pre-internship fears of music therapists. *Journal of Music Therapy, 36*, 17–25.

McClain, F. J. (1993). Student evaluations of practicum training in music therapy. *Dissertation Abstracts International, 54*(07), 2502A. (University Microfilms No. DA93332828)

McClain, F. J. (2001). Music therapy supervision: A review of the literature. In M. Forinash (Ed.), *Music therapy supervision* (pp. 9–17). Gilsum, NH: Barcelona.

Shulman-Fagen, T. (2001). The creative arts in group supervision. In M. Forinash (Ed.), *Music therapy supervision* (pp. 149–160). Gilsum, NH: Barcelona.

Spradley, J. P. (1979). *The ethnographic interview*. New York: Holt, Rinehart and Winston.

Stephens, G. (1984). Group supervision in music therapy. *Music Therapy, 4*, 29–38.

Stephens, G. L. (1987). The experiential music therapy group as a method of training and supervision. In C. D. Maranto & K. E. Bruscia (Eds.), *Perspectives on music therapy education and training* (pp. 169–176). Philadelphia, PA: Temple University, Esther Boyer College of Music.

Stige, B. (2001). The fostering of not-knowing barefoot supervisors. In M. Forinash (Ed.), *Music therapy supervision* (pp. 69–86). Gilsum, NH: Barcelona.

Thomas, C. B. (2001). Student-centered internship supervision. In M. Forinash (Ed.), *Music therapy* supervision (pp. 135–148). Gilsum, NH: Barcelona.

STUDY AND DISCUSSION QUESTIONS

1. What is a primary factor in the presentation of any research study?

2. According to Schleuter, doing qualitative research requires attention to what two elements?

3. Why did Schlueter use some element of quantification in her study?

4. How did Schleuter reduce concerns about subjectivity when assigning comments to curricular categories?

5. Why did Schleuter refer back to tapes for vocal nuance?

6. Why was Schleuter an unobtrusive part of her study?

7. Besides accounting for unanticipated observations, Schleuter feels the qualitative researcher must also do what to reduce subjectivity?

8. What advantage do clear questions offer a qualitative study according to Schleuter?

9. What is a phenomenological type of qualitative research?

10. What is the main concern of the qualitative study by Wheeler?

11. To what degree does the research literature address the concerns of practicum students in music therapy?

12. According to McClain (1993), about what are student therapists most concerned?

13. How many questions did Wheeler present at the beginning of her study, and were the answers presented in this order in the Results? Why or why not?

14. How many student participants were there in Wheeler's study?

15. How were the data gathered and transcribed in Wheeler's study?

16. How did Wheeler manage or transform the data so as to make sense of them?

17. By what process did Wheeler triangulate the data?

18. How did Wheeler minimize her role as investigator when she was also supervisor?

19. Why did Wheeler's original categories of investigation not work in the final analysis?

20. How would you summarize the findings regarding students' fear of new experiences?

SUGGESTED ACTIVITIES

1. Describe an activity in your own teaching situation where interviewing students might be helpful.

2. Qualitative research often appears easier to conduct than quantitative. Discuss the major problems of doing good qualitative research and why such research is not as easy to do as it may appear.

PART FOUR

Quantitative Research

CHAPTER 9

Principles of Quantitative Research

Modern-day scientific investigation has become the model for much of the research in music education and music therapy. Unfortunately, many people have become wary of scientific investigation especially in the medical field. The truth is that sloppy research can be found in any area of inquiry. The following of a strict protocol in all research is a basic assumption. Good research requires uncompromising principles.

THE SCIENTIFIC METHOD

The scientific method is known by all music students who have taken courses in the *hard* sciences. It is a method of investigation in which the suspected cause of a certain phenomenon is isolated and tested under highly controlled conditions. The purpose is to rule out all other causes except the one being tested. It often involves the comparison of an *experimental* group with a *control* group. The control group typically receives some type of placebo in place of the experimental *cause*, e.g., a sugar pill.

The field of medicine is familiar to most people as a place where scientific research is big business. Pharmaceutical companies spend millions of dollars on research developing new drugs and often end up with questionable results. It has become common for the news media to report that drugs once thought safe have been removed from sale because of problems discovered after the fact. These actions give the public a healthy skepticism about research in general.

Scientific research conducted in a laboratory setting is termed *pure* research (as opposed to *applied*). A scientist who studies the electrical makeup of the human heart may spend a lifetime investigating electrical pathways without producing any practical application of the findings. In such studies, the number of people being studied is typically quite small. The researcher is not concerned with having a large number of participants to observe because the control conditions of a laboratory are such that controlling for behavioral quirks is unnecessary.

There is not a lot of *pure* research conducted in music education. However, *The New Handbook of Research on Music Teaching and Learning* (Colwell & Richardson,

2002) contains three articles in Part VIII on "Neuroscience, Medicine, and Music." One of the general findings in this section states:

> There is fertile ground for research in the several theories of brain function and structure. These theories need to be tested, modified, and combined with research and new techniques of imaging the human brain. Students and scientists may use brain theories in their research by testing a theory in new situations or previously studied situations. (Flohr & Hodges, 2002, p. 1003)

The problem with doing such research is that most music educators are ignorant of the technology needed to run such experiments. However, collaborative efforts between musicians and scientists are becoming more common and can only lead to advances in both fields.

Some of the earliest experiments in pure research in music were done by Carl Seashore at The University of Iowa. Seashore was a psychologist with interests in music, especially in quantifying the vocal vibrato. Along with his students, he devised many instruments for the measurement of aural, visual, and kinesthetic perception. *The Seashore Measures of Musical Talent*, first published in 1919, was widely used for years as an important measure of musical aptitude. Carl Seashore was a pioneer in researching musical phenomena in the psychology of music (1938).

E. Thayer Gaston is recognized by music therapists as the pioneer researcher in their field (Johnson, 1981). Gaston encouraged and helped to develop principles of experimentation that became standard methods for investigating the effects of music on the human body. He believed that to understand music, people must first understand the nature of humankind from the viewpoints of the natural and behavioral sciences. Gaston edited a text (1968) on music therapy and established the first U.S. graduate degree program in music therapy at the University of Kansas (Lawrence). Like Seashore, Gaston was an early leader in studying the relationship of music and human response.

Much scientific inquiry exists as applied research in real-world settings. This involves application of a *treatment* to a population in a controlled environment. A study to lower cholesterol could begin as laboratory research for the development of a new drug. The applied phase might involve two groups of participants: one that receives the medication being tested and another receiving a placebo. Periodic checks of subjects' (people in the study) cholesterol levels would be made, quantified, and eventually analyzed using tests for significant differences between group mean scores. Unlike pure research, applied studies typically have large numbers of participants. It is important to establish the effectiveness of any new health-related product with a large enough sample to ensure a true representation of the population.

There is a growing interest among researchers in performing-arts medicine. "Unique to performing arts medicine is that a number of studies represent the joint work of scientifically and musically trained researchers" (Brandfonbrener & Lederman, 2002). Most of the work conducted thus far is related to the problems of instrumental players. Topics include health problems, the mechanics of performing, performance anxiety, abnormal muscular contraction, interactions of risk factors, and the relationship of stress and physical injury. This is a young field of applied research that shows much promise in helping musicians cope with medically related problems. Chapter 53 in *The New Handbook of Research on Music Teaching and Learning* (see Appendix B) should be read by anyone interested in this field of research.

It is the applied model of scientific investigation that is used most by music researchers in doing experimental research; strictly theoretical research is rare. The emphasis for researchers in music education and therapy is on behavioral change.

NONEXPERIMENTAL RESEARCH

Quantitative research that does not seek to establish cause-and-effect relationships falls into the nonexperimental genre. This type of research seeks to describe behaviors as they exist and also is used to establish relationships between or among factors. Because it is not experimental, it does not subscribe to the scientific method as far as controlling for the effects of extraneous influences on behaviors. The most common forms of nonexperimental research are *descriptive* and *correlation*.

Descriptive Research

Descriptive research is one of the major subclasses of quantitative research. As noted in Chapter 1, it describes "what is" rather than "what could be" under certain circumstances, i.e., cause and effect. Descriptive research presents information on one group or compares factors between or among groups and determines trends, needs, or changes. It is a "snapshot" of what is happening at the time the data are collected.

Data for descriptive study/quantitative research are numbers assigned to represent amounts or perceived degrees of things such as behaviors, objects, or events. Asmus and Radocy (2006) state: "Today, music educators use quantitative methods for such tasks as grading, student evaluation, contest and festival ratings, auditioning students for ensembles, and assigning chairs in an ensemble" (p. 96).

descriptive — what is being taught in G.M.

Survey Research

A survey is one of the most basic forms of descriptive research. It seeks to find out information from a particular group of persons. Cause-and-effect interpretation is not warranted. For example, surveys have shown that students who participate in music score higher on standardized tests of academic achievement (SAT, ACT, etc.). From such surveys it cannot be inferred that participation in music causes a person to score higher. To make such an inference would require an experimental investigation in which cause and effect are part of the research design. Survey research, even when groups are compared, tells us how things are but not "why" or what caused them to be.

Survey research is a form of quantitative investigation in which a numeric description of trends, beliefs, or opinions represents the responses of a certain group of people called the *population* (represented by the symbol N). For example, a researcher might want to know what styles of music sixth graders respond to best. Because it is impossible to survey all sixth-grade students, researchers choose a group, or *sample* (represented by the symbol n), of people from the population that would as closely as possible have

what % of curr. has singing

the same characteristics of the larger population. This *sampling* process involves choosing participants at random from the total group, thus ensuring a *representative* sample. If the researcher wants to generalize results of a survey to a population, it is important that the sample be chosen at random. Otherwise, the results may apply only to the sample itself.

The population is rarely the whole world. Rather, it might be all music education students in small colleges from the midwest region. Davis (1990) surveyed the career choices of high school honor band students in Nebraska. Out of a large population ($N = 296$) of possible participants, 65% of the population returned the survey and served as the sample ($n = 191$). As far as returns on surveys, this is considered a good rate of return. Anything over a 50% return rate is acceptable; smaller return rates can be acceptable with caution.

Surveys occur in basically four formats: (1) self-administered questionnaires, (2) interviews, (3) structured record reviews, and (4) structured observations. These are most often paper-and-pencil tasks, but Internet surveys are becoming more common. Figure 9.1 shows a portion of a paper-and-pencil task used by Phillips (2003) for soliciting answers from middle school students regarding their attitudes toward music.

SECTION ONE

Instructions: In this survey, you will be asked to describe how you feel about music. You may respond to each of the following statements in four ways: "Strongly Agree," "Agree," "Disagree," or "Strongly Disagree." Please mark your answer sheet with the answer that best fits the way you feel about the statement. Remember, all students think differently. There are no right or wrong answers.

   A. Strongly Agree
   B. Agree
   C. Disagree
   D. Strongly Disagree

1. I like to sing songs at home or at my friend's house.
2. I sing when I am happy.
3. I like learning about different kinds of music.
4. I like to play an instrument at home or at my friend's house.
5. I hate listening to music at school.
6. I watch musical shows on television.
7. I enjoy learning how music is put together, like the names of notes on the staff and how many beats in a measures.
8. Sometimes I like to make up my own songs and sing them for people. (p. 120)

Figure 9.1 Sample survey.

When putting together a survey it is important that the content be valid, rately represent what the researcher is investigating. This is accomplished l other persons in the field (e.g., fellow music teachers) to evaluate and provide feedback on the survey statements. Items that are unclear or ambiguous are identified, and eliminated or improved. A pilot study, or "dry run," is another means by which researchers check for validity and ease of understanding. The investigator should be expected to provide evidence as to how the validity was established for the survey instrument.

Administering a survey requires all participants to have equal understanding. For example, when given to a group of children, it is better that directions be read aloud by the investigator to ensure that everybody understands how they are to respond. In some cases, it is best for the researcher to read aloud each of the statements to ensure against children who read poorly or slowly. Caution must be taken that distractions do not impinge on the environment and that students are not sleepy, hungry, and so forth. In the written report the researcher should give the conditions under which the survey was given and how negative influences were handled. Where surveys are mailed, explicit directions are required to ensure uniform participation. The shorter the survey, the better chance that those contacted will complete and return it. It is almost impossible to have a 100% rate of return because some people immediately trash surveys upon receipt.

Other Forms of Descriptive Research

While the survey is the most common form of descriptive research, other forms exist: assessment, opinion polls, and evaluation research. Local, state, and national testing programs are all examples of assessment. The public is quite familiar with opinion polls, especially in the field of politics. Evaluation research is directed at determining whether or not a particular program, for example, "No Child Left Behind," has achieved its goals. These descriptive measures depict factors as they exist and do not attempt to manipulate them.

Historical, qualitative, and descriptive research genres are similar, in that they are all concerned with "what is" or "what was," and all rely on the narrative to "tell the story." However, descriptive research of the quantitative genre is based on numerical data, and this is what separates it from historical and qualitative research.

Analysis of Descriptive Data

The analysis of data from a survey can be as simple as the reporting of percentages, or it may involve the comparison of groups within the sample (e.g., males vs. females, accurate singers vs. inaccurate singers), in which case statistical tests are employed to determine significant differences (discussed in Chapter 10). Phillips (2003) reported that differences in attitudes toward music among middle school students could be attributed to home musical background (40%) and self-concept in music (45%), a reporting of simple percentages. However, Phillips went on to make group comparisons using statistical analyses and found:

> Results showed a slight decrease in music attitudes by grade level for all middle school students, and a significant decrease ($p < .05$) for low SES students. Girls' music attitudes, home musical environments and self-concepts in music were found to be significantly higher ($p < .05$) than boys' for all grades and SES levels. High-SES students

reported significantly richer ($p < .05$) home musical environments than low-SES students. Self-concept in music significantly decreased ($p < .05$) as grade level increased for all middle school students. (p. iii).

Significance and Probability

In research parlance the term *significance* has particular importance. When a research study reports a *significant difference* between two variables, it means an exacting statistical difference exists in favor of one of the two groups or variables. Also given is the *p*, or probability, level at which this statistical result occurs. When $p < .05$ is indicated, it is *probable* that the significant result could be expected 95% of the time and that a 5% chance exists that the significant result could have happened by chance. The .05 level of probability is the one most commonly used in behavioral research. Sometimes a stricter level of probability is reported, e.g., $p < .01$ or $p < .001$. In such a case, the probability of a significant finding happening by chance is 1 in a 100 or 1 in a 1000, respectively. Higher probability levels often appear in medical research, where the results are related to life and death issues. A drug that may fail 5% of the time is not desirable.

Those who do research know that research never *proves* anything. There are just too many uncontrolled variables in human behavior that may result in a finding's occurring by chance. Therefore, a probability of .05 provides some leeway in determining the statistical significance of a finding. If the result is 95% sure, it is likely true. However, we can never assume that it is without some measure of doubt, in this case 5%. This is why a researcher does not state that a finding *proves* something. "It suggests," "seems to show," "may indicate," and so forth are "softer" ways of saying "It appears that the instruction was successful in bringing about the desired results."

Correlation Research

Another common form of nonexperimental research is that of *correlation*, where relationships are established among factors or conditions. It does not imply cause and effect. There are three types of correlation research: simple, predictive, and modeling.

Simple Correlation

The *simple* form of correlation study employs an analysis that yields a single number known as the *correlation coefficient*. This number expresses the extent to which two factors are related. Coefficients range from $+1.0$ (a perfect positive correlation) to -1.0 (perfect negative correlation). A coefficient of 0.0 indicates no correlation at all. A positive correlation of .92 indicates a high level of correlation between factors; i.e., they are highly related. A correlation of $-.92$ indicates a high negative correlation; i.e., the factors run in opposite directions (as one score goes up, the other goes down, or vice versa).

According to Locke, Silverman, and Spirduso (2004), one of the powerful benefits of correlation research is that

> it allows the examinations of relationships among variables measured in different units (e.g., pounds and inches...). What matters in correlational research is not the actual units of measure but how the relative sizes of scores in different distributions relate to each other. (p. 138).

The authors state that simple correlation studies are used to answer such questions as "To what extent does educational level relate to the rate of unemployment for men and women?" (p. 137). Also, the results of simple correlation often accompany more sophisticated research analyses when the researcher wants to provide greater in-depth understanding of the descriptive data in the study.

Predictive Correlation

Predictive correlation is used when a researcher wants to know if a variable or set of variables can be used to predict another variable or set of variables. A common form of this research is found in studies that look at factors involving high school students' academic and personal success and their predicted achievement at the college or university level. Such variables as grade-point average, attendance, scores on the SAT or ACT, and school activities all have been linked to college success and have been used for predicting academic success.

Davis (1990) examined seven factors that might influence talented high school band students to select or reject careers in music teaching. He sought to determine if any of the factors (gender, personality, work values, socioeconomic status, influence of others, academic achievement, and music-related attributes) could be used to predict a teaching career in music. An investigator-designed survey and two standardized tests were completed by 191 high school honor band students ($N = 296$) from Nebraska. The analyses of the data were extensive and involved a variety of statistical measures. However, in the final analysis, Davis submitted the data to a stepwise discriminant function analysis, also known as a multiple-regression technique. This process allows the researcher to step-in, in a predetermined order, each of the variables to determine their individual and combined power in predicting the outcome variable. In the case of Davis's study, the seven preceding factors were involved in this stepwise analysis. The results showed that the strongest predictors of career choice related to the category "influence of others."

> The results of the stepwise discriminant analysis indicate that the following five subfactors were determined in rank order as the best predictors of career choices for high school senior honor band members in Nebraska: Band Director, High School Counselor, Private Music Instructor, Economic Rewards, and a Relative as a Professional Musician. (Davis, 1990, p. 148)

Studies like this of Davis often become buried in the literature and are largely unknown to music teachers. The power a teacher has to influence a student's choice in becoming a music teacher seems to be great. This is a good example of the successful employment of survey research.

Modeling Correlation

Modeling correlation is the third type of correlation research. According to Locke et al. (2004, p. 139), modeling correlation

> maps in graphic form (often in the familiar format of boxes with connecting arrows) the relationships among a number of variables, displaying the degree to which any one of them can be used to predict one or more of the others. Interlocking questions such

as "What is the best set of factors predicting whether or not a student will graduate from college?" "When placed in a diagrammatic model, how are those contributing factors most logically arranged? And "How much predictive power is exerted by the various lines of influence drawn from the factors?" illustrate the wonderfully complex sort of problem that can be addressed through the correlational procedures used in modeling research.

VALIDITY AND RELIABILITY

The concepts of validity and reliability are important to any research study, but the terms are sometimes confused. *Validity* is the degree to which something *actually measures* or *does* what it is intended to do; e.g., a valid test is one that measures the concept or construct it is designed to measure, or a valid study is one where the results represent the variable being measured and not something else. On the other hand, *reliability* refers to the *consistency* of a measure over time, across participants, tests, or observers, or within a test or scale.

does what its supposed

Reliability

A reliable measure is one that uniformly produces the same results when given repeated times. It is important for a researcher to report the reliability of any measures (e.g., tests) in a study, especially author-designed, nonstandardized measures. A statistic known as the *reliability coefficient* is computed through various techniques (e.g., split-half reliability, test–retest reliability, parallel forms, KR-20, coefficient alpha) and reported as a number ranging from 0 (complete unreliability) to 1.0 (complete reliability). Interjudge reliability is important when judges are involved in assigning scores to performances. A reliability coefficient of .94 would indicate a rather high degree of agreement among the judges, but a coefficient of .35 would indicate a low agreement among the raters, which should not be trusted. Data from these judges would not be reliable because their agreement as to what constituted a good or poor performance was not consistent. In this case the researcher would need to find other judges and carefully prepare them for the task.

Validity

The concept of validity is perhaps one of the most important areas of research that a consumer must understand. Studies often appear in the literature with tremendous holes that, in effect, negate the results, because the investigations were carried out in such a way as to make them invalid. Slavin (1984) explains:

> There are two principal criteria that a research design must satisfy if it is to add to knowledge. These are internal and external validity. Internal validity refers to the degree to which a research design rules out explanations for a study's findings other than that the variables involved appear to be related because they are in fact related. If a study high in internal validity finds a certain result, it is likely that the result is a true finding rather than a result of some flaw in the design. Any possibility that the

findings might be due to defects in the research design reduces internal validity. External validity, or generalization, refers to the degree to which the findings of a study using a particular sample have meaning for other settings or samples, particularly settings or samples in which we have some practical interest. (p. 109)

Thus, internal validity refers to the *internal* structure of the study, while external validity moves the results of the study *externally*, or beyond the sample to a population.

Internal Validity

Campbell and Stanley (1963) report eight threats to the internal validity of a study.

1. *History.* Specific events occurring between the first and second testing may somehow affect the outcome, e.g., students traumatized by some terrorist event.
2. *Maturation.* The passage of time may affect the outcome of a study; e.g., students tend to sing more accurately as they grow older.
3. *Testing.* The taking of the pretest may affect or sensitize students to the posttest. Also, comparability of tests must be ensured and ceiling and floor effects monitored.
4. *Instrumentation.* Changes in the calibration of a measuring instrument or changes in the observers or scorers may produce changes in the measurement,
5. *Statistical regression.* Students who score extremely low or high on the pretest may naturally regress toward the mean on the posttest.
6. *Selection.* Students are selected for the study who do not represent the normal comparison group, e.g., inner city students compared to all students.
7. *Mortality.* Loss of participants from the study may imbalance groups and/or affect normalcy.
8. *Interactions.* The combined influence of one internal factor with another, which may be mistaken for the effect of the experimental variable, e.g., a selection–maturation interaction.

Many a researcher will not report how he or she controlled for internal validity in a study. It may be that no problems were encountered, or it may be that threats to internal validity were ignored. It is important for the consumer to "read between the lines" and decide if violations to internal validity exist. Flagrant violations void research results.

External Validity

Campbell and Stanley (1963) report four threats to the external validity of a study.

1. *Reactive or interaction effect of testing.* A pretest might increase or decrease the participants' sensitivity to the experimental variable and thus make the results for a pretested population unrepresentative of the population (pp. 5–6). Campbell and Stanley do not favor pretesting.
2. *Interaction effects of selection biases and the experimental variable.* A biased sample may interact in a way with the treatment that is different and unrepresentative of the population.

3. *Reactive effects of experimental arrangements.* Students' reactions to being studied may not be the same reactions in the population.
    a. *Hawthorne effect.* Students do better or work harder when they know they are in a study.
    b. *John Henry effect.* Students in the control group work harder than usual to win.
    c. *Experimenter.* The researcher interacts differently with the participants than another person implementing the treatment in the population.
    d. *Contamination.* Something in the participants' background is peculiar to that setting but not common to the settings in the population.
    e. *Teacher effects.* The participants' teacher affects their responses in a manner not typical of the population, e.g., pressure to look good or do well.
    f. *Artificiality.* The research environment (e.g., classroom) of the study is different than that of the general population.
    g. *Class effects.* The effects that participants have on one another in the research environment is atypical of that in the population.
4. *Multiple-treatment interference.* Differing treatments may interfere with each other when the effects of prior treatments are not erasable.

Two additional threats to the external validity of a study are given by Campbell and Stanley: sampling and randomization.

5. *Sampling.* When the sampling procedure results in an atypical sample, the results of a study cannot be generalized to a population.
6. *Randomization.* When participants cannot be randomly assigned to groups, the groups may be unequal in their respective abilities. This also makes it difficult to generalize to a population. However, research is commonly conducted using intact classrooms of participants. In these cases, whole classes are assigned at random as either treatment or control, and attention is given to finding whether the classes are equal or not in the area being studied. If not equal, statistical procedures can correct for this inequality.

The ability to generalize research findings to a larger population is at the heart of experimental research. Unfortunately, investigations using intact classrooms of participants make this a difficult outcome. At the center of generalizing to a population is randomization. Research that does not involve randomized participants is not useless when it can show the efforts taken to equalize both intact groups. Caution, however, must be taken when applying the results beyond the basic study.

EXPERIMENTAL RESEARCH

Whereas descriptive research describes *what is*, experimental research describes *what could be* under carefully controlled conditions. Cause-and-effect relationships are explored to determine the influence of the *independent variable* (e.g., instruction) on the *dependent variable* (e.g., test). Experimental research exists in two forms: (1) true, where it is possible to randomize participants to groups, and (2) quasi, where randomization is not possible and existing intact groups are studied (e.g., classrooms of participants).

Independent and Dependent Variables

Two types of variables are involved in an experimental study: independent and dependent. An independent variable that is manipulated, e.g., a form of instruction, is labeled the treatment or *active* variable. Two other types of independent variables also exist: *organismic*, e.g., height, age, and gender, and *attribute*, e.g., grade level, occupation, and strong or weak readers. Typically the treatment variable is the primary focus of an experimental study. Gleason (1995/1996), in an experimental study of beginning band instruction, used the band method *Standard of Excellence* by Bruce Pearson (1993) as the independent variable for the treatment group. The testing of such instructional methods is rare in music education.

The dependent variable is the outcome or measured variable. It usually involves some type of testing. The Gleason study involved three achievement measures, two performances measures, two attitudinal measures, and a measure of retention. Experimental studies often have more than one dependent measure.

It is important that researchers focus their study on something with which they are knowledgeable and that the focus be narrowed to a manageable problem. Novice researchers often choose broad topics that result in studies that lack integrity. The narrowing of a topic often takes much consultation with a colleague or mentor.

Organismic and attribute variables are often included in studies to determine if the effects of the treatment are different for males and females, primary and intermediate students, accurate and inaccurate singers, and so forth. These questions are typically secondary to the main question: Does the treatment create a significant difference between groups (treatment and control)?

Subjects

People who participate in an experimental study are known as *subjects*. This term is pervasive in the research literature. However, the term *participants* is preferred in qualitative research.

The choice of subjects is one of the major decisions made by a researcher. College students are often used in music research because of their ready availability. The choice of minors is problematic because of the need for parental/guardian permission. Most colleges and universities require that all participants be approved by a review board. Studies done in music education and music therapy rarely employ treatments that are invasive, such as those found in medical areas, and receive rather easy approval. Researchers in the schools cannot be too careful in having their research approved by a governing board, a school administration, and parental authorities. A clear paper trail is a must, and some indication of this process should be mentioned in any research report making use of human participants.

Extreme caution must be taken when using underage students in any research study. The complete nature of the research must be revealed to the parents or guardians of all subjects, and written permission must be granted by them for the students to participate. Typically, parents must be given the option to withdraw the students at anytime from the investigation. As mentioned previously, every school of higher learning has an Institutional Review Board (IRB) that oversees all research using human subjects. A review document explaining the research project must be filed with them and permission received before the study can begin. Research that does not involve any type of invasive measures can expect to be approved rather easily. Research involving invasive measures (e.g., medical tests) are more intensively scrutinized for possible harm to the subjects. This process should be reported in any journal article, but it often is omitted due to space limitations.

When choosing subjects, a researcher must be careful that the pool of prospects is representative of the greater population. One of the purposes of experimental research is to externalize the results beyond the sample. If the sample is not a clear reflection of the population, a serious error has occurred. For example, if the study includes a high percentage of subjects who are ethnically different than the population at large, generalization is compromised. Results of studies in which subjects represent a balance of SES levels are more easily generalized than those in which lower- or upper-SES levels dominate. Any published research study should include information as to the makeup of the subject sample.

It is not always easy to find subjects for a school study. Parents who are suspicious of research will not give permission for their children to participate. Also, it is almost impossible to do a true experimental investigation in the schools. Most classrooms exist as intact groups, and participants cannot be reassigned. This is known as *convenience* sampling.

The number of subjects in any study should be reported. The total population from which a sample is drawn is represented by the capital letter N, which is italicized because it is a statistic. The sample size of each group is indicated by the lowercase letter n, again italicized. Investigators use a power analysis to determine the appropriate sample size for groups, a number that can be found in a statistical table. In general, the results from any study having fewer than 40 total subjects must be interpreted with caution.

Sometimes a researcher will encounter a group of subjects who are uncooperative and even hostile. At that point any results from such a study are compromised. If the researcher continues with the investigation, some indication in the report must address the compromised nature of the sample. Such research is hardly worth pursuing.

A person cannot sign away her or his rights via a permission slip. Unethical researchers who place subjects in harm's way are liable for damages and can be prosecuted regardless of what was signed and by whom.

Research Design

Two frequently used experimental research designs are the *true-experimental* design and the *non-equivalent* (quasi) control-group design. Both designs are the same except for one factor, randomization. Randomization of subjects is possible in the true design, whereas it is not in the quasi design. These designs both involve at least two groups (treatment and control), pre- and posttests, some type of active variable for the treatment group, and some other activity for the control. (In rare cases the control group does nothing.)

R Random Sample
O Pretest
Principles of Quantitative Research 165
X which group recieved treatment
O posttest *dependent variable*

True-Experimental Design

The *True-Experimental Design* controls for all sources of internal and most sources of external validity. The diagram for what Campbell and Stanley (1963) call a *Pretest-Posttest Control-Group Design* is as follows:

Group A	R	O	X	O
Group B	R	O		O

In this design the letter *R* stand for random assignment of participants. The letter *O* stands for the observations (dependent variable), pre and post, and *X* is the treatment or independent variable.

Two other designs exist in the true experimental research category: the *Posttest-Only Control Group Design*, and the *Solomon Four-Group Design*. Campbell and Stanley actually prefer the Posttest-Only Design to the earlier Pretest-Posttest Design because of pretest contamination that might occur if a participant learns something from taking the pretest that would help them do better on the posttest. However, when the treatment period is sufficiently long, it is doubtful that a carryover effect is lasting. The diagram of the *Posttest-Only Design* is as follows:

Can't randomly assign

Group A	R	X	O
Group B	R		O

The *Solomon Four-Group Design* involves the random assignment of participants to four groups. Campbell and Stanley recommend this design as a way of overcoming pretest carryover to the posttest. Note that pretests and treatments are varied among the four groups, and all four groups receive the posttest. Both internal and external validity are strong for the *Solomon Four-Group Design*.

Group A	R	O	X	O
Group B	R	O		O
Group C	R		X	O
Group D	R			O

Quasi-Experimental or Non-Equivalent Control-Group Design

The *Quasi-Experimental Design* is commonly used in educational research because of the availability of intact groups. It is weak in external validity because of the lack of randomization. Externalization of results must be handled with caution. Campbell and Stanley (1963) call this the *Non-equivalent Control-Group Design* and diagram it as follows:

Group A	O	X	O
Group B	O		O

Another quasi-experimental design is labeled the *Time Series*. In this design the researcher measures a single group a number of times before and following a treatment:

Group A	O	O	O	X	O	O	O

Campbell and Stanley note that this design is used more in the *hard* sciences, in which replication is prevalent. Because the design lacks a control group, use in the behavioral sciences is questionable without extensive replication.

Pre-experimental Design

Campbell and Stanley present a number of other designs, three of which are known as pre-experimental. A diagram of the *One-Shot Case Study* is as follows:

X   O

This is a weak design because no control group is present. Campbell and Stanley state: "Such studies have such a total absence of control as to be of almost no scientific value" (p. 6).

The second design in this pre-experimental category is the *One-Group Pretest–Posttest Design*. It is diagramed the same as the One-Shot Case Study but involves an "O" prior to the treatment "X," which represents the pretest. While this design is found in much educational research, it also is weak in both internal and external validity:

O   X   O

A third pre-experimental design is the *Static Group Comparison Design*. It is diagramed as follows:

Group A   X   O
            _____

Group B   O

This is a design in which a group which has experienced X is compared with one which has not, for the purpose of establishing the effect of X. Instances of this kind of research include, for example, the comparison of school systems which require the bachelor's degree of teachers (the X) versus those which do not; the comparison of students in classes given speed-reading training versus those not given it; the comparison of those who heard a certain TV program with those who id not, etc. (Campbell & Stanley, 1963, p. 12).

This design also is weak in external validity but somewhat stronger on internal validity than the other two designs in the pre-experimental category.

Reversal Design

Reversal designs are commonly used in applied behavioral analysis. A target behavior is established over time and is referred to as the baseline. Once the baseline is established, a treatment is administered and results observed. Observations then continue over time once the treatment has been removed. The *A-B-A Single Subject Design* involves multiple observations of one person.

Baseline A   Treatment B   Baseline A
                 X   X   X
O   O   O   O   O   O   O   O   O

In this design the independent variable has a positive effect if the behavior during the reversal period changes to almost the same level as observed during the first baseline period. One problem that may arise, however, is the irreversibility of the treatment effect once established. It also may be unethical to reverse a positive behavior once it is established. Many variations of the reversal design exist in the literature, including those with multiple treatments and/or multiple baselines.

Factorial Design

A final category of research design found commonly in music education and therapy studies is the *Factorial Design*. The word *factor* in this case refers to the independent variable. In a factorial design, at least two factors are involved, one of which must be an active treatment variable. The two factors can both be active, but typically the design involves one active variable and one stable variable, i.e., attribute or organismic. For example if a researcher wanted to determine if the Orff method of teaching sight-singing was superior to his or her own traditional method, the treatment variable would be the method of sight-singing used at two levels (Orff and traditional). However, if the researcher wanted to know if males or females responded better than the other, the organismic variable of "gender" would be added at two levels (male and female). This results in a *2 × 2 Factorial Design*, where each of the numbers stands for a variable (treatment and gender) at two levels each (Orff and traditional; male and female). If the researcher wants to compare Orff to Kodály and a traditional method of sight-singing, it would be a *3 × 2 Factorial Design* (Orff, Kodály, and traditional; male and female). But if the researcher does not care about gender and is more concerned with determining differences among grade levels three, four, and five, it would be a *3 × 3 Factorial Design* (two factors: sight-singing method and grade level, at three levels each: Orff, Kodály, traditional, and grades three, four, and five.). However, the researcher might want to include treatment, gender, and grade level, resulting in a three-factor design: *3 × 2 × 3*, where the first number (3) represents the three levels of sight-singing method, the second number (2) stands for two levels of gender, and the final number (3) stands for the three grade levels. Numerous variations of the Two-factor and Three-factor designs exist.

The benefit of factorial design is that it can be used to answer more than one research question in the same analysis. In the preceding 2 × 2 example, three research questions can be asked: (1) Is the Orff method superior to the traditional method? (2) Do males or females sight-sing better? and (3) Is there an interaction between the two independent variables; i.e., does a combination of the two independent variables account for significant differences? In this design the first two questions are labeled *main effects*, and the third question is labeled a *first-order interaction* or just *interaction*.

Whereas a two-factor design answers three questions, a three-factor design answers seven research questions: three main effects (one for each of the independent variables), three first-order interactions (A × B, A × C, B × C), and one second-order interaction (A × B × C). Three-factor designs become complicated to interpret; therefore, designs beyond three factors are rarely employed.

A simple picture of a two-factor (2 × 2) design appears in Figure 9.2. Notice the four boxes, or *cells*, in which the scores from a sight-singing test would be placed. In a classic true-experimental design with only one independent variable, only two groups of data would be compared for mean differences. In a factorial design the data

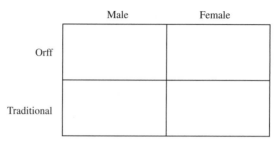

Figure 9.2 Two-way (2 × 2) factorial design (4 cells).

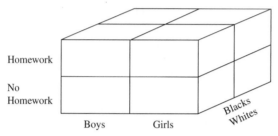

Figure 9.3 Three-way (2 × 2 × 2) factorial design (8 cells)

are split into four subgroups: (1) Orff and male, (2) Orff and female, (3) traditional and male, and (4) traditional and female. The first research question analyzes the difference between the top row (Orff) and the bottom row (traditional). The second research question analyzes the difference between the column on the left (male) and the column on the right (female). This question is important because it may be that one of the genders reads music better regardless of the method used. The final question analyzes differences between pairs of individual boxes to determine any significant interaction effect. For example, if a main effect were found in favor of the Orff approach, and then an interaction between Orff and female participants was reported, it may be that only the female scores were causing Orff to appear superior to the traditional approach. This observation would be missed if this study had not included gender as a factor. Factorial designs are more complicated, but they often help the researcher move beyond the surface of an investigation. When differences are suspected between genders or among grade levels, SES groups, and so forth, factorial analysis is warranted.

Figure 9.3 presents a picture of a three-way factorial design (2 × 2 × 2) with three factors at two levels each: treatment (homework, no homework); gender (boys, girls); race (blacks, whites). The shape is now three-dimensional and there are eight cells of data. As noted previously, this design generates three main effects and four interactions.

Understanding research design permits the reader of research to comprehend the framework of a study and how it is conceived. It also gives the reader an understanding of how internal validity may jeopardize the design, how the treatment was implemented, and how the results were reported.

Table 9.1 Summary of Experimental Research Designs

Pre-experimental Designs

One-shot case study
One-group pretest–posttest design
Static-group comparison design

True-Experimental Designs

Pretest–posttest control-group design
Posttest-only control-group design
Solomon four-group design

Quasi-Experimental Designs

Non-equivalent control-group design
Time series design

Reversal Designs

A-B-A single-subject design
Variations (multiple treatments and multiple baselines)

Factorial Designs

Two-factor design (2×2, 3×3, 2×3, etc.)
Three-factor design ($2 \times 2 \times 2$, $3 \times 3 \times 3$, $2 \times 2 \times 3$, etc.)

Table 9.1 is a summary of the basic designs common in behavioral research in music education and music therapy.

STUDY AND DISCUSSION QUESTIONS

1. What is the definition and purpose of the scientific method?
2. Why is the general public often skeptical about research results reported in the news?
3. Why is it difficult for music educators and therapists to do *pure* research?
4. Who were the pioneer researchers in music education and music therapy?
5. What is the difference between *pure* and *applied* research?
6. What is the difference between a sample and a population, and what is the statistical symbol for each?
7. What are two ways to check for the validity of a survey instrument?
8. How do you interpret the probability levels of $p < .05$ and $p < .01$?
9. What does it mean when a study reports a *statistical difference* between groups?
10. What is the difference between a general correlation study and a predictive correlation study?
11. What are the researcher's definitions of reliability and validity?
12. What is the difference between internal and external validity?

13. What are the Hawthorne and John Henry effects? What do they influence?

14. Sampling and randomization affect what type of validity? Why?

15. What is the difference between independent and dependent variables?

16. How do true experimental and quasi-experimental designs differ?

17. How do treatment, organismic, and attribute variables differ?

18. What is of utmost importance when a researcher chooses subjects for a study?

19. What are the three basic true-experimental designs?

20. Why are pre-experimental research designs considered weak designs?

21. What is the major advantage of a factorial design?

22. In a 2×3 factorial design, how many factors are there, and how many levels of each?

23. A 2×3 factorial design will include how many cells of data?

24. How many research questions can be addressed with a $2 \times 2 \times 2$ factorial design?

25. What are reversal designs, and what problems can result from using them?

SUGGESTED ACTIVITIES

1. Locate a report of research in your local newspaper. Can you identify the research design? Is it possible from the information given to determine if the sample was representative of a given population?

2. Consider each of the following brief descriptions of research, and assign each the label of one of the 12 experimental designs presented in this chapter.

   a. The study seeks to determine if there is a significant difference between treatment and control groups and males and females on a measure of singing accuracy.

   b. The study seeks to determine if there is a significant difference between treatment and control groups (intact classes) on directed vs. regular listening.

   c. The study seeks to determine if there is a significant difference between randomly assigned participants (treatment and control) on rhythm accuracy using numbers or "ta-tas" on both pre- and posttests.

   d. The study seeks to minimize pretest sensitization by comparing groups that are pretested to those that are not.

CHAPTER 10

Analysis of the Data

The word *statistics* often puts fear into the hearts of most novice readers of research. "We aren't statisticians—we're musicians, educators, therapists! What do we know about numbers?" Statistical terms like *mean, standard deviation, analysis of variance, F-test*, and so forth are possibly vague reminders of an assessment course taken in the past. Most music teachers and therapists are more interested in the aesthetic experience than significant *mean* differences between groups.

The problem is that you cannot understand quantitative research without knowing something about statistics. Results in studies use numbers as data. A little knowledge of statistical nomenclature can open to you a new world of discovery in quantitative investigation. Besides, music teachers and therapists are smart people. The study of statistics is something like the study of a foreign language—challenging but not impossible.

BASIC STATISTICAL CONCEPTS

Unlike qualitative research, in which the data are represented mainly by written narrative, data in quantitative research are represented by some form of numerical quantification.

Levels of Measurement

[handwritten annotation: nominal ordinal interval ratio, #, rankn]

There are four levels of numerical measurement: nominal, ordinal, interval, and ratio. The *nominal* scale uses numbers as labels or names for identifying certain categories or individuals, e.g., coding accurate singers as "1" and inaccurate singers as "2." The information can be increased if the frequency of each category is known, e.g., 10 accurate singers and 15 inaccurate singers. This is the lowest level of quantification—counted data, for which there is no hierarchy or order.

The second level of measurement, the *ordinal* scale, is slightly more sophisticated. In this form the data are "ranked"; i.e., things or persons are assigned to a relative position or hierarchy (1st, 2nd, 3rd, etc.). However, these ranks represent no absolute values, and the differences between ranks may not be equal, e.g., first, second, and third places in a race. Such rankings often occur at contests, when an ensemble ranked "first" might be only slightly better than the second-place group but much better than the third-place ensemble.

The *interval* scale produces "equal-interval" data and indicates the actual amount of a trait or characteristic being measured. In this third form of measurement, the differences in the amount between intervals are considered equal. In the study of vocal range, lowest and highest pitches sung are measured by assigning a number to every degree of the scale, by half-steps. Thus, the distances between numbers 16 and 20 and between 9 and 13 both represent a major third. Other examples of interval data are scores on music aptitude and achievement tests.

One limitation to the interval scale is the lack of a meaningful zero. For example, a score of zero on a test does not indicate that a student knows nothing about the subject. What the student knows might not have been on the test. Similarly, zero degrees in temperature indicates an arbitrary zero point because the temperature can fall below zero. Many aptitude and attitude tests use interval scales. "One person cannot be 'twice as smart' or 'twice as happy' as another, but scales can be constructed to have equal intervals between each score" (Slavin, 1984, p. 160). Interval scores can be added or subtracted and are commonly found in the behavioral sciences. This scale is far more sophisticated than nominal or ordinal scales.

The most sophisticated level of measurement and the most precise is the *ratio* scale. This also is a form of equal-interval data. However, this scale has a true zero; it is possible to indicate a complete lack of a property. For example, a person can have no money, and a person can have twice as much money as another. Music sounding at 100 decibels is said to be twice as loud as music at 50 decibels, and where there is a zero-decibel level no sound is audible.

The numbers of the ratio scale have the qualities of real numbers: They can be added, subtracted, multiplied, and divided and expressed in ratio relationships. The physical sciences use the ratio scale predominantly, but in practice the ratio and interval scales are considered as one in terms of procedures used.

Asmus and Radocy (2006) provide an excellent example of how data for a group can be expressed at different levels of measurement:

> [T]he members of a choir may be numbered for identity and ease in keeping records of robe assignments—a nominal level of measurement. This choir may be the first-place choir at a contest where the choirs were ranked—an ordinal level of measurement. The choir may also have received a 99 out of a possible 100 score at the contest—an interval level of measurement. Finally, the choir may also be said to have received a score twice as good as that for their previous performance —a ratio measurement. (p. 99)

Knowing these levels of measurement guides the researcher in determining the proper statistical test to use in the data analysis of a given study.

Elementary Statistics

Data are collected in quantitative studies as *raw scores*. However, data analysis is not focused on raw scores but, rather, on each group's combined or *average* score and the *dispersion* (average spread) of the scores. The average score (typically the *mean*) and the dispersion score (known as the *standard deviation*) are the two most important statistics for the beginning reader of research to understand.

In data analysis, a *statistic* is a number that represents or describes some characteristic of a measure, such as the *average* score or the *dispersion* score. The descriptive statistics most common in research articles are *measures of central tendency* (averages), *measures of variance* (dispersion or spread), *measures of relationships* (correlations), and *standard scores*, also known as *measures of relative position* (*z*- and *T*-scores).

Measures of Central Tendency

A measure of central tendency is a statistic that represents the *average* score of a group. The most common form is the **mean**, or arithmetic average. To determine the mean, the researcher adds all the scores and divides the total by the number of scores; e.g., $4 + 5 + 10 + 3 + 6 + 8 = 36 \div 6 =$ a mean of 6. The symbol for the mean is M or $\bar{X}$. (In reality there are two means, that of the population and that of the sample or group. In most instances, research studies report the sample or group mean.)

The **median** is the second most useful measure of central tendency. It represents the *middle score* in a *distribution* of scores, lowest to highest. Half the scores occur above the median score and half below. Since there is no middle score in the example given in the preceding paragraph, the median is the number halfway between the two middle scores, i.e., 5.5. The symbol for the median is either *Md* or *Mdn*.

The **mode** is the third measure of central tendency. It represents the most prevalent interval in a *distribution* of scores. The mode is useful when trying to give an accurate presentation of the average when the distribution is skewed. For example, it is reported that teachers' salaries in a school district are, on average, $45,000 a year. However, that figure is most likely inflated, because salaries of older teachers may be in the range from $50,000 to $65,000; when averaged in with lower salaries, they skew the average to be higher than it is in reality. In this case, the mode, or the salary figure that occurs most often in a distribution of all teachers' salaries, is most likely the better measure of central tendency. The symbol for mode is *Mo*.

Measures of Variability

In statistical terms, variability (or variance) represents the average amount of deviation (dispersion) of the raw scores from the *mean*. The greater the variance or dispersion of scores, the more difficult it becomes to find a significant difference between two means. In other words, when scores vary little from each other, the difference between means need not be great to be significant. However, when scores are spread out and the dispersion is great, it takes a greater difference between mean scores to find a significant difference. Therefore, researchers hope for as small a measure of variability as possible. The three most frequently used measures of variance (dispersion) found in research articles are *range*, *quartile deviation*, and *standard deviation*.

Range is the simplest and least accurate measure of variability. It is the difference between the highest and lowest scores in a distribution. For example, if a student has a vocal range reported as 15(d) to 42(f^2), the vocal range is 42 minus 15, or 27 half-steps (two octaves and a minor third). This is a useful statistic when charting students' vocal or instrumental ranges.

Quartile deviation, or semi-interquartile range, is a procedure in which the first 25% of the distribution of scores (lowest to highest) are assigned to the bottom, or first, quartile, the next 25% to the second quartile, the next 25% to the third quartile, and the top 25% to the fourth quartile (a total of 100%). The *quartile deviation* is the computed difference between scores in the second and third quartiles, with the highest and lowest quartiles eliminated. This helps to cancel the effects of extreme scores in the distribution. A normal distribution of scores results in a smaller deviation of scores, and vice versa. The symbol Q represents the quartile statistic.

Standard deviation is the most frequently appearing measure of variability in research articles. The variance of a set of scores is first calculated, and the square root of the variance is then computed, yielding the standard deviation (*SD*). The statistic for the sample's standard deviation is what appears most often in a study, but a separate standard deviation for the population is possible if the scores of every individual are known (or estimated) to whom results are to be generalized.

Two types of standard deviations are reported in the literature: the standard deviation *score* and the standard deviation *unit*. A standard deviation *score* is the average variability of all scores from the mean. For example, if a test has a total score of 100 and a standard deviation of only 2.5, then it could be said that the score dispersion is small and that students scored similarly on the test. If, however, $SD = 10.5$, it would suggest extreme scores affecting the distribution. In such a case, the mean could be skewed, i.e., an average score not representative of the "true" mean. As noted earlier, the mean and the standard deviation score are important statistics in the analysis process. Later it is discussed how they are used in statistical analysis.

Most teachers have not escaped contact with the "bell-shaped" curve (see Figure 10.1), or the common distribution of a population (normal probability curve). Given a normal distribution of scores, 68.2% of a population's scores fall between -1 and $+1$ standard deviation *units*. Another 27.2% fall between -2 and $+2$, another 4.2% between -3 and $+3$, and another 0.24% between -4 and $+4$ (total of 99.8%). Therefore, a score with a standard deviation unit of $+2$ means that a person scoring at this level has scored in the top 95.4% of the population. Since only 13.6% of people

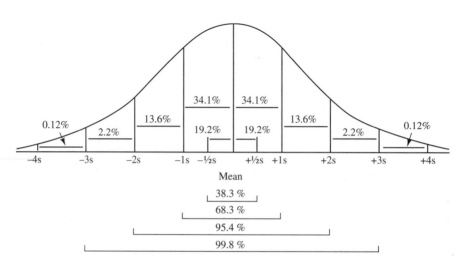

Figure 10.1 Normal curve distribution.

normally score at this level, this is an excellent achievement level. Several familiar scales are based on the normal curve, e.g., the *Scholastic Aptitude Test*.

Do not confuse the standard deviation score, often reported in research articles, with the standard deviation unit. The latter tells how a raw score relates to the normal curve of the population. If you see the *SD* being something like $+1$, you know this refers to *unit* and not score. $SD = 2.5$ (no plus or minus), however, indicates a standard deviation *score*. This is the statistic commonly reported in tables of data. The problem is that both terms are commonly referred to as standard deviation. Researchers want to know when comparing group means if mean differences are significantly (statistically) different, and an important part of the analysis involves the role of the standard deviation score, or the average dispersion of scores from the mean.

Measure of Relationship (Correlation)

A *measure of relationship* is used to determine whether or not a correlation exists between two or more variables and the degree to which the correlation exists. Correlations vary on a scale of $+1$ (positive correlation) to -1 (negative correlation). The more two factors agree, the higher the positive correlation. A negative correlation exists when one variable is positive and the other is negative. No correlation exists close to midrange between $+1$ and -1 (0). Therefore, a correlation coefficient of .34 would be a weak positive correlation, and a correlation coefficient of .94 would be a strong positive. A correlation coefficient of .01 would indicate almost no correlation at all, and a correlation coefficient of $-.85$ would show that as one score went up, the other went in the opposite direction, a negative correlation. The two most commonly used techniques for determining correlation are the Pearson product moment, with a symbol of r, and Spearman rank-difference, with a symbol of r_s (formerly rho).

If a correlation coefficient of .92 is reported between math and music achievement, it would suggest that music students are also good at mathematics, and vice versa. It does not suggest that studying music would cause students to be good at math. Correlation indicates relationship.

Measures of Relative Position (Standard Scores)

Standard scores are used primarily in standardized test measures and have the advantage of being directly comparable if groups are equivalent. For this purpose the raw score is changed into a standard score.

The most common standard score is the z-score. "If a mean and standard deviation are computed for a given set of raw scores, each raw score can be expressed in terms of its distance from the mean in standard deviation units, or z-scores" (Isaac and Michael, 1981, p. 105). Because standard scores are highly related to the normal curve, they should not be used with *skewed* populations. Also, the z-score involves decimals and plus-and-minus indicators, making them sometimes awkward to interpret, e.g., -1.5.

Another frequently used standard score is the T-score. The T-score is a transformed z-score. It is easier to interpret as a regular score than as a standard deviation unit, e.g., $z = +1.0$ transformed becomes $T = 60$.

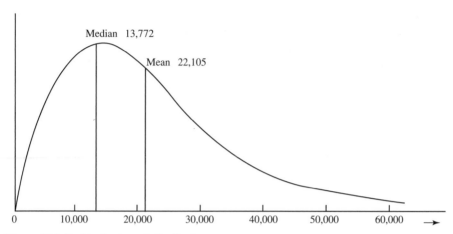

Figure 10.2 Positively skewed distribution.

Skewed Distributions

When a distribution of group scores is not normal (as reflected by the normal curve) it is said to be *skewed*. This is the result of scores bunching around the high or low ends of the distribution, e.g., too many grades of "A." Skewed distributions are problematic in research because the mean score (average) of the distribution is affected and no longer representative of the average. When scores are reflective of more high values than normally found in the normal population, the distribution is said to be *positively skewed* (see Figure 10.2); i.e., the computed mean is too high. When more low scores are present than in the normal population, the distribution is *negatively skewed;* i.e., the computed mean is too low.

Most tests for significant differences between means assume a normal distribution of scores. When this is not the case, using standard tests (such as *t* or *F*) for such analyses is not warranted. In such instances the researcher can elect to use the *median* or *mode* as the average. With today's computer programs, statistical tests are available that will correct for skewed distributions.

Researchers rarely report the normalcy of their data, and normalcy is assumed unless otherwise noted. Unfortunately, novice researchers are not always aware that their data are not normally distributed or that a skewed distribution can result in questionable conclusions.

Standard Error of the Mean

The standard error of the mean (S_m) is not a statistic commonly reported in research articles. It answers this question: How good an estimate of the population mean is a sample mean? This is an important question if results of an experimental study are to be generalized to a population. For example, in survey research it is important to know the *sampling error* if reports of the survey are to be believed. Sampling error is computed as twice the standard error of the mean. A survey stating that "37% of those responding favored corporal punishment in schools," with a sampling error of ±3%, would indicate a 95.4% chance (in relation to the bell-shaped curve) that the true mean (the mean of the population) would be within 3% of 37%. In this case, the standard error of the mean is very important for figuring sampling error, and survey reports without this information should be considered highly questionable.

DETERMINING SIGNIFICANCE BETWEEN MEANS

Thus far only statistics that describe a distribution of group scores have been presented. However, a researcher often wants to compare scores of two measures within one group or scores on one or more measures between two groups or among more than two groups. The following section discusses statistics used for such "mean difference" comparisons. Hold on—the ride becomes a bit rougher.

Hypothesis (H)

Scientific investigation begins with a *hypothesis*, i.e., a formalized "hunch" about the relationship of two or more things, e.g., that one way of doing something is better than another. The researcher writes a declarative *hypothesis* stating what he or she hopes to confirm in the investigation, e.g., "Teaching students to audiate will cause them to become more efficient at music reading." It assumes a cause-and-effect relationship. "A clearly stated hypothesis gives a fairly accurate idea of what we would have to do to provide evidence to confirm or disconfirm the hypothesis" (Slavin, 1984, p. 4).

For lack of space, journal articles frequently do not include the statement of hypotheses. Instead, a hypothesis can be incorporated in the purpose of the study, e.g., "The purpose of the study is to determine if teaching students to audiate will cause them to become more efficient at music reading." The ends are the same, and you can surmise the hypothesis even though it is not labeled as such.

Null Hypothesis (H_o)

For statistical purposes the researcher writes the hypothesis in negative form as a *null hypothesis*. The H_o involves a more rigorous statistical analysis. (It is statistically easier to accept a hypothesis than to reject a null hypothesis.) The preceding hypothesis now becomes a null hypothesis: "There will be no significant difference between means for students who are taught to audiate (group "A," or *treatment*) and those who are not (group "B," or *control*) on a measure of music reading." The researcher then determines the length of the study, the amount of instruction time, and the dependent measure (music-reading test) and employs the treatment with Group A and another treatment or the traditional approach with Group B. Assuming that both groups are randomly chosen from the same population, only posttests will be needed. When intact classes must be used, pretests are recommended to control for any initial group differences.

Again, journal articles often do not include the null hypotheses. These must be surmised from the results presented in the statistical analyses. For a beginning reader of research it can become confusing when neither the hypotheses nor null hypotheses are presented clearly in the text, but space constraints limit the statement of H and H_o.

Initial confusion as to hypotheses is often resolved on further reading of the article; it is best to keep on reading and not to give up too soon.

Probability and Significance

The scores entered into the data analysis are of two types: *gain scores* and *posttest scores*. A gain scores is the difference between the pretest and posttest score when a pretest is given. Gain scores are not popular among statisticians. These scores are easily influenced by "ceiling" and "floor" effects. A ceiling effect occurs when subjects score so high on the pretest that there remains little room to improve on the posttest. The opposite occurs with the floor effect, when subjects score so low on the pretest that the posttest is likely to show gain even when little improvement has occurred.

The most common raw scores entered into a data analysis for determining significance between or among means are those of the posttest, assuming that subjects have been randomized. Group means and standard deviations are computed and form the basis of the analysis. If the computer program via a statistical test determines that a significant (or "true") difference exists between groups in favor of one or the other, a statistic will be reported (most typically t or F) and a *level of significance* (.05, .01, .001) will be stated, e.g., $p < .05$. This level of significance needs to be at least at the *level of probability* set by the researcher before the study, e.g., $p = .05$ (see Chapter 9). (*Note*: Statistical symbols (e.g., t, F, p, N) are always italicized or underlined)

When a *significant difference* is found between conditions or groups, a level of significance is always reported with the analysis statistic (t, F, etc.). This is determined mathematically by the computer program, which tells the researcher whether or not the null hypothesis of "no difference" can be rejected safely because the level of probability has been met. If a researcher sets .05 as the level of probability and the level of significance is reported to be .059, the null hypothesis cannot be rejected—it is probable the results would not be the same a true 95% of the time. Sometimes such levels of significance are reported as having "approached significance," but this means very little—the null hypothesis cannot be rejected if probability is greater than .05. However, if the level of probability is set at $p = .05$ and the level of significance is reported to be $p < .01$ or $p < .001$, then the researcher can be even more confident that the results of the study are open to sampling error only 1 in 100 or 1 in 1000 replications. Rarely are levels of significance reported to be $p < .000$, but it does happen because the numbers reported for probability do not extend beyond three places.

When a researcher rejects a null hypothesis, he or she is then able to say, "There is a *significant* difference between groups." The word *significant* is important because it has been determined that the difference is not a matter of chance, at least not much of a chance! That is why behavioral researchers shy away from saying "the research results *prove* that this way is better than the other way." When dealing with people, there is always a chance, however slight, that the results could fall within the 5% unknown.

The Importance of Standard Deviation

The standard deviation (*SD*) of each group is extremely important when determining if means are significantly different. Slavin (1984) presents an excellent example of how the standard deviation impacts group differences even when the group means are identical

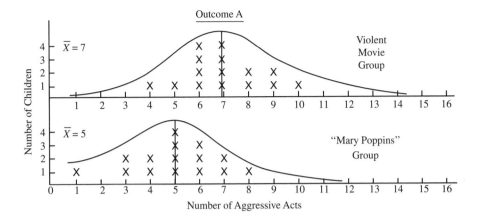

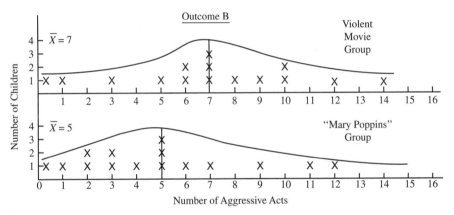

Figure 10.3 Two distributions yielding identical means but differing results. (From Slavin (1984). *Research Methods in Education.* Reprinted by permission of Allyn & Bacon, Boston, MA. Copyright © 1984 by Pearson Education.)

(see Figure 10.3). The experiment in the example concerns the effects of viewing different movies on preschoolers' aggressive behavior.

> Thirty preschool children were randomly assigned to see either the violent movie or "Mary Poppins." Afterwards, they were allowed to play with a set of toys, and the number of aggressive acts committed were observed by observers who did not know which movie the children had seen. Two possible sets of outcomes are depicted [in Figure 10.3]. Each "X" represents the number of aggressive acts for a single child.... [E]ven though the means for the groups are the same in Outcomes A and B, Outcome A clearly shows that students who saw the violent movie exhibited more aggressive behavior than those who saw "Mary Poppins." The null hypothesis (which states that the means of the two groups are the same) does not appear to be tenable; sample-to-sample variation in means would probably not produce such a sharp difference in distributions by chance.
>
> In Outcome B the distributions of scores overlap too much for us to be able to say that the means are not different due to mere chance variation. (pp. 172–73)

In Outcome A because the dispersion of scores is not as spread out as for Outcome B, the standard deviation will be smaller than for Outcome B. It takes a smaller mean difference in Outcome A to produce a significance difference between means because of this smaller standard deviation. In Outcome B the standard deviation will be larger, requiring a larger difference between means to produce a significant difference. In this example, Outcome B is not as likely to result in significant difference due to the dispersion of scores and the larger, standard deviation.

Type I and Type II Errors

It is possible for a researcher to reject a null hypothesis when it should be accepted (false positive). This is known as a *Type I error* (or *alpha error*). A *Type II error* (or *beta error*) occurs if the researcher accepts the null hypothesis when it should be rejected (false negative). The chance of a Type I error can be reduced by increasing the *alpha*, or probability level (e.g., from .05 to .01). However, this also can result in a greater chance of committing a Type II error. These errors are more likely to happen when the sample size is small. Having a large enough sample ($n = 40$ or more) helps to guard against both. Type I and Type II errors rarely emerge in an article, but knowledgeable readers should be aware they exist, especially with small samples.

STATISTICAL TESTS

Two categories of statistical tests are used to determine mean differences between or among groups: *parametric* and *nonparametric*. Parametric tests use interval and ratio data, while nonparametric tests use nominal and ordinal data (review the beginning of this chapter). Most analyses in experimental research are parametric, which means that a parameter (i.e., a characteristic such as a test score) of the group distribution meets certain assumptions, e.g., normal or near-normal distribution (i.e., "bell curve"). Results, therefore, can be generalized to the population. Parametric tests are considered more powerful and should be used when possible to test mean differences. In nonparametric analysis, parameters do not represent an evenly distributed population.

Statistical tests are used in two types of quantitative studies: nonexperimental and experimental. Nonexperimental research (descriptive and correlation) reports "what is" and does not include a treatment component. The data describe and do not infer "cause and effect." Examples of such research are survey, interrelational, and developmental. Parametric or nonparametric tests are employed, based on the type of data collected.

Experimental research is *inferential*; i.e., it draws conclusions (or infers) about populations based on observations of samples. This type of research follows the scientific method. True-experimental and quasi-experimental research also use parametric or nonparametric tests, but parametric is far more common.

One-Tailed and Two-Tailed Tests of Significance

Sometimes the reader will come upon the statement that a "one-tailed" or "two-tailed test" of significance was used in the analysis of means. Phelps (1980) explains this concept nicely:

> Two-tailed and one-tailed tests of significance relate to the direction of difference of the hypotheses. Tests of significance are almost always two-tailed. The null hypothesis states that there will be no difference between the groups (X = Y) being compared. The two-tailed test indicates that the difference may be in either end of the tail, in other words, the mean of X may be higher than that of Y, or the mean of Y may be higher than that of X. In a one-tailed test the difference appears only in the end of one tail, either in the direction of X or Y. (p. 190)

If a research investigation is designed knowing that results can go in only one direction (e.g., measuring students' heights over a year-long period means subjects will probably grow taller), then a one-tailed test is appropriate. However, if for some reason the researcher thinks the subjects can shrink (e.g., the elderly), then a two-tailed test would be appropriate.

Parametric Tests

Besides using interval and ratio data, parametric tests assume a normal or near-normal distribution of the sample. Hopefully the subjects are chosen at random, resulting in groups that have equal or nearly equal variances. The most common parametric tests found in behavioral research are the *t*-test, the *F*-test, and Pearson's *r*.

t-Test

The *t*-test is the simplest way to compute the difference between two means. This test can be done by use of a hand calculator, but computer programs make the computation even easier. One important assumption behind the *t*-test is *homogeneity of variance*, which requires the samples being compared to be similar, or homogenous.

Two drawbacks exist for using the *t*-test: it is appropriate with no more than 30 subjects per group, and it can compare only two means at a time. The once popular *t*-test is rarely seen today in journal articles.

There are two types of *t*-tests: *dependent* samples (paired or correlated) and *independent* samples (nonpaired or noncorrelated). With the dependent-samples test, a researcher can compare the same group to itself, e.g., pretest to posttest. The independent-samples *t*-test must be used when two different groups of subjects are being compared.

Table 10.1 presents a summary of a two-group, independent samples *t*-test. The two groups (meaningful-term method and nonsense-term method) and three statistics (mean, standard deviation, *t* statistic) are shown. The study involved subjects being

Table 10.1 Achievement in Identifying Selected Sounds in Spoken Words Following Two Training Methods

Group	M	SD	t
Meaningful-term method	4.7	2.2	3.2*
Nonsense-term method	6.3	1.6	

*$p < .01$

randomly assigned to two groups. The experimental group was given practice in identifying sounds in nonsense words, while the control group was given practice in identifying the same sounds in meaningful words.

The title indicates the dependent variable or measure ("identifying selected sounds in spoken words") and two independent or treatment variables (the instructional approaches). The mean is given for each group (4.7 and 6.3) as well as the standard deviations (2.2 and 1.6). The t statistic (3.2) is the computed value for t. This value has an asterisk (*), indicating a significant difference exists between means and refers the reader to the notation below the table body that indicates the result is significant at $p < .01$. Therefore, the null hypothesis is rejected—there is a significant difference between groups. In Table 10.1, the mean for the nonsense-term method (6.3) is higher than that for the meaningful-term method (4.7). Therefore, the nonsense-term method is determined to be significantly superior (Huck, Cormier, & Bounds, 1974, p. 54).

Analysis of Variance (ANOVA)

Analysis of variance is the procedure most commonly used in journal articles today for analyzing mean differences. Unlike the t-test procedure, it can compare *two or more* samples. The statistical measure used to compute an analysis of variance is Fisher's F-ratio test.

Like the t-test, ANOVA requires homogeneity of variance as a basic assumption. This is accomplished through randomization of samples. However, ANOVA also requires that observations within sets be mutually independent. There is no such thing as a dependent-samples F-test.

The ANOVA procedure is more rigorous than the t-test because it accounts not only for between-group variance but also for within-group variance in the analysis. Isaac and Michael (1981, p. 182) present this explanation:

> It [ANOVA] answers the question, is the variability between groups large enough in comparison with the variability within groups to justify the inference that the means of the populations from which the different groups were sampled are not all the same? In other words, if the variability between group means is large enough, we can conclude they probably come from different populations and that there is a statistically significant difference in the data. The particular statistical test yielding the answer is the F-ratio:

$$F = \frac{\text{Between-Group Variance}}{\text{Within-Group Variance}}$$

The simplest form of ANOVA is the *one-way analysis of variance*. This is similar to the classic pretest–posttest control-group design, where the effect of one independent variable (treatment) on one dependent variable (measure) is analyzed between two groups. With ANOVA, however, differences between two or more groups can be analyzed.

An ANOVA summary table for a one-way analysis of variance with three groups is presented in Table 10.2 (Huck et al., 1981, p. 59). The title relates that in this experiment there were three groups, each using a different test form measure of different item arrangements. In one test the items were arranged from easiest to most difficult, the second reversed the first order, and the third contained items in random order. The dependent variable was the score on each test for each individual. The independent variable was the mode of arrangement of the items.

Table 10.2 ANOVA Summary Table for Experiment
Comparing Scores on Three Test Forms of
Different Item Arrangements

Source	df	SS	MS	F
Test forms	2	16	8	4*
Within-groups	15	30	2	
Total	17	46		

*p <.05

The ANOVA table looks similar to but different from the *t*-test results shown earlier. For one thing, the "Source" column lists "Test forms" (between-groups variance) and "Within-groups" (within-groups variance). A third row is labeled "Total."

There are four statistics in the table: *df, SS, MS,* and *F*. The degrees of freedom column (*df*) has three numbers: 2 for Test forms, 15 for Within-groups, and 17 for Total. The *df* for Test forms represents 1 less than the number of groups in the study (3). The *df* for Total (17) is 1 less than the total number of subjects in the study (18). The *df* for Within-groups is found by subtracting the *df* for Test forms (2) from the *df* for Total (17), which equals 15. These statistics are important for computing the *F* statistic but are of little importance to the reader except in knowing how to find the total number of groups (3) and subjects in the study (18).

The column marked *SS* (sum of squares) is determined by a rather complicated formula. Suffice it to know that the sum of the first two *SS* should always equal that of the Total *SS* (in this case, $16 + 30 = 46$).

MS stands for mean squares, and the two numbers in this column are found by dividing each *SS* by its *df*. Therefore the *SS* for Test forms is 16, and when divided by its *df* (2) equals the *MS*, 8. The Within-groups *MS* is 2 ($30 \div 15$).

The statistic in the last column is the computed *F* of 4, which was found by dividing the two mean square numbers ($8 \div 2 = 4$). Note the asterisk after the 4, indicating a significant difference at a probability level shown below the table body as $p < .05$. The null hypothesis of "no difference" is rejected. The groups are different.

To determine whether a calculated *F* value is significant or not, the researcher refers to a critical *F* table found in the back of most quantitative research books. (When a computer is used, this critical table is included in the program.) This table contains critical values for *F* (expressed as whole numbers and decimals, e.g., 5.29) positioned in rows and columns based on degrees of freedom (*df*) for within-groups and between-groups errors. Critical values are listed for both .05 and .01 levels of probability. If the calculated *F* value is larger than the critical value in the table, there is significant difference and the null hypothesis is rejected. The same is true in the opposite direction— if the critical value is larger, the null hypothesis is accepted. The use of computers in data analysis makes critical value tables almost obsolete.

When three or more groups are being compared, it is not possible to refer back to the means to determine which are significant. The first mean could be significantly larger than the second, the third, or both, or the second could be larger than third. When ANOVA is calculated for more than two groups, some type of follow-up test is used to determine what group or groups are significantly different from the other(s). Therefore, a follow-up analysis is computed, e.g., Tukey's HSD, and reported in an additional table.

Analysis of Covariance (ANCOVA)

The *analysis of covariance* (ANCOVA) is an analysis that uses the *F*-test as its basis. It is similar to ANOVA but involves accounting for variance due to a *covariate*. It is especially helpful in quasi-experimental research when the initial variance of groups is unequal. The ANCOVA procedure can take out, or *covary*, from the analysis the difference on pretest scores. Covariance also can be used when trying to balance group variance due to inequality on some given measure, such as IQ. The means that are reported for the ANCOVA are "corrected means"; i.e., they have been adjusted.

For example, say that a research study concerns sight-reading accuracy. The investigator gives the subjects in the groups a sight-reading test as a pretest. The researcher has had to use intact groups and fears that the subjects might vary unequally on the pretest because they were not randomized. When he or she analyzes the pretests by means of an independent-samples *t*-test, a significant difference between groups is found—one group sight reads better than the other. However, if the difference between groups on the pretest is used as a covariate when the posttest scores are analyzed (ANCOVA), this initial difference is removed, thus balancing and accounting for the initial difference. Computer analysis makes covariance calculation easy.

Factorial Analysis

Two-way and three-way analyses of variance (ANOVAs) and covariance (ANCOVAs) also exist. These are known as *factorial analyses*, the designs for which are discussed in Chapter 9. In these analyses the groups are submitted to two or more independent variables, one of which must be active (i.e., the treatment). Other variables often include organismic (e.g., age) and attribute (e.g., grade level). In these cases there will be an *F* statistic for each of the independent variables (a minimum of two) and one for each of the interactions between the independent variables. One benefit of two- and three-way ANOVAs is the increase of possible research questions.

The two-way ANOVA permits three research questions: two main effects (one for each independent variable and one interaction [A × B]). The three-way ANOVA permits seven questions (three main effects, three first-order interactions [A × B, A × C, B × C], and one secondary interaction [A × B × C]). The results tables for two-way and three-way ANOVAs are similar to the one-way ANOVA (which permits only one research question), except a lot more information is included. Table 10.3 (Huck et al., 1981, p. 80) is an example of a two-way ANOVA results table for two main effects (Item order and Time limit) and the interaction of these two independent variables. The dependent measure or variable is the subjects' test scores on each of the treatment variables (Item order and Time limit).

Significant interactions are often unwanted, for they can interfere with and even cancel main effects (main research questions). For example, if two grade levels were involved in a study and grade level interacted with one treatment variable, the main effect for that treatment, if significant, could be jeopardized because the interaction, if significant, could indicate that the treatment was effective for only one grade, not both.

Table 10.3 Model Summary Table for a Two-Way
ANOVA Analysis

Source	df	SS	MS	F
Item order	2	10	5	10**
Time limit	1	8	8	16**
Interaction	2	4	2	4*
Within-group (error)	54	27	0.5	
Total	59	49		

**p <.05
*p <.01

However, researchers sometimes ask research questions that involve interactions and, in these cases, are looking for significant interactions.

Table 10.3 reports the analysis as factorial (3 × 2), with three levels of the first factor (Item order) and two levels of the second factor (Time limit). (Remember that df represents 1 less that the total number of levels in each factor). The df for the interaction (2) represent the results of multiplying the df of the two factors. The total df (59) are one less than the number of subjects in the study (60).

It is impossible for the reader to check the accuracy of the numbers given in the SS (sum of squares) column. Remember, however, that the total in this column should always be equal to the sum of those above (49).

The numbers in the MS (mean squares) column are found by dividing the corresponding number in the SS column by its df. There is no MS given for the Total. If a number appears for Total in this column, it is wrong.

The F column indicates significant differences for the two main effects at $p < .05$ and for the interaction at $p < .01$. This shows a significant difference among the three levels of the Item order main effect, a significant difference between the two levels of the Time limit main effect, and an interaction between these two factors (independent variables).

A further step is needed to find out what this all means, which is to check the table of means as presented in Table 10.4 (Huck et al., 1981, p. 77). Table 10.4 has means for six groups of subjects ($n = 10$) who each took a 100-point test under one of six conditions: Syllabus/Yes, Syllabus/No, Backwards/Yes, Backwards/No, Random/Yes, or Random/No. The scores are grouped by three levels of the first factor (Item order) and two levels of the second factor (Time limit), thus the 3 × 2 nature of the factorial design, which yields six cells of data (3 × 2 = 6). The group means are given outside the box in rows (for Item order) and columns (for Time limits). It is these group means that are analyzed in the test for mean differences (F-test).

The results in Table 10.4 indicate a significant difference for both factors. Three group means are reported: for the factor Item order: 72, 71, and 67. By looking at the means in Table 10.4, a slight difference can be seen between the syllabus-group mean (72) and the backwards-group mean (71). Therefore it is safe to assume there is no significant difference between groups. However, the syllabus-group mean (72) is 5 points higher than the Random-group mean (67), and the Backwards-group mean (71) is 4

Table 10.4 Test Score Means for a Two-way,
3 × 2 Factorial ANOVA Analysis

		Time Limit		
		Yes	**No**	
Item Order	Syllabus	$M = 69$	$M = 75$	$M = 72$
	Backwards	$M = 68$	$M = 74$	$M = 71$
	Random	$M = 61$	$M = 73$	$M = 67$
		$M = 66$	$M = 74$	

points higher than the Random-group mean (67). Could both of these be significant? We do not know without doing some type of follow-up test. Having three levels of any factor always creates this problem; it cannot be told from a table of means just where the significance difference lies.

Now look in Table 10.4 at the two columns for Time Limit. The Yes-group mean is 66 and the No-group mean is 74. Because we know from Table 10.3 that there is a significant difference (main effect) between these two levels, the No-group did significantly better than the Yes-group on the variable Time order.

However, Table 10.3 also reports a significant interaction between Item order and Time limit. This confounds the two main effects (one of whose results we do not know without a follow-up test). This necessitates an inspection of the individual means in the six cells of data. Huck et al. (1981) explain:

> We must look at the individual cell means and ask, "Do the differences among the levels of one factor remain constant as we move from one level to another of the second factor?" At the first level of item order (syllabus), the difference between the time limit group ($\overline{X} = 69$) and the no time limit group ($\overline{X} = 75$) is 6 points. Moving to the next level of item order (backwards), the difference between the time limit group ($\overline{X} = 68$) and the no time limit group ($\overline{X} = 74$) is again 6 points. So far, no interaction. However, when we move to the third level of item order (random), we find that the difference between the means is 12 points. Thus, the differential effect of having a time limit as opposed to not having a time limit does not remain constant for all three test forms. For this reason, an interaction may be said to exist between item order and time limit. (pp. 78–79)

The authors go on to state that you could also calculate the differences among the means within each column. They conclude: "No matter how we look at the cell means, we come up with the same conclusion—there is some degree of interaction present in the data" (p. 79). Again, some type of follow-up test is used, e.g., a test of simple main effects, where each of these tests may be likened to a one-way ANOVA that compares the various levels of one factor at a particular level of the second factor.

Multivariate Analysis of Variance (MANOVA) and Multivariate Analysis of Covariance (MANCOVA)

Things become much more complicated when a researcher wants to include more than one dependent variable in a study. This is done when the dependent measures are highly related and thus share variance (e.g., high pitch, low pitch, and total vocal range). The analysis becomes *multivariate analysis of variance* (MANOVA) and *multivariate analysis of covariance* (MANCOVA) when covariance analysis is warranted. These remain one-way, two-way, or even three-way investigations of the effects of one, two, or three factors on two or more *dependent* measures considered as a "set." When significance is found, follow-up univariate tests are required to sort out the answers.

Pearson's r

The Pearson product-moment correlation (*r*) is the most common parametric statistic used when a researcher wants to know the relationship between two observations expressed in interval or ratio data. As mentioned earlier, correlations are presented as numbers ranging from +1 to −1. A plus number indicates a positive relationship; a minus number indicates a negative relationship (as one score goes up the other goes down). Anything close to a "0" correlation indicates no systematic relationship.

Sometimes a number of correlations are presented in a table called a *correlation matrix*. Table 10.5 is an example of a correlation matrix in which correlations among six variables are shown. Half of the table is blank because these would be the same correlations in inverse order. Variables 1–6 across the top of the table are the same variables 1–6 down the side of the table. The correlation matrix in Table 10.5 shows that the strongest relationships exist between English and Music (.85), Algebra and Music (.82), and Science and Music (.75).

Correlations can be difficult to interpret. One thing to remember is that a strong positive correlation does *not* indicate that a causal relationship exists between variables. Just because music students score high on their SATs does not mean that studying music makes people smart. It more likely means that smart people study music!

Nonparametric Tests

Besides using nominal or ranked data, nonparametric tests have less power than parametric tests, and they are not as likely to reject a null hypothesis. The population distribution is not thought to be normal, so these tests are known as being "distribution free." The most common nonparametric tests include: *chi square* (X^2), *median test, Mann-Whitney test, sign test, Wilcoxon,* and the *Spearman rank-order coefficient of correlations*.

Table 10.5 Correlations Among Grade Point Averages

Variables	1	2	3	4	5	6
1. English	—	.63	.58	.50	.67	.85
2. Social Studies		—	.45	.35	.42	.51
3. Latin			—	.65	.35	.65
4. Algebra				—	.72	.82
5. Science					—	.75
6. Music						—

Chi Square (X^2)

Chi square is the most widely used nonparametric statistic. It is employed whenever data consist of frequency counts, such as the number of responses, objects, or people that fall in two or more categories (nominal data). This test indicates whether the results obtained are significantly different from those that might be expected by chance at a given probability level (e.g., $p < .05$). This test is sometimes called a "goodness-of-fit" statistic.

> Suppose ... that a college administrator wanted to determine if there is a significant difference between the number of students who actually sign up for six elective courses (the observed number) and the number expected by chance. The administrator might expect that by chance alone an equal number of students would enroll in each elective course. The null hypothesis for this study thus becomes that an equal number of students sign up for all six elective courses. (Huck et al., 1981, p. 217)

Often, chi-square results are reported within the text without an accompanying table. The following is an example of reporting results of a single sample X^2 test within the text. "A one-sample chi-square test was used to determine whether the frequency of correct test responses differed among the four treatment groups. The obtained $X^2 = 15.89$, $df = 3$, was significant at the .01 level" (Huck et al., 1981, p. 218).

The chi-square test also can be used with two or more independent samples. Here again the researcher is interested in determining whether the observations are significantly different from what might be expected by chance. In these cases the design looks similar to a factorial model, but it is called a *contingency table* (e.g., 2×2, 3×4). The chi-square test permits the comparing of responses between one or more groups when the data are nonparametric.

Spearman Rank-Order Correlation Coefficient (r_s)

The Spearman r_s is the nonparametric correlation test analogous to the parametric Pearson product-moment correlation. It also reports a two-digit number from $+1$ to -1, and serves as a test for significant differences. The data used in the computation of this test are ordinal/ranked. This procedure could be useful for testing the relationship of one judge's rankings of ensemble performances with another's.

Sign Test ($+ - 0$)

The sign test is used to determine whether two conditions are different for related samples when the data for each pair are ranked. For example, a researcher might want to know if husbands consume more caffeine than wives. Couples are sampled and the results charted as H $>$ W (husband has greater consumption than wife), which results in a $+$sign. H $<$ W would yield a $-$sign, and H $=$ W is a 0 sign. The hypothesis states that an equal number of plus and minus signs are present.

Wilcoxon Matched-Pairs Signed-Ranks Test (T)

The Wilcoxon test is the equivalent of the dependent- or paired-samples t-test (parametric). It is a more powerful test than the sign test because more weight is given to a pair that shows a larger difference.

Median Test

The median test is analogous to the parametric independent-samples *t*-test. Instead of the mean as the measure of central tendency, the median is used. The median test is usually chozen when *N* is between 20 and 40. It involves nominal data.

Mann-Whitney U Test

This test is analogous to the parametric independent-samples *t*-test. Like the independent-samples *t*-test, the Mann-Whitney can work with samples of unequal number. This test uses ordinal or ranked data.

Summary

Without an extensive research background it is impossible for the novice reader to know whether or not the researcher has chosen the correct statistical test for use in any study. However, names of parametric and nonparametric tests appear regularly in journal articles and should at least be recognizable as tests used in quantitative research.

STUDY AND DISCUSSION QUESTIONS

1. What are the four levels of measurement, and what does each represent?
2. How does a raw score differ from a statistic?
3. What are the three measures of central tendency, and what does each represent?
4. How does a standard deviation score differ from a standard deviation unit?
5. Why is the standard deviation an important statistic reported in research articles?
6. What does the standard error of the mean represent?
7. Why is a null hypothesis used in experimental research rather than a hypothesis?
8. How does a probability level differ from a level of significance?
9. What is the importance of the degrees of freedom (*df*) statistic?
10. What are Type I and Type II errors?
11. How do parametric and nonparametric tests differ?
12. What are the characteristics of the *t*-test?
13. What are the characteristics of the *F*-test?
14. How is the *F* statistic computed?
15. How can a researcher know if the *F* calculated value is significant?
16. In a two-way ANOVA, how many independent variables are there?
17. How many research questions can be asked using a two-way ANOVA?
18. How many levels of each factor are there in a 3×2 ANOVA?
19. What is meant by the main effects of a research analysis?
20. What causes a significant interaction in a factorial analysis?
21. What is an ANCOVA, and when it is used in an analysis of data?

22. A Pearson's *r* of .95 would indicate what type of correlation between variables?

23. Why are nonparametric tests less powerful than parametric tests?

24. For what purpose could a researcher use a chi-square test?

25. When would a researcher use the sign test?

SUGGESTED ACTIVITIES

1. Discuss the meaning behind the following statement: "Behavioral researchers refrain from having 'proven' anything, even when significant results are found in a study."

2. What type of statistical test would be used in the following example? The researcher wants to know what method of teaching sight-singing (Orff, Kodály, Gordon) might be best in grades 3 and 4.

CHAPTER 11

Quantitative Research

Descriptive

Descriptive studies are easier to read than experimental studies. For that reason, we begin our reading of quantitative research with a survey report. Don't be concerned at this point if you do not understand some terms. Just keep reading and try to comprehend as much as you can. While the results presented in the following article are somewhat dated, this study is a good example of survey research.

READING DESCRIPTIVE RESEARCH: A COMMENTARY

A survey is one of the most common forms of descriptive research. It can be deceptive, however, because a good survey requires an understanding of how to formulate and present the questions. Also, identifying and acquiring an adequate and representative sample of the population is extremely important. The following article by Gfeller, Hedden, and Darrow (1990) is an excellent example of survey research.

Perceived Effectiveness of Mainstreaming in Iowa and Kansas Schools

Kate Gfeller, The University of Iowa; Steven K. Hedden, *The University of Arizona*; Alice-Ann Darrow, *The University of Kansas*

Journal of Research in Music Education, 38(2), 90–101.

Reprinted by permission of MENC: The National Association of Music Education.
Copyright © 1990, by MENC.

Since the 1978 implementation of Public Law 94–142 (the Education for All Handicapped Children Act of 1975), music educators have faced the challenge

---

of integrating handicapped students into regular music classes. This law has required that education for handicapped children take place in the "least restrictive environment" commensurate with their needs. In other words, the selected placement must be as close to a "normal" educational situation as possible while still providing adequate support for educational progress. In many instances, this has meant placement of the handicapped child in a regular music classroom (Jellison, 1979).

Although the basic spirit of mainstreaming is admirable, pragmatic music educators have become increasingly aware that successful mainstreaming is not simply a matter of proximity. Past studies have investigated factors such as age-group level and music specialty area (Gilbert & Asmus, 1981; Lerner, 1981; Shehan, 1977; White, 1981/1982), which appear to affect the attitudes of music educators working toward mainstreaming. Another factor in successful mainstreaming is that of teacher preparation in working with the handicapped (Gilbert & Asmus, 1981; Lerner, 1981; Shehan, 1977; White 1981/1982). In past inquiries, teachers have reported lack of adequate preparation (be it through formal classroom work or in in-service training) concerning implementation of mainstreaming or development of adaptive teaching methods and materials.

While adequate teacher preparation is certainly an important factor in successful mainstreaming (Lerner, 1981; Nocera, 1972), another critical factor is that of instructional support. According to Lerner (1981), a coordinated effort by all school personnel is essential to successful mainstreaming. She further stated that the special educator should be the major party responsible for coordination of special programs, including the education of the rest of the staff through in-service training and consultation.

While previous studies (Atterbury, 1986; Gilbert & Asmus, 1981) allude to inadequate instructional support in terms of numbers of handicapped students, assistance by teacher aides, and participation in IEP development, these studies are inconclusive in terms of success in mainstreaming. Furthermore, they do not address all of the specific supports recently recommended by the Music Educators National Conference (MENC).

The second edition (1986) of MENC's *The School Music Program: Description and Standards* makes specific recommendations for instructional support when a handicapped child is mainstreamed into regular music classes. These recommendations include active educator involvement in the initial placement of the child, with placement based primarily on musical achievement; provision of in-service or preservice training for teachers; convenient access to trained consultants in special education; and a general recommendation for adequate teacher preparation time.

In addition to teacher preparation and instructional support, the success of mainstreaming ultimately should be judged on the outcome in terms of educational objectives. In the true spirit of P.L. 94–142, the intent of mainstreaming is the exposure of handicapped students to "normal" educational opportunities. As Thompson (1982) pointed out, there are overlapping procedures and materials in music therapy and music education. He emphasized, however, that music educators should focus on the development of aesthetic potential rather than nonmusic behaviors. To date, studies have not addressed the basic issues of curriculum goals and objectives when a child is mainstreamed into a music. Specifically, to what extent do music educators perceive mainstreaming practices in music education as meeting the true spirit of P.L. 94–142?

In summary, past studies have examined mainstreaming practices in music education in view of grade level and the teacher's area of specialization as well as preparation. These studies, conducted more than 7 years ago, indicated that there was inadequate preparation for work with the handicapped. Has there been a change in this status? Further questions remain concerning instructional support as it relates to successful mainstreaming of the exceptional child in music education, as well as actual adherence to the spirit of P.L. 94–142. Therefore, this study examined the following research questions:

1. Are there differences among music educators who work predominantly within different specialty areas (general music, choral, instrumental) on the overall questionnaire or the following subscales: instructional support, musical objectives, or perceived success of mainstreaming?

2. Are there differences among music educators with varied experience in working with mainstreamed students?

3. What extent of educational preparation for mainstreaming exists among music educators in Iowa and Kansas?

4. What is the present extent of instructional support for music educators who have handicapped students mainstreamed into music classes? Support is defined as available consultation and in-service training, aides, preparation time, and teacher participation in placement decisions.

5. Does amount of instructional support correlate positively with perceived success in mainstreaming?

6. Do music educators perceive specific types of handicapping conditions as more difficult than others to integrate into the mainstream?

Commentary

The authors introduce their article/study with a review of the literature regarding the implementation of mainstreaming in the music education classroom. They report a number of factors that have arisen from other studies in relation to mainstreaming: age-group level and music specialty area, teacher preparation, adaptive teaching methods and materials, instructional support, assistance by teacher aides, participation in IEP development, and educational goals and objectives, e.g., development of aesthetic potential. The authors reveal the purpose of their study to be the examination of perceived status of mainstreaming among music educators in Iowa and Kansas, and they present six research questions as the basis for the investigation. These questions become the implied hypotheses and null hypotheses for which the data are later analyzed.

The Article *(continued)*

Method

A questionnaire was developed for distribution to music educators in Iowa and Kansas. These states were chosen because they both use music specialists to teach music in the public schools, and they have similar population profiles in terms of rural and urban demographics.

Development of the Questionnaire

Items for the questionnaire were developed by (1) reviewing research literature on mainstreaming in music education; (2) examining the suitability of items from extant questionnaires that would address this study's research questions (Sudman & Bradburn, 1982); (3) examining guidelines specified in the MENC document *The School Music Program: Descriptions and Standards* for music education of an exceptional child; and (4) professional experiences of the authors and their colleagues in the public schools.

No previous questionnaire fully addressed the research questions for this study, so series of questions were developed for the following areas: (1) demographic information on age group, specialty taught, and extent of experience with handicapped students; (2) amount of educational preparation in special education, using a scale of 1 to 5 to determine amount of formal classroom, in-service, or workshop education; (3) extent of instructional support in mainstreaming students in regular music classes, measured through frequency ratings of "never" to "always"; (4) the extent to which musical and nonmusical goals are primary concerns for mainstreamed students, measured through frequency ratings of "never" to "always"; (5) the degree of difficulty in mainstreaming students with various handicapping conditions, measured through frequency ratings of "strongly disagree" to "strongly agree"; and (6) perceived success in mainstreaming, measured through frequency ratings of "strongly disagree" to "strongly agree."

The questionnaire was submitted to a panel of three judges from the fields of music education, speech pathology, and administration. The judges were asked to critique the device for format and relevance to the research questions. Several questions were reworded due to lack of clarity, and ambiguous questions were eliminated. This adjusted form was then submitted to three more judges. Additional recommendations were integrated, and a final form sent to music educators in the public schools in Iowa and Kansas.

Commentary

The method for data collection is disclosed as the questionnaire or survey. This is one of the primary procedures for conducting descriptive research. Unfortunately, for lack of space the questionnaire is not included in the article. This is a common place occurrence in journal articles.

Development of the questionnaire evolved from four information sources: review of the literature, extant questionnaires, guidelines published in a professional document, and experiences of the authors and their colleagues. These sources represent a rigorous and scholarly process for building a valid survey instrument.

The questionnaire encompassed six question areas: information about the participants, amount of educational preparation in special education, extent of instructional support in mainstreaming students in regular music classes, the extent to which musical and nonmusical goals are primary concerns for mainstreamed students, the degree of difficulty in mainstreaming students with various handicaps, and perceived success of teachers in mainstreaming. The measures for these areas also were included.

To validate the questionnaire it was submitted to a panel of three judges for their comments. This is a common and necessary process when developing a survey. Based on the judges' feedback, several questions were reworded to enhance clarity and ambiguous questions were eliminated. To further validate the final document, the revised version was given to three different judges, and additional comments from them helped to determine the final form of the questionnaire, which was sent to music educators in public schools in Iowa and Kansas.

The Article (continued)

Procedure

Five percent of the elementary and secondary music educators in each state ($N = 350$) were surveyed using a stratified random sample. Two attempts were made to obtain responses from the sample. There was a return rate of 76% from the Iowa sample and 70% from the Kansas sample. Of those who returned surveys, 41.5% of the Iowa respondents and 58.5% of the Kansas respondents were involved in mainstreaming handicapped students. These surveys provided the data for statistical analysis.

Commentary

The questionnaire was sent to 5% of music educators in both states. The total population of music teachers in these states is not given, but the sample size was 350. The sampling procedure was a "stratified random sample," meaning equal numbers of elementary and secondary teachers were selected by a random process to receive the survey.

It is difficult to get people, in general, to return questionnaires, and a follow-up contact was conducted to elicit more responses. There was a final return rate of 76% from Iowa teachers and 70% from the Kansas group. These response rates would be considered "good." However, not all teachers had contact with mainstreamed students.

Therefore, the final response rate was 41.5% from Iowa and 58.5% from Kansas. The total number of persons included in the data analysis is not given, but from the ANOVA table that appears later in the article it can be determined that 72 persons were included in the final data analyses.

The Article (*continued*)

Results

In the investigation of the reliability of the questionnaire, the items were grouped according to the following areas of inquiry: type of mainstreaming experience, primary educational objectives, level of instructional support, and perceived success of mainstreaming. Each of these areas was analyzed for reliability using the Cronbach Alpha. Table 1 indicates reliability coefficients for the total questionnaire and areas of inquiry.

Table 1 Reliability for Questionnaire Subscales

Questionnaire and Subscales	Reliability (Coefficient Alpha)
Total questionnaire minus demographic information (Items 6–37)	.76
Music objectives (Items 17–22)	.42
Instructional support (Items 6–16, 24)	.56
Perceived success of mainstreaming (Items 25–28)	.79

Commentary

Reliability refers to the consistency of a measure to reproduce the same results each time it is given. The survey in this study was not a standardized one and a published reliability was not available. Recognizing the need to calculate the reliability of the questionnaire, the investigators calculated the reliability using a standard statistical test, Cronbach Alpha.

The reliability coefficients that appear in Table 1 vary from .42 to .79, or moderately low to moderately high. Of the four the reliability of .76 for the total questionnaire is the most important. This moderately high reliability coefficient indicates a fairly reliable instrument, one that can be trusted to yield similar results repeatedly.

The Article (*continued*)

1. The greatest percentage of respondents had combination assignments with regard to area of teaching (general, vocal, instrumental).

2. The greatest percentage of respondents had teaching assignments that included grades K–6.

3. Nearly 50% of the respondents had been teaching for 10 or fewer years.

Table 2 Demographic Data on Respondents

Classifications	Percentage of Respondents
Area of Teaching	
General	13
Vocal	25
Instrumental	23
Combination	39
Primary Teaching Responsibility	
K–6	38
7–12	22
K–12	10
Other	29
Years of Teaching Experience	
1–5	23
6–10	22
11–15	23
16–20	13
21–25	11
More than 25	8
Special Education Preparation	
No formal training	38
Workshops and in-service	15
A college course	25
A college course with additional in-service/workshops	10
Several college courses with ongoing in-service/workshops	6
Other	6

Research Questions

1. *Are there differences among music educators in different specialty areas on the overall questionnaire, or the following subscales: instructional support, musical objectives, or perceived success of mainstreaming?*

   The differences were nonsignificant with one exception. The instrumental teachers indicated significantly greater instructional support than the teachers of general music or choral music (Tables 3 and 4). Percentage responses on musical objectives and perceived success (Table 5) indicate a general lack of consensus concerning emphasis on musical objectives and perceived success of mainstreaming.

Table 3 ANOVA Summary Table for Instructional Support for Instrumental, Choral, and General Music Educators

Source of Variance	Sum of Squares	df	Mean Squares	F	p
Between groups	186.43	2	93.21	4.84	.010[*]
Within groups	1,327.57	69	19.24		
Total	1,514.00	71			

[*]$p < .01$

Commentary

The one-way ANOVA summary presented in Table 3 is an excellent example of using parametric statistics in descriptive, nonexperimental research (Chapter 10). Under the heading "Source of Variance" is first listed "Between groups." This represents the variance found between the three subgroups (general music, choral, and instrumental). By looking at the degrees of freedom (*df*) for "Between groups" we see that the number "2" is given, which is 1 less than the total numbers of groups in this analysis (3). The "Total" for *df* is 71, which is 1 less than the total number of subjects in this analysis (72). Only two other numbers are of importance in this table: the *F* statistic (4.84) and the level of probability, $p = .010$, which is significant at $p < .01$ (shown below the table). Do you remember from Chapter 10 how to compute the *F* statistic? You divide the mean squares of between groups by the mean squares of within groups ($93.21 \div 19.24 = 4.84$). The probability level at which the significant results were identified is $p = .010$, which matches the probability level established by the researchers, $p < .01$.

Because the analysis involved three groups, it is not possible to tell where the significance occurs among the three. Therefore, a follow-up analysis was conducted, which appears in Table 4. Notice in Table 4 that the test results for "Elementary Music Educators" and "Vocal Music Educators" are underscored. This indicates that no significant differences were found between these groups. However, the result for "Instrumental music educators" is not underscored, indicating that this group is significantly different from the other two. In other words, the instrumental teachers indicated significantly greater instructional support than the teachers of general music and choral music.

The Article (*continued*)

Table 4 Newman Keuls Multiple Range Test for Mean Level of Instructional Support

Elementary Music Educators	Vocal Music Educators	Instrumental Music Educators
20.60	22.26	24.81

Rule under values indicates nonsignificance. All other comparisons significant ($p < .01$).

2. *Are there differences among music educators who have worked with "few," "some," or "many" mainstreamed students?*

The differences were not significant for all comparisons.

3. *What extent of educational preparation for mainstreaming exists among music educators in Iowa and Kansas?*

The average music educator in these states has received little preparation in terms of course work pertinent to working with mainstreamed students. The mean score for the group of five questionnaire items was 10.78 (standard deviation of 3.95), where a mean score of 5.00 would have indicated no preparation and 25.00, maximal preparation.

Table 5 Percentage of Respondents on Items Concerning Effectiveness of Mainstreaming and Emphasis on Music Objectives

Questionnaire Items	Percentage of Respondents
Handicapped students are effectively integrated in music.	62
Handicapped students' music education needs are being met in regular music.	52
Handicapped students' music education needs are better met in special education classes.	50
Having handicapped students in regular music hampers progress of nonhandicapped students.	61
My primary objective with the handicapped child is development of nonmusical goals.	67
I am expected to adapt regular music education goals/objectives for handicapped students.	57
I expect handicapped children to participate in the same musical objectives and programming as nonhandicapped children.	63
I grade handicapped children on the same standards of musical achievement as nonhandicapped students.	32

4. *What extent of instructional support for mainstreaming in music exists in Iowa and Kansas?*

The data reveal little participation by music educators in placement procedures, limited support through in-service education, and lack of preparation time for individualizing programs for the handicapped (see Tables 6 and 7).

5. *Does amount of instructional support correlate positively with perceived success in mainstreaming?*

A positive but slight correlation was found between perceived success in mainstreaming and the amount of instructional support ($r = .40$).

Table 6 Instructional Support

Item	Percentage of Respondents
Included in IEP programming	13
Participate in placement courses	21
Placement of students based on level of musical achievement	16
Assistance of aides when required	27
Write IEP goals for musical achievement	3
Given extra preparation time	1
Expected to mainstream all handicapped students	65
Adequate consultation with special education teachers	27
Adequate time to individualize	18
Adequate resource materials	31
School administrator is sensitive to concerns	36

6. *Do music educators perceive specific types of handicapping conditions more difficult to integrate into the mainstream?*

Respondents were asked to indicate the difficulty of working with specific handicaps, but only if they had previous direct teaching experience with students having that condition. Responses indicated that students with emotional or behavioral disorders and hearing impairments are the most difficult to mainstream, while students with speech communication and other health impairments are the least difficult to mainstream (Table 8).

Table 7 Provision of In-Service

Frequency of Provision	Percentage of Respondents
Each month	1
Once a semester	1
Once a year	6
Upon request of staff	33
Not at all	54
No response	5

Table 8 Percentage of Respondents Reporting Difficulty in Working with Various Handicaps

Handicapping Conditions	Percentage of Respondents
Emotional or behavioral disorders	56
Hearing impairment	40
Educably mentally retarded	37
Learning disabled	35
Trainably mentally retarded	33
Visually impaired	25
Physical handicaps	21
Speech/communication disorders	21
Other health impairments (e.g., sickle-cell anemia, cystic fibrosis)	9

Commentary

The way in which question 2 is answered reflects a null hypothesis of "no difference" among those educators who worked with "few," "some," or "many" mainstreamed students. It was not significant.

The third question is answered by inspecting the mean scores, and no apparent analysis was conducted. The results indicate little preparation for teachers in working with mainstreamed students.

Question 4 is answered by citing simple percentages. However, question 5 shows that a correlation analysis was used to determine relationship of instructional support and perceived success in mainstreaming. The correlation coefficient of $r = .40$ indicates that a slight positive correlation exists. Correlation analysis is one of the main statistical procedures used in nonexperimental research.

Finally, question 6 is answered by means of simple percentages, and results indicate that students with emotional or behavioral disorders and the hearing impaired are cited as being the most difficult to mainstream. This is to be expected.

The Article (continued)

Discussion

The results of this study indicate lack of consensus among music educators concerning effectiveness of mainstreaming (Table 5). While 62% of the respondents reported that handicapped students are effectively mainstreamed, at least 50% of the educators indicated that handicapped students' music education needs are better met in special classes. Furthermore, 61% feel that handicapped students hamper progress of nonhandicapped peers. What are possible interpretations for this lack of consensus? Perhaps there is lack of clarity among educators concerning what actually constitutes successful mainstreaming. According to P.L. 94–142, a student should be mainstreamed only in the regular classroom setting provides adequate educational support. Moreover, successful mainstreaming practices should not hinder the progress of nonhandicapped students. The data from this study suggest that these criteria for effective mainstreaming are not being met consistently.

Lack of consensus among educators may also be related to differences across handicapping classifications. As the data in Table 8 indicate, certain handicapping conditions are perceived as more problematic. Furthermore, while this study did not address the issue of the continuum of severity among handicapped students, it is possible that the level of severity of handicaps is also influencing perceived success of mainstreaming. Future studies might investigate the extent to which severity influences effective integration.

Responses concerning emphasis on music objectives suggest that the true spirit of P.L. 94–142 is not always maintained. Of the respondents 67% reported that their primary objective is the development of nonmusical goals and objectives; 63%

expected handicapped students to meet the same musical objectives; but only 32% reported that they grade on the same musical standards (Table 5).

The reliability coefficient of subscales dealing with music objectives and instructional support indicate that conclusions regarding these subscales should be interpreted with care. However, the data suggest that music educators may have difficulty determining appropriate educational objectives for handicapped students. To what extent should musical as opposed to nonmusical objectives be emphasized when working with a handicapped student? Unfortunately, if this question has not been addressed, it is not only difficult to plan instructional units, but also to evaluate achievement or the extent to which mainstreaming has been successful. While the selection of educational objectives and criteria for grading must certainly vary depending on the nature and severity of the handicap, the music educator could better establish educational expectations if learning objectives for music are discussed and clearly stated at the time of placement.

Another issue that appears to influence the effectiveness of mainstreaming is extent of educational support. Data in Table 6 indicate limited resources in terms of aides, extra preparation time, and consultation. Perhaps most critical, however, is the small percentage of respondents who reported what placement of students was based on level of musical achievement and the large percentage of respondents expected to mainstream all handicapped students. P.L. 94–142 does not mandate "mainstreaming"; it does, however, require education in the "least restrictive environment." Mainstreaming may very well be the most restrictive environment if placement of handicapped students is not based on musical achievement. Appropriate placement decisions constitute a serious responsibility for the music educator. Failure to mainstream a handicapped student should be a decision based on musical criteria rather than a lack of desire to adapt teaching procedures.

The issue of placement based on level of musical achievement appears to be important in terms of perceived instructional support. When comparing differences among music educators within general, vocal, or instrumental settings, the data analysis (Table 3) revealed that instrumental teachers perceived greater instructional support than did general or vocal teachers. Further analysis (using a chi square) indicated that a significantly greater ($<.01$) number of handicapped students are laced in instrumental classes according to level of musical achievement than in general or vocal classes. This finding may, in part, explain the significant differences in perceived instructional support among these areas of specialization.

On the topic of placement, it is interesting to note that nearly one-half of the respondents indicated that handicapped students are not mainstreamed into their classes. The data do not indicate whether music educators do not mainstream because there are no handicapped students in their school or because mainstreaming practices are not employed in their school. However, since relatively few (21%) music educators are actually involved in placement decisions, it could be that many music educators are, to some extent, uninformed concerning criteria for mainstreaming in their school. Clarification regarding this question may require inquiry of school administrators as well as music educators.

Another factor that appears to influence the perceived success of mainstreaming is that of teacher preparation in working with handicapped students. Only 25% of respondents have had even one college course related to teaching handicapped students. The course most often listed was child psychology, which typically does not focus specifically on handicapping conditions. Furthermore, in-service education is a relatively rare occurrence. In short, most music educators are attempting to meet the educational needs of handicapped students with little or no educational preparation. Moreover, the data from this study do not suggest that greater exposure or experience with handicapped students significantly changes perceptions of mainstreaming. Therefore, it seems that teachers will not achieve greater satisfaction with mainstreaming simply as a matter of accumulated experience with special students.

While a survey course that deals with various handicaps would be a welcome change over no preparation at all, perhaps academic preparation should include courses in classroom management and/or behavior modification procedures for students with severe behavior disorders; a large number of respondents noted that students with behavioral and emotional disorders are difficult to mainstream. Furthermore, educators working with hearing-impaired students might request in-service or continuing education in basic sign language skills or instructional strategies appropriate for hearing-impaired students.

Commentary

The results of the study indicate what most music educators know—criteria for effective mainstreaming are not being met consistently in the music classroom. Neither are musical objectives being met. Lack of educational support in terms of aides, extra preparation time and consultation also are notably lacking.

The ANOVA and follow-up analysis reveal greater instructional support for instrumental teachers than for general music and vocal teachers. A new finding is revealed that does not appear in the Results section: Chi-square analysis shows that a significantly greater number of handicapped students are placed in instrumental classes according to level of musical achievement than in general or vocal classes. The authors say that this finding may, in part, explain the significant difference for instructional support in favor of instrumental teachers. It also may show that students unable to play band instruments cannot function in an instrumental class.

The finding that only 25% of respondents had even one college course related to teaching handicapped students is not surprising given the date of this article (1990). Most states, colleges and universities have now increased requirements for teachers in the area of students with disabilities. However, much remains to be done in order to help music teachers feel really qualified to work with mainstreamed learners.

The Article (*continued*)

Conclusions and Recommendations

This study points to several key areas that influence perceived success of mainstreaming in music education: (1) the need for clear educational objectives and expectations; (2) the need for adequate instructional support, particularly in terms of the music educator's participation in placement decisions; and (3) the need for better educational preparation—especially for handicapping conditions deemed to mainstream.

If music educators are to uphold the true spirit of P.L. 94–142, mainstreamed students should be graded on similar standards and expected to achieve the same musical objectives set for nonhandicapped students. At present, it appears appropriate. If music educators abandon regular musical objectives to accommodate the handicapped students in the mainstream, they are, at least in part, responsible for the continued poor implementation of mainstreaming practices.

To teach students with special needs effectively, however, music educators need an adequate level of instructional support and educational preparation. This includes requesting consultation and aides when necessary and informing administrators of the desire to be included in placement decisions. The music educator also needs information concerning methods and materials appropriate for integrating the special student. This study indicates that in-service training is usually offered only upon request. Therefore, in addition to attending workshops or courses as part of continuing education, the music educator may wish to request in-service training in the school, specifying information on those particular handicapping conditions that are most problematic.

In closing, while mainstreaming has been implemented for over ten years, music educators in the states of Iowa and Kansas show a lack of consensus concerning its effectiveness. Factors that may contribute to the less than overwhelming success of mainstreaming include limited educational preparation, poorly defined educational objectives, and lack of instructional support.

While this study surveyed only Iowa and Kansas music educators, there are important implications for music educators across the country. It is possible that the weaknesses in mainstreaming identified in this study may be amplified in other areas of the country where mainstreaming practices in music education have not been fully implemented. The study described in this article should give impetus and direction for others to examine the progress of mainstreaming in their respective states. In addition, further research is necessary to identify specific types of classes or in-service education most effective in preparing the teachers to work with handicapped students, as well as the differential needs related to severity of handicaps.

Commentary

The authors conclude by pointing to three key issues that influence the perceived success of mainstreaming among music educators in Iowa and Kansas: lack of clear educational objectives, inadequate instructional support, and little educational preparation. While the authors do not attempt to generalize these results to the population of music educators in the United States (this is not an inferential study), they do recommend that others examine the progress of mainstreaming in their respective states. They also recommend that research be conducted to explore the types of classes or workshops that would best prepare music educators to work with the disabled.

The Article (continued)

REFERENCES

Atterbury, B. (1986). A survey of present mainstreaming practices in the southern United States. *Journal of Music Therapy, 23*(4), 202–207.

Gilbert, J. P., & Asmus, E. P., Jr. (1981). Mainstreaming educators' participation and professional needs. *Journal of Research in Music Education, 25*, 283–289.

Jellison, J. A. (1979). The music therapist in the educational setting. Developing and implementing curriculum for the handicapped. *Journal of Music Therapy, 16*(3), 128–137.

Lerner, J. (1981). *Children with learning disabilities* (3rd ed.). Boston: Houghton Mifflin.

Music Educators National Conference (1986). *The school music program: Descriptions and standards* (2nd ed.). Reston, VA: Music Educators National Conference.

Nocera, S. (1972). Special education teachers need a special education. *Music Educators Journal, 58*(8), 73–75.

Shehan, P. (1977). A brief study of music education for exceptional children in Ohio. *Contributions to Music Education, 5*, 47–53.

Sudman, S., & Bradburn, H. (1982). *Asking questions: A practical guide to questionnaire design.* San Francisco, CA: Jossey-Bass Publishers.

Thompson, K. (1982). Music for every child: Education of handicapped learners. *Music Educators Journal, 68*(8), 25–28.

White, L. D. (1981/82). A study of the attitudes of selected public school music educators toward the integration of handicapped students into music classes. *Contributions to Music Educaton, 9*, 36–47.

STUDY AND DISCUSSION QUESTIONS

1. Was the study by Gfeller, Hedden, and Darrow quantitative or qualitative? Why?

2. Was the study nonexperimental or experimental? Why?

3. Was the study descriptive or inferential? Why?

4. Did the study use parametric or nonparametric data?

5. What was the purpose of the brief review of literature that introduced the study?

6. Why were the research questions not stated as hypotheses?

7. What was the process for data collection?

8. How was validity established for the questionnaire?

9. What was the process used for sampling? What was the return rate?

10. How many teachers were sent the questionnaire?

11. What reliability coefficient was reported for the total questionnaire?

12. What result was reported for the analysis of variance?

13. At what level was the *F* statistic reported significant?

14. Why was a follow-up test needed for the ANOVA results?

15. What type of statistic is chi square, parametric or nonparametric?

16. The majority of statistics in the study were reported as what?

17. What were the three general findings of the study?

18. Why did the researchers not attempt to generalize the results?

19. What two recommendations did the authors makes for future research?

20. How does your current teaching environment relate to the findings of this study?

READING DESCRIPTIVE RESEARCH: PATTERNS OF INSTRUCTION

The following is an example of a descriptive study that uses a very basic form of data quantification: percentages. The simplicity of the data presentation, however, should not be confused with the value of the research. This article has much to say regarding the effectiveness of teaching styles.

Sequential Patterns of Instruction in Music

Cornelia Yarbrough, *Louisiana State University*
Harry E. Price, University of Alabama
Journal of Research in Music Education, 37(3), 179–187.

Reprinted by permission of MENC: The National Association for Music Education.
Copyright © 1989 by MENC.

Results of recent research support the notion that effective teaching involves the ability to sequence teaching and learning events in an optimal pattern of instruction. This optimal pattern, labeled *direct instruction* by Rosenshine (1976), was observed and first experimentally tested in reading and mathematics instructional situations at the primary level and later at the secondary level.

> The teaching of a task can be broken into three components: (1) before the task is presented, the teacher gets the child's attention; (2) the task is presented in a routine designed to teach the task and to require the children to respond to a "do it" signal; and (3) the children are reinforced for right responses and corrected on wrong responses. (Becker, Englemann, & Thomas, 1971, 306–315)

Comparisons of the direct instruction approach to other teaching approaches (e.g., open classroom model, cognitively oriented curriculum model, response education model, parent education model, behavior analysis model) clearly demonstrate its superiority in terms of producing student achievement of basic skills, cognitive understandings, and positive attitudes toward learning. Furthermore, teachers who were viewed as effective in helping students learn were those who were engaged in direct instruction (Berliner & Rosenshine, 1976; Brophy, 1979; Good & Brophy, 1974; Medley, 1977; Powell, 1978; Rosenshine, 1976, 1979).

Direct instruction requires that a great deal of time be spent on academic activities and that teachers provide immediate and relative feedback using praise. The earliest model for direct instruction defined interactive units of teaching in which the sequential order of events, or patterns of instruction, was of paramount importance. Specifically, the pattern began with the teacher's presentation of the task to be learned, followed by student interaction with the task and the teacher, and solidified by immediate praise or corrective feedback related to the task presented (Becker, Englemann, & Thomas, 1971).

Results of recent studies in music have substantiated the presence of the direct instruction model in elementary music teaching (Moore, 1981; Rosenthal, 1982) and ensemble rehearsals (Yarbrough & Price, 1981). Early research revealed a significantly greater amount of intonational improvement when children were given instruction and contingent reinforcement, versus no instruction and noncontingent reinforcement (Madsen & Madsen, 1972). Later, researchers found that ensemble conductors who used a sequential pattern of instruction with musical task presentation followed by student performance of the task and immediate, related reinforcement were most effective in producing good performances, a high rate of student attentiveness, and positive student attitudes (Price, 1983). Results of other research showed that students clearly favored a teaching style in which the teacher structured a music concept and presented it verbally, allowed an opportunity for students to respond, and reinforced student responses (Jellison & Wolfe, 1987; Price, 1983). Jellison and Kostka (1987) studied elementary students' written recall of teaching content in music teaching cycles. Results indicated that the information recalled was specific musical information (as compared to nonspecific social information).

Music research isolating the effect of the complete and correct teaching cycle on student behavior is scant because, to date, the observation and control of the cycle has been difficult and cumbersome. The complexities involved in studying teaching effectiveness are recognized, and various researchers continue to grapple with these problems toward the goal of enabling those who train teachers to use complete, correct cycles so that effects may be studied. Although efforts toward this end have been unsuccessful up to now, progress has been made in the observation and isolation of the effects of each of the three components of the complete teaching cycle—teacher presentation of musical information (verbalization), student response (participation), and reinforcement (approvals versus disapprovals).

Verbalization used in presenting musical information have been analyzed in recent research. Verbal-technical directions, demonstration/modeling, questioning, and instruction concerning musical elements (e.g., rhythm, dynamics, pitch) have been counted and timed (carpenter, 1987; Moore, 1987; Thurman, 1978). Several researchers have examined the use of teaching time in music classes and rehearsals. Thurman (1978) analyzed five choral rehearsals and found that the conductors devoted approximately 40% of their rehearsal time to verbal communications. In other research, observers found that experienced teachers gave fewer directions than inexperienced teachers (Wanger & Strul, 1979). In general, research results suggest that verbal behavior should be kept to a minimum, since it seems to be associated with increased student off-task behavior (Forsythe, 1977; Yarbrough & Price, 1981).

Furthermore, research in music has shown the effectiveness of active participation by students in increasing attentiveness and creating better attitudes toward instruction (Yarbrough & Price, 1981). Students were more on-task while involved in music activities compared to involvement in other academic work regardless of the teaching style used (Forsythe, 1977; Madsen &Alley, 1979; Sims, 1986; Spradling, 1985).

The effectiveness of the praise component of the model is well documented in music research, which demonstrates that student attentiveness is better under highly approving teachers than under highly disapproving ones (Forsythe, 1975; Kuhn, 1975) and that approval reinforcement significantly increased positive attitudes toward choral rehearsals (Murray, 1975). Still other researchers have supported using specific or descriptive praise as reinforcement following student responses (Madsen & Madsen, 1983; Madsen & Yarbrough, 1985). In spite of the overwhelming evidence of the efficacy of praise, recent descriptive research data showed that teacher-conductors were more disapproving than approving and that theses disapprovals were more likely to be directed at musical behaviors than at social behaviors (Carpenter, 1987).

Although active participation and reinforcement have produced greater attentiveness and more positive attitudes, the presence of each component in the teaching cycle (presentation of task, student response, and reinforcement) in the correct sequence may be important in producing musical achievement (Jellison & Kostka, 1987; Jellison & Wolfe, 1987; Price, 1983). A large volume of research in education and a relatively few studies in music education substantiate a theory of effective teaching that proposes that effective teaching involves the application of interactive units of teaching in which the sequential order of events, or pattern of instruction, is of utmost importance. Specifically, the pattern begins with the teacher's presentation of the task to be learned, followed by student interaction with the task and the teachers. Student learning was then solidified by immediate praise or corrective feedback. Therefore, the purpose of this study was to determine whether music teachers were applying in their own classrooms what has been demonstrated through research to be effective teaching. Specifically, rehearsals of experienced and preparatory instrumental and choral teachers were analyzed to determine how much time was being spent in various activities and whether teachers were using the correct sequence of teacher presentation of task, student response, and reinforcement. Comparisons of these observations to the research-established theoretical model of effect teaching were made to determine the potential for student achievement, attitude, and attentiveness.

Procedure

Subjects were freshman music education majors ($n = 30$), sophomore music education majors ($n = 19$), experienced instrumental teachers ($n = 15$), and experienced choral music teachers ($n = 15$). Freshman music education majors were videotaped teaching a song to preschool children; sophomores were trained to use direct instruction techniques (teacher presentation of musical task followed by student response and teacher reinforcement) and videotaped rehearsing their peers; and experienced instrumental and vocal teachers were videotaped in the regular rehearsal rooms at the normal rehearsal times. Experienced teachers were from New York, Georgia, Florida, Alabama, and Louisiana. Students were enrolled in music education degree programs at the University of Alabama, Tuscaloosa; Louisiana State University, Baton Rouge; and Florida State University, Tallahassee.

Verbatim typescripts ($N = 79$) of each of the above teaching situations were prepared. The typescripts were used to analyze, count, and time units of teaching and student performance. Units of teaching were categorized as teacher presentation of a task, student response, or teacher reinforcement.

Teacher presentation was coded "1" and was divided into subcategories as follows: 1a = academic musical task presentation (explaining musical aspects of the score, describing how the music is to be performed); 1s = social task presentation (telling students how to behave, presenting rules, planning social activities); 1d = giving directions (telling students who will play/sing, where to begin playing/singing); 1dc = counting beats, usually ending in "reading, play/sing," commonly known in other subjects areas as "do it" signals; 1q = questioning (asking students questions about musical, social, or directional tasks); and 1o = interruptions in rehearsal such as teacher off-task statements and intercom announcements.

Student response was coded "2" and was divided into three subcategories, which were coded and defined as follows: 2p = performance by the entire ensemble or by sections; 2v = verbal response; and 2nv = nonverbal response.

Teacher reinforcement was coded "3" and was divided into two subcategories: 3va = verbal academic or social approval (positive statement about student behavior); and 3vd = verbal academic or social disapproval (negative statement about student behavior). Errors of reinforcement (such as approving of inappropriate behavior and disapproving of appropriate behavior) and specificity of reinforcement were also noted.

Teaching cycles were then analyzed for correct sequencing and content. All cycles that followed a 1–2–3 sequence without error were considered correct. Cycle mistakes occurred (a) when cycles contained only directions with no musical task content; (b) when directions interrupted the flow between musical task presentation and student performance; (c) when reinforcement was not related to the task presented; and/or (d) when a reinforcement mistake occurred.

An independent observer completed reliability observation for 25% of the videotaped teachers. Reliability was computed using the formula of agreements divided by agreements plus disagreements. Average reliability across all categories and teachers was .94 with a range of reliability from .74 to .99.

Results

Using the direct instruction-theoretical model for effective teaching as a guide, the authors calculated (in seconds) the time spent in correct and incorrect teaching cycles, presentation of musical tasks, directions, presentation of social information, questioning, classroom interruptions, student performance, student verbalization, student nonverbal responses, teacher approval/disapprovals, and specific/nonspecific reinforcement for experienced band and choral directors, trained sophomore music education majors, and freshman music education majors. Percentage of time spent during each rehearsal was computed for each category (see Table 1).

Table 1 Percentage of Time Spent in Teaching-Pattern Components

Components of Patterns	Band	Chorus	Teachers Sophomores (trained)	Freshmen (untrained)
Cycles to Teaching				
Correct	18.39	34.52	36.51	70.25
Incorrect	81.61	65.48	63.91	29.75
Presentation of Tasks	43.54	40.98	46.74	52.96
Musical information	18.11	17.22	26.47	18.75
Directions	20.19	16.30	16.75	20.36
Social information	0.56	1.23	0.91	2.08
Questioning	1.33	1.99	1.80	0.99
Interruptions	3.35	4.24	0.81	10.78
Student Responses	47.91	53.06	45.60	40.88
Performing	45.95	49.23	42.26	37.36
Verbalizing	1.44	2.65	2.79	3.45
Nonverbal responses	0.52	1.18	0.55	0.07
Reinforcement	8.55	5.96	7.65	6.16
Approvals	1.62	2.44	5.60	5.47
Disapprovals	6.93	3.52	2.05	0.69
Approval/disapproval ratio	19/81	41/5	73/27	89/11
Specific/nonspecific ratio	70/30	59/41	57/43	47/53

Within the category of presentation of tasks, an almost equal amount of time was spent giving directions as compared to presenting musical tasks except in the trained sophomore group. The sophomores spent approximately 10% more time presenting musical tasks than giving directions. There was little attention to the presentation of social information and little questioning. Interruptions seemed to be numerous during rehearsals conducted by experienced teachers and by freshmen but were negligible during rehearsals conducted by sophomores.

Student responses for all groups were mostly performance-oriented, with few verbalizations and nonverbal responses. Almost half of the rehearsal time for all groups was spent in student performance. Interestingly, the percentage of time spent in giving directions plus the time spent in student performance equals well over half of the total rehearsal time (band = 66.14; chorus = 65.53; sophomores = 59.01; freshmen = 57.72).

Very little time, comparatively, was spent on reinforcement. If one considers the presentation of musical information and reinforcement for the correct performance of the musical task presented to be the primary components of teaching in the rehearsal situation, then it would seem that more structured practice than actual teaching occurred in the rehearsals observed. The percentage of time spent in presenting musical information plus the time spent in appropriate reinforcements was little more than one-fourth of the total rehearsal time except in the case of the sophomores (band = 26.66; chorus = 23.18; sophomores = 34.12; freshmen = 24.91).

Experienced teachers were highly disapproving, while preparatory teachers were highly approving. All groups were more specific when using disapprovals as reinforcement.

Discussion

The purpose of this study was to observe and analyze regular rehearsal situations and to determine whether music teachers were applying the results of research that demonstrates that there is a pattern of teaching (i.e., direct instruction) that results in high levels of student achievement, attitude, and attentiveness. Thus, occurrences of those variables of teaching effectiveness, as defined by the direct instruction model, were timed. Percentages of time spent for each component of the three-part sequential pattern of instruction (task presentation, student response, and reinforcement) were computed (see Table 1).

The presentation of musical information in rehearsals is occurring at a very slow rate (less than 20% for all groups except the trained sophomores). The ability to speak appropriately about the musical score to students and to describe creatively what the music should sound like to young students is an art that may not have been developed in teacher training programs or through experience. Experienced teachers were very conscientious about catching the mistakes of students.

It was particularly disturbing to observe this high rate of disapproval among the experienced teachers. Numerous research studies have demonstrated that disapproval is not an effective feedback technique and, indeed, may even be counterproductive. The alternative, according to the theoretical model of direct instruction, may be to present corrective feedback. For example, instead of verbally punishing students for wrong notes, one might point out the correct notes and provide another opportunity for the student to get the wrong ones right. Also, a correct model might be presented to students to help them learn the musical task. Regardless, the authors recommend that those responsible for music teaching training programs examine the results of research in direct instruction and consider the importance of *initiating* student responses rather than simply *reacting* to them.

In addition, there seems to be too much extraneous verbalization, primarily in giving directions. Over half of the rehearsal time in settings examined in this study was devoted to structured practice, i.e., the teacher gave directions regarding where to begin and who should play, then set tempo by counting one or more measures aloud (usually ending in "Ready, play/sing"). Subsequently, students would play until stopped by the teacher. This pattern of giving instructions without musical information and cueing the response of students was the most common pattern observed among all groups of teachers.

The ability of sophomore and freshmen to maintain a highly positive reinforcement ratio is encouraging. However, specifying approvals is a skill that needs attention by these students as well as by experienced teachers. In addition, when an increase in the amount of musical information presented is achieved, a concomitant decrease in directions and increases in the amount of positive reinforcement must be sought.

Mistakes in correct sequencing (i.e., cycle mistakes) occurred most often in two ways: (a) when directions were given (that is, students' attention was focused on a particular place in the musical score), then musical information was presented followed by a "ready play/sing" signal, students played/sang, and the teacher stopped them with a disapproval for incorrect performance of something not presented to them before they responded; and (b) when musical information was given and then followed by a long list of directions concerning where students were to begin and who was to play. In the first instance, it would seem appropriate to recycle the objective and to give corrective feedback to those who had not. In the second instance, the lengthy list of directions disrupted the students' concentration on the musical information given. It might have been difficult for them to remember the musical task. Often, we select music that is so logistically difficult that we may be forced to spend too much time in "gathering the forces" and consequently have little time left to address musical issues.

Give the amount of research data supporting the use of complete and correct teaching cycles, the authors believe it is of paramount importance to develop techniques for teaching prospective teachers to present musical information, allow student response time, and appropriately reinforce the acquisition of the information. Future research will examine more closely the content and frequency of occurrence of musical information presented by experienced teachers toward the goal of developing training models for student teachers. In addition, it may be necessary to examine differences among teachers' reinforcement patterns in relation to ages of children being taught. Finally, the authors of this study must express appreciation and admiration for the experienced teachers who so graciously submitted themselves to such close scrutiny. These teachers also share the belief that, through research, we may be able to improve the quality of teaching in music education settings to enhance students' achievement, attentiveness, and attitudes.

REFERENCES

Becker, W. C., Englemann, S., & Thomas, D. R. (1971). *Teaching: A course in applied psychology.* Chicago: Science Research Associates.

Berliner, D. C. & Rosenshine, B. (1976). *The acquisition of knowledge in the classroom. Beginning Teacher Evaluation Study: Technical Report IV-1.* San Francisco, CA: Far West Laboratory for Educational Research and Development. (ERIC Document Reproduction Service No. ED 146 158)

Brophy, J. E. (1979). Teacher behavior and its effects. *Journal of Educational Psychology, 71,* 733–750.

Carpenter, R. A. (1987, March). A descriptive analysis of relationships between verbal behaviors of teacher conductors and ratings of selected junior high and senior high school band rehearsals. Paper presented at the Research in Music Behavior Symposium, Logan, Utah.

Forsythe, J. L. (1975). The effect of teacher approval, disapproval, and errors on student attentiveness: music versus classroom teachers. In C. K. Madsen, R. D. Greer, & C. H. Madsen, Jr. (Eds.), *Research in music behavior.* New York: Teachers College Press, 49–55.

Forsythe, J. L. (1977). Elementary student attending behavior as a function of classroom activities. *Journal of Research in Music Education, 25,* 228–239.

Good, T. L., & Brophy, J. E. (1974). Changing teacher and student behavior: An empirical investigation. *Journal of Educational Psychology, 66,* 390–405.

Jellison, J. A., & Kostka, M. J. (1987, March). Student or teacher content within music teaching units. Paper presented at the Research in Music Behavior Symposium, Logan, Utah.

Jellison, J. A., & Wolfe, D. E. (1987). Verbal training effects on teaching units: An exploratory study of music teaching antecedents and consequences. In C. K. Madesen & C. A. Prickett (Eds.), *Applications of research in music behavior*. Tuscaloosa, AL: University of Alabama Press.

Kuhn, T. L. (1975). The effect of teacher approval and disapproval on attentiveness, musical achievement, and attitude of fifth grade students. In C. K. Madsen, R. D. Greer, & C. H. Madsen, Jr. (Eds.), *Research in music behavior*. New York: Teachers College Press, 40–48.

Madsen, C. H. Jr., & Madsen, C. K. (1983). *Teaching/Discipline: Behavioral principles toward a positive approach*. Raleigh, NC: Contemporary Publishing.

Madsen, C. K., & Alley, J. M. (1979). The effect of reinforcement on attentiveness: A comparison of behaviorally trained music therapists and other professionals with implications for competency-based academic preparation. *Journal of Music Therapy, 16*, 70–82.

Madsen, C. K., & Madsen, C. H., J., (1972). Selection of music listening or candy as a function of contingent versus noncontingent reinforcement and scale singing. *Journal of Music Therapy, 9*, 190–198.

Madsen, C. K., and Yarbrough, C. (1985). *Competency-based music education*. Raleigh, NC: Contemporary Publishing.

Medley, D. M. (1977). Teacher competence and teacher effectiveness. A review of process-product research. Washington, DC: American Association of Colleges for Teacher Education. (ERIC Document Reproduction Service No. ED 143 629).

Moore, R. S. (1981). Comparative use of teaching time by American and British elementary music specialists. *Bulletin of the Council for Research in Music Education, 66–67*, 62–68.

Moore, R. S. (1987, March). The use of rehearsal time by a model conductor and children's choir. Paper presented at the Research in Music Behavior Symposium, Logan, Utah.

Murray, K. C. (1975). The effect of teacher approval/disapproval on musical performance, attentiveness, and attitude of high school choruses. In C. K. Madsen, R. D. Greer, & C. H. Madsen, Jr. (Eds.), *Research in music behavior*, New York: Teachers College Press, 165–180.

Powell, M. (1978). Research on teaching. *The Educational Forum, 43*, 27–37.

Price, H. E. (1983). The effect of conductor academic task presentation, conductor reinforcement, and ensemble practice on performers' musical achievement, attentiveness, and attitude. *Journal of Research in Music Education, 31*, 245–257.

Rosenshine, B. V. (1976). Recent research on teaching behaviors and student achievement. Journal of Teacher Education, *27*, 61–64.

Rosenshine, B. V. (1979). Content, time, and direct instruction. In P. L. Peterson & H. J. Walberg, (Eds.), *Research on teaching*. Berkley, CA: McCutchan Publishing, 28–56.

Rosenthal, R. K. (1982). *A data-based approach to elementary general music teacher preparation*. Unpublished doctoral dissertation, Syracuse University.

Sims, W. L. (1986). The effect of high versus low teacher affect and passive versus active student activity during music listening on preschool children's attention, piece preference, time spent listening, and piece recognition. *Journal of Research in Music Education, 34*, 173–191.

Spradling, R. L. (1985). The effect of timeout from performance on attentiveness and attitude of university band students. *Journal of Research in Music Education, 33*, 123–127.

Thurman, V. L. (1978, April). *A frequency and time description of selected rehearsal behaviors used by five choral conductors*. Paper presented at the MENC National Biennial In-Service Conference, Chicago.

Wagner, M. J., & Strul, E. (1979). Comparisons of beginning versus experienced elementary music educators in the use of teaching time. *Journal of Research in Music Education*, 27, 113–125.

Yarbrough, C., & Price, H. E. (1981). Prediction of performer attentiveness based on rehearsal activity and teacher behavior. *Journal of Research in Music Education*, 29, 209–217.

STUDY AND DISCUSSION QUESTIONS

1. Did this research involve parametric or nonparametric data?

2. How was the review of literature related to the purpose of the study?

3. What was the purpose of the study?

4. What did the statistic $N = 79$ indicate?

5. How were the data collected and presented?

6. Why would the freshmen (untrained) music education majors show the greatest percentage of correct (70.25) cycles of teaching?

7. Why would experienced teachers be highly disapproving while preparatory teachers were highly approving?

8. What was the finding for the subjects' ability to speak appropriately about the score?

9. What did this study find regarding the amount of extraneous verbalization?

10. Why is it inappropriate to generalize the results of this study to a population?

SUGGESTED ACTIVITIES

1. Consider how a survey might be useful in finding information about your program.

2. Think of the ensemble directors you have experienced and their approaches to the rehearsal. Are there any that stand out in your mind as being especially effective rehearsal conductors? If yes, what made them outstanding? Did their approaches reflect any of the characteristics identified in the article by Yarbrough and Price?

CHAPTER 12

Quantitative Research

Experimental

The focus of this chapter is on experimental research in which treatment and control groups are part of the design. These studies are quantitative in nature; i.e., the empirical observations are presented in some form of numerical data. Quantitative research is based on the scientific method common to the natural sciences. True-experimental research involves assigning subjects to groups at random, while quasi-experimental design typically uses intact groups.

READING EXPERIMENTAL RESEARCH: A COMMENTARY

The following article is an example of experimental research in which subjects serve as their own control. This is quasi-experimental research—intact groups serve as subjects for treatment and control. One group of seventh-grade boys and one group of eighth-grade boys were each tested under two different singing conditions to determine if their singing responses (traditional and use of distinct vocal registers) would differ.

Vocal Registration as It Affects Vocal Range for Seventh- and Eighth-Grade Boys

Kenneth H. Phillips and Steven W. Emge, *The University of Iowa*
Journal of Research in Singing and Applied Vocal Pedagogy, 18(1/1994), 1–19.

Reprinted by permission of the International Association for Research in Singing.

The changing voice of the adolescent boy has been a persistent challenge to music educators. Early twentieth-century music educator John Dawson (1919) observed,

"So complicated is it that even today, after the lapse of centuries, it is misunderstood, neglected, and abused" (p. 7). The same remains true at the end of the twentieth century.

Phillips (1992a) relates seven different pedagogical approaches to the boy's changing voice. While similarities exist among these practices, differing opinions remain as to the best mode of instruction. This is due, in part, to the authors' views concerning the vocal limitations imposed upon the pubertal voice because of the voice change. This study addresses one such issue—the limits of vocal range for singing (highest to lowest pitch comfortably sung) among seventh- and eighth-grade boys.

Two basic "schools" of thought have been identified by Phillips (1992a) regarding the limits of vocal range for singing among adolescent boys. "School A" believes that the boy's voice changes rather predictably; it lowers gradually, losing some of its top pitches while slowly gaining more lower range. The pubertal boy's comfortable vocal range is limited to what might be called a mid-voice tessitura of an octave or less around middle C. This "school" is represented by such authors as Don Collns (1981), John Cooksey (1992), Irvin Cooper (1953), Duncan McKenzie (1956), and John Yarrington (1990).

"School B" believes that the boy's voice may change slowly or very quickly, and is not limited to a mid-voice comfort range of an octave or less. Authors in this school include Sally Hermann (1988), Frederick Mayer and Jack Sacher (1964a, 1964b), and Frederick Swanson (1977). These writers believe that wider singing ranges are possible for the pubertal boy when the boy is instructed in the proper use of his vocal registers.

The impact of vocal registers on singing range requires some understanding of how vocal registration is reflected in the singing voice. Vocal registers have been defined by Reid (1983) as "a group of like sounds or tones whose origin can be traced to a special kind of mechanical (muscular) action" (p. 296). This "mechanical action" involves a process by which the vocal folds become longer and thinner for higher pitches, and shorter and thicker for lower pitches. When the vocal folds vibrate in either of these modes, or a combination of both, the resulting sound waves couple with the vocal tract (pharynx and oral cavity) to produce "like sounds," which are heard as similar types of vocal quality.

There is strong scientific evidence to support the existence of vocal registers (Beard, 1980; Large, 1972; Reckford, 1982; Schoenhard and Hollien, 1982; Titze, 1983; Vennard, Hirano, and Ohala, 1970). Appelman (1967) states, "In the human voice, registration is a physiological and acoustical fact. Years of research . . . have contributed evidence of its existence and have verified that all voices have three registers that may be utilized in singing" (p. 86). These three registers have been commonly referred to as upper/head, middle, and lower/chest.

The process of puberty causes the male larynx to grow substantially (Kahane, 1975), which brings about a lowering of the male singing range by at least an octave. The soprano register (c^2 to c^3)[*] is basically lost because the vocal folds are becoming longer and thicker, while the pitches below middle C strengthen and extend downward into the mature male singing range. During this voice change (the "peak"

[*]Pitches are designated using c^1 as middle c.

of which is usually in the eighth grade), adolescent boys often experience vocal discomfort and voice "cracking." This is due to the readjustment of the muscles that govern the "mechanical action" of the vocal folds in response to vocal fold growth. The results are heard in changes of vocal registration as the pubertal boy learns to sing with different use of the vocal muscles.

Central to this study is how the adolescent boy learns to sing during the period of changing vocal registration. "School A" believes that physiological problems in the changing voice necessitates a "go slow" approach in which outer extremes of range are not exercised. Rather, the voice is kept in its "middle" register as it lowers gradually during puberty. This results in the use of only one vocal register (middle) and a rather limited vocal range. In contrast, "School B" believes that adolescent boys should be exercised vocally in all three vocal registers (upper, middle, and lower), resulting in a rather expansive vocal range. They do note, however, that for some boys, the middle register may be lost until such a time as the voice settles and becomes more stable. Hollien (1977) found that one-third to one-half of all subjects studied did not have overlapping lower and upper registers. "For these individuals there was a gap in the consecutive frequencies they could produce when they shifted out of one register toward the other" (p. 113).

Proponents of "School A"

One of the earliest proponents of the gradual, predictable lowering of the adolescent boy's voice was Duncan McKenzie (1956), who called his approach the "Alto-Tenor Plan." McKenzie taught that the boy's voice lowered to an alto-tenor range of g to g^1, then lowered to baritone. In senior high school the voice could raise to tenor, lower to bass, or remain a baritone. McKenzie advocated that boys with changing voices could sing the tenor part of four-voice music (SATB), but noted that the tenor would sound more like a low alto than a true tenor.

The dominant voice of "School A" in the 1950s and 1960s was that of Irvin Cooper, who used the word "cambiata" to denote the male changing voice. Cooper (1970), like McKenzie, believed that adolescent boys should sing within a limited middle vocal tessitura, and that no real bass or tenor voices existed in junior high. Unlike McKenzie, Cooper did not advocate that adolescent boys sing tenor, but rather, a special "cambiata" or changing voice part written for them.

Don Collins (1981) was a student of Irvin Cooper, and continued the work of his mentor. Collins founded the Cambiata Press in 1972 to produce choral music written specifically for the changing voice, especially the "cambiata" part. While Collins suggests that help for "uncertain singers" may be found in exercising the upper register voice, the vocalizes in his approach all remain within a five- or six-note mid-voice range (pp. 46–50).

John Cooksey (1984; 1992) was another student of Irvin Cooper, but unlike Collins, disagreed with the limitations of the "cambiata" voice part. In a series of four articles published in the *Choral Journal* (1977–1978), Cooksey presented a voice classification system that he called "The Contemporary Eclectic Approach for the Training of the Junior High School Male Changing Voice." This "system" identifies three changing voice parts, and Cooksey admonishes the teacher to move the adolescent boy from part to part as his voice lowers according to a rather slow and predictable pattern. Exercise of the upper register is to be avoided for fear of "hyper-functioning" of the larynx, and Cooksey's voice classification system has been advocated by several authors, including Barresi (1984), Rutkowski (1984), and Yarrington (1990).

Proponents of "School B"

Mayer and Sacher (1964a; 1964b) are among the first writers on the subject of the boy's changing voice to challenge the idea of limited vocal range. They suggest that many boys, when instructed in the proper use of their lower register, are capable of immediately producing tones a fourth, fifth, and sometimes a sixth lower than their initial range test might indicate. Mayer and Sacher note that limiting adolescent boys to a "cambiata" or "alto-tenor" range may be detrimental to the proper development of the singing voice. They further state that "the difference between our suggested tenor range (d-flat to g^1) and that advanced by proponents of the 'cambiata' theory is rather that the latter suggests an improperly taught lower register" (1964b, p. 10). In addition to developing the lower voice, Mayer and Sacher advocate the training of the "upper extension" of the boy's voice in order to promote the ability to move freely from the lower register to the upper, and vice versa.

Frederick Swanson (1982) was a leading authority on the adolescent male voice in the 1970s and 1980s. He stated that the voice change could occur slowly, or quickly within a few weeks. Swanson, like Mayer and Sacher, believed that limiting the vocal range of the adolescent boy did not fit the facts, and, like Hollien (1977), found that in a significant number of cases there might be blank areas around middle C where no tones can be produced. Swanson was famous for his boys' choruses in the Moline, Illinois, area.

Sally Hermann (1988), another proponent of "School B," agrees that the adolescent bass is real and can be developed. For the boy with changing voice, she advocates a "Voice-Pivoting Approach" whereby the boy switches voice parts as the notes of one part become difficult to sing comfortably. She also teaches that the boy's upper register must be strengthened and used by the adolescent male to realize the full potential of the singing range. It is, she states, the secret of developing the tenor voice.

Medical authorities Sataloff and Spiegel (1991) also believe that adolescent boys should keep the upper vocal register functioning throughout the voice change. They suggest vocalizing across the "break," from lower to upper register, without trying to blend the registers for awhile. "This produces a tolerable choral sound, and they can continue singing safely in whichever mode is most relaxed for any given note" (p. 60).

Phillips (1992a; 1992b) is a proponent of "School B." He states, "The parameter of vocal registration is one that is very important, especially when considering appropriate vocal ranges for young singers. In fact, most studies that have investigated children's singing ranges have not taken into account the influence of vocal registration on range, and the results of such studies must be viewed with caution" (1992a, p. 571). Based on the conflicting nature of the research findings that explore the adolescent male's changing voice. Phillips suggests that a greater emphasis on empirical research is needed in the profession.

Research on Voice Change

A wealth of literature is available on vocal registers and how they affect the vocal ranges of adults. Few studies, however, have addressed registration events in the voices of children and adolescents. Notable exceptions in the area of children's voices are studies by Brown (1988), and Wurgler (1990). Brown (1988) found that training students in the use of the upper register could increase the child's singing range. No research is known to have studied this phenomenon among adolescent boys.

Wurgler (1990) sought to confirm the existence of registers in children's voices. Based on measures of aural perception she states, "The singing voices of children do exhibit perceptually distinct registers, the production of which affects the usable singing range. Children can sing in chest register and in head register, the two primary registers of vocal production" (p. 140).

Most early research on the adolescent male's singing voice has been descriptive in nature (Beall, 1958; Ekstrom, 1959; Joseph, 1959). The researchers have presented information based on observations of "what is," as opposed to "what could be." One exception is a study by Swanson (1959).

Using a classic pretest–posttest quasi-experimental design, Swanson assigned general music classes of eighth-grade boys to either experimental or control groups. A yearlong training program was instituted for the experimental group, which consisted of daily vocalizes to help establish correct breath management, free the vocal tract, increase range, eliminate the voice "break," and increase vocal resonance. This was in addition to the regular general music curriculum (singing, listening, reading), which the control group received. Swanson found that the experimental group surpassed the control group in gaining control of the voice, retaining use of the treble register, eliminating the "break" between registers, and increasing overall vocal range (1959, p. 214).

Cooksey (1984) conducted a three-year descriptive study to classify the singing voices of adolescent males. The study built upon his previous work (Cooksey, 1977, 1978), and resulted in a revision of the ranges and tessituras of his six-stage sequence of voice development of the adolescent male. Cooksey (1984) reported that "range was the most effective criterion for classifying the voices in developmental stages" (p. 25). "The register and vocal quality criteria were not utilized in the development of the Index of Voice Classification; however, both factors were found to be very important in the voice maturation process" (p. 223). Cooksey's work is purely descriptive in nature, measuring male voices as he found them. It is not known the type of vocal training the subjects had prior to testing, if any, and how instruction in vocal registration might have influenced Cooksey's classification system.

Addressing vocal registration and its affect on vocal range, Cooksey (1984) states, "[B]y proper vocal training, the two registers can be melded together within the passagio [sic] (head region) and excessive tension and voice breaks can be avoided. The question, of course, is how this can best be achieved in the young male adolescent singer" (p. 40). Cooksey goes on to argue that "I do not believe that one should rely exclusively upon the falsetto register to extend range or consolidate the upper range" (p. 41). He proposes that the modal (lower) register be strengthened first, and that the music teacher attempt to find choral music that will allow the adolescent male to sing primarily in the modal register.

Wolverton (1985), like Cooksey, studied those vocal parameters that were the best predictors of adolescent voice classification. The author-designed "Individual Subject Profile" was used to identify the variables of range, register change, tessitura, and vocal quality. Thirty-nine high school directors were asked to view a videotape of students vocalizing, and then to classify the 40 eleventh- and twelfth-grade students (20 female and 20 males) as soprano, alto, tenor, or bass. Results indicated that "one of the main findings...was that tessitura emerged as an important predictor for both boys' and girls' singing voices" (p. 73). In addition, register shifts were found to be stronger predictors of appropriate voice classification than vocal range.

Chapman (1989) investigated the use of a "Vocal Behavior Training" methodology with adolescent boys. While the results were not significant, Chapman found in his review of literature "the lack of and the need for a viable method for training the male adolescent voice.... While many methodologies involved some analytic processes and modification skills, they mainly categorized or classified the voices during the various stages of change" (p. 64).

While the "action research" of Mayer and Sacher (1964a) lacks an empirical basis, their little "study" serves as the basis for the present investigation. Mayer and Sacher relate:

> In a summer camp where Dr. Mayer recently conducted the junior high school chorus, there was one 12-year-old boy singing soprano and five boys singing alto on the advice of their teachers. The five altos, when first tested, were capable of reaching about "a" below middle "c," but, when they were introduced to the use of the lower register in their voices, three of them were immediately capable of singing "d" below middle "c." One sang to "e flat" and the other maintained a bottom pitch of "a." ... The following morning, during the demonstration, the boy soprano sang as expected, but the five "altos" all sang with ease to "d" below middle "c." These voices did not develop overnight, but, by finding the use of the lower register, which was already a reality when the boys first came to the camp, they were able to sing about a fifth lower in a day's time. (p. 11).

Commentary

The authors introduce their study with a fairly long review of literature on the male changing voice. Two schools of thought are discussed and leading proponents of each are presented. "School A" believes that boys' vocal ranges are rather limited during the voice change period, while "School B" believes the opposite—boys can have wide or extended ranges if taught to use their vocal registers correctly. The authors conclude their introduction by citing the limited research that exists on the male adolescent voice change. The "action research" conducted by Mayer and Search sets up the design of the study.

The Article *(continued)*

Purpose of the Study

The present study was conducted to replicate, in an empirical design, the "experiment" of Mayer and Sacher (1964a) in determining the vocal ranges of seventh- and eighth-grade boys prior to and immediately following a brief period of vocal register modeling by the investigators. Specifically, the researchers wanted to know if adolescent boys could adapt quickly to using different adjustments of the vocal mechanism, and what impact such adjustments might have on the highest and lowest pitches of their vocal range.

Procedures

Subjects were 26 seventh- and 26 eighth-grade boys enrolled in choral programs at two different midwestern junior high schools. It was determined that the subjects in both schools had received no special training in register adjustment, and were relatively homogeneous with regards to vocal instruction. Both schools reflected the "cambiata" concept of Cooper, the boys being generally assigned to a "cambiata" part of most of the music in their repertoire.

   Prior to the testing the subjects were told by their respective choral directors that it was important to obtain vocal range information for each boy in the chorus, and that the researchers would collect the data. Each subject was given a form for use in charting his vocal range. The form listed all pitches from C up to c^3. For analysis purposes, each pitch was assigned a number: C = 1, C# = 2, D = 3, and so forth. Individual subjects were directed to one of two practice rooms, where the two researchers awaited them.

   To alleviate tension and to codify the data, researchers asked each subject their grade level, age, and how the year was going. Each subject was then told that the researcher was going to determine how high and low the subject could sing. The lower range was tested first; using the piano the researcher played the pitch c^1 and asked the subject to sing the pitch on an "ah" vowel. The exercise continued, descending by half-steps, until it was determined that the subject could no longer produce a comfortable musical pitch. The researcher then played a pitch that was three or four half-steps higher than the lowest pitch sung, and the subject again sang down to his lowest comfortable pitch until it was determined that it was indeed the lowest pitch the student could sing. The corresponding number was circled on the subject's range form.

   The upper range was then tested; starting at c^1 a three-note ascending arpeggio (1, 3, 5) was played, and the subject was instructed to sing the three pitches on an [u] vowel (oo). The pitch was raised by half-steps until it was determined that the subject could not sing comfortably. Going back several half-steps, the subject sang ascending arpeggios again until it was clear that the top of the singing range had been established. The pitch and corresponding number were registered on the subject's form. This process established each subject's traditional vocal range.

Each researcher then briefly discussed the vocal maturation process, explaining that the subject would soon be singing with an adult male voice, which may now be emerging. The lower/chest register was demonstrated by the investigator using what Phillips (1992b) calls a "lower wheelie." Subjects were directed to imitate the sound of an automobile engine with a dead battery; the subjects produced a low rolling pulse on "yah-a-a-ah." The researcher had each subject attempt the exercise several times to discover the sound of the "thicker" chest register. The lower pitch range again was measured as before with each subject aware of using a more distinct lower chest register, if possible.

The subjects were then led to find their upper/head register. The investigator explained that the upper voice could be found by imitating a siren, the sound of which demonstrated by the researcher on a vocal glissando. Each subject repeated the exercise several times until they were able to discover and make the "hook" into the upper register. Following this model, each subject's upper range was rechecked using the same procedure as for the pretest. Data for the posttest ranges were marked in red on the subject's form.

Commentary

The purpose of the study was to replicate Mayer and Sacher's "experiment" in a more controlled setting according to quasi-experimental research guidelines. Phillips and Emge proposed to compare the singing of seventh- and eighth-grade boys while the boys were singing in two modes: traditional (control) and distinct vocal registers (treatment). Each grade level represented a separate group for the analyses, and each group was compared to itself; grades were not compared to each other.

The boys in both grades met with the researchers individually (each researcher saw half the boys), and the boys were told that the researchers simply were interested in how their vocal ranges were progressing. First, each boy was asked to sing in his regular voice downwards and then upwards. This constituted the control condition. Then it was explained that boys their age were approaching or were into the voice change and that the researchers wanted to hear if a difference might exist in the vocal range of the boy if he could "find" and sing in more adult male voices (registers). This constituted the treatment condition. Each investigator modeled the "chest" voice for the boy using a "dead-battery" technique and asked each boy to respond in like manner. Once the "chest" voice was established, the boy was tested again for the lower vocal range. Each investigator then modeled the upper vocal register for the boy, using a glissando technique in the upper voice. Once this was established, the boy was tested in this register for the upper vocal range. Numbers were assigned to each lowest and highest pitch sung by each voice, and these were the data submitted for computer analysis for each grade.

The Article (*continued*)

Results

The seventh-grade descriptive data for the tests of traditional and use of distinct registers are presented in Table 1. Each score is presented as a pitch number followed by the actual pitch in parentheses. The traditional and knowledge (of registers) ranges in column six indicate the number of half-steps in the total range (i.e., the highest pitch score minus the lower pitch score plus 1). The total gain score in column seven is the difference between the traditional and distinct register scores in column four, and represents the total number of half-steps gained in vocal range between the two vocal-range tests.

Table 1 Seventh Grade Traditional and Use of Distinct Registers for Highest Pitch, Lowest Pitch, and Total Gain Scores

Subject	Traditional Lowest Pitch	Registers Lowest Pitch	Traditional Highest Pitch	Registers Highest Pitch	Traditional Registers Range	Total Gain Half-Steps
701	20(g)	20(g)	35(a♯¹)	36(b¹)	16–17	1
702	23(a♯)	21(g♯)	42(f²)	43(f♯²)	20–23	3
703	20(g)	20(g)	39(d²)	40(f♯²)	20–21	1
704	22(a)	21(g♯)	40(d♯²)	40(d♯²)	19–20	1
705	18(f)	18(f)	41(e²)	43(f♯²)	24–26	2
706	22(a)	22(a)	36(b¹)	36(b¹)	15–15	0
707	18(f)	17(e)	36(b¹)	39(d²)	19–23	4
708	22(a)	21(g♯)	39(d²)	40(d♯²)	18–20	2
709	17(e)	17(e)	39(d²)	40(d♯²)	23–24	1
710	25(c¹)	23(a♯)	39(d²)	39(d²)	15–17	2
711	18(f)	18(f)	41(e²)	43(f♯²)	24–26	2
712	18(f)	17(e)	43(f♯²)	43(f♯²)	26–27	1
713	12(B)	12(B)	24(b)	39(d)	13–28	15
714	08(G)	08(G)	20(g)	20(g)	13–13	0
715	14(c♯)	13(c)	41(e²)	43(f♯²)	28–31	3
716	19(f♯)	15(d)	35(a♯¹)	37(c²)	17–23	6
717	20(g)	16(d♯)	41(e²)	43(f♯²)	22–28	6
718	19(f♯²)	19(f♯)	38(c♯²)	41(e²)	20–23	3
719	10(A)	08(G)	41(e²)	41(e²)	34–36	2
720	20(g)	16(d♯)	41(e²)	42(f²)	22–27	5
721	18(f)	09(G♯)	42(f²)	44(g²)	25–36	11
722	20(g)	19(f♯)	41(e²)	42(f²)	22–24	2
723	19(f♯)	16(d♯)	41(e²)	42(f²)	23–27	4
724	16(d♯)	15(d)	39(d²)	43(f♯²)	24–29	5
725	18(f)	13(c)	44(g²)	44(g²)	27–32	5
726	10(A)	06(F)	25(c¹)	41(e²)	16–36	20

The means and standard deviations for the seventh-grade subjects' lowest and highest pitches sung (traditional and with distinct registers) are presented in Table 2. The seventh-grade boys had an average "low" pitch of "f" on the traditional measure, and a "d♯" on the distinct registers measure, a difference of two half-steps, or a major second. For the highest pitch, the seventh-grade boys average a "c♯^{2}" on the traditional measure, and "d♯^{2}" on the register measure, a difference of four half-steps, or a major third.

Table 2 Means and Standard Deviations for Seventh-Grade Traditional and Registers Pitches

	Traditional Lowest Pitch	Registers Lowest Pitch	Traditional Highest Pitch	Registers Highest Pitch
Mean	18(f)	16(d♯)	38(c♯^{2})	40(d♯^{2})
SD	4.15	4.62	6.015	4.74

The means and standard deviations for the seventh-grade subjects' traditional and register total ranges and gain are presented in Table 3. The average traditional range was a score of 20.96 pitches, or almost an octave and a sixth. The average register range was a score of 25.08 pitches, or two octaves. The total difference in range from traditional to register was 4.12 half-steps, or slightly more than a major third.

Table 3 Means and Standard Deviations for Seventh-Grade Traditional and Registers Total Range and Total Range Gain (in half-steps)

	Traditional Total Range	Registers Total Range	Total Gain for Range
Mean	20.96	25.08	4.12
SD	4.98	6.17	

The eighth-grade descriptive data for the tests of traditional and use of distinct registers are presented in Table 4. The setup of Table 4 is the same as for Table 1.

The means and standard deviations for the eighth-grade subjects' lowest and highest pitches sung (traditional and use of distinct registers) are presented in Table 5. The eighth-grade boys had an average "low" pitch of "c♯" on the traditional measure, and a "B" on the registers measure, a difference of two half-steps. For the highest pitch, the eighth-grade boys average a "a♯^{1}" on the traditional measure, and "d^2" on the registers measure, a difference of four half-steps, or a major third.

Table 4 Eighth-Grade Traditional and Use of Distinct Registers for Highest Pitch, Lowest Pitch, and Total Gain Scores

Subject	Traditional Lowest Pitch	Registers Lowest Pitch	Traditional Highest Pitch	Registers Highest Pitch	Traditional Registers Range	Total Gain Half-Steps
801	15(d)	13(c)	42(f^2)	43(f$_\sharp^2$)	28–31	3
802	17(e)	15(d)	43(f$_\sharp^2$)	43(f$_\sharp^2$)	27–29	2
803	11(A$_\sharp$)	11(A$_\sharp$)	36(b^1)	39(d^2)	26–29	3
804	11(A$_\sharp$)	11(A$_\sharp$)	36(b^1)	37(c^2)	26–20	1
805	7(F$_\sharp$)	7(F$_\sharp$)	36(b^1)	36(b^1)	30–30	0
806	13(c)	13(c)	29(e^1)	34(a^1)	17–22	5
807	12(B)	12(B)	32(g^1)	41(e^2)	21–30	9
808	17(e)	17(e)	39(d^2)	42(f^2)	23–26	3
809	18(f)	17(e)	39(d^2)	44(g^2)	22–28	6
810	6(F)	5(E)	34(a^1)	34(a^1)	29–30	1
811	13(c)	9(G$_\sharp$)	31(f$_\sharp^1$)	36(b^1)	19–28	9
812	7(F$_\sharp$)	5(E)	30(f^1)	41(e^2)	24–36	13
813	12(B)	7(F$_\sharp$)	32(g^1)	32(g^1)	21–26	5
814	18(f)	17(e)	20(g)	20(g)	13–13	1
815	20(g)	19(f$_\sharp$)	38(c$_\sharp^2$)	38(c$_\sharp^2$)	19–20	1
816	21(g$_\sharp$)	21(g$_\sharp$)	35(a$_\sharp^1$)	39(d^2)	18–19	1
817	16(d$_\sharp$)	16(d$_\sharp$)	39(d^2)	40(d$_\sharp^2$)	24–25	1
818	7(F$_\sharp$)	7(f$_\sharp$)	28(d$_\sharp^1$)	41(e^2)	22–35	13
819	12(B)	10(A)	29(e^1)	39(d^2)	18–30	12
820	11(A$_\sharp$)	9(G$_\sharp$)	26(c$_\sharp^1$)	26(c$_\sharp^1$)	16–18	2
821	11(A$_\sharp$)	08(G)	42(f^2)	44(g^2)	32–37	5
822	15(d)	15(d)	34(a^1)	40(d$_\sharp^2$)	20–26	6
823	20(g)	17(e)	35(a$_\sharp^1$)	44(g^2)	16–28	12
824	13(c)	12(B)	40(d$_\sharp^2$)	41(e^2)	28–30	2
825	18(f)	17(e)	38(c$_\sharp^2$)	40(d$_\sharp^2$)	21–24	3
826	14(c$_\sharp$)	14(c$_\sharp$)	32(g^1)	44(f$_\sharp^2$)	19–30	11

Table 5 Means and Standard Deviations for Eighth-Grade Traditional and Distinct Registers Pitches

	Traditional Lowest Pitch	Registers Lowest Pitch	Traditional Highest Pitch	Registers Highest Pitch
Mean	14(c$_\sharp$)	12(B)	35(a$_\sharp^1$)	39(d^2)
SD	4.25	4.48	4.83	4.24

The means and standard deviations for the eighth-grade subjects' traditional and registers total ranges and gain are presented in Table 6. The average traditional range was a score of 22.73 pitches, or almost an octave and a minor seventh. The average registers range was a score of 26.96 pitches, or two octaves and a minor third. The total difference in range from traditional to use of distinct registers was 5.00 half-steps, or a perfect fourth.

Table 6 Means and Standard Deviations for Eighth-Grade Traditional and Distinct Registers Total Range and Total Range Gain (in half-steps)

	Traditional Total Range	Registers Total Range	Total Gain for Range
Mean	22.73	27.73	5.00
SD	4.51	4.76	

Results of paired samples t-tests (Table 7) on traditional and distinct registers for vocal ranges of seventh-grade boys show significant differences for highest pitch ($p < .006$), lowest pitch ($p < .001$), and total difference in range ($p < .001$). In each case the subjects averaged a higher and lower vocal pitch on the use of distinct registers measure, and an overall increase in vocal range between traditional and use of registers.

Table 7 Results of Paired Samples t-Tests Between Traditional and Distinct Registers for Ranges of Seventh-Grade Boys

	Traditional Registers Highest Pitch	Traditional Registers Lowest Pitch	Traditional Registers Total Range
t	2.976*	4.177**	4.512**
df	25	25	25

*Significant at the .006 level.
**Significant at the .001 level.

Results of paired samples t-tests (Table 8) on traditional use of registers for vocal ranges of eighth-grade boys show significant differences for highest pitch, lowest pitch, and total difference in range, all at the $p < .001$ level of significance. In each case the subjects averaged a higher and lower vocal pitch on the knowledge measure, and an overall increase in vocal range between traditional and knowledge of registers.

Table 8 Results of Paired-Samples t-Tests Between Traditional and Distinct Registers for Ranges of Eighth-Grade Boys

	Traditional Registers Highest Pitch	Traditional Registers Lowest Pitch	Traditional Registers Total Range
t	4.638*	4.386*	5.944*
df	25	25	25

*Significant at the .001 level.

Commentary

Descriptive data for the seventh-grade boys are presented in Table 1 (raw scores) and Tables 2 and 3 (means and standard deviations). Table 2 shows that for seventh-grade boys the lowest pitch sung in the traditional (control) response was "f" below middle c. When using the distinct register response the mean pitch dropped to "d♯" below middle c, or one whole step. The highest pitch when sung in the traditional and distinct register responses increased from "c♯^{2}" to "d♯^{2}," again one whole step. The total range gain for seventh-grade subjects was 4.12 half-steps (Table 3).

The descriptive data for eighth-grade boys are presented in Table 4 (raw scores) and Tables 5 and 6 (means and standard deviations). Table 5 shows the lowest pitch sung in the traditional voice to be "c♯" below middle c, following a whole step to "B" using the register approach. The highest pitch sung traditionally was "a♯^{1}," expanding a major third to "d^2" when using the distinct register approach. The eighth-grade subjects had a slightly larger total range gain of 5.0 half-steps.

Paired-samples t-tests were used to determine significant differences between means (treatment and control conditions) for both groups separately. Table 7 reports significant differences for the seventh-grade boys on all three pitch measures: highest pitch ($t = 2.976$, $p < .006$), lowest pitch ($t = 4.177$, $p < .001$), and total range ($t = 4.512$, $p < .001$). Inspection of means in Tables 2 and 3 shows that the boys sang with higher and lower range and with greater total range when using the distinct register approach. Similar results for eighth-grade boys are reported in Table 8.

The Article (continued)

Conclusions

Based on the results of this study, the following conclusions are presented:

1. Distinct use the upper register of the voice for the adolescent male has a significant effect in increasing the upper pitch of the vocal range.

2. Distinct use of the lower or chest register of the voice for the adolescent male has a significant effect in increasing the lowest pitch of the vocal range.

3. Distinct use of the upper and lower registers of the voice for the adolescent male has a significant effect increasing overall vocal range.

Discussion

The present study was conducted to determine the vocal ranges of seventh- and eighth-grade boys under two conditions: traditional and use of distinct vocal registers. The results support the extended range theory advocated by proponents of "School B" and Mayer and Sacher (1964a, 1964b), which suggests that the adolescent boy's voice displays a wider range through distinct use of upper and lower registers.

The most dramatic increases were revealed between the traditional measure and the registers measure on highest pitch. For example, subject 726 (see Table 1) had a traditional highest pitch of 25 (c^1), while his registers score increased to 41 (e^2), an increase of 17 half-steps. The majority of subjects, however, increased the upper pitch by two or three half-steps. Only 13 of all 52 subjects showed no increase for highest pitch.

While the lowering of range was not as dramatic, it was significantly different for both grades. As might be expected, the eighth-grade boys had a lower average range for both the traditional and registers approaches than that of the seventh-grade boys. However, both groups lowered their vocal ranges when singing in chest-voice production. The seventh-grade boys went from a traditional pitch of "f" to a distinct register pitch of "d♯," while the eighth-grade boys sang from a traditional pitch of "c♯" to a "B" when singing in the chest register.

Nine of the seventh graders sang no lower using the distinct registers approach, but one subject (#721) sang from an "f" to a low "G♯," a dramatic drop of nine half-steps. Ten of the eighth-grade boys sang no lower when using the chest-voice production. The greatest increase was for subject #813, who sang a low "B" using the traditional approach, and a low "F♯" using the registers approach. The majority of seventh- and eighth-grade boys increased their lower vocal ranges by one to three half-steps.

The results of this study support the belief of Swanson (1982) that the concept of a limited vocal range for all adolescent males does not fit the facts. The subjects in this study were capable of demonstrating an average range of two octaves when they were singing in both lower and upper registers.

Mayer and Sacher (1964b) state that "a boy singing in the 'cambiata' classification with a production based primarily on the upper register, or his 'boy's voice,' will be interfering with the very change which is taking place" (p. 10). Rather than sing the notes below "e^1" in a boy's vocal quality or as an alto, the voice must be treated like a tenor, shifting more into the chest register as it descends. "It is primarily a difference in quality rather than range. In working in the general tessitura of "a-flat" to "e-flat^1," the boy will be encouraged to develop his lower register, which will be the voice he uses as a man" (Mayer and Sacher, 1964b, p. 10).

This study sought to determine if wider vocal ranges were possible for adolescent males while using distinct lower and upper register vocal production. Results indicate that seventh- and eighth-grade boys can significantly increase their singing ranges, both upper and lower, when they use the upper and lower mechanisms involved in voice production in those areas of the singing range.

REFERENCES

Appelman, R. D. (1967). *The science of vocal pedagogy: Theory and application.* Bloomington, IN: Indiana University Press.

Barresi, A. L. (1984). From uncertainty to understanding: A new approach to instruction about changing voice. In M. Runfola & L. Bash (Eds.), *Proceedings: Research symposium on the male adolescent voice* (pp. 155–165). State University of New York at Buffalo.

Beall, L. M. (1958). Elementary and junior high school voice training. (Doctoral dissertation, American University, Washington, DC (1958). *Dissertation Abstracts, 19,* 469.

Beard, C. J. (1988). Recognition of chest, head, and falsetto isoparametric tones. *The NATS* *Bulleti, 37*, 1–10.

Brown, C. J. (1988). *The effect of two assessment procedures on the range of children's singing voices.* Unpublished masters thesis, Indiana University, Bloomington.

Chapman, R. T. (1990). Training the male adolescent singing voice prior to, during, and following voice mutation using the "Vocal Behavior Training" methodology. (Doctoral dissertation, New York University, 1989). *Dissertation Abstracts International, 50*(9), 2820.

Collins, D. L. (1981). *The cambiata concept.* Conway, AR: Cambiata Press.

Cooksey, J. M. (1977–1978). The development of a contemporary eclectic theory for the training and cultivation of the junior high school male changing voice. *Choral Journal,* October, *18*, 5–14; November, *18*, 5–14; December, *18*, 5–15; January, *18*, 5–17.

Cooksey, J. M. (1992). *Working with the adolescent voice.* St. Louis, MO: Concordia.

Cooksey, J. M. (1984). *The male adolescent changing voice: Some new perspectives.* In M. Runfola & L. Bash (Eds.), *Proceedings: Research symposium on the male adolescent voice* (pp. 4–59). State University of New York at Buffalo.

Cooper, I. (1953). *Changing voices in junior high: Letters to Pat.* New York: Carl Fischer.

Cooper, I., & Kuersteiner, K. O. (1970). *Teaching junior high school music* (2nd ed.). Boston: Allyn and Bacon.

Dawson, J. J. (1919). *The voice of the boy.* New York: Laidlaw Brothers.

Ekstrom, R. C. (1959). Comparison of the male voice before, during, and after mutation. (Doctoral dissertation, University of Southern Californina, Los Angeles). *Dissertations Abstracts 20*(09), 3569.

Hermann, S. (1988). *Building a pyramid of musicianship.* San Diego: Curtis Music.

Hollien, H. (1977). The registers and ranges of the voice. In M. Cooper & M. H. Cooper (Eds.), *Approaches to vocal rehabilitation* (pp. 76–121). Springfield, MO: C. C. Thomas.

Joseph, W. A. (1959). The relationship between vocal growth in the human adolescent, and the total growth process. (Doctoral dissertation, Boston University Graduate School, 1959). *Dissertations Abstracts, 20*, 1388.

Kahane, J. C. (1975). The developmental anatomy of the human prepubertal and pubertal larynx (Doctoral dissertation, University of Pittsburgh). *Dissertation Abstracts International, 36*(7B), 4966.

Large, J. (1972). Towards an integrated physiologic-acoustic theory of vocal registers. *The NATS Bulletin 28*, 18–25.

Mayer, F. D., & Sacher, J. (1964a). The changing voice. *American Choral Review, 6*(2), 8, 10–12.

Mayer, F. D., & Sacher, J. (1964b). The changing voice (II). *American Choral Review, 6*(3), 9–11.

McKenzie, D. (1956). *Training the boy's voice.* New Jersey: Rutgers University Press.

Phillips, K. H. (1992a). Research on the teaching of singing. In R. Colwell (Ed.), *Handbook of research on music teaching and learning.* New York: Schirmer Books.

Phillips, K. H. (1992b). *Teaching kids to sing.* New York: Schirmer Books.

Reckford, L. P. (1982). Leo P. Reckford, M. D. In J. Hines, *Great singers on great singing.* Garden City, NJ: Doubleday.

Reid, C. (1983). *A dictionary of vocal terminology: An analysis.* New York: Joseph Patelson.

Rutkowski, J. (1984). Two-year results of a longitudinal study investigating the validity of Cooksey' theory for training the adolescent voice. In M. Runfola & L. Bash (Eds.), *Proceedings: research symposium on the male adolescent voice* (pp. 86–96). State University of New York at Buffalo.

Sataloff, R. T., & Spiegel, J. (1991). The young voice. In R. T. Sataloff & I. F. Titze (Eds.), *Vocal Health and science: A compilation of articles from The NATS Bulletin and The NATS Journal.* Jacksonville, FL: The National Association of Teachers of Singing.

Schoenhard, C., & Hollien, H. (1982). A perceptual study of registration in female singers. *The NATS Bulletin, 32*(1), 22–26.

Swanson, F. J. (1959). Voice mutation in the adolescent male: An experiment in guiding the voice development of adolescent boys in general music classes. (Doctoral dissertation, University of Wisconsin). *Dissertation Abstracts, 20,* 2718.

Swanson, F. J. (1982). Growlers, fryers, and other rejects. *Choral Journal, 23,* 5–10.

Titze, I. R. (1983). Vocal registers. *The NATS Bulletin, 39,* 21.

Vennard, W., Hirano, M., & Ohala, J. (1970). Chest, head, and falsetto. *The NATS Bulletin,* 27, 30–37.

Wolverton, V. D. (1986). Classifying adolescent singing voices. (Doctoral dissertation, The University of Iowa, Iowa City, 1985). *Dissertation Abstracts International, 47*(3), 708.

Wurgler, P. S. (1991). A perceptual study of vocal registers in the singing voices of children. (Doctoral dissertation, The Ohio State University, 1990). *Dissertations Abstracts International, 52*(2), 461.

Yarrington, J. (1990). *Building the youth choir: Training & motivating teenage singers.* Minneapolis: Augsburg Fortress.

STUDY AND DISCUSSION QUESTIONS

1. What two "schools" of thought regarding the changing voice of adolescent males do the authors identify in the review of literature?

2. What did Wurgler's research (1990) state concerning registers in children's voices?

3. What type of research design did Swanson (1959) use in his study of the adolescent male voice?

4. What aspect of the changing voice did Cooksey not account for in his research on the adolescent male changing voice?

5. Why did the authors of the present study want to replicate the "experiment" of the authors Mayer and Sacher?

6. What was the total sample of the present study? What was the population?

7. What type of experimental research was the design of this study, true or quasi?

8. What does "subjects as their own control" mean in research design?

9. What was the main research hypothesis of the adolescent voice study?

10. What type of data were collected, interval or ratio?

11. Was the total range gain larger for the seventh graders or the eighth graders?

12. What level of significance was reported for t as total range in Table 8?

13. Why were paired- (dependent-) samples t-tests used instead of independent samples?

14. In Table 8, the three computed t statistics were all significant at what level?

15. What were the results of this study?

READING TRUE-EXPERIMENTAL RESEARCH

True experimental research in education is not common. The problem is finding student populations that can be assigned at random. Most school populations are assigned to classrooms prior to the start of the school year, and there is not much that can be done about that. Therefore, studies in education often assign intact classrooms to either treatment or control conditions, resulting in quasi-experimental research designs.

I was fortunate to be the principal of a private elementary school when I did my dissertation. Because I was the "boss," I could require that all students in grades 2, 3, and 4 be in choir, and I could arrange the master schedule so that members of the choir could be randomly assigned to either treatment or control conditions, each group meeting on Tuesday and Thursday for 30 minutes. While one group was meeting, the other was involved in a project where students visited residents of a nursing home located directly behind the school. In addition to choir, all students had general music class for a half-hour on Mondays, Wednesdays, and Fridays with their regular music teacher. Therefore, all students had music a half-hour every day! Who but a music educator could design such a schedule!

The Effects of Group Breath-Control Training on the Singing Ability of Elementary Students[*]

Kenneth H. Phillips, *The University of Iowa*
Journal of Research in Music Education, 33(3), 179–191.

Reprinted by permission of MENC: The National Association for Music Education.
Copyright © 1985 by MENC.

Singing is recognized by music education as a basic part, if not the most important part, of the elementary music curriculum. That many children never learn to use their singing voices is a persistent problem in the field of music education. It was the purpose of this study to investigate breath-control training as a means by which this basic skill of singing could be improved among elementary students.

Coleman (1980), in a study that surveyed public school music teachers' ratings of the effectiveness of their undergraduate training in music education, found that training for teaching a beginning vocalist was among the lowest-rated areas of preparation. Similarly, the present review of literature on children's singing revealed (a) a lack of specific methodology in current elementary methods texts and (b) a substantial amount of writing and research on the child voice that has been largely unknown or

---

[*]Outstanding Dissertation Award in Music Education (1983) from the Council for Research in Music Education, The University of Illinois, Champaign-Urbana.

ignored by current textbook writers. Evidence was found among current publications (Farrell, 1977; Fortunato, 1981; Greenberg, 1979; Jacobs, 1948/1981; Joyner, 1969; Richner, 1976; Swanson, 1977), and especially among authors writing before 1950 (Bates, 1907; Behnke & Browne, 1885; Curtis, 1895; Dann, 1936; Dawson, 1902; Giddings, 1919; Hardy, 1906; Howard, 1895/1923; Johnson, 1935; Mason, 1939; Rix, 1909), that the training of the child voice using specific breathing exercises and associated vocalizes was considered to be appropriate. Little evidence was found, however, that such techniques were subjected to the rigors of scientific investigation.

Wilson, in "An Overview of Vocal Maturation from Infancy through Adolescence" (1978), notes six vocal evaluative criteria as standards for measuring voice development: "muscular tonus and coordination, laryngeal tone, loudness, pitch, resonance, and intelligibility" (p. 8). Of these six, the present study concerned measures of muscular coordination, loudness, and pitch. Also included were measures of maximum duration of phonation, and musical frequency range, which Wilson also notes as aspects of the child's voice that have been measured and analyzed.

Studies of children's singing that have investigated the area of respiration are those of Brody (1948), Gembizkaja (1962), Jersild and Bienstock (1932), and Nelson (1955). Training in breathing measures other than for singing has been demonstrated by Simpson and Nelson (1972), in a study of hyperactive children ages 6 to 8. These studies suggest the appropriateness of breath-control training with children.

Problem

Two problems were investigated in this study. The first of these concerned specific vocal training and the effects of such training upon the singing ability of elementary students in grades 2, 3, and 4. The vocal training, in addition to the traditional song materials to which the subjects in the study were exposed, included techniques that involved posture and breathing exercises. Those measures of singing ability studied included vocal range, intensity of tone, duration of tone, and pitch accuracy.

The second problem concerned the appropriateness of the prescribed training at these grade levels. Vocal development has long been linked to maturation (Boardman, 1964; Williams, Sievers, & Hattwick, 1932), but Shuter and Taylor (1969) note that "Many motor skills may be learned more easily earlier than later, because of the possibility of negative transfer from previously practiced activities" (p. 35). Those measures used to verify the effectiveness of the training on breath control and to control for maturation were vital capacity and pneumograph tracings of thoracic and abdominal displacement during inhalation preparatory to singing. It was the goal of the breath-control training exercises to increase the abdominal displacement (expansion) of the subjects while decreasing the amount of thoracic expansion or "chest heaving." This approach to breathing for singing was verified by a lengthy review of methodologies advocated by leading authorities and medical professionals.

Procedures

Forty-four subjects, representing all of the students in grades 2, 3, and 4 in a private elementary school, were randomly assigned to the two treatment groups. The subjects were considered representative of the population as no socioeconomic, ethnic, racial, or academic ability requirements were used for admission to the school other than the parents' desire of a parochial education for their children.

The two treatment groups met twice weekly for half-hour sessions during 18 weeks of instruction. In addition to the singing of songs, the experimental group's rehearsal contained 10 to 12 minutes of specific training in breath-control exercises, which were selected from those recommended by leading vocal authorities. The emphasis in this group was on the development of psychomotor techniques as they apply to the physiology of breathing for singing. Peters and Miller (1982) define psychomotor skills as "organized patterns of muscular activities controlled by changing stimuli from the environment" (p. 149). The control group's instruction was that of the traditional song approach, in which technique is taught mainly through the singing of songs. Both groups received the same total instruction time of 30 minutes per session, and both groups were taught by the investigator with the assistance of students' regular music teacher at the piano. Experimenter bias was controlled through the use of identical song materials, vocalizes, and end-of-year concert objectives for both groups. As the investigator was the subjects' regular choir director, concert preparation provided the necessary motivation to prepare both groups equally for their combined presentation. Only in the matter of breath-management exercises were the groups differentiated.

Physical-conditioning exercises were the first part of the training sequence used with the experimental group. These were intended to "activate" the body for singing through "muscle movers" (stretching, bending, etc.) and posture-development exercises. Breathing exercises involved establishing a correct "breathing motion" of the muscles of the torso and application of breath to singing tone through breath-management exercises. The tone-production part of the training sequence added phonation on vocalizes to breath management. Much emphasis was placed on the aspirate "h" in staccato and marcato vocalizes to encourage the proper working of the support muscles at the onset of phonation. Long phrases were also emphasized to discourage the wasting of breath upon controlled exhalation.

As the emphasis of the study was on the benefits of breath-control training to children's singing, the effects of the vocalizes on the singing had to be considered. Several studies (Cary, 1949; Joyner, 1969; Smith, 1961) have noted that children improve in singing once they find their "upper," or "head," voices, regardless of breath-control training. As the vocalizes in the present study did assist the children in exercising their "head" voices, the benefits of training would be difficult to differentiate between probable causes: breath-control training vs. vocalizes. However, most vocal authorities agree that breathing exercises by themselves are useless without application to vocalization. Therefore, in order to control for the possible variable of tone production, the control group also was instructed with identical vocalizes and range-register coordination exercises. In this way, the variable of breath-control training was isolated as the only factor that the experimental group alone received.

At all times a group approach was used during the study. Although individual subjects were occasionally called upon to demonstrate a particular technique or exercise for the groups, no subjects were given individual instruction outside of the usual rehearsal sessions.

Data Collection

Pre- and posttests of the four dependent measures (range, intensity, duration, and pitch accuracy), as well as vitalometer and pneumograph readings, were obtained from each subject. The vocal-range test was administered in a separate session by the investigator and the regular music teacher. The other five measures were taken in a second session during the 2-week pre- and posttest periods. In these sessions, the investigator was assisted by a speech scientist who operated equipment for obtaining the vital capacity and body-wall displacement (pneumograph) measures. The speech scientist and the procedures were all introduced to the subjects prior to the actual testing sessions in order to prepare the subjects and to lessen their concerns during the testing. All of the testing was done on an individual basis, and all of the singing trials were tape-recorded using standard reel-to-reel equipment.

For the vocal-range test, each subject was tested for optimum musical frequency range as defined by Wilson (1978): "the range from the highest musical tone a child can match to the lowest tone he can match accurately" (pp. 9–10). An electrical piano or the assistant's voice were used as the models for pitch matching, as Clegg (1966) found that a female voice and a piano were the easiest modes for children when matching pitch. The investigator recorded the lowest and highest musical pitches (as determined by the assistant) sung by each subject on three separate trials. Statistical analysis was done on the mean of the three trials.

In the second test session, each subject was first tested for vital capacity using a Collins six-liter vitalometer. A score in liters was averaged from three separate trials for each subject.

The measures of thoracic and abdominal displacement followed. Subjects were asked to remove bulky clothing such as sweaters or vests, but blouses or shirts were retained. Two pneumographs were then strapped around the subject's torso; one at chest level and one at medial abdominal level. These positions were confirmed by Brody (1948), Ross (1955), Gould and Okamura (1974), Baken and Cavallo (1979), and Wilder (1979).

The conventional pneumograph (Manning type) is used to measure bodily movements associated with respiration. The actual device consists of a small, accordion-like rubber cylinder that surrounds a helical spring attached to end plates. These may be placed around the body and held taut by end straps. No removal of clothing is necessary. A length of thin tubing leads from the cylinder to a transducer, thereby creating a pneumatically coupled, air-tight system. The transducer connects electronically to a polygraph (motor-driven pen-writer that permits the moving of recording paper at a constant speed). The pressure change created within the cylinder by the movement of the pneumograph is communicated to the polygraph and recorded. In the present study, one channel of the polygraph recorded thoracic movement while the other channel recorded abdominal movement.

Upon attaching the pneumographs to the subjects, each was told that he or she would be tested for "how long" (duration) and "how loudly" (intensity) they could sing a single pitch. The pitch used was the subject's midrange pitch as determined by the previous vocal-range test. Each subject was instructed to sing the pitch on the vowel "ah," which Miller (1973) noted as being the loudest vowel throughout most of the singing range.

The assistant recorded the voice level (in decibels) that the subject maintained the longest. The level indicator of the sound level meter was shielded from the subject. The procedure was repeated for a total of three trials, the final score representing the average.

The measure of duration was taken simultaneously with that of the intensity level. The investigator timed the length of each pitch sung with a standard stopwatch for the average of three trials.

For the pitch-accuracy test, two phrases were selected from the song repertoire of the previous semester. One phrase was chosen for its disjunct motion and one for its conjunct motion. Combined ranges of the two phrases was a tenth. Phrases used for the posttest were drawn from the repertoire learned during the course of the study. Gould (1968) noted that using the same song material for pre- and posttests may result in a carryover effect of bad habits. Phrases for the pre- and posttests were matched as closely as possible for key, range, and motion. Musical phrases were chosen to test pitch accuracy because previous research (Updegraff, Heiliger, & Learned, 1938) showed the "phrase test" to be the most discriminating test of singing ability. Words were used because Boardman (1964) noted that children sang more accurately with words than music alone.

Scoring for the three pitch-accuracy trials used a numerical rating scale (1–5), which reflected both accuracy of pitches and pitch direction. Each trial was rated separately from the recorded tapes by the investigator and two other judges whose musical backgrounds qualified them as reliable raters. The judges were told to rate pitch accuracy without regard to vocal quality, and the necessary precautions were taken regarding subject identity. Reliability among the judges was calculated using a HOYT program for interjudge reliability, which showed a combined pretest alpha of .96 and a combined posttest alpha of .975. In the final analysis of the data, the mean score for each subject's pitch accuracy was represented by the composite mean of the three judges' ratings on all phrases.

The pneumograph recordings of body-wall displacement were made immediately before phonation for each vocal test trial (duration, intensity, and pitch accuracy). There were three trials per tests, and statistical analysis was performed on the mean of the three trials.

Design and Analysis

The data from this study were subjected to a two-way multivariate analysis of covariance (MANCOVA). The scores analyzed were only those of the posttest for each variable, with the error variance in the pretest measure "covaried" from the final analysis. Such factors as subjects' physical characteristics or pretest performance levels were then taken into account. The remaining "corrected values" became the scores upon which the analyses were performed.

The "corrected" posttest means of the four dependent variables (range, intensity, duration, and pitch accuracy) were each analyzed for the effects of the three covariate breathing measures. The posttest mean for each dependent measure and each of the covariate measures constituted a "set" of variables, resulting in a multivariate procedure. In this way, the effects of the breath-control training itself could be substantiated by scores reflecting the breathing process. To state that a change in singing ability was due to the training variable without substantiating a change in the training variable (as reflected in the breathing measures) would open the question of whether or not improved singing ability was due to the results of breath-control training or to some other uncontrolled variable. Thus, the multivariate nature of the design analyzed, as a "set" of variables, the effects of each breathing measure with each singing measure. The two independent variables, breath-control training and grade level, constituted a 2 × 3 design with two groups (experimental and control) and three grade levels (second, third, and fourth). A computer program titled NYMBULA (Finn, 1974) was used to perform this analysis.

The multivariate analysis of covariance was done by means of a step-down procedure in which the variables were considered in a predetermined order. At each stage, only the unique contribution of the additional variable was estimated and tested. There were a total of four steps in each of the step-down analyses.

In Step 1, the dependent variable posttest was tested with effects of the given covariate related to a pretest characteristic controlled. Statistical significance at this first step would mean that the two groups (experimental and control) were drawn from different populations and, therefore, unequal before training began. If this were the case, the analysis would stop at the first step because further analysis would be needless in this procedure. If Step 1 revealed nonsignificant findings, then analysis proceeded to Step 2, with the interpretations of significance or nonsignificance for another pretest characteristic being the same as in Step 1. If Steps 1 and 2 both showed nonsignificance, then analysis proceeded to Step 3, in which both pretest measures (Steps 1 and 2) were covaried out (controlled) while testing for the effects of training on the dependent variable. If Step 3 revealed significance, then that aspect of training differentially affected the dependent variable. If Step 3 showed nosignificance, then it was assumed that training did not affect the dependent variable. In Step 4, the dependent variable was tested independently of the covariates in the three other steps. Significance at this step was interpreted to mean that training, as a whole, did affect the dependent variable, but not specifically as a result of the covariate. The third step, therefore, was the most critical step in the analysis. Separate analyses also were performed to determine any significant interaction between the independent variables.

Results

Group-by-grade analyses revealed no significant findings. Consequently, any main effects of group training or grade level that were found to be significant were not contaminated by interaction between the two independent variables.

Summaries of the multivariate analyses of covariance results for main effects by group appear in Tables 1, 2, and 3 as follows: Table 1—abdomen displacement on all four dependent vocal measures; Table 2—thorax displacement on all four dependent vocal measures; Table 3—vital capacity on all four dependent vocal measures. Results of Steps 1 and 2 of each of the four dependent vocal analyses per table show no significance and therefore indicate that both groups were drawn from the same population.

Table 1 Summary Table of MANCOVA Main
Effects by Group for Abdomen
Displacement on Dependent Measures

Step	Source		df	MS	F
		Effects on Vocal Range			
1	Abdomen	1	1,38	30.75	1.76
2	Range	1	1,38	18.70	0.98
3	Abdomen	2	1,38	636.18	27.85*
4	Range	2	1,38	14.65	0.01
		Effects on Vocal Intensity			
1	Abdomen	1	1,38	30.75	1.76
2	Intensity	1	1,38	0.98	0.02
3	Abdomen	2	1,38	636.18	26.77*
4	Intensity	2	1,38	76.70	2.10
		Effects on Vocal Duration			
1	Abdomen	1	1,38	30.75	1.76
2	Duration	1	1,38	38.54	2.80
3	Abdomen	2	1,38	636.18	21.76*
4	Duration	2	1,38	0.31	0.60
		Effects on Vocal Pitch Accuracy			
1	Abdomen	1	1,38	30.75	1.76
2	Pitch accuracy	1	1,38	0.99	0.37
3	Abdomen	2	1,38	636.18	21.53*
4	Pitch accuracy	2	1,38	1.47	0.01

$*p < .05$

The effects of breath-control training on vocal range are reported at Step 3 in each of the first step-down analyses of Tables 1, 2, and 3. A significant difference between groups at the $p < .001$ level was found for the effects of abdominal and thoracic displacement on range. The effects of vital capacity on range in Step 3 of Table 3 found significant difference at the $p < .05$ level. Body-wall displacement, for the experimental group, was shown to have a significant effect upon the subjects' increased vocal range (20.30 pitch pre- to 20.97 pitch posttest) in the direction of training with increased abdominal displacement (2.98 mm pre- to 6.02 mm posttest) and decreased thoracic displacement (17.48 mm pre- to 11.88 mm posttest).

Table 2 Summary Table of MANCOVA Main
Effects by Group for Thorax Displacement
on Dependent Measures

Step	Source		df	MS	F
		Effects on Vocal Range			
1	Abdomen	1	1,38	3.53	0.08
2	Range	1	1,38	18.70	0.99
3	Abdomen	2	1,38	465.47	11.55*
4	Range	2	1,38	14.65	0.53
		Effects on Vocal Intensity			
1	Abdomen	1	1,38	3.53	0.08
2	Intensity	1	1,38	0.98	0.04
3	Abdomen	2	1,38	465.47	11.70**
4	Intensity	2	1,38	76.70	8.16**
		Effects on Vocal Duration			
1	Abdomen	1	1,38	3.53	0.08
2	Duration	1	1,38	38.54	3.06
3	Abdomen	2	1,38	465.47	11.51**
4	Duration	2	1,38	0.31	0.89
		Effects on Vocal Pitch Accuracy			
1	Abdomen	1	1,38	3.53	0.08
2	Pitch accuracy	1	1,38	0.99	0.87
3	Abdomen	2	1,38	465.47	10.65**
4	Pitch accuracy	2	1,38	1.47	0.01

*$p < .001$.
**$p < .01$.

The opposite was true for the control group as abdominal displacement decreased (1.09 mm pre- to 2.09 mm posttest) and thoracic displacement increased (16.25 mm to 18.57 mm posttest). Vital capacity showed a slight decrease for the experimental group (1.95 mm pre- to 1.83 mm posttest) and a slight increase for the control group (1.85 mm pre- to 1.88 mm posttest), substantiating most vocal authorities' belief that the amount of air one breathes is relatively unimportant as compared to how one controls that air.

The effects of breath-control training on vocal intensity are reported in the second step-down analyses as summarized in Tables 1, 2, and 3. A significant difference between groups at Step 3 was found for each analysis at the reported levels of confidence. Abdominal displacement, for the experimental group, was shown to have a significant effect upon the subjects' increased vocal intensity (68.35 dB pre- to 69.53 dB posttest) in the direction of training as previously stated. The effect of thoracic

Table 3 Summary Table of MANCOVA Main
Effects by Group for Vital Capacity
Displacement on Dependent Measures

Step	Source		df	MS	F
		Effects on Vocal Range			
1	Abdomen	1	1,38	0.09	0.82
2	Range	1	1,38	18.70	0.93
3	Abdomen	2	1,38	0.03	4.48*
4	Range	2	1,38	14.65	0.58
		Effects on Vocal Intensity			
1	Abdomen	1	1,38	0.09	0.82
2	Intensity	1	1,38	0.98	0.15
3	Abdomen	2	1,38	0.03	4.33*
4	Intensity	2	1,38	76.70	5.61*
		Effects on Vocal Duration			
1	Abdomen	1	1,38	0.09	0.82
2	Duration	1	1,38	38.54	2.59
3	Abdomen	2	1,38	0.03	5.57*
4	Duration	2	1,38	0.31	0.01
		Effects on Vocal Pitch Accuracy			
1	Abdomen	1	1,38	0.09	0.82
2	Pitch accuracy	1	1,38	0.99	0.73
3	Abdomen	2	1,38	0.03	4.59*
4	Pitch accuracy	2	1,38	1.47	0.04

*$p < .05$.

displacement in Table 2 is unclear, as significance was found at both Steps 3 and 4. The control group showed a decrease in vocal intensity (68.75 dB pre- to 66.74 dB posttest), with greater "chest" elevation and less abdominal extension as stated. Again, the slightly greater vital capacity of the control group and the slightly less vital capacity of the experimental group seemingly had no effect upon vocal intensity. This is confirmed by the significance found in Step 4 of Table 3 for vital capacity on intensity.

The effects of breath-control training on vocal duration are reported in the third step-down analyses of Tables 1, 2, and 3. A significant difference between groups at Step 3 of each analysis was found at the levels reported for all three breathing measures. Comparison of means show, however, that vocal duration decreased for the experimental group (12.23 sec. pre- to 10.83 sec. posttest) and increased slightly for the control group (10.44 sec. pre- to 10.47 sec. posttest). The effects of increased abdominal expansion and decreased thoracic expansion apparently had a negative effect for the experimental group, while decreased abdominal expansion and increased thoracic expansion had little effect on the control group. A factor that may have influenced the decrease of duration in the experimental group was the group's increase on the intensity measure. As greater vocal intensity also calls for an increase in breath pressure (Bouhuys, Proctor, & Mead, 1966), it can be reasoned that more breath pressure may have been used when singing louder. Therefore, the experimental group sang with more intensity on the posttest but with less duration. It was perhaps a limitation of the study to have vocal intensity and duration measures taken simultaneously. The effects of the one upon the other were not foreseen. Conversely, the control group sang with less intensity on the posttest but with slightly longer duration.

The effects of breath-control training on vocal pitch accuracy are reported in stepdown analyses in Tables 1, 2, and 3. A significant difference between groups was found in the third step of each analysis at the reported levels of confidence. Bodywall displacement, for the experimental group, was shown to have a significant effect upon the subjects' increased pitch accuracy (2.75 pre- to 3.66 posttest) in the direction of training as given. Vital capacity, although significant at the $p < .05$ level of confidence, appears to be relatively unimportant, considering the slight decrease in vital capacity demonstrated by the experimental group.

In the 12 analyses involving the effects of breath-control training on vocal range, intensity, duration, and pitch accuracy, the results were not significantly different among grade levels. Therefore, the students in grade 4 did no better after training than the students in grade 2, and the students in grade 2 did no worse after training than the students in grade 4. Significant differences were found only between groups, not among grades.

Discussion

The results of the present study show that breath-control training had significant effects on the singing ability of students in grades 2, 3, and 4. The finding that training as early as the second grade was effective is of particular interest. No other studies are known to have investigated the effectiveness of breath-control training as early as the second grade, although various writers on the child voice recommend that such training begin when a child is approximately 8 years old.

The effectiveness of psychomotor breath-control training in this study demonstrates that such training can be effective in approaching child voice training. The exercises and vocalizes used in the training helped develop abdominal-diaphragmatic-costal breathing, as advocated by such vocal authorities as Alderson (1979), Klein and Schjeide (1972), and Vennard (1967). The absence of a significant grade-by-training interaction and the means of the three breathing measures for the experimental group show that subjects at each grade level responded to the breath training in the same manner; abdominal expansion increased, thoracic expansion decreased, and vital capacity remained stable. Brody (1948) found similar results to breath-control training in her study of subjects in Grades 4 through 12. The fact that vocal training in a group setting at the elementary level was possible is an important observation of this study. This supports the belief of Swanson (1977) that child vocal training may be successfully carried on in a group setting.

A greater group participation among all students also was observed by the investigator during the sessions of the study. Boys in the experimental group seemed to respond, especially to the training exercises that involved physical or "muscular" activities.

Conclusions

Based upon the limitations and results of this investigation, the following conclusions are presented for consideration:

1. Group breath-control training for children's singing in the second, third, and fourth grades has a significant effect in changing from "chest" to abdominal-diaphragmatic-costal breathing.

2. Group breath-control training for children's singing in the second, third, and fourth grades has a significant effect on singing ability, especially on measures of vocal pitch range, vocal intensity, and pitch accuracy.

REFERENCES

Alderson, R. (1979). *Complete handbook of voice training*. West Nyack, NY: Parker Publishing.

Baken, R. J., & Cavallo, S. A. (1979). Chest wall preparation for phonation in untrained speakers. In Van Lawrence (Ed.), *Transcripts of the Eighth Symposium [on] Care of the Professional Voice* (part 2). New York: Voice Foundation.

Bates, J. (1907). *Voice culture for children*. London: Gray & Novello.

Behnke, E., & Browne, L. (1885). *The child's voice*. Boston: Oliver Ditson.

Boardman, E. L. (1964). An investigation of the effect of preschool training on the development of vocal accuracy in young children. *Dissertation Abstracts, 25*, 1245. (University Microfilms 64–8354)

Bouhuys, A., Proctor, D. F., & Mead, J. (1966). Kinetic aspects of singing. *Journal of Applied Physiology, 21*, 483–496.

Brody, V. A. (1948). An experimental study of the emergence of the process involved in the production of sound. *Dissertation Abstracts, 15*, 90. (University Microfilms No. 13–1417)

Cary, D. (1949). *A study of range extension in the voices of third grade children with singing deficiency*. Unpublished master's thesis, University of Kansas, Lawrence.

Clegg, B. (1966). *A comparative study of primary grades children's ability to match tones*. Unpublished master's thesis, Brigham Young University, Provo, UT.

Coleman, H. (1980). Perceptions of music teacher competencies through a survey of public school music teachers in selected school districts: A positive response to accountability for higher education. *Dissertation Abstracts International, 80*, 3861A. (University Microfilms No. 80–01179)

Curtis, E. H. (1895). *Children's voices*. New York: John Church.

Dann, H. (1936). Hollis Dan song series: Conductor's book. Boston: American Book.

Dawson, J. J. (1902). *The voice of the boy*. New York: E. I. Kellog & Co.

Farrell, M. F. (1977). An examination of the training techniques and related factors in selected outstanding boy-choirs in the United States. *Dissertation Abstracts International, 38*, 688A. (University Microfilms No. 77–16,868)

Finn, J. D. (1974). *A general model for multivariate analysis.* New York: Holt, Rinehart, and Winston.

Fortunato, C. (1981). *Children's music ministry.* Elgin, IL: David C. Cook.

Gembizkaja, E. (1962, April). Systematic development of the child's singing voice in Russia. *International Music Educator, 5,* 146–148.

Giddings, T. P. (1919) *Grade school music teaching.* New York: C. H. Congdon.

Gould, A. O. (1968, August). *Developing specialized programs for singing in the elementary school.* Final Report. Washington, DC: Research in Education. (ERIC Reproduction Service No. ED 025530 24 TE 499967)

Gould, W. J., & Okamura, H. (1974). Respiratory training of the singer. *Folia phoniatrica, 26,* 275–286.

Greenberg, J. (1979). *Young children need music.* Englewood Cliffs, NJ: Prentice-Hall.

Hardy, T. M. (1906). *How to train children's voices.* London: J. Curwen and Sons.

Howard, F. E. (1923). *The child voice in singing.* New York: H. W. Gray. (originally published 1895)

Jacobs, R. K. (1981). *The successful children's choir.* Chicago: H. T. FitzSimons. (originally published 1948)

Jersild, A. T., & Bienstock, S. F. (1932). Training and growth in the development of children. *Child Development Monographs, 10,* 39–42; 49–61.

Johnson, C. E. (1935). *The training of boys' voices.* Boston: Oliver Ditson.

Joyner, D. R. (1969). The monotone problem. *Journal of Research in Music Education, 17,* 114–125.

Klein, J. J., & Schjeide, O. A. (1972). *Singing technique: How to avoid vocal trouble.* Anaheim, CA: National Music Publishers.

Mason, L. (1839). *Manual of the Boston Academy of Music* (5th ed.). Boston: J. J. Wilkins & R. B. Carter.

Miller, L. W. (1973). An experimental study of the effectiveness of supplemental calisthenics as an aid in the teaching of breath support for singing. *Dissertation Abstracts International, 34/03-A,* 1114. (University Microfilms No. 73–16,500)

Nelson, R. C. (1955). A physiologic study of the utilization of the vital capacity in phonation, resonation, and articulation and its effect on tone quality in the adolescent. *Dissertation Abstracts, 15,* 518.

Peters, G., & Miller, M. (1982). *Music teaching and learning.* New York: Longman.

Richner, S. S. (1976). The effect of classroom and remedial methods of music instruction on the ability of inaccurate singers in the third, fourth, and fifth grades to reproduce pitches. *Dissertation Abstracts International, 37,* 1447-A. (University Microfilms No. 76–19, 898)

Rix, R. F. (1909). *A manual of school music in elementary grades for supervisors and class teachers.* New York: Macmillan.

Ross, W. E. (1955). An objective study of breathing for singing. *Dissertation Abstracts, 15,* 1628. (University Microfilms No. 55–284)

Shuter, R., & Taylor, S. (1969). Summary of discussion of the International Seminar on Experimental Research in Music Education. *Journal of Research in Music Education, 17,* 32–38.

Simpson, D. D., & Nelson, A. E. (1972). *Breathing control and attention training: A preliminary study of a psychophysical approach to self-control of hyperactive behavior in children.* Final report. Washington, DC: National Center for Educational Research and Development. (ERIC Reproduction Service No. ED 063 723 24 ED 04229)

Smith, R. B. (1961). A study of the effect of large-group vocal training on the singing ability of nursery school children. *Dissertation Abstracts, 21,* 3811.

Swanson, F. J. (1977). *The male voice ages eight to eighteen.* Cedar Rapids, IA: Laurance Press.

Updegraff, R., Heiliger, L., & Learned, J. (1938). Effect of training upon the singing ability and musical interest of three-, four-, and five-year old children. *University of Iowa Studies in Child Welfare, 14,* 83–131.

Vennard, W. (1967). *Singing, the mechanism and the technique.* New York: Carl Fischer.

Wilder, C. N. (1979). Chest wall preparation for phonation in trained speakers. In Van Lawrence (Ed.), *Transcripts of the Eighth Symposium [on] Care of the Professional Voice* (part 2). New York: Voice Foundation.

Williams, H. M., Sievers, C. H., & Hattwick, M. S. (1932). The measurement of musical development. *University of Iowa Studies in Child Welfare, 7,* 1–191.

Wilson, D. K. (1978). An overview of vocal maturation from infancy through adolescence, In B. Weinberg and Van Lawrence (Eds.), *Transcripts of the Seventh Symposium [on] Care of the Professional Voice* (part 2). New York: Voice Foundation.

STUDY AND DISCUSSION QUESTIONS

1. What was Coleman's (1980) finding in a survey of music teachers' preparedness?

2. What were the two problems put forth by Phillips in this study?

3. How were the subjects assigned to groups? Why was this possible?

4. How did the treatment group's instruction differ from that of the control group's?

5. What were the two independent variables and the four dependent variables?

6. What is a pneumograph, and how was it used?

7. What was the factorial design used in Phillips's study?

8. What was the statistical analysis used by Phillips?

9. How did the intensity measure confound the duration measure?

10. What was Phillips's observation regarding boys in this study?

READING QUASI-EXPERIMENTAL RESEARCH

One of the problems in educational research, in general, is that so many people who receive the Ph.D., which prepares a person for a career in research, rarely do research beyond the doctoral dissertation. When the thesis becomes a terminal investigation, development of the area investigated sometimes continues by others, but much is lost when a person with a doctorate does not continue to develop as a researcher.

Researchers in the "hard" sciences often have students who choose to continue in their mentors' lines of investigation. This is not commonly found in educational research.

The following article by Dr. Karin Sehmann, however, is one such example. Karin Sehmann is presently professor of music education at Eastern Kentucky University.

Sehmann was a student horn player who was interested in my research in the area of breathing and its effects on children's singing. Since the horn is a wind instrument, she saw similarities between how students breathe for singing and for horn playing. Her research uncovered a number of exercises recommended for horn students, and along with some of the exercises I used she developed her own methodology for use with elementary brass players. Her situation was that found in most schools—intact groups of students existing for instrumental lessons. However, she was able to assign at random the treatment and control conditions to the groups. This, then, is a good example of quasi-experimental research. The article appears in the Summer 2000 issue of JRME.

The Effects of Breath Management Instruction on the Performance of Elementary Brass Players

Karin Harfst Sehmann, *The University of Iowa*
Journal of Research in Music Education, 48(2), 136–150.

Reprinted by permission of MENC: The National Association for Music Education.
Copyright © 2000 by MENC.

Instrumental music in the United States has become a basic part of the music curriculum in most schools. The importance of this early instruction to the total school instrumental music program has been noted by the Music Educators National Conference (now MENC—The National Association for Music Education) in The School Music Program: Description and Standards (MENC, 1986). Recommendations in this document include beginning wind instruction no later than grade 5.

Given the importance of this instruction, little is found in the research literature concerning effective teaching techniques for beginning instrumentalists. Areas that have been investigated include strategies for rehearsals (Caimi, 1981; Price, 1983; Witt, 1986; Yarbrough & Price, 1981) and curriculum for instrumental lessons (Kendall, 1988). Several authors have commented about the lack of research concerning the psychomotor process of learning to play an instrument (O'Donnell, 1987; Rainbow, 1973).

Experts in wind playing, especially brass teachers, stress the importance of psychomotor skills. Johnson, in his 1981 book *The Art of Trumpet Playing*, states that "highly developed motor skills are critical in implementing fine musical performance" (p. 6). The well-known trombonist Denis Wick (1971) writes, "Playing any brass instrument for an extended period at a high standard is very much an athletic pursuit. It demands prolonged concentration, precise coordination" (p. 25). Of the motor skills involved, the respiration process often is mentioned as the most important physical aspect of brass playing (Farkas, 1956; Johnson, 1981; Wick, 1971). Kleinhammer (1963) states that "breath control is directly related to everything the trombonist plays" (p. 15). Kohut (1985), in his book *Musical Performance: Learning Theory and Pedagogy*, discusses all aspects of musical performance. He stresses the importance of breathing for the musician, writing that "breath directly affects intonation, articulation and diction, vibrato, dynamic level and intensity of the tone as well as phrasing, accents, and other aspects of musical expression" (p. 163). Arnold Jacobs, longtime tubist with the Chicago Symphony, became known for his work with musicians on the topic of respiration (Bobo, 1981a, 1981b; Jacobs, 1991: Kelly, 1983; Russo, 1973; Stewart, 1987). He taught the same mode of abdominal/diaphragmatic breathing that has been described by the previously mentioned writers on brass pedagogy (Kohut, 1985), stressing that the rib cage can be expanded simultaneously with the abdomen. Jacobs instructed the instrumental teacher to "start mechanical movements without the instrument so the student experiences change in the abdominal/diaphragmatic relationship" (Kelly, 1983, p. 11).

Kohut (1985), in his writing on instrumental pedagogy, notes the lack of concise, accurate writing about musical performance. He stresses that perceptual-motor learning is a large part of musical performance, but that it is neglected as a research topic and in pedagogical sources. He gives a thorough explanation of the breathing process for musicians and cites relevant research. Medical authorities, specialists in respiration, acousticians, and master teachers have studied the breathing process. The research and knowledge from these sources have not been synthesized into a systematic methodology for teaching brass players.

Taylor (1968/1969) is perhaps the first to have surveyed the 20th-century scientific and pedagogical sources on breathing as related to wind playing. Taylor reported the most common type of respiration used by most teachers and players of brass instruments to be abdominal/diaphragmatic breathing. Later scientific findings and expert opinions support this survey.

Medical researchers have conducted studies on the breathing process as to efficiency and functioning. Vellody, Nassery, Druz, and Sharp (1978) studied the functions of the chest and abdominal regions in breathing, finding that both areas of the torso contribute to the possible capacity of the lungs. Such scientific knowledge has provided a basis for an understanding of the breathing process as it relates to musical performance. Druz and Sharp (1981) studied the effect of body position on lung capacity and noted that an upright, standing posture allowed the greatest amount of air to be inspired into the lungs. Watson and Hixon (1985) found that active breathing of the type used by singers and wind players involves different action and uses different muscles than passive breathing.

Advances in technology for measuring respiration (Bouhuys, 1964; Cugell, 1986; Konno & Mead, 1967) have made the study of breathing more objective and quantifiable. The instrumentation used by Cugell (1986) in a study of brass players (respiratory inductive plethysmography, or RIP) was similar to that used in the present study to measure movement of the chest and abdomen during brass playing. This method (RIP) was originally developed for medical personnel, but has been used for studying respiratory activity in musicians (Cugell, 1986; Fuks & Sundberg, 1999; Phillips & Sehmann, 1990; Phillips & Vispoel, 1990). The RIP equipment consists of one elastic band placed to measure chest expansion and one to measure abdominal expansion during respiration. All researchers found that wind playersand singers use a combination of abdominal and thoracic lung expansion to perform.

In several studies, investigators have measured respiratory function in wind instrumentalists (Berger, 1965; Bouhuys, 1964; Cugell, 1986; Huttlin, 1982; Smith,

Kreisman, Colacone, Fox, & Wolkove, 1990; Van Middlesworth, 1978). Results from several of these studies indicate that brass players have larger lung capacities than the average nonplayer; only Van Middlesworth reported no significant difference between the lung capacities of wind players and nonwind players. Staples (1988) investigated the effects of different conditions placed on brass players during inspiration and found that restricting the chest and shoulders decreased measured lung capacity. Dennis (1987/1988) researched the use of instruction in the Alexander technique with brass players, noting that a short amount of instruction did not alter musical performance or respiratory function, but was highly regarded by the participants of the study. Smith et al. (1990) found that trained musicians had a much higher level of control over breathing than the average population. A study by Phillips and Sehmann (1990), which served as a pilot study for the present research, was an investigation of the effects of breath management instruction on college-level brass players. These investigators found that instruction in breath management significantly improved breathing mode and some measures of musical performance for those subjects receiving the experimental treatment (breath management instruction). All of the studies cited used adults as subjects.

The mode of breathing used in the present study was based on the one recommended by most leading authorities on brass playing and breathing physiology (Brown & Thomas, 1990; Jacobs, 1991; Kelly, 1983; Kohut, 1985; Sataloff, Spiegel, & Hawkshaw, 1990; Taylor, 1968/1969), which emphasizes abdominal/diaphragmatic breathing. The technique is characterized by a lowered diaphragm, laterally extended lower ribs, and an expansion of the abdominal wall during inhalation. Proper breathing motion allows for more air to be inspired than is required for normal respiration.

Many authors have commented on the need for correct breathing (Farkas, 1956; Jacobs, 1991; Johnson, 1981; Kleinhammer, 1963; Kohut, 1985; O'Donnell, 1987; Wick, 1971), but few have proposed methods to teach breathing. Rainbow (1973) notes the shortage of research on the physical aspects of instrumental performance, stating that "one of the most urgent needs in instrumental music education is the development of a theory of instruction based on fact and not speculation" (p. 9).

A review of older method books intended for elementary-age brass students reveals that most traditional methods include little discussion about breathing (Erickson, 1988; Feldstein & O'Reilly, 1988; Froseth, 1984; Pearson, 1982; Swearingen & Buehlman, 1984). The writers of these books may assume that instrumental music teachers cover the psychomotor aspects of playing, or the absence of this information may reveal a lack of understanding as to the importance of breathing for young brass players. Even the more recently published methods, such as *Essential Elements* (Rhodes, Biershank, & Lautzenhauser, 1993), *Standard of Excellence* (Pearson, 1993), and *Accent on Achievement* (O'Reilly & Williams, 1997), include little about breathing in the student books. In a descriptive study of beginning brass pedagogy, O'Donnell (1987) also notes a lack of psychomotor instruction for elementary brass players.

Teaching students to breath properly for instrumental playing may be the most important part of the teaching sequence. The ability to perform articulations, dynamics, phrasing, and most other "musical" aspects of wind playing are contingent upon correct breath management. Kohut (1985) stated that "correct breathing, therefore, is an essential requisite to good performance, since it affects practically every aspect of tone production and musical expression" (p. 163).

The purpose of this study was to investigate the effects of breath management instruction on the breathing technique and musical performance of elementary level brass players in grades 4, 5, and 6. Specifically, the investigator sought to determine if instruction in breath management would effect a significant change in the physical breathing mode and lung capacity of brass players and would significantly improve the following performance measures: tone quality, range, and duration. To this end, an instructional manual was developed to present a logical, sequential method of instruction in breathing.

Method

Subjects

The subjects in this study were all of the 64 brass students representing five elementary schools within a moderate-size Illinois school district. Prior to the beginning of the study, the researcher set a minimum attendance level of eight lessons during the 10-week instructional sequence. Three students did not complete the study: one did not meet the minimum attendance requirement, one student moved out of the district, and one student dropped out of the instrumental program. Therefore, 61 students completed all the requirements of the study.

Subjects were grouped by instrument class for lessons, and these same groups were used in the study so as not to disrupt the school schedule and possibly bias the results (since students might have realized they were in an experimental research setting). The instrumental lesson groups were randomly assigned to experimental (breath management instruction) and control groups. The lesson groups were matched for group size prior to assignment to treatment or control; that is, groups of five students per lesson were assigned equally to treatment or control, groups of four students per lesson were assigned equally to treatment or control, and so forth. The 61 subjects that completed the study included 34 trumpet students, 6 horn students, and 21 trombone/baritone students; tuba students were not students part of the study due to the lack of tuba players in these grades and the small number of tubists in elementary schools in general.

The subjects received 30-minute group lessons once each week in the semester preceding this research project. The group structure remained the same for the duration of the second semester, the period of this study. Lesson groups were assigned to either the experimental or the control group. There were a total of 24 lesson groups involved in the study. All subjects were taught by the same instrumental instructor that they had had prior to the beginning of the study. The experimental group received 5, 6, or 7 minutes of instruction, depending on the length of treatment in breath management during each group lesson, whereas the control group continued group lessons in the same format as had been used the previous semester. The total amount of treatment time within lessons for the experimental group was 65 minutes.

Duration of the Study

The duration of this study was 16 weeks. During the first week, all preliminary dependent measures were taken. There followed 5 weeks of breath management instruction in weekly group lessons. This treatment period was followed by 4 weeks during which the subjects prepared for a solo and ensemble contest. No treatment was given during this 4-week period. During the final 6 weeks, treatment resumed for 5 weeks, and the final week of the study was given to posttesting.

Instructional Procedures

The psychomotor instructional sequence, as devised by the investigator, was a combination of psychological and physiological approaches for achieving the optimum breathing mode for brass playing. Specifically, the psychomotor instruction included parts of a sequence used with college-level brass players (Phillips & Sehmann, 1990), practice with breathing tubes (Staples, 1988), instructional aids used with school children in a previous study on breathing (Phillips, 1983), recommended exercises for improving breathing (Zi, 1986), and researcher-devised instruction suggested by scientific respiration research.

Since the material from the investigator-devised instructional manual was taught by the regular instrumental teachers, the investigator conducted two 1-hour training sessions with the two instrumental teachers. These training sessions were designed to make the instruction from the manual as identical as possible, since there were two different teachers involved in teaching the treatment groups involved in the study. The investigator explained the goals and theories behind the development of the manual, the physical characteristics of proper breathing and posture, and the procedures to be followed for record keeping. The teachers were given demonstrations and tried specific exercises and activities for each lesson.

The first portion of the instructional sequence included postural exercises to reduce muscle tension. The next part of the instruction was the establishment of the technique of abdominal/diaphragmatic breathing, the type of breathing recommended by almost all brass experts (Taylor, 1968/1969). The students' instruments were not used in the first exercises.

The second set of breathing exercises were designed to improve the exhalation portion of the breathing process, which determines the actual tone production on brass instruments. These exercises were intended to improve the action of the muscles involved in breath management. Activities such as deflating the abdominal area with the hands, exhaling in varied counting patterns, and exhaling while tonguing imaginary quarter notes ("toh, toh, toh," etc.) were part of these lessons. The instruction manual included instructions that the chest should remain expanded as much as possible and should not be restricted in any way for maximum volume of air (Staples, 1988). The application of breath management instruction to the subjects' instrumental playing occurred during the second 5-week period of lessons. Students performed long tones throughout their ranges while the instructors checked for application of abdominal/ diaphragmatic breathing to tone production. Another exercise consisted of tongued patterns designed to ensure that the breath management remained the same in all styles of playing.

The sequence of treatment exercises were presented to all of the lesson groups in the experimental group. Depending on the lesson, 5, 6, or 7 minutes were spent on this instruction during the regular 30-minute lesson; the remainder of the lesson was spent playing out of the method book or working on solo and ensemble pieces. The control group played only out of the method book or worked on solo and ensemble literature.

Data Collection

Pretests and posttests of the three dependent measures of breathing (thoracic displacement, abdominal displacement, and lung capacity) as well as the three dependent measures of performance (tone quality, range, and duration) were obtained for each subject. All of the measures were taken individually during separate sessions by the investigator and an assistant during the 1-week pretest and posttest periods.

The measures of thoracic and abdominal displacement were obtained using respiratory inductive plethysmography. This method was originally developed for monitoring medical patients, but has been used for studying respiratory activity in singers and wind players (Cugell, 1986; Fuks & Sundberg, 1999; Phillips & Sehmann, 1990; Phillips & Vispoel, 1990). The instrument used was a Respitrace unit (Ambulatory Monitoring, Inc., Ardsley, NY). This breath measurement device consists of two gauze-like Respibands placed around the subject's torso, one at upper chest level and one at the abdominal level. The Respibands contain sensors that, when connected to a pen chart writer (called a "penwriter"), are able to transmit the amount of torso displacement at these two levels. Measures of displacement were produced by the penwriter tracings and were measured in millimeters. These measurements were made during the performance of long tones. A statistical analysis of the sum of the measurements for the three trials was done for both thoracic and abdominal displacements.

Lung capacity was measured before and after the treatment period with a Respiradyne pulmonary function monitor. The investigator recorded the lung capacity, called "vital capacity" in the medical world, in liters on three separate trials. Statistical analysis was done on the total of the three trials. Three trials have been used in previous studies (Bencowitz, 1984; Huttlin, 1982; Phillips, 1983; Staples, 1988) and have been accepted as reliable. Lung capacity was included in the study to determine if taking a "deeper" breath (abdominal/diaphragmatic mode) increased subjects' lung capacity. A significant increase in capacity was not expected.

Tone quality was assessed using an etude from a beginning-level band book, *Best in Class* (Pearson, 1982). The subjects' performances were recorded and later scored by judges experienced in working with beginning brass students. Prior to listening to the taped examples, the judges attended a training session and practiced using the rating scale on sample etudes. Four items from a multiple-item 5-point rating scale (Abeles, 1973) for clarinet performance were used.

The range test consisted of subjects playing scales from music provided by the investigator. The investigator recorded the highest and lowest pitches played by each subject on three trials. The number of half-steps between the highest and lowest pitches was calculated, and the total number of half-steps for the three trials was the score for the range measure.

The measure of duration determined how long each subject could sustain a pitch. The same concert pitch (the concert B-flat nearest middle C) was played in the same register by each instrument (on the staff, these appeared for the trumpet, as middle C; for the horn, as the F above middle C; and for the trombone, as the B-flat just below middle C). Research shows that equivalent concert pitches produce the same airflow rate on all brass instruments (Cugell, 1986; Bouhuys, 1964). To ensure similar playing levels, the subjects first practiced the pitch while looking at a decibel meter (100 dB at one meter). When the reading on the decibel meter dipped to the line below the set level, the subject was instructed to stop playing. This procedure was repeated three times.

Results

Reliability estimates for thoracic displacement, abdominal displacement, vital capacity, range, and duration range from .85 to .99. The interjudge reliability estimate (coefficient alpha) for judges' scores of the tone quality ratings was .92.

A two-by-three-by-three factorial design was used in the study. The three independent variables were Group (experimental and control), Instrument (trumpet, horn, and trombone), and Grade (fourth, fifth, and sixth grade). The data were analyzed using multivariate and univariate analyses of covariance on the SAS computer program (SAS, 1989). The results are shown in Table 1. The results for main effects showed that the experimental group had significantly higher scores than the control group ($p < .05$) on breathing and performance measures. Among the breathing measures, significant differences were found for abdominal displacement, but not for lung capacity and thoracic displacement. These results were expected, since the instruction stressed increased abdominal expansion and did not work toward increased thoracic expansion. Among the performance measures, significant differences were observed for range and duration, but not for tone quality.

There were no significant grade level main effects for either the breathing or performance measures according to a MANCOVA analysis. However, there were significant effects for instrument classification. In both duration and tone quality, differences were noted. The horns had significantly higher duration scores than either the trombones or trumpets. Tone quality scores were significantly lower for trombones when compared with horns, but only marginally lower when compared with trumpets.

Discussion

The results of this study show that breath management instruction is effective in improving both breathing and performance aspects of brass playing. Group main effects for the dependent measures were found to be significant for the sample of fourth- through sixth-grade brass players. The results of the study reinforce the view that improving the brass players' breathing will improve the players' performance (Dale, 1965; Johnson, 1981; Kohut, 1985; O'Donnell, 1987).

Table 1 MANCOVA and ANCOVA Results for Breathing and Performance
Measures

Measure	Treatment (T)	Instrument (I)	Grade (G)	T × I	T × G
		Multivariate			
	$F = 6.35**$	$F = 0.44$	$F = 1.90*$	$F = 0.73$	$F = 0.98$
	(6, 40)	(12, 80)	(12, 80)	(12, 80)	(12, 80)
		Univariate			
Thoracic displacement					
	$F = 0.03$	$F = 0.01$	$F = 0.19$	$F = 0.48$	$F = 0.09$
	(1, 50)	(2, 50)	(2, 50)	(2, 50)	(2, 50)
Abdominal displacement					
	$F = 8.83**$	$F = 0.20$	$F = 1.82$	$F = 0.35$	$F = 0.24$
	(1, 50)	(2, 50)	(2, 50)	(2, 50)	(2, 50)
Vital capacity					
	$F = 2.72$	$F = 1.15$	$F = 0.28$	$F = 0.67$	$F = 2.22$
	(1, 50)	(2, 50)	(2, 50)	(2, 50)	(2, 50)
Range					
	$F = 12.51**$	$F = 0.11$	$F = 1.92$	$F = 0.57$	$F = 0.55$
	(1, 50)	(2, 50)	(2, 50)	(2, 50)	(2, 50)
Duration					
	$F = 21.63**$	$F = 6.30*$	$F = 0.33$	$F = 0.60$	$F = 1.19$
	(1, 50)	(2, 50)	(2, 50)	(2, 50)	(2, 50)
Tone quality					
	$F = 1.45$	$F = 3.59*$	$F = 0.13$	$F = 0.65$	$F = 1.14$
	(1, 50)	(2, 50)	(2, 50)	(2, 50)	(2, 50)

*$p < .05$.
**$p < .01$.
Note: Multivariate tests were run using the GLM procedure from SAS (1989). Pretest scores on all six dependent variables served as covariates in the MANCOVA analysis. A single covariate (the appropriate pretest measure) was used in the follow-up ANCOVA analysis.

Among the breathing measures, abdominal displacement was found to be significantly higher for members of the experimental group (mean, +5.59 millimeters; standard deviation [*SD*] of 6.47) when compared to the control group (mean, –1.37 millimeters; *SD* = 6.82). The control group still exhibited abdominal contraction, meaning the abdominal area got smaller when taking a breath. Therefore, the regular instrumental instruction does not seem to aid the development of abdominal breathing.

Among the performance measures, the range measure showed significantly higher scores for the experimental group. The experimental group showed an average range of almost 22 half-steps (*SD* = 3.91). The control group (18.72 half-step mean scores, *SD* = 4.22) improved slightly with a semester of regular instruction, but the larger increase in range for the experimental group seems to be due to the specific instruction in breathing. The experimental group also improved on the duration measure from pretest to posttest. The posttest experimental group averaged 13.92 seconds per held pitch. The control group showed a lower score for duration on the posttest (mean, 9.39 seconds) than they had on the pretest (mean, 11.47 seconds). The treatment appears to be responsible for the increase in duration for the experimental group.

The instruction in breathing mode was successful in improving abdominal displacement. Both the experimental and control groups showed a lack of abdominal movement on the pretest, but the experimental group was able to change from a thoracic mode of breathing to an abdominal/diaphragmatic mode of breathing. Both groups showed about the same thoracic displacement on the posttest as they had on the pretest. This was expected, since the breath management instruction did not stress chest movement, and the students were already actively using the thoracic mode of breathing.

Various researchers have measured lung capacity among instrumentalists (Brown & Thomas, 1999; Huttlin, 1982; Staples, 1988; Tucker, Faulkner, & Horvath, 1971; Van Middlesworth, 1978), but only the Brown and Thomas study explored the effects of breath training upon the subjects. The control group in the present study increased their lung capacity slightly from an average of 1.81 liters to 1.97 liters. The experimental group also increased their lung capacity, although not quite reaching the significance level set by the researcher (1.85 liters to 2.17 liters; $SD = 0.46$). These results may have been due to the practice in taking deeper breaths by the experimental group or general maturity.

Among the performance measures, significant differences were found for range by group. The exercises in the instructional manual stress using the airstream to produce higher pitches instead of using embouchure (or mouthpiece) pressure. An inspection of the means for the range measure shows that the control group increased about 1 half-step in overall range, while the experimental group increased their range about 5 half-steps.

Significant group differences also were found for the duration measure. The control group did show a decrease in their duration scores; perhaps the effects of improper breathing cause the inconsistency in both inspiration and expiration and can have a negative effect on this aspect of playing. The results of these two measures show that the treatment (breath management instruction) made a positive difference in an important component of brass-playing duration. This may have occurred because certain of the exercises stressed the control or slow emission of the air. These techniques enable the subjects to learn to relax the diaphragm more slowly, permitting the subject to conserve breath.

Among the experimental group, the horns had significantly better scores on the duration test than either the trumpets or trombones. This is probably due to the initial bore size of the instrument. The horns, of all the instruments in this study, have the narrowest leadpipe and, therefore, the most resistance and less air expended on the same airflow rate, allowing subjects to play slightly longer. More resistance makes it easier to slow the flow of air through the aperture.

Tone quality varied little from pretest to posttest between groups. It may take longer than 16 weeks to see any change in the tone quality of elementary brass players, or the rating scale used for judging may be too imprecise to measure small differences in tone. Also, tone quality may be a function of other variables than just breathing style; these variables might include instrument, aural memory, aural tone model, articulation, and embouchure.

The tone quality scores for the trombone players were significantly lower than those for horn or trumpet players. Tone quality may be a function of variables other than just breathing style (e.g., instrument, aural memory, aural tone model, articulation, and embouchure). The young trombonists are playing in a range lower than their own singing range, and this may cause a difference in aural perception of the pitches as well.

Taken as a whole, the results indicate that the addition of some breath management instruction is more effective than traditional instruction alone for enhancing breathing and performance skills. The absence of group-by-instrument and group-by-grade interactions, coupled with the significant group main effects, indicates that the breath management instruction was equally effective with all grade levels and instrument classes. Brass teachers should be focusing on teaching breathing skills to their students to obtain the most growth in their performance abilities. Future research might focus on high school students and the benefits of breath instruction for increasing their performance skills.

REFERENCES

Abeles, H. F. (1973). Development and validation of a clarinet performance adjudication scale. *Journal of Research in Music Education, 21*, 246–255.

Bencowitz, H. Z. (1984). Inspiratory and expiratory vital capacity. *Chest, 85*, 834–835.

Berger, K. (1965). Respiratory and articulatory factors in wind instrument performance. *Journal of Applied Physiology, 20*, 1217–1221.

Bobo, R. (1981a). Arnold Jacobs. *Brass Bulletin, 33*, 43–50.

Bobo, R. (1981b). Arnold Jacobs. *Brass Bulletin, 34*, 37–44.

Bouhuys, A. (1964). Lung volumes and breathing patterns in wind instrument players. *Journal of Applied Physiology, 19*, 967–975.

Brown, S. E., & Thomas, M. (1990). Respiratory training effects in wind and brass instrumentalists. *Medical Problems of Performing Artists, 5*, 146–150.

Caimi, F. (1981). Relationships between motivation variable and selected criterion measures of high school band directing success. *Journal of Research in Music Education, 29*, 183–198.

Cugell, D. W. (1986). Interaction of chest wall and abdominal muscles in wind instrument players, *Cleveland Clinic Quarterly, 53*, 15–20.

Dale, D. A. (1965). *Trumpet technique*. London: Oxford University Press.

Dennis, R. J. (1988). Musical performance and respiratory function in wind instrumentalists: Effects of the Alexander technique of musculoskeletal education (Doctoral dissertation, Columbia University Teachers College, 1987). *Dissertation Abstracts International, 48*, 1689A.

Druz, W. S., & Sharp, J. T. (1981). Activity of respiratory muscles in upright and recumbent humans. *Journal of Applied Physiology, 51*, 1552–1561.

Erickson, F. (1988). *Belwin comprehensive band method*. Miami: Belwin Mills.

Farkas, P. (1956). *The art of horn playing*. Evanston, IL: Summy-Birchard.

Feldstein, S., & O'Reilly, J. (1988). *Yamaha band student*. Van Nuys, CA: Alfred.

Froseth, J. O. (1984). *Listen, move, sing, and play*. Chicago: G.I.A. Publications.

Fuks, L., & Sundberg, J. (1999). Using respiratory inductive plethysmography for monitoring professional reed instrument performance. *Medical Problems of Performing Artists, 14*, 30–42.

Huttlin, E.J. (1982). A study of lung capacities in wind instrumentalists and vocalists (Doctoral dissertation, Michigan State University, 1982). *Dissertation Abstracts International, 43*, 301A.

Jacobs, A. (1991). Arnold Jacobs master class. *Instrumentalist, 45*, 21–24.

Johnson, K. (1981). *The art of trumpet playing*. Ames, IA: Iowa State University Press..

Kelly, K. (1983). The dynamics of breathing with Arnold Jacobs and David Cugell, M.D. *Instrumentalist, 38*, 6–12.

Kendall, M. J. (1988). Two instructional approaches to the development of aural and instrumental performance skills. *Journal of Research in Music Education, 36*, 205–219.

Kleinhammer, E. (1963). *The art of trombone playing*. Evanston, IL: SummyBirchard.

Kohut, D. L. (1985). *Musical performance: Learning theory and pedagogy*. Englewood Cliffs, NJ: Prentice-Hall.

Konno, K., & Mead. (1967). Measurement of the separate volume changes of rib cage and abdomen during breathing. *Journal of Applied Physiology, 22*, 407–422. MENC Committee on Standards. (1986). *The school music program: Description and standards*, 2nd ed. Reston, VA: Music Educators National Conference [now MENC—The National Association for Music Education].

O'Donnell, J. F. (1987). Beginning brass instruction: Teaching strategies for selected skills and concepts (Doctoral dissertation, Ball State University, 1987). *Dissertation Abstracts International, 48*, 1411A.

O'Reilly, J., & Williams, M. (1997). *Accent on achievement*. Van Nuys, CA: Alfred.

Pearson, B. (1982). *Best in class*. San Diego, CA: Kjos West.

Pearson, B. (1993). *Standard of excellence*. San Diego, CA: Kjos.

Phillips, K. H. (1983). The effects of group breath control training on selected vocal measures related to the singing ability of elementary students in grades two, three, and four (Doctoral dissertation, Kent State University, 1983). *Dissertation Abstracts International, 44*, 1017 A.

Phillips, K. H., & Vispoel, W. (1990). The effects of class voice and respiration instruction on vocal knowledge, attitudes, and vocal performance among elementary education majors. *The Quarterly, 1* (1 & 2), 96–105.

Phillips, K. H., & Sehmann, K. H. (1990). A study of the effects of breath management instruction on the breathing mode, knowledge of breathing, and performance skills of college-level brass players. *Bulletin of the Council for Research in Music Education*, no. 105, 58–71.

Price, H. E. (1983). The effects of conductor academic task presentation, conductor reinforcement, and ensemble practice on performers' musical achievement, attentiveness and attitude. *Journal of Research in Music Education, 31*, 245–247.

Rainbow, E. (1973). Instrumental music: Recent research and considerations for future investigations. *Bulletin of the Council for Research in Music Education*, no. 33, 8–20.

Rhodes, T., Bierschenk, D., & Lautzenheiser, T. (1993). *Essential elements*. Milwaukee, WI: Hal Leonard Publishing.

Russo, W. (1973). An interview with Arnold Jacobs. *The Instrumentalist, 27*, 28–30.

SAS Institute, Inc. (1989). *SAS software release 5.18*. Cary, NC: Author.

Sataloff, R. T., Spiegel, J. R., & Hawkshaw, M. (1990). The effects of respiratory dysfunction on instrumentalists. *Medical Problems of Performing Artists, 5*, 94–99.

Smith, J., Kreisman, H., Colacone, A., Fox, J., & Wolkove, N. (1990). Sensation of inspired volumes and pressures in professional wind instrument players. *Journal of Applied Physiology, 68*, 2380–2383.

Staples, T. W. (1988). A comprehensive performance project in horn literature with an essay consisting of the effects of inspiratory conditions on the vital capacity of brass players (Doctoral essay, University of Iowa, 1988). *Dissertation Abstracts International, 49,* 3198A.

Swearingen, J., & Buehlman, B. (1984). *Band plus.* Dayton, OH: Heritage Music Press.

Taylor, R. B. (1969). A study of the concepts of breathing as presented in literature dealing with tone production for orchestral brass-wind instruments (Doctoral dissertation, Columbia University Teachers College, 1968). *Dissertation Abstracts International, 29,* 2296A.

Tucker, A., Faulkner, M. E., & Horvath, S. M. (1971). Electrocardiography and lung function in brass instrument players. *Archives of Environmental Health, 23,* 327–335.

Van Middlesworth, J. L. (1978). *An analysis of selected respiratory and cardiovascular characteristics o wind instrument performance.* Unpublished master's thesis, Eastman School of Music, Rochester, NY.

Vellody, V. P., Nassery, M., Druz, W. S., & Sharp, J. T. (1978). Effects of body position change on thoracoabdominal motion. *Journal of Applied Physiology, 45,*581–589.

Watson, P. J., & Hixon, T. J. (1985). Respiratory kinematics in classical (opera) singers. *Journal of Speech and Hearing Research, 28,* 104–122.

Wick, D. (1971). *Trombone technique.* London: Oxford University Press.

Witt, A. C. (1986). Use of class time and student attentiveness in secondary instrumental music rehearsals. *Journal of Research in Music Education, 33,* 34–42.

Yarbrough, C., & Price, H. E. (1981). Prediction of performer attentiveness based on rehearsal activity and teacher behavior. *Journal of Research in Music Education, 29,* 209–217.

Zi, N. (1986). *The art of breathing.* New York: Bantam Books.

STUDY AND DISCUSSION QUESTIONS

1. What longtime tubist with the Chicago Symphony was known for his work on the topic of breathing? What did he advocate (Kelly, 1983)?

2. What did Middlesworth (1978) report regarding the lung capacities of wind and nonwind players?

3. Who were the subjects in Sehmann's study, and how were these assigned to groups?

4. What differentiated the instruction between the treatment and controls groups?

5. Who provided the instruction to the subjects in Sehmann's study? What did Sehmann provide for them?

6. What were the dependent variables, and how were these measured?

7. Why was it important to use both pre- and posttests?

8. What was the research design in Sehmann's study?

9. What were the independent variables?

10. How were the data analyzed?

11. What were the results of Sehmann's study?

12. At what level of probability was abdominal displacement significant?

SUGGESTED ACTIVITIES

1. Explain and demonstrate the process of breath management for both singers and wind players. Detail the function of the diaphragm and abdominal muscles.

2. Study Table 1 in Sehmann's study, and explain why it was necessary to do so many univariate tests (ANCOVAs) following the multivariate analysis (MANCOVA).

3. Explain why Phillips's dissertation study is considered classic, or "true," experimental research while Sehmann's is quasi-experimental research.

CHAPTER 13

Quantitative Research

Clinical

Not all research is carried out in natural settings, i.e., places where people work, live, or play on a daily basis. Scientific research is typically carried out in laboratories, where the controls are higher and human reaction does not depend on a natural setting (e.g., a classroom) for authentic results. When behavior is studied in this type of lab setting, it is known as clinical research.

STUDYING BEHAVIOR IN A CLINICAL ENVIRONMENT

Clinical research in music education is not very common; it is more so in music therapy because of the connection to mental and physical health. This type of study often involves specialized testing equipment that is not readily available to most music researchers. People in music electing to do this type of investigation typically need help in finding the instrumentation and in learning how to operate it.

A clinical study is often a type of trial run that uses a sample of far fewer than 40 subjects. Such a clinical trial is done in anticipation of replication with a greater number of subjects. Clinical trials are common in the drug industry, where the search for new medications begins with a small sample of subjects. Such trials lead to larger studies when there is evidence that a drug is found to be useful for its intended purposes, e.g., lowering cholesterol levels. Both of the articles presented in this chapter are of the clinical-trial genre.

Clinical researchers are not as concerned with threats to external validity as those doing behavioral research in natural settings. Because the natural environment (e.g., a classroom) presents many challenges to generalizing results, the researcher must be cautious of problems caused by possible threats to external validity, i.e., sample normalcy, randomization, size of sample, and so forth. The clinical environment is far easier to control and results from clinical trials are typically not generalized. Such trials serve as a type of pilot study. Clinical research is quantitative in nature and common to the natural sciences.

READING CLINICAL RESEARCH

The following study by music therapist Rebecca Engen, Ph.D., was carried out at The University of Iowa. Ms. Engen studied child and adolescent voice pedagogy and being a singer herself became interested in singing as a means for helping improve the quality of life for senior citizens. In an earlier study, Ms. Engen used a number of vocal techniques from *Teaching Kids to Sing* (Phillips, 1992) with residents of a home for senior citizens. She found older people were able to learn the vocal techniques quite easily and benefited from using them. Knowing this, Ms. Engen devised a study for the use of the same vocal techniques with persons suffering from emphysema. This study by Dr. Rebecca Engen is good example of behavioral research as clinical research.

The Singer's Breath: Implications for Treatment of Persons with Emphysema

Rebecca L. Engen, *Queens University of Charlotte*

Journal of Music Therapy, XLII(1), 20–48.

Reprinted by permission of American Music Therapy Association. Copyright © 2002 by AMTA.

The occurrence of chronic obstructive pulmonary disease (COPD) is on the rise in the United States. This degenerative disease, currently affecting over 13.5 million Americans, is the fourth leading cause of death in America (Swyberius, 2001; U.S. Department of Health and Human Service Centers for Disease Control and Prevention, 1999). As recently as 1993, the National Institutes of Health (NIH, 1993) listed COPD as the fifth leading cause of death in the United States. The economic impact of this disease is enormous when considering lost workdays and decreased productivity, visits to the doctor, hospitalization, prescriptions, oxygen, and home health assistance (Ahlheit, 1995; Craig, 1988; Higgins, 1984; NIH, 1993). Economic issues are not the only concern; emotional costs are also considerable. Persons with emphysema (a type of COPD) typically experience social withdrawal, anxiety, and fear related to breathing difficulties, and perhaps most significantly, loss of control and feelings of helplessness (Connelly, 2001). Powers (1997) states,

> The experience of chronic illness is unique to the individual and not limited to the pathophysiology of the disease. While disease may be the problem from the health care provider's perspective, the issue for older adults with various incurable conditions is how to live with and respond to symptoms and disabilities. (p. 136)

Emphysema

Emphysema is one of two types of chronic obstructive pulmonary disease (COPD). Chronic bronchitis is the other form. While emphysema certainly presents a serious medical problem, the nature of the disability is often primarily functional rather than medical. By nature, emphysema poses daily limits on activity and is a chronic problem; chronic bronchitis more often results in acute attacks. Because of these differences in symptom presentation, this study limited itself to persons with a physician's diagnosis of emphysema or COPD, probable emphysema.

In most cases, smoking is the most important risk factor for developing COPD. Since only 15% to 20% of smokers develop the disease, other risk factors such as age, repeated environmental exposure to smoke or pollution, frequent respiratory infections in childhood, low socioeconomic living conditions, and other yet unknown factors also contribute to its development (Hercules, Lekwart, & Fenton, 1979; Higgins, 1984; Hong & Ingram, 1998; NIH, 1993). There is also a rare form of emphysema caused by an inherited deficiency of a blood component, alpha-l-antitrypsin. It is estimated that 1% to 3% of all emphysema cases are due to this deficiency (NIH, 1993).

COPD is a degenerative disease that worsens over time. Among the first and most prominent of symptoms is dyspnea, or shortness of breath, with onset generally after the third or fourth decade of life (Hercules et al., 1979; Wilkins, Krider, & Sheldon, 1995). A cough and increased effort required for respiration follows, and as the disease progresses, the heart may be affected. When the heart and lungs no longer function effectively enough to supply the vital organs and tissues with oxygen, death is likely to occur.

Another physiologic feature of COPD is airway obstruction, which results from damage to the alveoli (tiny air sacs in the lungs) and collapse of the bronchioles (the smallest airways). This damage is due to the loss of elastin, a protein that helps maintain the strength of the alveolar and bronchiole walls. The result of this damage is difficulty in moving air out of the lungs.

Expiration is normally a passive process, but with the loss of elastic recoil, persons with COPD require a greater work effort to expel air. Respiratory muscle oxygen consumption can be as much as 10 to 20 times normal (Rochester, 1984). Additional effort to breathe can lead to greater airway collapse and compounds, rather than alleviates, the problem. Inspiratory muscles pull the air in through obstructions, but the air does not leave without assistance and is easily trapped by collapsed airways. Upon exhalation, use of abdominal and auxiliary thoracic muscles aid expiration. The added workload increases oxygen demand and contributes to diaphragmatic fatigue (Hercules et al., 1979; Taylor, 1987). Breaking this vicious cycle of increased oxygen demand and fatigue is an important treatment concern for COPD patients (Lutz, 1987). "Full utilization of his available pulmonary energy for activities important to him is the patient's right—his right to breathe" (McCarthy, 1967, p. 783).

Treatment Standards

Standard treatment for emphysema recognizes and addresses the added stress of emotional and economic costs associated with a diagnosis of COPD. Typical treatment recommendations are to stop smoking, take medication, and, in severe cases, use oxygen therapy. Beyond these medical interventions are three additional areas of recommended treatment: breathing (respiratory) instruction, relaxation exercises for anxiety control, and group support to encourage active participation in the treatment process (NIH, 1993; Stanescu, Nemery, Venter, & Maréchal, 1981; Taylor, 1987). Treatment of emphysema often amounts to amelioration of symptoms, and the areas addressed are well suited to music therapy interventions.

Related Findings in Traditional Approaches

Intuition and tradition have indicated that adoption of a diaphragmatic breathing mode can benefit persons with COPD. As a result, brief breathing mode instruction has become a standard treatment recommendation. Amazingly, the benefit of diaphragmatic breathing has yet to be established. Research on the effects of diaphragmatic breathing has demonstrated mixed results and an increase in energy output for the patient. Few controlled studies on the diaphragmatic breathing mode have been done (Gosselink & Wagenaar, 1993), and no studies focusing on the entire breath cycle (means of inspiration and of expiration) have been found.

The health effects of diaphragmatic breathing are so commonly accepted that lay publications (e.g., *Prevention, Redbook*) even describe the technique. In Kolodzey (1982), several physicians describe the technique in a clear, simple way that tells of their clinical experience. Similar to vocal instructors, they use imagery and observational feedback to help their patients learn a relaxed, diaphragmatic mode of breathing. Moreover, these physicians acknowledge the importance of practice in obtaining and maintaining a healthy breathing mode.

> The way we breathe has a profound effect on the way we feel....Many stress-related complaints, whether physical, mental, or emotional, are caused by improper breathing. But fortunately, many of these complaints can be reversed simply by learning to breathe properly.... [O]ne way to alleviate this stress response is simply by consciously switching to a pattern of slow, deep, diaphragmatic breathing. (Kolodzey, 1982, pp. 139–140)

However, in a review of common medical texts (Byers, 2000; Fischer, Fegelman, & Johannigman, 1999; French, Painter, & Coury, 1994; Larsen, Accurso, Deterding, Halbower, & White, 1999; Micromedex, 2000; Odom, 1999; Wong, Hockenberry-Eaton, Wilson, Winkelstein, Ahmann, & DiVito-Thomas, 1999), there was little or no direction for monitoring patient success in breathing or for educating the patient in proper technique. (Lamaze breathing was excluded from this search because of its detailed and specific training and application to childbirth.)

Nursing and patient education texts often provide more detail on how to instruct the patient in breathing. In most cases they provide an explanation as to why deep breathing is useful for these procedures. One important technique these texts recommend is to begin a deep breath by first exhaling completely. This technique also is used for singers (Phillips, 1992; Satoloff, 1998; Smith & Sataloff, 2000). Nursing instructions frequently mention either breathing through the mouth or through the nose, depending upon the purpose of the breath, and will provide exercises for the patient to practice their breathing (Ahlheit, 1995; Bolander, 1994; Byers, 2000; Cahill, 1987; Diamond Headache Clinic (n.d.); French et al., 1994; Kleiber, 2001; Micromedex, 2000; Seaton, 1970; Taylor, Lillis, & LeMone, 1997; Wilkins et al., 1995; Wong et al., 1999).

Pursed-lip breathing is a technique often recommended for persons with emphysema; it helps to manage anxiety and stave off an acute attack. This breathing technique also provides upstream resistance so airways remain open during expiration. Directions are to use this technique anytime, "if it makes you feel better" (Shayevitz & Shayevitz, 1985). In this manner of breathing, inspiration is through the nose and the breath is let out through pursed lips, as if blowing through a straw. Using this technique prolongs the expiration and serves to reduce the expiratory airflow. A lower flow rate maintains subglottal pressure and prevents airway collapse (Byers, 2000; Hugh-Jones & Whimster, 1978; Shayevitz & Shayevitz, 1985).

A few studies have attempted to measure the effects of learning to control the breath. Breathing rate and mode as applied to yoga practice in clinical populations and compared to healthy controls yielded encouraging results. Bernardi et al. (1998) concluded that six breaths per minute was the optimum rate for improving oxygen saturation and the other pulmonary functions measured in both chronic heart failure patients and in healthy adults. Stanescu et al. (1981) found that "[v]oluntary control of breathing may be a useful adjuvant in the treatment of patients with chronic obstructive pulmonary disease" (p. 1629).

The physiological process of breathing, often from the standpoint of whether the inspiration was abdominal as well as perceived effort, has been addressed, with inconclusive and contradictory results. Gosselink, Wagenaar, Rijswijk, Sargeant, and Decramer (995) used a small sample $(n = 7)$ in an ABA design to show that diaphragmatic breathing can be learned in a brief period of study (3 weeks). Using the protocol of a previous study (Collett, Perry, & Engel, 1985), Gosselink et al. measured the mechanical efficiency of the inspiratory muscles through a variable load inspiratory threshold device, similar to the one employed in the present study. Subjects were able to breathe diaphragmatically under load, though compared to a "natural breathing mode." "No positive effects were observed after a learning period of diaphragmatic breathing in patients with severe COPD" (p. 1411). Using healthy subjects Ward, Danziger, Borica, Allen, and Bowes (1966) found that a single held breath (similar to a yawn or sigh), as opposed to a simple deep breath or even several deep breaths, was most efficient in keeping the lungs ventilated and perfused (filled with blood). This expanded the findings by Ferris and Pollard (1960) that breath measures varied day to day, with position, and that lung expansion and compliance decreased 26% to 40% after a period of quiet breathing.

Ventilations and perfusion are not the only breathing concerns for persons with COPD. Because of the increased effort exerted in the process of breathing, fatigue is also a problem. Grassino, Belle-mare, and Laporta (1984) found that some COPD patients routinely breathe close to their fatigue threshold. Airflow through the mouth was measured in some subjects, and they found that with exercise airflow in both directions increased, as did dyspnea. However, diaphragmatic activation decreased and diaphragmatic fatigue was avoided. When these same subjects were asked to consciously alter their breathing for a prolonged inspiration and brisk expiration, diaphragmatic fatigue ensued, with concurrent employment of auxiliary breathing muscles. Dyspnea was late to appear, and recovery was much quicker than in the exercise condition.

In a well-controlled study with a design similar to the present research, O'Donnell, McGuire, Samis, and Webb (1998) measured pulmonary function, peripheral muscle strength and endurance, as well as dyspnea in 20 outpatients with COPD. The authors concluded that positive changes in perception of breathlessness during exertion, exercise endurance, and muscle strength, while providing functional improvement, were likely a result of reduced ventilatory demands rather than a direct effect of mechanical change or improved muscle strength. Subjects served as their own controls, and O'Donnell et al. found that, for their measures, the slopes before and after the control period were virtually identical or had slightly increased (representing a minor loss in function). Similar baseline results were discovered by Gosselink et al. (1995). For this reason baseline data were collected only once, as a pretest, in the present study.

Related Findings in Music Approaches

Without detailed instruction, musicians, unlike medical personnel, would not expect someone to breathe naturally in the expected manner (Christy, 1979; Phillips, 1992; Roma, 1956; Sataloff, 1998; Schmidt, 1998; Smith & Sataloff, 2000; Stanton, 1983; Titze, 1986; Vennard, 1967; Wormhoudt, 1981). In addition to creating a better understanding of the correct breathing pattern, vocal music teachers provide feedback on the quality and approximation of the respiratory technique. These are critical to continued application of the preferred breathing mode. Not one of the medical sources cited earlier indicates a method of assessment or provision for feedback. However, many of the medical reasons for using the deep breathing mode require a repetitive pattern of full lung inflation, as in the prevention of pneumonia following surgery.

While breath instruction is more consistent and thorough when teaching music, few studies have been done while instructing a clinical population. What follows is a brief review of literature demonstrating the efficacy of the instructional techniques employed in the present study, as well as the few studies that do look at breathing with medically ill subjects.

Instrumental.   Prior to this author's investigations, limited research, primarily with wind instruments, was available. Studies and reports from the '60s and '70s found that playing wind instruments uses a breathing pattern that is similar to singing (Bouhuys, Proctor, & Mead, 1966) and utilizes large volumes of air at high internal pressure, but that it does not present a heavy workload for the respiratory system itself (Bouhuys, 1964). Controlling the breath and airflow were crucial to success (Bouhuys) and led to beneficial results among children with asthma as reported by parents and teachers (Marks, 1974).

These early studies helped guide music therapists, who have begun to document the results of their clinical practices. Griggs-Drane (1999) developed a treatment protocol for introducing wind instruments to patients with respiratory problems,

Nornhold (1999) studied adults with COPD as they learned to play recorders, and Lipawen (2000) taught children with asthma to play the harmonica. Coffman and Adamek (1999) surveyed senior center band members, who indicated the importance of social and health benefits from playing in the group. There were limited but positive results in each of these studies.

One additional study in the development of elementary school brass players does deserve mention. Sehmann (1990) used an instructional method developed for teaching singing at the elementary school level (Phillips, 1992) and found the breathing exercises to be effective. Sehmann's study demonstrated that Phillips' method was suitable for different applications.

Vocal.   Phillips' (1992) method for vocal instruction, originally developed through his dissertation (1983), has been field-tested extensively in teaching vocal music within general music and choral settings (Aaron, 1990/1991; Cox, 1992; Fett, 1993/1994; Gackle, 1987; Henry, 1995; Phillips & Aitchison, 1997a, 1997b, 1998, 1999; Phillips, Aitchison, Bergman, & Western, 1999; Phillips, Aitchison, & Nompula, 2001; Phillips & Emge, 1994; Phillips & Vispoel, 1990). These studies have consistently demonstrated that with brief but regular practice, students improve on the exercises administered in the study, but that these skills translate into improved quality of tone, pitch accuracy, and enjoyment of music. Additionally, there is evidence for improved breath support and control.

Learning Theories

Older adults often have not been in a formal educational setting for some time. Pratt (1988) recognized that adults enter an educational setting with varying levels of dependency for both support and direction. Providing the right instructional situation to match each learner's characteristics is a challenge for the instructor (Pratt). A learner who feels they have tried everything and yet the illness continues to affect their every move is likely to require teacher-directed study and a high level of support. Someone seeking information about the disease process and options for lessening its impact may be more self-directed in their study and require a lower amount of support from the instructor. Flexibility within the small-group setting of the present study allowed the investigator to discover and address the individual needs of the subjects.

The net sum of positive and negative forces is said to determine motivation and participation among adult learners (Miller, 1967). According to Miller's force field analysis model, the magnitude and direction of social forces and personal needs combine to predict participation in formal learning environments. When both types of forces are strong in favor of an educational objective, initial and continued participation is expected to be high. Some considerations of the present study included offering a choice of times to participants in a convenient and familiar setting. Where transportation or parking expenses were an issue, vouchers were arranged through the Red Cross and local volunteers. Notebooks, complete with a pen, schedule, lined paper, and large-print song lyrics, were provided to each participant, as were props to assist in visualizing the breath and to serve as a reminder to practice. The treatment protocol included a time for community building, since social connections are one of the primary factors influencing adult education participation (Merriam & Caffarella, 1991; Morstain & Smart, 1974).

Phillips' method (1992) was pilot-tested on healthy senior citizens (Engen, 2000), then again with senior volunteers diagnosed with COPD (Engen, 2001). Participants in both of these studies responded favorably, improved breathing habits, increased breath control and support, stated perceived health benefits, and noted the support of the group treatment process. The method for the clinical pilot (Engen) was identical to the current study (Engen, 2003).

Method

Subjects

Outpatients in a gerontology clinic and a pulmonary rehabilitation clinic in a southeastern metropolitan area were invited to participate in this project. To qualify for this study subjects were required to have a physician's diagnosis of emphysema or COPD probable emphysema and agree to be present for 10 out of 12 group lessons. Additionally, potential subjects were screened for smoking and respiratory related hospitalization and tested for $FEy1$ ($\geq 35\%$ and $\leq 7\%$ of predicted values; Morris, Koski, & Johnson, 1971). Twelve persons participated in the program, though only seven completed the requirements for inclusion. Of the additional five, one was dropped due to absences for a family emergency, two had initial breath measurements too low for inclusion, and two had measurements too high for inclusion. The four participants with measurements outside the inclusion limits signed the consent, requested to participate, and completed the program. The seven subjects included three males with an average age of 80.67 years and four females, who averaged 72 years of age.

Duration of the Study

This study spanned a period of 9 weeks during the summer of 2002. Pretesting took place the week prior to the beginning of the treatment phase. The pretest measures were administered individually and each session was 45 minutes in duration. Following the pretest week, the treatment phase of the study began. Subjects met in two small groups for two sessions per week. Each session was identical and ran for 45 minutes. The treatment phase lasted for a total of 6 weeks (for a total of 12 instructional sessions). A 2-week no-contact period followed the treatment phase, which was followed by the final data collection. In addition to the pretest and final data collection times, repeated measures of the same battery of tests were administered following weeks 2, 4, and 6 of the treatment phase. Data collected at 2-week treatment intervals were independent of, and did not interfere with, the regular vocal music/treatment sessions.

Instructional Procedures

Subjects met in small groups twice per week for 6 weeks of singing instruction. Each group received the same sequence of instruction in equal duration of time. Subjects were assigned to a small group based on their preference for scheduling (day of week, time of day). Each session was 45 minutes in length, with testing scheduled on an individual basis. All sessions were held in a classroom at the Presbyterian Senior Health Center and were conducted by the researcher.

The methodology consisted of posture and breath management exercises from Phillips's (1992) vocal instruction program as pilot-tested with this population by Engen (2000, 2003). The specific exercises were chosen for their appropriateness to an adult population and connection to predetermined goals. In addition to the aforementioned warm-up exercises, the bulk of the treatment sessions consisted of choral speaking and singing.

Specific songs and keys were chosen in an extended process. The researcher's experience as a music therapy clinician provided a framework for presenting appropriate musical choices to participants. The two pilot studies provided feedback on song and style preferences, pitch ranges, and pacing for skill acquisition. Two experienced music therapists assisted the researcher in key choice and determination of stylistic variety as well as representation of musical concepts (e.g., syllabic vs. sustained text setting). Additionally, participants stated their musical experience and preferences in the screening interview. This information confirmed the appropriateness of the song choices.

The first part of each treatment session focused on respiration (posture and breath management). A relaxed and stable body position is necessary for optimizing the breath. To lessen demands on the subjects, all exercises and singing were done from a seated position as described by Phillips (1992). A brief series of warm-up exercises was used to help subjects relax, stretch, and attain proper body alignment for the breathing and singing that followed.

Breath management is subdivided into breath control and breath support. Breath support is the power behind a voice. Activation of the abdominal and oblique muscles during exhalation creates an internal pressure and energizes the air column. The purpose of breath control is to be able to maintain an energized air column while slowly emitting the air. Both support and control are necessary for a good singing tone, but more importantly, in this study they provide skills for dealing with dyspnea and promoting confidence for meeting life's challenges.

It was anticipated that, due to the nature of the disease being studied, subjects might be reluctant to sing and would initially have difficulty in applying the breathing techniques being taught. For this reason, the treatment included choral speaking to ease inhibitions and begin connecting the breath to voice. (Research has shown a relationship between the production of the singing voice and the speaking voice; Gould, 1968.) All singing was expected to be in unison, unless someone harmonized spontaneously; participants were not singled out for solo singing. The emphasis of instruction was on the application of the breath—vocal performance was not emphasized.

The use of props, such as soap bubbles, a pinwheel, or a pipe and ball, provided lighthearted practice in controlling airflow. A substantial amount of breath support and airflow were required for use of such props. These gadgets offered visual feedback and improvement that could be detected in the ease of operation, duration, and steadiness of the floating ball or spinning pinwheel. Each subject was given these props to take home. It was hoped that having the toys around the house would prompt the subjects to remember their breathing mode and remind them to practice the exercises on a regular basis. Evidence from journals and conversation indicated that this was in fact a very helpful technique, as subjects responded positively to this visual reminder.

Once posture and the breath were established within a treatment session, exercises for connecting the breath to the voice were taught. While breathing is a vital skill, isolated breathing exercises serve a limited purpose. Applying the breath management skills to the speaking voice can affect breathing mode throughout the day, and provides a functional outcome for subjects who may question the value of the exercises or of the singing. Techniques for this portion of the session combined the use of vocal sounds, abdominal contraction, and vocal register shifts, without specific pitch requirements. These exercises were planned to help the learner notice the physical sensation of breath management and how breath demands can vary with the task. Vocalizing in this manner was less clearly appreciated by the participants. While they understood the concept of warming up the voice, they were anxious to get to the singing and apply the "same" techniques.

The final phase of the warm-up included vocalises and echo singing. These exercises stimulated the vocal folds and provided an application for practicing the exercises previously discussed. For nonsingers, as the subjects for this study were, vocalises can build confidence in the singing voice and reinforce posture and breath management issues. Additionally, the exercises chosen (see Engen, 2003) were easily done in a single breath, with time allowed for concentrated effort on the next breath. Subjects seemed to appreciate singing vocalises, as it was more musical than the previous exercises. By varying tempo, duration, and dynamics, support and control were challenged. Subjects regularly described situations such as speaking when winded or reciting a long line of prayer in church and compared these situations to how it felt when practicing the vocalises.

A 10-minute intermission was an integral part of each session. In addition to allowing time for restroom breaks or getting a drink, this time provided a breathing respite for the subjects who found the activities tiring. Though this time was considered an intermission, additional function within the framework of this study was inherent. This downtime was less structured than the formal exercises or singing, and socialization among participants was encouraged. Group bonding improved subjects' investment in the program and provided positive social interaction that is crucial to self-perception of general well-being. An additional benefit to the researcher was the sharing of applications of the techniques from class to their daily lives. These stories of success and struggle were taken into account by the researcher as the sessions progressed. Though no formal agenda was apparent to the subjects during intermission, the investigator facilitated group discussion on topics related to music (e.g., background, memories, preferences, etc.) or coping skills (e.g., problem solving/sharing, breathing, nutrition, fitness, etc.).

The final part of the instructional period focused on the singing of songs. This began with easy songs (narrow range, movement mostly stepwise or small intervals, and simple rhythms) in a call-and-response format. Again, to increase probability of success, this song structure allowed for short phrases, with an extended period in which to prepare the breath. Finally, a variety of standard folk, sacred, and pop songs were sung, with continued attention to breath mechanics and phrasing. Because many of the participants were ill at ease with their singing voices or had trouble with respiratory activity, little emphasis was placed on tone quality or pitch matching. Singing in this study was viewed as a means to an end—ease of respiratory function, resulting in improved quality of life.

The specific sequence of the exercises and vocalises was: (a) respiratory activities (posture and breath management); (b) phonatory exercises (application of breath to speaking voice); (c) vocalises (sustained tones, arpeggios, and scales), (d) intermission (discussion of music/singing in subjects' lives); and (e) songs. Sessions were always ended with a review of any new exercises, a summary of topics discussed, and a reminder to practice. While this sequence served to structure each singing lesson, subjects' performance and preference affected the choice of materials.

Data

The collection of data took place every 2 weeks as repeated measures, for a total of five testing periods. Subjects were tested individually within 24 hours after a session by the investigator, and every effort was made to provide the same testing conditions for all subjects. The timed walk and threshold loading were administered first and last during the testing since these were the most physically demanding tasks. The order of presentation for other tests was flexible, and participants regularly requested a specific test to be offered next. Many of the measures were familiar to the subjects, due to their clinical history. The investigator demonstrated those that were unfamiliar or new, and subjects had an opportunity to practice using the equipment.

Physical health. Three of the dependent variables in this study looked at physical health. During this battery of breathing tests, subjects were monitored with pulse oximetry for their medical safety; data were not formally analyzed. The oximetry provided continuous feedback of blood-oxygen content (SpO_2) and heart rate. Its unobtrusive ease of use and clinical value as an assessment tool are well documented (Ehrhardt & Graham, 1990; McConnell, 1994; Melini, 1989).

1. Forced expiratory volume (FEV) was measured by a handheld Respiradyne pulmonary function meter. This test was familiar to all subjects, but the investigator offered to demonstrate the maneuver for the subjects. To insure accurate readings, each subject had one breathing tube that was used for all three testing dates. For each testing date, three trials were recorded and the best score was used for reporting results. This "best-of-three" score was then compared to normative data based on age, gender, and height (Morris et al., 1971).

2. Inspiratory threshold, an indication of diaphragmatic strength and endurance, was measured with an inspiratory muscle trainer (Threshold IMT), a spring-loaded device that can incrementally increase inspiratory resistance. Research has shown that there is an initial training effect, and subjects should be allowed to experience the test before actual measurement begins (Baarends, Schols, Nusmeier, van der Grinten, & Wouters, 1998; Eastwood, Hiliman, & Finucane, 1994; Eastwood, Hillman, Morton, & Finucane, 1998; Gosselink et al., 1995; Gosselink, Wagenaar, & Decramer, 1996; Grassino et al., 1984; Hopp, Kim,

Larson, & Sharp, 1996; Johnson, Cowley, & Kinnear, 1997; Larson et al., 1999; Pardy, Rivington, Despas, & Macklem, 1981). There is a learning curve reported for this measure, and minimally loaded practice trials were offered. During testing, subjects wore a nose clip and breathed for two minutes at a given level of resistance. After each 2-minute interval, they received one minute of rest before a trial with increased resistance. This pattern continued until a subject was unable to maintain breathing without breaking their seal on the mouthpiece. Load was measured in centimeters of water displaced and was limited on the device to loads between 7 and 41 cm H_2O, in 2-cm increments.

3. The third measure of physical health was the distance walked in six minutes. Timed walking is a standard assessment tool for persons with emphysema. The length of time allotted varies in the literature from 6 to 12 minutes (Eakin, 1994/1995; O'Donnell et al., 1998; Pardy et al., 1981). Subjects were asked to walk as far as possible. They were allowed to rest if needed and were monitored by pulse oximetry. One subject was given mandatory resting instructions if her oxygen saturation level fell to 85%. All others were able to self-monitor their exertion.

Functional outcomes.   Three functional outcomes were addressed as a practical indicator of improvement, that is, outcomes that would directly affect the subjects' ability to perform activities of daily living.

1. Breath control was defined as the ability to extend the expiratory process and utilize the breath efficiently. Subjects were asked to count out loud as high as possible without taking another breath. A metronome set at 92 beats per minute (bpm) cued the subjects and paced their counting. Falling behind by more than one beat stopped the count. This measure was previously used by Engen (2000, 2001) and was reported as the mean of three trials.

2. Breath support was defined as the power behind the breath and was measured as intensity of speech. Persons with emphysema are known to have a breathy vocal quality. As a measure of vocal support, intensity of speech, in decibels, was measured. A RadioShack® digital sound level meter was placed on a table about a yard from the subject's mouth to record the maximum decibel level during recitation of the "Pledge of Allegiance" delivered as if speaking to a large audience.

3. A simple visual check was taken at each measurement period to determine whether or not the subjects could learn to breathe diaphragmatically. Subjects were asked to place two fingers on the abdomen, exhale, then inhale as if to begin singing. The investigator observed the subject for evidence of abdominal displacement (desired) and for clavicular displacement (not desired). This method has been previously used by Phillips and Aitchison (1999) and Engen (2000, 2001).

Quality of life.   Quality of life was a third area investigated in this study; four measures were used.

1. The Modified Borg Symptom Rating Scale, used during the timed walk, is a self-report scale of dyspnea ratings that have been used extensively in the literature (Eakin, 1995; Gosselink et al., 1995; Hopp et al., 1996; O'Donnell et al., 1998;

Thornby, Haas, & Axen, 1995). This scale has been demonstrated to be highly reliable in test–retest conditions and valid when compared to other measures of dyspnea (Borg, 1982; Eakin, 1995). Borg symptom ratings are on a 10-point ratio scale from 0 = nothing at all to 10 very, very severe/almost maximal.

2. Visual analog scales (VAS) are a self-report measure of whatever is indicated by the endpoint labels. For the purposes of the present investigation, endpoints indicated the subjects' current state of breathlessness or perceived difficulty as a result of the breathlessness. This scale was easy to use and was available for daily recording; all that was required for this measure was to mark across the linear scale at the current level of the indicated factors (Ahlheit, 1995; Eakin, 1995; Gift, 1989a, b).

3. The Duke Health Profile© (Parkerson, 1999), used by permission (G. R. Parkerson, personal communication, May 15, 2001), addressed quality of life and general well-being by asking about self-perception, relationships, breathlessness, overall health, and socialization. Scores are scaled in two broad categories of "function" and "dysfunction." In the present study, four of the six functional scales were scored: physical health score, mental health score, social health score, and self-esteem score. Additionally, three of the five dysfunctional scales were considered: anxiety score, depression score, and anxiety depression (DUKE-AD) score. The outcomes on these scales for each individual were converted to age-group and gender quartiles and compared to a reference population of 1997 primary care adult patients (Parkerson, 1999).

Additional data were collected in the form of free-response journal entries and a satisfaction survey. Following the six weeks of group vocal instruction, a survey was mailed to participants. This form was used by Nornhold (1999), and was slightly modified by Engen (2001) to reflect the needs and institutional support of the current investigation. The survey was used with permission (Debbie Cestaro-Seifer, personal communication, May 13, 2001). Throughout the duration of the treatment, subjects were asked to keep a journal. Information on practice times, musical preferences, frustrations, health comments, and so forth, were gathered in an effort to evaluate and modify the treatment program for future applications. These comments were not analyzed as a dependent measure, but were reflected descriptively, to monitor subjects' reactions. Journal sheets were provided to all participants, but were not equally used. The men only made entries when reminded during a treatment session, while the frequency and quality of entries by women varied widely.

Design and Analysis

The independent variable for this study was time (repeated measures), with singing instruction as the mode of treatment. The study investigated numerous dependent variables measuring breathing mode, pulmonary function, diaphragmatic endurance, breath management, and perception of symptoms in a one-group pretest–posttest design with repeated measures. The data in this study were collected over a period of 9 weeks, with the first measures taken prior to treatment. Every 2 weeks throughout the treatment sessions additional measures were taken. A follow-up measurement was taken 2 weeks after the last treatment session. The results of these measures were analyzed using eight repeated-measures analyses of variance (ANOVA). Tukey's honestly significant difference (HSD) test was applied to significant F-ratios to determine which mean differences were significant. For these analyses the independent variable was time and the dependent measures included FEV_1, inspiratory threshold, distance on a timed walk, extent of counting on one breath, and average intensity of speech. While the present study had, of necessity, a small number of subjects, the data generated over five trials were large. Therefore, the initial weakness of the design was tempered by the statistical power engendered by the subjects' repeated testing. In comparison to similar clinical studies with this population, the sample from this study was of average size.

Results

Repeated-measures ANOVAs were used to analyze the measures of physical health (see Table 1). None of these, FEV_1, inspiratory threshold, or distance walked, were significantly different across time. Functional outcomes of breath management and breathing mode were analyzed with paired-samples t-tests and descriptive statistics (see Table 1). Counting as a measure of breath control was significant ($p < .05$ for 7 subjects; $p < .01$ for all 11 participants), as was intensity as a measure of breath support ($p < .01$ for 7 subjects and for all 11 participants). The breathing mode of subjects showed a clear shift from predominantly clavicular to 100% diaphragmatic that was maintained in all but one subject two weeks after the treatment sessions ended (see Figure 1).

Table 1 Repeated Measures ANOVA Results

	SS	df	MS	F	p
FEV_1	70.990	4	17.748	1.318	.292
Inspiratory threshold	25.867	4	6.467	.632	.645
Walk distance (pre-)	829,348.643	1	29,348.643	3.253	.121
Walk (all 11)	85,313.636	1	85,313.636	10.545	.009**
Counting	84.700	4	21.175	3.021	.038*
Counting (all 11)	161.356	4	40.339	5.769	.001**
Intensity	234.309	4	58.577	12.104	.000**
Intensity (all 11)	349.362	4	87.340	15.983	.000**

*$p < .05$
**$p < .01$.

Quality of life as measured by subjects' ratings of perceived breathlessness on both the Borg scale and the VAS were not significantly different across time. A paired-samples t-test on subjects' VAS ratings of interference in daily activity did show a significant decrease between the first three weeks of treatment and the last three weeks of treatment ($p < .01$ for 7 subjects; $p < .05$ for all 11 participants). The DUKE scores were converted to quartile scores for each subscale based on a comparative sample of primary care patients separated by age and gender. Two of the seven subscales analyzed, mental health and social health, showed an upward shift in quartile scores.

(a)

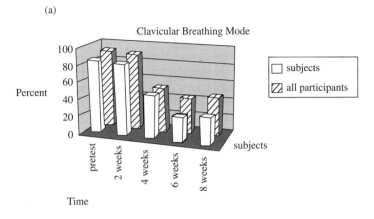

(b)

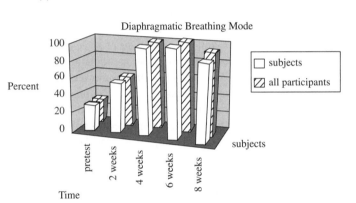

Figure 1 Frequency distribution for breathing mode. **(a)** The clavicular breathing mode. **(b)** The diaphragmatic breathing mode.

Free-response journal entries and a satisfaction survey provided additional data. Journal comments were classified into four categories: investment in the program, group support, improvement, and socialization. Satisfaction survey results were analyzed with descriptive statistics (see Table 2). The six responses with the highest ratings were all to questions directly related to the program content or relationships with the therapist or other subjects within the group. The six responses receiving the lowest ratings came from questions that dealt with generalizing treatment topics to daily life or that were not specifically addressed in the treatment protocol (relaxation and family involvement).

Discussion

The idea of asking persons who experience a chronic state of breathlessness to attend vocal music classes was less startling to potential clients than was expected.

By applying an established methodology for teaching breath management and vocal control (Phillips, 1992), the importance of and connection between the breath and the voice was of logical interest to the subjects. Given the lack of musical experience and absence of active listening among participants, as reported during the screening process, the level of participation and universal enthusiasm and perseverance in the program was remarkable. One participant presented the researcher with a cassette recording of himself singing through the entire songbook.

A rigid time schedule for each treatment session was established for the purpose of consistency and research reliability between the two small groups of subjects. Within each session the sequence of skill introduction was effective; however, more elasticity in time spent on each type of skill may have been useful. Participants took the instruction seriously and often had questions or asked to work on something longer. In an effort to meet their needs while maintaining the integrity of the research protocol, those skills were readdressed during the singalong portion of the treatment session. Similarly, subjects often had tales to relate about breathing, singing, or practicing of the techniques. The intermission allowed ample time for such discussions; however, it was often necessary to defer these tales until the intermission, thus losing the timeliness of their narration.

The measure of FEV_1 was used initially as a means of screening persons who were either not very ill or who may have been so ill that participation could be either risky or to no avail. As it turned out, four persons fell into those extreme categories and chose to participate anyway. As was demonstrated in the presentation of results, in most cases including these persons in the data analyses did not alter the outcome. In fact, on walking distance all four outliers improved so much that they brought a nonsignificant finding for the other seven subjects to a level of significance ($p < .01$) when all 11 participants were counted. One of the subjects was a 1-year post lung transplant, while the most severe outlier was on a transplant waiting list. Sharing between these two persons was motivational not only to themselves, but to the whole group. Similarly, one of the outliers had been an avid distance runner until the last ten years, since her diagnosis. Her determination to stay active and in control of her life was inspirational to less motivated and optimistic subjects. It is doubtful that including these extreme cases compromised the treatment for the subjects and a clinical diagnosis of emphysema, regardless of severity, could determine eligibility for this type of treatment.

In addition to serving as a screening tool, FEV_1 was also used as a measure of physical health. While as a group there were no significant changes in the expiratory volume, certain individuals did improve. Four of the seven subjects achieved a higher percent of the expected value for their age and gender after 8 weeks. There was more variance than expected between measurement periods. Results for the four additional participants showed more stable numbers, with three of the four improving or remaining stable and one (the most severe case) showing a moderate decline from 20% of the expected value to 17.6%. There is no definitive answer for what the expected rate of decline would be for these individuals; adding a delayed treatment group as a control could help clarify these results.

Findings from inspiratory threshold testing were not significant; however, there were problems with this measure that could have hidden real change from the mathematical analysis. The device did not allow for minimal levels of resistance, and started at 7 cm H_2O. One subject and two of the extra participants were unable to sustain that minimum level of resistance for the required 2 minutes. Without a precise baseline measurement for comparison, data for these subjects could not he included in the ANOVA analysis. Conversely, by the fourth week one of the healthiest participants was able to complete 2 minutes at the greatest resistance offered by the device, 41 cm H_2O. Therefore, the participant's inspiratory threshold was unable to be assessed. More sophisticated computerized equipment is available to analyze the airflow associated with use of the threshold device. While still bound to the load limits of the Threshold IMT device, computerized analysis of peak mouth pressure and maximum inspiratory pressure could have continued to show progress, if not the true threshold due to limitations of the measurement tool.

Table 2 Selected Satisfaction Survey Results

Rank	*M*	*SD*	(all 11)	*M SD*	Question
1	4.00	0	3.91	.29	I have learned about a variety of activities and techniques that help me to feel less short of breath.
2	3.86	.35	3.82	.39	The music therapist gives information that is clear and useful.
2	3.86	.35	3.73	.45	The instruction I get fits into my routines and activities at home.
4	3.71	.45	3.82	.39	I feel participation in the Music Therapy Program has been worthwhile.
4	3.71	.45	3.73	.45	The music therapist listens and responds to my needs, concerns, questions, and ideas.
4	3.71	.45	3.73	.45	The class allows me to feel less like a "sick patient" and more like an individual with special challenges.
4	3.71	.45	3.73	.45	I feel my overall mood/outlook has improved.
20	3.29	.45	3.27	.62	I feel the Music Therapy Program provides activities and information that is important to my partner/family.
20	3.29	.45	3.27	.62	I feel less alone as a person with emphysema.
22	3.14	.35	3.27	.45	I am more able to relax.
22	3.14	.35	3.18	.57	I feel I am more likely to pursue activities outside my home (e.g., go shopping, go to a restaurant, go to the movies, etc.).
22	3.14	.35	3.09	.51	I have less fatigue and shortness of breath.
25	3.00	0	3.27	.45	I feel I am more likely to pursue musical activities on my own time.

A timed walk is a familiar assessment tool to COPD patients. While no significance was found for the seven subjects, results were significant ($p < .01$) when all 11 participants were considered. No particular trend for those who improved and who did not was apparent for the seven subjects, but in looking at the raw data for the four extra participants there is a clear trend. All four improved by 8–50%. Even the healthiest participant increased her walking distance by 24%. Two of the seven subjects stated orthopedic complaints rather than breathlessness as a reason for pausing during the walks. Perhaps the advanced age and frailness of some participants caused the physical demands of this measure to overshadow potential gains in respiratory fitness.

Being able to extend the expiratory process without further increasing the sensation of breathlessness is both recommended and problematic for persons with emphysema. Singing and counting both offer this experience and the fact that there was significant growth in this area has important implications for symptom management. Because subjects continued to improve on measures of vocal control and support throughout the treatment, and for some, even beyond, the potential benefits from the treatment may be even greater than assessed in this study. These results provide evidence that a longer treatment period may be beneficial.

One of the research questions posed for this study was whether the singing instruction would lead to a change in breathing mode. As expected, all but one subject used clavicular breathing on the pretest, and two subjects demonstrated both diaphragmatic and clavicular breathing modes. Simultaneous use of both breathing modes is not a relaxed state and is indicative of cognitive understanding without physical mastery of the skill. Engen (2001) also found this phenomenon after treatment sessions ended. In the present study only half of the participants were using a clavicular breathing mode after week 4 of the treatment, while 100% demonstrated diaphragmatic breathing. After six weeks the diaphragmatic mode was maintained, with a continued drop in the use of clavicular motion. Two weeks after the end of the treatment sessions there was a slight regression toward clavicular breathing, but only one subject did not employ the diaphragmatic breathing mode. Two things stand out in this analysis: (a) it is clear that there was a change in breathing mode, and (b) it took four weeks of treatment to produce the change.

One benefit of exploratory research such as this project is the generation of more specific questions based on the findings. How can progress be maintained once the research project has ended? Is six weeks of treatment enough? For breathing mode and the other measures for which there was a positive change, it appeared to take at least four weeks to occur and for some measures, for example, intensity, there was a steady increase through the end of treatment, possibly indicating that maximum benefit had not yet been reached. Anecdotal evidence would suggest that participants' satisfaction with this program was high. Staff from both the Senior Health Center and the Pulmonary Rehabilitation Center sat in on some of the treatment sessions to see what their patients were talking about. When visiting the pulmonary rehabilitation program, patients not in the study would ask the investigator questions about some of the treatment techniques they had heard subjects discuss. Ratings from the satisfaction survey were mixed. Overall, the ratings were clustered between "agree" and "strongly agree," but were lower than expected. Nevertheless, the open-ended comments section at the end of the survey produced uniformly positive statements. The time demands of the study, five measurement periods and twelve treatment sessions, plus practicing and journaling, were a negative aspect of the treatment voiced by more than one subject. Some of the lowest-ranked questions were as expected, since the topics, like relaxation or family roles, were indirectly addressed in the treatment. The journal comments were neutral or positive in regards to satisfaction.

REFERENCES

Aaron, J. (1991). The effects of vocal coordination instruction on the pitch accuracy, range, pitch discrimination, and tonal memory of inaccurate singers (Doctoral dissertation, The University of Iowa, 1990). *Disseriation Abstracts International, 51*(9), 2912–3A.

Ahlheit, B. D. (1995). Interventions for clients with lower airway problems. In D. D. Ignatavicius, M. L Workman, & M. A. Mishler (Eds.), *Medical surgical nursing:A nursing process approach* (2nd ed.,Vol.1, pp. 673–728). Philadelphia: W. B. Saunders.

Baarends, E. M., Schols, A. M., Nusmeier, C. M., van der Grinten, C. P. M., & Wouters, E. F. M. (1998). Breathing efficiency during inspiratory threshold loading in patients with chronic obstructive pulmonary disease. *Clinical Physiology, 18*(3), 235–244.

Bernardi, L., Spadacini, G., Bellwon, J., Hajric, R., Roskamm, H., & Frey, A. W. (1998). Effect of breathing rate on oxygen saturation and exercise performance in chronic heart failure. *Lancet, 351,* 1308–1311.

Bolander, V. B. (1994). Sorensen and Luckmann's basic nursing: A psychophysiologic approach (3rd ed.). Philadelphia: W. B. Saunders.

Borg, G. A. V. (1982). Psychophysical basis of perceived exertion. *Medicine and Science in Sports and Exercise, 14*(5), 377–381.

Bouhuys, A. (1964). Lung volumes and breathing patterns in wind-instrument players. *Journal of Applied Physiology, 19*(5), 967–975.

Bouhuys, A., Proctor, D. F., & Mead, J. (1966). Kinetic aspects of singing. *Journal of Applied Physiology, 21*(2), 483–496.

Byers, J. F. (2000). Respiratory care modalities. In S. C. Smeltzei, & B. G. Bare (Eds.), *Brunner & Suddarth's Medical Surgical Nursing* (9th ed., pp. 490–528). Philadelphia, PA: Lippincott.

Cahill, M. (Ed.). (1987). *Patient teaching.* Springhouse, PA: Springhouse.

Christy, V. A. (1979). Foundations in singing: A basic textbook in the fundamentals of technic and song interpretation. Dubuque, IA: Wm. C. Brown.

Coffman, D. D., & Adamek, M. S. (1999). The contribution of wind band participation to quality of life of senior adults. *Music Therapy Perspectives, 17*(1), 27–31.

Collett, P. W., Perry, C., & Engel, L.A. (1985). Pressure–time product, flow, and oxygen cost of resistive breathing in humans. *Journal of Applied Physiology, 58,* 1263–1272.

Connelly, C. (2001). You can feel better!: How pulmonary rehabilitation helps people with COPD. *Breathe Well, 5*(4), 8, 11–12, 16.

Cox, M. J. (1992). *An investigation of how vocal exercises affect the range, respiration, and pitch accuracy of junior high students.* Unpublished master's thesis, University of Nebraska at Omaha.

Craig, K. (1988). The role of research in respiratory care. In R. L. Cliatburn & K. C. Craig (Eds.), *Fundamentals of respiratory care research* (pp. 3–14). Norwalk, CT: Appleton and Lang.

Diamond Headache Clinic. (nd.). *Biofeedback exercises.* Chicago, IL: Autonomic Feedback.

Eakin, E. G. (1995). Clinical assessment of shortness of breath in chronic obstructive pulmonary disease (Doctoral dissertation, University of California, San Diego, San Diego State University, 1994). *Dissertation Abstracts International, 55*(9), 4165.

Eastwood, P. R, Hillman, D. R., & Finucane, K. E. (1994). Ventilatory responses to inspiratory threshold loading and role of muscle fatigue in task failure. *Journal of Applied Physiology, 76*, 185–195.

Eastwood, P. R., Hillman, D. R., Morton, A. R., & Finucane, K. E. (1998). The effects of learning on the ventilatory responses to inspiratory threshold loading. *American Journal of Respiratory and Critical Care Medicine, 158*, 1190–1196.

Ehrhardt, B. S., & Graham, M. (1990). Pulse oximetry: An easy way to check oxygen saturation. *Nursing, 20*(3), 50–54.

Engen, R. (2000*). The effects of breath training, via vocal pedagogy, oxygenation and breath control.* Unpublished manuscript, The University of Iowa, Iowa City.

Engen, R (2001*). The singer's breath: A preliminary investigation into the effects of singing on persons with chronic obstructive pulmonary disease.* Unpublished manuscript, The University of Iowa, Iowa City.

Engen, R. (2003). *The singer's breath: Implications for treatment of persons with emphysema.* Unpublished doctoral dissertation, The University of Iowa, Iowa City.

Ferris, B. G., Jr., & Pollard, D. S. (1960). Effect of deep and quiet breathing on pulmonary compliance in man. *The Journal of Clinical Investigation, 39*, 143–149.

Fett, D. L. (1994). The adolescent female voice: The effect of vocal skills instruction on measures of singing performance and breath management (Doctoral dissertation, The University of Iowa, 1993). *Dissertation Abstracts International, 54*(7), 2501.

Fischer, J. E., Fegelinan, E., & Johannigman, J. (1999). Surgical complications. In S. I. Schwartz, U. T. Shires, F. C. Spencer, J. M. Daly, J. E. Fischer, & A. C. Galloway (Eds.), *Principles of surgery* (7th ed., pp. 441–484). New York: McGraw-Hill.

French, C. M., Painter, E. C., & Coury, D. L. (1994). Blowing away shot pain: A technique for pain management during immunization. *Pediatrics, 93*(3), 384–388.

Gackle, M. L. (1987). The effect of selected vocal techniques for breath management, resonation, and vowel unification on tone production in the junior high school female voice (Doctoral dissertation, University of Miami, 1987). *Dissertation Abstracts International, 48*(4A), 862.

Gift, A. G. (1989a). Visual analog scales: Measurement of subjective phenomena. *Nursing Research, 38*(5), 286–288.

Gift, A. G. (1989b). Validation of avertical visual analog scale as a measure of dyspnea. *Rehabilitation Nursing, 14*(6), 323–325.

Gosselink, R., & Wagenaar, R. C. (1993). Efficacy of breathing exercises in chronic obstructive pulmonary disease and asthma: A metanalysis of the literature. *Journal of Rehabilitation Sciences, 6*, 66–87.

Gosselink, R., Wagenaar, R. C., & Decramer, M. (1996). Reliability of a commercially available threshold loading device in healthy subjects and in patients with chronic obstructive pulmonary disease. *Thorax, 51*, 601–605.

Gosselink, R., Wagenaar, R. C., Rijswijk, H., Sargeant, J., & Decramer, M. L. A. (1995). Diaphragmatic breathing reduces efficiency of breathing in patients with chronic obstructive pulmonary disease. *American Journal of Respiratory and Critical Care Medicine, 151*(4), 1136–1142.

Gould, A. O. (1968). Developing specialized programs for singing in the elementary schools. Final Report. Washington, D.C.: Research in Education, August, 1968. (ERIC Reproduction Service No. ED 025530 24 TE 499967)

Grassino, A., Bellemare, F., & Laporta, D. (1984). Diaphragm fatigue and the strategy of breathing in COPD. *Chest, 85*(6, supplement), 51S–54S.

Griggs-Drane, E. R. (1999, November). Music Therapy in the treatment of respiratory diseases. Paper presented at the meeting of the American Music Therapy Association in cooperation with the WorldFederation of Music Therapy: 9th World Congress of Music Therapy, Washington, DC.

Henry, J. E. (1995). The effectiveness of Kenneth Phillips' strategies on the singing development of students in grade five. Unpublished master's thesis, The Pennsylvania State University, College Park.

Hercules, P. R., Lekwart, F. J., & Fenton, M. V. (1979). *Pulmonary restriction and obstruction: A programmed text.* Chicago, IL: Year Book Medical.

Higgins, M. (1984). Epidemiology of COPD: State of the art. *Chest, 85*(6), 3S–8S.

Hong, E. G., & Ingram, R. H., Jr. (1998). Chronic bronchitis, emphysema, & airway obstruction. In A. S. Fauci, E. Braunwald, K. Isselbacher, J. D. Wilson, J. B. Martin, D. L. Kasper, S. L. Hauser, & D. L. I.ongo (Eds.), *Harrison's principles of internal medicine,* Vol. 2 (14th ed., pp. 1451–1459). New York: McGraw-Hill.

Hopp, L. J., Kim, M. J., Larson, J. L., & Sharp, J. T. (1996). Incremental threshold loading in patients with chronic obstructive pulmonary disease. *Nursing Research, 45*(4), 196–202.

Hugh-Jones, P., & Whimster, W. (1978). State of the art: The etiology and management of disabling emphysema. *American Review of Respiratory Disease, 117*(2), 343–378.

Johnson, P. H., Cowley, A.J., & Kinnear, W.J. M. (1997). Incremental threshold loading: A standard protocol and establishment of a reference range in naïve normal subjects. *Eurapean Respiratory Journal, 10*, 2868–6871.

Kleiber, C. (2001). Distraction. In M. Craft-Rosenberg & J. Denehy (Eds.), *Nursing interventions for infants, children, and families* (pp. 315–327). Thousand Oaks, CA: Sage.

Kolodzey, J. (1982). The most overlooked health secret. *Prevention,* Dec., 136, 138, 140, 142–143.

Larsen, G. L., Accurso, F. J., Deterding, R. R., Halbower. A. C., & White, C. W. (1999). Respiratory tract and mediastinum. In W. W. Hay Jr., A. R. Hayward, M. J. Levin, and J. M. Sondheimer (Eds.), *Current pediatric diagnosis and treatment* (pp. 418–64). Stamford, CT: Appleton & Lange.

Larson, J. L., Covey, M. K., Berry, J., Wirtz, S., Alex, C. G., & Matsuo, M. (1999). Discontinuous incremental threshold loading test: Measure of respiratory muscle endurance in patients with COPD. *Chest, 115*(1), 60–67.

Lipawen, P. J. (2000, November). The effects of harmonica playing on lung function in asthmatic children. Unpublished masters thesis, Drexel University, Philadelphia, PA.

Lutz, M. M. (1987). Extrapulmonary problems: Causes of ineffective breathing patterns. In V. P. Peck (Ed.), *Nurse review: Respiratory problems* (pp. 115–136). Springhouse, VA: Springhouse.

Marks, M. B. (1974). Musical wind instruments in rehabilitation of asthmatic children. *Annals of Allergy, 33*(6), 313–319.

McCarthy, J. A. (1967). Immobility: Effects on respiratory function. *American Journal of Nursing, 67*(4), 783–784.

McConnell, E. A. (1994). Performing pulse oximetry. *Nursing, 24*(10), 23.

Melini, L. (1989). A noninvasive way to measure oxygen saturation. *RN, 52*(1), 79.

Merriam, S. B., & Caffarella, R. S. (1991). *Learning in adulthood.* San Francisco: Jossey-Bass.

Micromedex. (2000). Advice for the patient: Drug information in lay language (20th ed., Vol. 2). Englewood, CO: Micromedex.

Miller, H. L. (1967). Participation of adults in education: A force-field analysis. Boston: Center for the Study of Liberal Education for Adults, Boston University.

Morris, J. F., Koski, W. A., & Johnson, L. C. (1971). Spirometric standards for healthy nonsmoking adults. *American Review of Respiratory Disease, 103*(1), 57–67.

Morstain, B. R., & Smart, J. C. (1974). Reasons for participation in adult education courses: A multivariate analysis of group differences. *Adult Education, 24*(2), 83–98.

National Institutes of Health. (1993). *Chronic obstructive pulmonary disease*. [Brochure]. Bethesda, MD: National Institutes of Health.

Nornhold, N. A. (1999*). Chronic obstructive pulmonary disease: A music therapy pilot project*. (Manuscript in preparation).

Odom, J. (1999). Postoperative pain care and complications. In M. H. Meeker & J. C. Rothrock (Eds.), *Alexander's care of the patient in surgery* (11th ed., pp. 239–262). St. Louis, MO: Mosby.

O'Donnell, D. E., McGuire, M., Samis, L., & Webb, K. T. (1998). General exercise training improves ventilatory and peripheral muscle strength and endurance in chronic airflow limitation. *American Journal of Respiratory and Critical Care Medicine, 157*, 1489–1497.

Pardy, R. L., Rivington, R. N., Despas, P. J., & Macklem, P. T. (1981). Inspiratory muscle training compared with physiotherapy in patients with chronic airflow limitation. *American Review of Respiratory Disease, 123*(4), 421–425.

Parkerson, G. R. (1999). *User's guide for the Duke Health Measures*. Durham, NC: Department of Community and Family Medicine, Duke University Medical Center.

Phillips, K. H. (1983). The effects of group breath control training on selected vocal measures related to the singing ability of elementary students in grades two, three, and four (Doctoral dissertation, Kent State University, 1983*). Dissertation Abstracts International, 44A*, 1017.

Phillips, K. H. (1992). *Teaching kids to sing*. New York: Schirmer Books.

Phillips, K. H., & Aitchison, R. E. (1997a). The relationship of inaccurate singing to pitch discrimination and tonal aptitude among third-grade students. *Contributions to Music Education, 24*(1), 7–22.

Phillips, K. H., & Aitchison, R. E. (1997b). The effects of psychomotor instruction on general music singing performance. *Journal of Research in Music Education, 45*(2), 185–196.

Phillips, K. H., & Aitchison, R. E. (1998). The effects of psychomotor skills instruction on attitude towards singing and general music among students in grades 4–6. *Bulletin of the Council for Research in Music Education, 137*, 32–42.

Phillips, K. H., & Aitchison, R. E. (1999). Second-year results of a study relating singing instruction, pitch accuracy and gender to aural acuity, vocal achievement, musical knowledge, and attitude towards singing among general music students. *Contributions to Music Education, 26*(1), 67–85.

Phillips, K. H., Aitchison, R. E., Bergman, J. F., & Western, B. A. (1999). First-year results of a longitudinal study of the relationship of singing instruction, pitch accuracy and gender to aural acuity and vocal achievement among general music students. *Research Perspectives in Music Education, 1*, 32–37.

Phillips, K. H., Aitchison, R. E., & Nompula, Y. P. (2001). The relationship of music aptitude to singing achievement among fifth-grade students. *Contributions to Music Education, 29*(1), 47–58.

Phillips, K. H., & Emge, S. (1994). Vocal registration as it affects vocal range for seventh- and eighth- grade boys. *Journal of Research in Singing and Applied Vocal Pedagogy, 18*(1), 1–10.

Phillips, K. H., & Vispoel, W. P. (1990). The effects of class voice and breath management instruction on vocal knowledge, attitudes, and vocal performance among elementary education majors. *The Quarterly Journal of Music Teaching and Learning, 1*(1 & 2), 96–105.

Powers, B. A. (1997). Social support, social networks, and the problem of loneliness in elder care. In E. A. Swanson & T. Tripp-Reimer (Eds.), *Chronic illness and the older adult* (pp. 136–158). New York: Springer.

Pratt, D. D. 1988). Andragogy as a relational construct. *Adult Education Quarterly, 38* (3), 160–181.

Rochester, D. F. (1984). The respiratory muscles in COPD: State of the art. *Chest, 85*(6), 47S–50S.

Roma, L. (1956). *The science of singing.* New York: G. Schirmer.

Sataloff, R. T. (1998). *Vocal health and pedagogy.* San Diego, CA: Singular.

Schmidt, J. (1998). *Basics of singing* (4th ed). New York: Schirmer Books.

Seaton, R. M. (1970). *A study to determine whether preoperative instruction in deep breathing and coughing produced more effective deep breathing and coughing postoperatively.* Unpublished master's thesis, The University of Iowa, Iowa City.

Sehmann, K. H. (1990). The effects of breath management instruction on the performance of elementary brass players (Doctoral dissertation, The University of Iowa, 1990).

Shayevitz, M. B., & Shaveviti, B. R. (1985). *Living well with emphysema and bronchitis: A handbook for everyone with chronic obstructive pulmonary disease.* Garden City, NY: Doubleday.

Smith, B., & Satalof. R. T. (2000). *Choral pedagogy.* San Diego, CA: Singular.

Stanescu, D. C. Nemers. B., Venter, C., & Maréchal, C. (1981). Pattern of breathing and ventilatory response to CO_2 in practicing hatha-yoga. *Journal of Applied Physiology, 51,* 1625–1629.

Stanton, R. (1983). *Steps for singing for voice classes* (3rd ed). Behnont, CA: Wadsworth.

Swyberius, S. J. (2001). Spirometry: Learning if your lungs are healthy. *Breathe Well, 5*(4), 6–7.

Taylor, C., Lillis, C., & LeMone, P. (Ed.). (1997). *Fundamentals of nursing: The art and science of nursing care* (3rd ed.). Philadelphia: Lippincott.

Taylor, J. D. (1987). COPD: A debilitating problem. In V. P. Peck (Ed.), *Nurse review: Respiratory problems* (pp. 40–51). Springhouse, VA: Springhouse.

Thornby, M. A., Haas, F., & Axeis, K. (1995). Effect of distractive stimuli on exercise tolerance in patients with COPD. *Chest, 107*(5), 1213–1217.

Titze, I. (1986). Voice research: Some notes on breath control in singing. *The NATS Journal, 43*(2), 28.

U.S. Department of Health and Human Services Centers for Disease Control and Prevention. (1999). Chronic diseases and their risk factors: The nation's leading causes of death [Brochure]. Atlanta, GA: Author.

Vennard, W. (1967). *Singing: The mechanism and the technic* (Rev. ed.). New York: Carl Fischer.

Ward, R. J., Danziger, F., Bonica, J. J., Allen, C. A., & Bowes, J. (1966). An evaluation of postoperative respiratory maneuvers. *Surgery, Gynecology & Obstetrics, 123*(1), 51–54.

Wilkins, R. L., Krider, S. J., & Sheldon, R. L. (Eds.). (1995). *Clinical assessment in respiratory care* (3rd ed.). St. Louis, MO: Mosby.

Wong, D. L., Hockenberry-Eaton, Wilson, D., Winkelstein, M. L., Ahmann, E., & DiVito-Thomas, P. A. (1999). *Whaley & Wongs nursing care of infants and children* (6th ed., pp. 1131–1209, 1456–1532). St. Louis, MO: Mosby.

Wormhoudt, P. S. (1981). *Building the voice as an instrument.* Oskaloosa, IA: William Penn College.

STUDY AND DISCUSSION QUESTIONS

1. Who were the subjects, how many were in the sample, and what were their ages?

2. Why is emphysema considered a chronic disorder?

3. What was the duration of the treatment period, and of what did the treatment consist?

4. Why were the data collected as "repeated measures"?

5. What categories of measurements did the dependent variables reflect?

6. What were the four measures used to collect data for quality of life?

7. What was the design of Engen's study? Was this a weak or a strong design?

8. What type of analyses were used to determine significant differences?

9. What were the results found for (1) physical health, (2) functional/breathing measures, and (3) quality of life?

10. What were the levels of significance reported in Table 1 for extent of counting for 7 subjects and for 11 subjects?

11. What did Engen conclude about improving the quality of life for persons with emphysema?

12. How did the subjects in the study respond on the satisfaction survey?

Benefits Seen in Acoustic Hearing + Electric Stimulation in Same Ear

Chris Turner, Bruce Gantz, Mary Lowder, and Kate Gfeller, The University of Iowa

The Hearing Journal, 58(11), 53–55.

Reprinted by permission of Lippincott, Williams & Wilkins., Copyright © 2006 by LWW.

More than 28 million Americans suffer the effects of hearing loss. Of primary concern to most of them is their difficulty understanding speech. Hearing aids are the most common treatment for most sensorineural hearing loss, while cochlear implants are the treatment of choice for the patient with a severe-to- profound hearing loss.

In general, when the hearing loss is less than severe, the patient is presumed to have sufficient existing inner hair cells and accompanying neural connections to allow simple amplification of sound to transmit speech information to the brain. When the loss is greater, transmitting the pattern of basilar membrane vibrations in the cochlea to the brain can be problematic due to damaged or missing inner hair cells. In such cases, a cochlear implant, which bypasses the basilar membrane vibrations and transductions of the inner hair cells to stimulate the auditory nerve directly, can be a very effective solution.

However, the electric stimulation used in cochlear implants has several disadvantages in comparison with amplification. These disadvantages are related to the limited frequency resolution provided by current electrode arrays, in which even the best users behave as if they are receiving only six to eight independent channels of frequency information when listening to speech, compared with the more precise frequency resolution provided by acoustic hearing. Speech can sound "fuzzy" to implant users, and other signals, such as music, may be nonmelodic and often unpleasant. This also can make it difficult to separate people's voices when several people are talking at once.

Another disadvantage of traditional implants is that any residual hearing is usually destroyed as a result of the implantation surgery; and subsequently the patient needs the implant and processor to be "powered up" for basic sound awareness.

The most common form of adult hearing loss is a high-frequency sensorineural deficit, caused by damage to hair cells in the basal end of the cochlea. In these individuals, the apical hair cells still function normally for the perception of low-frequency sounds. If the hearing loss is severe in the high-frequency region (severe damage to the inner hair cells), the patient may be unable even with amplification to distinguish the higher-frequency sounds of speech (such as consonants) that are crucial for human communication.[1-2] What is needed for these patients then is a way to bypass the missing or damaged inner cells at the basal half of the cochlea and get high-frequency speech in formation to the brain.

One strategy is to preserve the low-frequency acoustic hearing during implantation surgery and provide electric stimulation for the transmission of the higher-frequency regions of speech. In the past, there have been isolated cases of patients with some response to acoustically presented sound after implant surgery. However, surgical techniques and devices designed to preserve residual acoustic hearing in cochlear implant patients are a more recent development.[3-6] One of several options is usually chosen today to minimize potential damage to the apical (low-frequency) region of the cochlea. In one approach, an electrode of standard length is inserted only partially into the cochlea.[7]

A Short-Electrode Device

The University of Iowa adopted a different approach, which is to insert a specifically designed short electrode into the cochlea.[8] Patients implanted in this way hear sounds through combined acoustic and electric stimulation. Depending upon the degree of hearing loss in the lower frequencies, some of these patients require a hearing aid for the low frequencies, while some do not. The electrode currently used by the Iowa Group is only 10 mm in length and has six channels of electric stimulation assigned to transmit the sound information corresponding to frequencies above the audiometric cutoff, usually near 750 to 1000 Hz.

An interesting finding of our research so far is that in patients who have sufficient residual hearing in the nonimplanted ear to match the pitch of the electrical stimulation to a tone in the contralateral ear, the electrical stimulation of the most apically located electrode provides pitch sensations, on average, of about 1200 Hz, even though the 10-mm electrode resides in the basal first turn of the cochlea.

In a multicenter FDA clinical trial, 24 patients have been implanted with short electrodes to date, and residual hearing was preserved to within a median value of +/–10 dB postoperatively. In one patient, residual hearing disappeared about 2 months after surgery following a viral infection. However, in every case, the patient's speech-recognition performance (using combined electric and acoustic hearing) is better now than it was preoperatively. These results have been so encouraging that the FDA clinical trial has been extended and expanded to include patients with normal hearing up to 1500 Hz and severe losses in the higher frequencies.

Improved Speech Recognition

For most of our patients, speech recognition continues to improve (for combined acoustic and electric hearing) for 6 to 9 months after the initial hookup of the implant. We now have speech-recognition results from 12 patients who have been using the device for at least a year. Comparing these patients' speech-recognition scores for CNC words between 12 months after hookup and before the surgery showed that all patients have improved with the addition of the electrical stimulation, including the one patient who lost his residual acoustic hearing. The mean improvement in CNC word recognition observed from adding the electric stimulation is 40%; the range of improvement across patients was from 18% to 66%.

We are currently investigating the possible factors contributing to the success of the device in individual patients. We suspect that the quality of residual acoustic hearing and the survival pattern of auditory nerve fibers in the base of the cochlea are important factors.

The acoustic-only (preoperative) score represents the best the patient had been able to achieve, even with advanced hearing aids. Thus the improvements observed from adding electrical stimulation represent an advance in the treatment of sensorineural hearing loss that was previously unavailable. Analysis of errors from our consonant-recognition test shows that the primary benefit on speech recognition of adding electrical simulation is improved perception of the place of articulation feature in consonant recognition. Many patients report after receiving the hybrid implant that "speech sounds very much like it used to, only clearer." Since these patients perceive the lower frequencies through their residual hearing, it's no surprise that speech sounds the way it used to.

We have also measured the ability of the short-electrode patients to understand speech in a background of other talkers, a situation in which the ability to separate different voices is crucial.[8] We used an adaptive task in which the listener is asked to identify simple spondee words, and the level of the background signal (competing speech from two other talkers or steady noise) is adjusted to find the signal-to-noise ratio (SNR) at which 50% of the spondees can be accurately identified. We also tested users of traditional cochlear implants, listeners with sensorineural hearing loss, and normal-hearing subjects for comparison.

The spondees were highly understandable by all subjects when presented in quiet, so this test primarily reflects listeners' ability to resist background noise. Normal-hearing listeners do extremely well on this task, and listeners with moderate to severe hearing loss show a disadvantage of approximately 15 to 20 dB compared with normals. However, users of long-electrode cochlear implants show, on average, a 35-dB disadvantage compared with normals. In contrast, the short-electrode users perform approximately the same as the moderate-hearing-loss group.

In another analysis, we matched the 10 highest-performing traditional implant users with the 12 long-term short-electrode users on their ability to understand speech in quiet. In this comparison, the short-electrode patients showed a 6-dB advantage for speech understanding in the competing-talker background and a 5.5-dB advantage for speech in a steady background noise. The best short-electrode patients could understand speech in backgrounds with an SNR 10 dB more adverse than could the best traditional, long-electrode implant users.

Better Music Perception

An added benefit is that music remains more natural in tone quality and important structural features of music such as pitch and timbre are preserved in the frequency range stimulated by acoustic energy. The fundamental frequencies played by many musical instruments—which are also those that make up many melodies and harmony—lie below 750–1000 Hz. Therefore, these patients, as a group, do considerably better than traditional cochlear implant patients on discriminating musical intervals, perceiving directions of pitch changes, and recognizing familiar melodies.

Research by Kate Gfeller's research team here at Iowa has measured melody recognition in these patients, and they score over 80% correct on their standard test. Compare this with 87% correct for normal-hearing subjects and only 25% correct for patients wearing traditional long-electrode cochlear implants. One of our short-electrode patients is an audio engineer, and preserving his residual hearing and the associated musical perception abilities has helped him function at his job.

Conclusion

These findings strongly suggest that the advantage for speech in noise shown by the acoustic-plus-electric patients is a result of their preserved residual hearing and their ability to separate the target voice from the background. This advantage in noise, and the related preservation of the esthetic qualities of music and other sounds, is a compelling reason to preserve residual hearing in patients when possible.

The new short-electrode or hybrid cochlear implant appears to offer an opportunity for improving the lives of many patients who, in the past, had to choose between wearing hearing aids that provided little benefit and, if their hearing was poor enough, sacrificing the natural sounds of acoustic hearing to use a traditional long-electrode cochlear implant. Therefore, preserving residual acoustic hearing during future cochlear implant surgeries will most likely become a common practice in treating sensorineural hearing loss.

REFERENCES

1. Ching T, Dillon H, Byrne D: Speech recognition of hearing-impaired listeners: Predictions from audibility and the limited role of high-frequency amplification. *J Acoust Soc Am* 1998:103:1128–1140.
2. Hogan C, Turner CW: High-frequency amplification: Benefits for hearing-impaired listeners. *J Acoust Soc Am* 1998:104:432–441.
3. Gantz BJ, Turner CW: Combining acoustic and electric speech processing: Iowa/Nudeua Hybrid Implant. *Acta Otolaryngol* 2003:124:344–347.
4. Gantz BJ, Turner C, Gfeller K, Lowder M: Preservation of hearing in cochlear implant surgery. Electrical/acoustic hearing. *Laryngoscope* 2004:115:796–802.

5. Von Ilberg C, Kiefer J, Pfenningdorff T, et al.: Electric-acoustic stimulation of the auditory system. *ORL* 1999:61:334–340.

6. James C, Albegger K, Battmer R, et al.: Preservation of residual hearing with cochlear implantation: How and why. *Acta Otolaryngol* 2005:025:481–491.

7. Kiekr J, Pok M, Munka O, et al.: Combined electric and acoustic stimulation of the auditory system: Results of a clinical study. *Audiol Neuroto* 2005:10:134–144.

8. Gantz BJ, Turner CW: Combining acoustic and electric hearing. *Laryngoscope* 2005:113:1726–1730.

9. Turner CW, Gantz BJ, Vidal C, Behrens A: Speech recognition in noise for cochlear implant listeners: Benefits of residual acoustic hearing. *J Acoust Soc Am* 2004:115:1729–1735.

STUDY AND DISCUSSION QUESTIONS

1. What has been the perception of music when using the traditional cochlear implant?

2. What is the most common form of adult hearing loss?

3. How does the short-electrode cochlear implant differ from a standard cochlear implant?

4. How do patients using the short-electrode implant hear sounds?

5. What genre of research does this study represent?

6. What is the FDA, and why is this support important?

7. What was found regarding patients' speech-recognition performance using combined acoustic and electric hearing stimulation?

8. Why was consonant recognition so dramatically improved for patients?

9. What benefits are there for music perception when using the short-electrode implant?

10. How have patients with the short-electrode implant scored on a test of melody recognition?

11. How have patients with the traditional implant scored on a melody-recognition test?

12. What is the overall conclusion of this study as presented by the authors?

SUGGESTED ACTIVITIES

1. Do you know of anyone who has a loss of hearing and has had a cochlear implant? If so, what have been the results?

2. Discuss other types of studies in music education and music therapy in which clinical research could be beneficial.

3. Speculate on why the traditional cochlear implant has not been successful in helping people with severe hearing loss to perceive music with any clarity.

CHAPTER 14

Mixed Methods Research

The two articles in this chapter are examples of concurrent procedures in which the researchers use quantitative and qualitative data in order to provide a comprehensive analysis of the research problem. The data are collected simultaneously and then integrated in the interpretation of the results. This permits the researchers to analyze different types of questions within the same study. Creswell (2003) states:

> With the development and perceived legitimacy of both quantitative and qualitative research in the social and human sciences, mixed methods research employing the data collection associated with both forms of data is expanding. A new *Handbook of Mixed Methods in the Social and Behavioral Sciences* (Tashakkori & Teddlie, 2003) and journals reporting and promoting mixed methods research (e.g., *Field Methods*) exist as outlets for discussions about mixed methods research. With increased frequency, published articles are appearing in social and human science journals.... Entire books now exist about procedures for conducting mixed methods studies—similar books were not available a decade ago. (p. 208)

READING A MIXED-DESIGN RESEARCH STUDY

The following article is from the Center for Music Research, Florida State University, Tallahassee, where Clifford Madsen is Robert O. Lawson Distinguished Professor of Music. The abstract has been omitted to save space and to challenge you to read beyond the summary.

First Remembrances of Wanting to Become a Music Teacher

Clifford K. Madsen and Steven N. Kelly, *Florida State University*

Journal of Research in Music Education, 50(4), 323–332.

Reprinted by permission of MENC: The National Association for Music Education.
Copyright © 2002 by MENC.

In an attempt to address issues concerning recruitment of music teachers, identifying factors that lead students to become music educators is both timely and important.

The choices that young people make and the context in which they make these choices are worthy of investigation. Although a number of social and musical factors that may influence how music teachers are prepared and what it is they bring to the university have been investigated, exactly what "causes" a student to want to become a future music teacher has not received the same attention.

There are studies concerning what prospective music teachers already bring to their formal teacher training programs and some studies investigating how certain variables may predict success. These variables include high school grade point average (LeBlanc, 1971); personality characteristics (Bergee, 1992a; Cutietta & McAllister, 1997); self-concept, empathy, interest in people, flexibility, and creativity (Griffin, 1986); social interaction within ensemble participation (Koutz, 1987); and family incluence, peer pressure, gender stereotypes, and future occupational choice (Castelli, 1986; Kourajian, 1982). Other researchers have investigated factors that contribute to attrition, including grades in music theory and applied music (Brown & Alley, 1983). Madsen and Hancock (2002) examined attrition in relationship to how supported young teachers felt by parents, administrators, and others within their early teaching experience.

Another issue might well be influential "role models" that music students perceive to be important. In a study published in 2002, Kantorski described his survey of undergraduate music education majors about their perceptions of their "best" teacher. Forty-eight percent of the respondents selected a music teacher as their "best" teacher, whereas 52% selected a nonmusic teacher. However, respondents indicated music teachers were more influential than nonmusic teachers in their decision to become a teacher.

Recently, MENC: The National Association for Music Education sponsored a survey by Bergee et al. (2001) to examine what influenced collegiate MENC members' decisions to become music educators. As is true of other studies, Bergee et al. found that most students made the decision to become a music teacher while in high school and their high school music teacher was the most influential person on their making that decision. Respondents indicated the primary reason for their decision was a "love of music." Paul et al. (2002) investigated how strongly the role of teacher was developed by students based on initial teaching experiences. Student responses from a role development questionnaire were compared to video recordings of student teaching examples. The author found that judges evaluating the recorded teaching episodes did not necessarily rate students who perceived themselves as strong teachers in the questionnaire as highly.

More specific to the present investigation are studies by Bergee (1992b) and Kelly (2000), who investigated factors influencing undergraduate music education students' attitudes toward teaching and found the major sources of encouragement came from family members, peers, and teachers. However, the authors concluded that these measures might not be sufficient in predicting future success and that other variables, such as personality traits, motivation, and socioeconomic status, should also be considered in evaluating potential success at the undergraduate level.

Researchers have determined that individual interest in teaching music initially emerges because of early interaction and reaction to environmental experiences (Hidi & Harackiewicz, 2000). Accordingly, as knowledge and positive feelings develop over time, an individual's initial interest becomes a relatively stable motivational force; while this research examines diverse variables, the researchers in these studies have not investigated initial reasons affecting the decisions to pursue music education as careers.

In three studies, investigators examined subjects' first remembrances of music teachers and of teaching in general (Edenfield, 1989; Madsen, 1994; Madsen & Duke, 1999). This line of inquiry is based on the premise that important information is contained in the strong early memories relating to music, including time, place, occasion, who was there, how the individuals felt about it, and what their thoughts were at the time. Edenfield (1989) asked 55 students (all nonmusic majors) enrolled in a music appreciation class at a large university to describe their first-remembered music experience during their first 10 years of life. Subjects were asked a series of 12 questions about their music memories. Results showed that musical experiences were vividly recalled, that remembered experiences occurred toward the end of this first decade, that experiences involving peers were remembered more than those with family, and that 30% of the subjects indicated the experience was either negative or of no significance.

Madsen and Duke (1999) surveyed 103 undergraduate and graduate music students (all nonmusic education majors) about their earliest musical remembrances concerning their age, the place, who was with them, how they felt, and what their thoughts were at the time. As a reliability check 1 month after the initial survey, 44 of the subjects were asked to do the identical task again. Responses were again vivid and often described in exactly the same detail. The first remembered responses were from around ages 3 to 5 (earlier than in Edenfield's study), all of the experiences were positive, and a family member was almost always present.

The authors concluded that it was difficult to isolate early musical experiences from family or other sociological influences. It seems apparent that factors such as family and peer interaction, age, place, and time significantly influence an individual's earliest musical experiences. Results of previous research (Bergee, 1992b; Kelly, 2000) suggest that these same types of experiences may also affect musical decisions such as why individuals choose to become music teachers. However, no researcher has heretofore sought to determine these effects.

The variety of responses given in previous research suggests that almost everyone has a "story" concerning early musical memories, which might include reasons to pursue music education. In this study, we attempted to ascertain those salient aspects of initial experiences that might affect decisions by individuals to pursue teaching as a career by isolating students' first remembered experiences of wanting to become a music teacher.

Method

Methodology used in this study combines both qualitative and quantitative approaches. An open-ended essay was used to elicit each musician's earliest and most natural remembrances of when he or she decided to become a music teacher. We were careful not to put unnecessary constraints on individual interpretations or force arbitrary classifications. Wishing to avoid the type of questionnaire in which respondents must "fit" their responses into a priori classifications, we deemed it important to provide more freedom to allow respondents to add, omit, or redefine the question through their prose, making it personal for the individual.

Subjects ($N = 90$) were undergraduate music education majors enrolled at a large comprehensive school of music in the southeastern United States. Subjects were instructed using a template similar to that used previously concerning first remembered responses to music (Edenfield, 1989; Madsen & Duke, 1999) and responded to the following:

> Please write on the sheet of paper in front of you a time line. On this time line, please indicate, in your own words, your earliest remembrances of when you first considered becoming a music teacher. Please indicate your age, place, who was there with you, how you felt, what your thoughts were at the time, and any other aspect you consider important.

No time limit was given and a few subjects wrote an extended essay (2–3 pages); most others wrote a short paragraph. Each essay was read carefully several times by both authors in an attempt to delve into the richness of individual responses. While each respondent had a unique "story," after many discussions between the authors several "patterns" seemed to emerge. To develop those aspects deemed important to the profession and to make sense out of these patterns, a classification system was used to group responses according to the questions asked in the instructions. After this first classification, a revised taxonomic structure was devised that collapsed many categories as agreed upon by the authors. The taxonomy was changed several times until we were satisfied with the clarity of the taxonomy and our final classifications (see Table 1).

Two additional researchers then read all responses and classified them according to frequency into this taxonomic structure. Reliability for this frequency distribution was .96, determined by counting the number of identical response classifications and comparing the two lists using the formula agreements/agreements + disagreements (Madsen & Madsen, 1998). As an additional reliability check, after 2 months, 27 of the original subjects were asked to do the identical task. Reliability was .94, computed as above.

Data were analyzed according to percentage classification, but since this study dealt with open-ended written responses, much of the information could not be effectively collapsed into percentage classifications and was treated more qualitatively. Several essay excerpts are included that demonstrate some of these important nuances not captured in the percentage data.

Results

Many of the music education students answered all questions. However, as would be expected with an "open written response," many subjects did not answer all questions, yet we assumed that what each respondent wrote or did not write was important. For example, while a respondent's age concerning when she or he wanted to become a music teacher was answered by almost all respondents, a few did not mention age. Also, many did not provide any information about the place where their decision was made or how they felt, or who was with them when this decision was made. Analysis of the data relating to age demonstrates that many subjects decided to become a music teacher early in their music study, with 56% of respondents listing high school or the high school ages of 15–18; 14% listed middle school or middle school ages (11–14); and 6% listed elementary school (ages 5–10). These data indicate that 76% of students decided to become a music teacher before entering a teacher preparatory program. Only 22% of subjects indicated that they decided to become a music teacher in college (see Table 1).

Although many participants (39%) did not indicate the location or place where they made this decision, 44% identified the location as being the school band/chorus/orchestra rehearsal room or at school. Honors groups, auditioned groups, or summer music camp accounted for only 8% of the sample, and private lesson teacher/giving lessons accounted for 6%.

In answering the question "Who was with you at the time?," the highest percentage of respondents (51%) indicated that they were with students and teachers in band/chorus/marching band/orchestra. People with them at this time were fellow students in the music group, directors, and others involved in the program. Thirty-six percent did not list any information, perhaps indicating that for these subjects this was not a salient issue, or perhaps indicating that this question had been answered elsewhere, i.e., in the Place category (see Table 1). Only 4% indicated "parents," 4% indicated "private teacher," and 4% indicated "professor."

The category of "How You Felt" elicited some of the most interesting and wide-ranging responses. The highest percentage of subjects (25%) indicated that they liked and wanted to teach. Twenty-two percent indicated that they liked and wanted to emulate their director. Interestingly, 21% did not provide information in this category. Fourteen percent of subjects indicated "emotional, happy, excited," etc. The same percentage (14%) expressed a "love for music and music experiences." Three percent of the respondents indicated that they wanted to go into teaching because they had been subjected to a "bad" music teacher.

Other aspects of the data were treated in a qualitative manner because the written responses were unique to each person and could not be effectively collapsed into categories. Individual "thoughts at the time" responses were most often expressed with conviction, e.g., "I can do this," "I'm good at this," "I should do this," "This is what I was meant to do," "Teaching would be fun." Indeed, most of the respondents had extremely vivid memories expressing almost a "musical epiphany" concerning the realization that they wanted to teach.

Table 1 First Remembrances of Wanting to Become a Music Teacher

Group	Percentage
Age	
High school (ages 15–18)	56%
College (ages 19–30)	22%
Middle school (ages 11–14)	14%
Elementary school (ages 5–10)	6%
No information	2%
Place	
Band/Chorus/School/Marching Band/Orchestra	44%
No information	39%

Allstate/Tri-state/Audition groups/Summer camps	8%
Practice with lesson teacher/other students	6%
At home	3%
Who Was with You	
Students in class (band/chorus/marching band/orchestra, including directors and staff)	51%
No information	36%
Private lesson teacher	4%
Parents	4%
Professor	4%
How You Felt	
Liked and wanted to teach	25%
Wanted to emulate director	22%
No information	21%
Emotional, happy, excited, etc.	14%
Love for music and music experiences	14%
Aggravated at director	3%

When the decision to become a music teacher was made gradually over time, it usually corresponded with increased performance abilities or leadership roles. Analysis of these data indicates that there is often a time in middle or high school at which prospective teachers experience a profound music performing music experience that motivates them to continue their studies and to take music more seriously. Students identified and received reinforcement from their peers and especially from their music director. They then began to practice more, increase their skill level, and began a continuing positive cycle that carried on to their future major. To provide a more personal expression, the following written excerpts are provided from a choral, band, general K–6, and a string person:

> In elementary school 4th grade, we were practicing in the after-school recorder choir. There were about 15 us; I knew all of the others, because most of us were in the same class. We were preparing to do a concert at the local mall, and I was excited and happy and proud at how amazing we sounded on our really hard recorder pieces with three, four, and five different parts. I've been an admirer of the music teacher, Mrs. G., ever since. And I was thinking that music was the greatest thing ever and that she must like her job better than anything, and I wanted to be just like her.

> I was in 10th grade and it was the month of January. I was 15 (and 1/2) and was participating in our county's Honor Band. Mr. W. was the guest director and was the best. We were working on music and Mr. W. was reading us passages from a book of short stories, all in an attempt to get us to try and experience better musicianship, when he asked, "How many of you want to be music teachers when you grow up?" I saw hands go up and I noticed my band director looking at me, I raised my hand too—I realized I like[d] the idea.

> Music education as a career choice first came to mind my senior year of high school. The thought going through my head at the time was "Do you want to do this for the rest of your life?" I had no doubt that whatever my life decision

would be, it would have to involve music. Through the years I have really enjoyed working with others, especially children. So I figured, why not put the two together?

When I truly decided to be a music teacher, I was working with some students with special disabilities. Up to this point, I had given some thought, but never really considered teaching. But when I saw those kids' happy faces and how they filled up with joy. I realized that this is what I really wanted to do for the rest of my life. Even though most students w/disabilities don't become Yo Yo Ma's, just knowing that I have done something worthwhile for them is enough for me.

While most of the respondents were very committed to teaching, some were still undecided. Another string person wrote the following:

I knew that music would be integral in my future, but I didn't know where or what. I entered a conservatory; my thoughts of teaching at this point shifted to a studio setting only. My private teacher from home and I explored other options for my future besides performance. Now, I may be interested in education from the podium, but I honestly don't know my exact focus. I'm still working on it.

Discussion

The results of the present study show that age level and influential people were the factors having the greatest impact on the decision to become a music teacher. The decision is made early and is primarily influenced by an elementary/middle school/high school music teacher and by teacher-like activities such as supervising a sectional rehearsal or being a student conductor. Most subjects made this decision when in high school and in the presence of their teacher or conductor. Others made the decision based on intense feelings felt through performing music. It seems that the "power of music," when combined with a genuine respect and appreciation of a music teacher, culminates in the decision to emulate that teacher. For many students, this decision to become a music teacher is not based on extensive thought, but a sudden realization of their life for music and helping others; others make the decision gradually over time. It is ironic that a very few individuals thought that their music educator did not work hard enough or care enough about them, and therefore they decided to work to "right the world" for the benefit of future students.

Observing exemplary music educators, getting compliments from others, an awareness of one's performance ability, realizing the powerful effect music has on one's life, and not wanting to give up music seem to be major factors in making the decision to become a teacher. Since most of the responses were positive and often expressed with great emotional conviction, it seems that after subjects made their initial decision to teach music, they did not consider changing careers—if the decision was made when they were young. One prominent finding of this study is the almost complete absence of wanting to become a music teacher as a second choice or because the individuals did not have other options; this is especially true for those who chose their profession early. These data indicate that decisions were not forced on prospective teachers, at least in the present sample.

Many college-age students outside music wait to declare a major until the junior year, and some students change majors repeatedly. This situation gives college and university personnel the opportunity to influence the best students to enter their field, or at least a chance to attempt to persuade them. Yet, if our music profession is to recruit the "best and brightest" as well as the most musically competent, then the influence of a formidable elementary, middle school, or high school teacher, combined with good performances, seems extremely important.

In the current teacher shortage, there are individuals who advocate taking nonmusic education majors and putting them in the music classroom. There will be some individuals who decide relatively late in their long music careers to become music educators and do very well—especially if they enjoy teaching when given the opportunity, regardless of when it comes. However, the tenuous ambivalence evidenced by those in the current sample who waited until their college careers to decide, or are still deciding whether to go into music education, does not seem to be equivalent to that evidenced by those who decide much earlier. One important aspect of the data indicates that when students are uncertain about being a teacher until their college years, they often remain ambivalent concerning their decision.

Additional studies need to be done to determine how best to encourage prospective teachers to make the very best decisions possible. Sometimes college music teachers identify those few students who have a tremendous desire but evidence few other "talents" musically and/or interactively. Additionally, while many students wanted to enter the profession because they wanted to teach, there seem to be few examples of youngsters wanting to go into the profession because they already demonstrated a recognized high-level ability to teach.

We recommend that a larger sample, more representative of the nation, be studied, even though in Bergee et al. (2001), there were no major differences among the various components of the national sample. More important, additional investigations concerning the complex interrelationships between and among the many variables that influence the decision-making process should be made. Free written responses, while difficult to manage and classify, still provide a plethora of important information. To address the important issues in music education, we suggest that qualitative as well as quantitative methodology be used to tease out important relationships.

REFERENCES

Bergee, M. J. (1992a). The relationship between music education majors' personality profiles, other education majors' profiles and selected indicators of music teaching success. *Bulletin of the Council for Research in Music Education*, no. 112, 5–15.

Bergee, M. J. (1992b). Certain attitudes toward occupational status held by music education majors. *Journal of Research in Music Education, 40*, 104–113.

Bergee, M. J., Coffman, D. D., Demorest, S. M., Humphreys, J. T., & Thornton, L. P. (2001). Influences on collegiate students' decision to become a music educator. (Summary available on the MENC Web site at http://www.mench.org/networks/rnc/Bergee-Report.html)

Brown, A. L., & Alley, J. M. (1983). Multivariate analysis of degree persistence of undergraduate majors. *Journal of Research in Music Education, 31*, 271–281.

Castelli, P. A. (1986). *Attitudes of vocal music educators and public secondary school students on selected factors which influence a decline in male enrollment occurring between elementary and* secondary public school vocal music programs. Unpublished doctoral dissertation, University of Maryland, College Park.

Cutietta, R. A., & McAllister, P. A. (1997). Student personality and instrumental participation, continuation, and choice. *Journal of Research in Music Education, 45,* 282–294.

Edenfield, T. N. (1989). A descriptive analysis of nonmusicians' early music experience. *Southeastern Journal of Music Education, 1,* 33–43.

Griffin, G. A. (1986). Issues in student teaching: A review. In J. D. Raths & L. G. Katz (Eds.), *Advances in teacher education* (Volume 2, pp. 239–272). Norwood: Ablex.

Hidi, S., & Harackiewicz, J. M. (2000). Motivating the academically unmotivated: A critical issue for the 21st century. *Review of Educational Research, 70*(2), 151–179.

Kelly, S. N. (2000). Social and musical influences of prospective undergraduate music teacher candidates. In R. R. Rideout & S. J. Paul (Eds.), *On the sociology of music education II* (pp. 121–130). Amherst, MA: University of Massachusetts.

Kantorski, B. J. (2002*). Music education majors' perceptions of the "best teacher I ever had."* Poster session presented at the National Biennial In-Service Conference of MENC: The National Association for Music Education, Nashville, TN.

Kourajian, B. J. (1982). Nonparticipation of freshmen and senior boys in high school choir. *Missouri Journal of Music Education, 5,* 108–117.

Koutz, T. A. (1987). *An analysis of attitudinal differences toward music performance classes in secondary schools by nonparticipants, current, and former participants.* Unpublished doctoral dissertation, University of Missouri—Columbia.

LeBlanc, J. R., Jr. (1971). *The ACT test battery as a predictor of completion of a baccalaureate degree of music education.* Unpublished doctoral dissertation, University of Southern Mississippi, Hattiesburg.

Madsen, C. K. (1994). Developing a research agenda in general music: A personal perspective. *General Music Today, 7,* 13–18.

Madsen, C. K., & Duke, R. A. (1999). First remembered responses. *General Music Today, 13*(1), 19–20.

Madsen, C. K., & Hancock, C. B. (2002). Support for music education: A case study of issues concerning teacher retention and attrition. *Journal of Research in Music Education, 50,* 6–19.

Madsen, C. K., & Madsen, C. H., Jr. (1998) *Teaching discipline: Behavioral principles toward a positive approach.* Raleigh, NC: Contemporary Publishing Co. of Raleigh, Inc.

Paul, S. J., Teachout, D. J., Sullivan, J. M., Kelly, S. N., Bauer, W. I., & Raiber, M. A. (2002). Role development activities and initial teaching performance. *Contributions to Music Education, 29*(1), 85–89.

STUDY AND DISCUSSION QUESTIONS

1. What did Kantorski (2002) find in relation to the influence that music teachers have on students wanting to become music teachers?

2. What did Bergee (2001) find as the main reason for collegiate MENC members to choose music education as a career?

3. Why did the Madsen and Kelly choose to study *initial* reasons affecting students' decision to pursue music education as a career?

4. Do you think this is an important research question? Why or why not?

5. What type of data-collection instrument was used? Why was this chosen?

6. What was the *N* for this study? Is this sufficient to generalize results?

7. When was the taxonomy of response classifications developed? Is this indicative of quantitative or qualitative research?

8. Was it possible to collapse all of the subjects' responses into the taxonomy in Table 1? Why or why not?

9. When did the results show that most students first thought about being a music teacher?

10. How were the quantitative data analyzed in this study? The qualitative data?

11. Did this study confirm Kantorski's (2002) finding that the main influence on a student choosing to become a music teacher is their high school music teacher?

12. "[D]ata indicates that when students are uncertain about being a teacher until their college years, they often remain ambivalent concerning their decision." Why is this?

READING MIXED RESEARCH

The following article by Lois Schleuter (1991) is another example of mixed methodology where both quantitative and qualitative data analyses are involved. The study sought to determine how student teachers in elementary general music thought (before and after student teaching) about school music curricular issues.

Student Teachers' Preactive and Postactive Curricular Thinking

Lois Schleuter, *Indiana University, Bloomington*
Journal of Research in Music Education, 39(1), 46–63.

Reprinted by permission of MENC: The National Association for Music Education.
Copyright © 1991 by MENC.

The cognitive tasks of teaching have been given increasing research attention over the past 10 years (Clark & Peterson, 1986; Clark & Yinger, 1979b; May 1986; Morine-Dershimer, 1978–1979; Neale, Pace, & Case, 1983; Oberg, 1976; Shavelson & Stern, 1981; Yinger, 1979). In an effort to determine curricular effectiveness and curriculum implementation, researchers have documented the significance and relative autonomy of individual teachers and their plans for the classroom.

Instructional planning is considered in both comprehensive and short-range (incremental) thinking (Clark & Yinger, 1979a; 1979b), includes determination of objectives (Peterson, Marx, & Clark, 1978; Sardo, 1982; Zahork, 1975), and involves pupil evaluation (Taylor, 1970; Yinger, 1977), thus including the elements but not the order of Tyler's rationale (1949). Teacher perceptions of their students' needs, interests, and abilities were also found to be significant factors in teacher planning of instruction (Crocker & Banfield, 1986; Germano & Peterson, 1982; Grohosky, 1984/1985; Malone, 1979; McCutcheon, 1980; Oberg, 1976; Richey, 1983; Shavelson & Borko, 1979).

Student teachers and experienced teachers do not share the same responsibilities for teaching in the classroom (DiNapoli 1984) or for presenting music instruction (Krueger, 1985) even though teachers are more autonomous than other apprentices (Rosenfeld, 1969; Tabachnik & Zeichner, 1984). The conceptualization processes of student teachers when regarding the teaching process also differ from experienced teachers (Calderhead, 1983; Hill, Yinger, & Robbins, 1983; Housner & Griffey, 1985; Yinger & Clark, 1982, 1983). Furthermore, the study of student teachers emphasizes the need to consider individual cases when determining what student teachers do when planning and thinking about teaching (Broeckmans, 1986; Bruitink & Kemme, 1986; Calderhead, 1983). The use of qualitative and ethnographic research has emerged as an insightful way to obtain these findings about teachers and their craft. "Education is a process whose features may differ from individual to individual, context to context, and is best addressed by theories which embrace artistry" (Eisner, 1976, p. 149).

The information about the thinking of classroom teachers just cited may not generalize well to the thinking of general music teachers, and even less to student teachers in elementary general music. Elementary general music teachers are responsible for planning and presenting instruction to far greater numbers of pupils than are classroom teachers, meet their classes on an intermittent schedule that allows them relatively little time with any one group of pupils, may teach the same pupils across several years' schooling, and may be the only people to plan and/or interpret the music curriculum experienced by the pupils of one or more schools. For those reasons, a study of the curricular thinking of student teachers in elementary general music was undertaken.

Limitations were established on the sources and availability of data. Only the preactive and postactive thinking of subjects were studied. Preactive and postactive thoughts are defined by Clark and Peterson (1986) as "the thought processes that teachers engage in prior to classroom interaction but also includes the thought processes or reflections they engage in after classroom interaction that then guide their thinking and projections for future classroom interaction.... Thus, because the teaching process is a cyclical one, the distinction between preactive and postactive thoughts has become blurred" (p. 258).

Terminology and Research Questions

Terminology used in discussion of curriculum forms the basis for the questions posed in this study. Essential terms are defined here for clarification:

Aims/goals/objectives: "reference is being made to some terminal point toward which we are moving, working, or traveling" (Zais, 1976, p. 298). Aims are typically more broadly stated and refer to distant outcomes. Objectives, at the opposite end of the continuum, tend to be more specifically stated and immediate.

Activity: that in which students are actively engaged; typified by such directions as *think, move, describe, sing, listen, clap,* and so forth, "An 'activity' is a connected whole of teaching and learning activities of a certain kind, performed upon a part of the lesson content" (Broeckmans, 1986, p. 219); the manner in which students encounter the content or concept.

Content/concept: "such substantives as information, ideas, concepts, generalizations, principles and the like" (Zais, 1976, p. 3324); the "what" that is to be learned. "This component is defined...as the *musical concept.* A musical person will possess basic concepts about the elements of music that may be combined into more complex concepts regarding the musical whole" (Meske, 1987, p. 45).

Nature of the learner: characteristics of pupils pertaining to their abilities, interests, needs, development, and learning style.

Program evaluation: "the determination of how well a curriculum performs when measured against certain criteria or when compared with another curriculum" (Zais, 1976, p. 379).

Pupil evaluation: determining "standards to judge relative success or failure" of students (Zais, 1976, p. 373).

Scope: "the extent and arrangement of curriculum elements that occur at the same time" (Zais, 1976, p. 439).

Sequence: "describes their [curriculum elements] progressive, level-to-level organization over a period of time" (Zais, 1976, p. 439).

Student teacher evaluation: assessment of the progress/performance of the student teacher as part of the student teaching experience.

Three questions were formulated to guide the study of music student teacher curricular thinking:

1. Given the curricular categories of (a) aims/goals/objectives/scope/sequence; (b) content/concept; (c) activities; (d) nature of the learner; and (e) pupil, program, and self-evaluation, what aspects of curricular decision making do elementary general music student teachers address in their student teaching, and how do they address them?

2. What is the distribution of the foci stated in Question 1 among curricular concerns evidenced in the preactive and postactive thinking of elementary general music student teachers?

3. Are there shifts in emphasis on these foci during the student teaching experience? Categories included in Question 1 were derived by Shavelson and Stern (1981) after extensive meta-analysis of studies of teacher thinking.

Method

Drawing on research underscoring the individual and unique nature of teacher thinking, the researcher selected a case-study approach. Case study, a form of ethnographic research, is "the in-depth investigation of an individual, group, or institution with the primary purpose...to determine the factors, and relationships among the factors, that have resulted in the current behavior status of the subject of the study" (Gay, 1987, p. 225). Carini (1975) states that reflection on such cases can yield significant data that are sharable and generalizable. Shulman (1981) describes two forms of generalizability, stating that the most frequently discussed is that in which findings derived from the study of a presumably representative sample of individuals apply to a larger population. This is generalizability "across people" (Shulman, 1981, p. 9) and is not appropriate for ethnographic research. Limitations of the present study fall into those peculiar to studies in which generalization is "across situations" (Shulman, 1981, p. 9).

Goetz and LeCompte (1984) clarify the assumptive modes of ethnographic research as follows:

1. Ethnographic research is an inductive process. The researcher begins with the collection of data, looks for similar and dissimilar phenomena, and develops a theory to explain what was studied.

2. Ethnographic research is inductive in nature. The intent is to discover constructs and propositions from data collected from various sources.

3. Ethnographic researchers use the strategy of construction, that is, the proposal of categories or constructs derived from observation of events, persons, and behaviors.

4. Ethnography is a subjective form of inquiry. "The goal is to reconstruct the specific categories that participants use to conceptualize their own experience and world view" (p. 6).

It should be noted, however, that the categories of curricular thinking used here were established through prior research.

Students attending a northeastern Ohio university were selected as subjects. All student teachers whose 10-week student teaching assignment included elementary general music ($N = 3$) were included. No special placement considerations were made to accommodate the study. This selection process is in keeping with those of naturalistic inquiry in which "variables influencing inquiry...may or may not be manipulated, controlled, or randomized" (Miller, 1986, p. 3). Also, individual differences and diversity are expected.

Two of the three student teachers were placed with experienced cooperating teachers. Two were male, but one, "Rick," was a traditional student, and the other, "Phil," was an older student returning for certification after completing a music performance degree. "Bev," the third subject, was a traditional female student. Rick and Bev were vocal majors. Phil was a keyboard major. Each subject was assigned to a secondary school setting in the morning and completed their day in an elementary school for the duration of the 10 weeks. Each had been instructed in elementary music methods by the same instructor, who emphasized a creative approach to planning rather than reliance on music textbooks, and each was placed with a cooperating teacher who had taken coursework from this same instructor.

The elementary methods class for Rick and Bev included campus-based instruction in conjunction with a supervised early field experience of 2.5 hours per week. Phil's early field experience included 5 fewer hours of field experience and was completed in a different field site.

All three subjects had positive attitudes toward the teaching of elementary music prior to student teaching. Each, however, indicated a preference for becoming a high school choral director upon graduation. Positive feelings about their own accomplishments in school music, enjoyment received from recognition of their musical talent by others, and the desire to work with people were major factors leading all three subjects to enter music education.

Selected quotes are included to add insight into the subjects as they approached student teaching:

> *Bev:* I think it's [music] is important. On a main level for the children it's just an enjoyment and a break from the routine... They're learning but it's a sneaky way to learn 'cause they won't always know that they're learning. [I hope my students will] think that I do know what I'm talking about or that if I don't know the answer I will go find it or tell them how to find the answer... basically friendly—that you can ask a question at any time. [I hope to become] close to them... it takes a while to get to know them and there it's a gradual process of treating them with respect. [I would want my teaching to include] singing, and I'd like to get a lot more hands-on experience with Orff and tonal instruments like Autoharp, recorder, and use movement—and I feel that's important—and listening. When you get in the upper levels you can also get into ethno music or a true sense of understanding.

> *Phil:* I think music education is important to education and anybody at any age. I believe music is an important experience that everybody has in their life and I don't know anybody who has never experienced music. I think it's important that it start as soon as possible.... [I hope my students will see me] as somebody that inspired them, especially when it came to music.... I want to teach music through working with choruses—[and to teach much more than] just learning to sing music. Time permitting, I would cover everything and the time would be the determining factor or when it stopped. [When relating to students,] I intend to be as professional as I can be, but then I don't want to be cold and separate from the students. But I think I will be very cautious about being too terribly close, and where that line is. [Shrug]

> *Rick:* [Music education is important] because a music course is a compilation of everything that we're trying to bring across in the educational system.... Anyone can be in your class—a blind student, a hearing-impaired [youngster, and so forth]—they can all be in your course equally... it's a time where everyone comes together as an ensemble to work together and that's important—working together. [I hope students will see me as maintaining] strong discipline but yet when I try to teach them something it comes across in a nice way.... I don't want to be so easy on them that they just say, "Oh, you know, he's fly-away" or "You can get away with anything with him." I feel that a role model as a singer, that's a strong emphasis on my part and I like that. [One thing I would like to include,] other than just covering the basics of

rhythm, melody, harmony, and texture in class, [is] programs. [There should be an opportunity] for them to do performance for parents because you're teaching them music, but if they never get to perform it for anyone, it seems like such a waste.

(An in-depth case study was compiled for each subject and is available on request from the author.)

The researcher was also the university supervisor for the elementary portion of each subject's teaching. Thus, participant observation was one of the data-gathering procedures since the supervisor was involved in audiotaped conferences within the limitations of preactive and postactive thinking. "Participant observation is a technique in which the investigator enters the social world of those studied, observes, and tries to find out what it is like to be a member of that "world" (Biddle & Anderson, 1986, p. 237).

Data were gathered through examination of lesson plans and daily planning journals kept by each subject (document analysis). Subjects were asked to keep a journal describing the planning process, factors influencing their selection/exclusion of content and activities, and concerns or questions that rose during the planning process. Audiotapes of conferences between student teachers, cooperating teachers, and the supervisor were transcribed to increase the capacity for analysis not restricted to the limitations of on-the-spot reaction. Structured interviews conducted before, at midpoint, and after student teaching, as well as informal interviews during conferences, were used to solicit opinions or values, reveal feelings, ascertain knowledge, elicit perspectives, and illuminate the background of the students' current circumstances. Stimulated recall was used: a large number of cues were provided to each subject to enable them to recall vividly and describe in more detail their reactions to events that occurred as part of an original situation. Weekly triangulation of all data sources was completed (Guba, 1978). The design is shown in Table 1.

Results

The ensuing descriptions are condensed examples from the three case studies. Qualitative analysis of data indicated that, in some respects, the three subjects were similar. All three began student teaching by observing during the first half of Week 1 and then presented their first lesson or portion of a lesson in the latter half of the week. Whole-group instruction was used exclusively throughout the student teaching experience. Shared instruction time was varied, however: Phil immediately became responsible for all instruction, Rick gradually assumedfull instructional time, and Bev shared instruction for nearly the total experience.

Planning considerations for the first lesson included all categories except program evaluation. Each student teacher followed a lesson-plan format including objectives and activities but not a specific plan for pupil evaluation. Evaluation was, however, quite prominent in their thoughts after teaching, as was expressed in these excerpted comments from their recall of events during teaching:

Table 1. Design of the Study

Research Question	Data Source	Analysis
1. Given the curricular categories of (a) aims/goals/objectives/scope/ sequence; (b) nature of the learner; and (c) pupil, program, and self-evaluation, what aspects of curricular decision making do elementary general music student teachers address in their preactive and post active thinking and how do they address them?	Student teacher journals Taped conferences of the student teacher, cooperating teacher and university supervisor. Interview Stimulated recall Lesson plans	Content analysis for reference by category Triangulation
2. What is the distribution of the above curricular concerns evidenced in the preactive and postactive thinking of elementary general music student teachers?	Student teacher journals Taped conferences of the student teacher, cooperating teacher, and university supervisor Interview Stimulated recall Lesson plans	Percentage of content devoted to each curricular focus
3. Are there shifts in emphasis on these foci during the student teaching experience?	Student teacher journals Taped conferences of the student teacher, cooperating teacher, and university supervisor. Interview Stimulated recall Lesson plans	Comparison of percentage by week and overall Examination for evidence of change in nature of Consideration given

Bev: I feel that the students were very strong as a class when it came to producing accel., and rit.... Once they get the rhythms down, they can echo the rhythm perfectly, and they can put the patterns together well, but when it comes to singing it, they screw up the ending measures every single time.

Rick: Easily they still performed the task. Real sharp!... I didn't think the singing part went very well.... They had more trouble than I thought they would.... They were having trouble with the octave displacement. Because of the slumful attitude, learning was not quick.

Phil: I thought it was pretty good, but they're the only ones I've seen do it.... This lesson was particularly successful and interesting for the students.... They were aware, and if I saw they knew it and because of losing a lot of time, but I could see that they knew it.

The thought process used in determining the lesson plan included unpredictable amounts of reference to any category, and there was no predictable pattern to the order in which categories were considered. This random pattern of integrated thought was noted throughout the student teaching experience and is not unlike thinking shifts of experienced teachers (May, 1986; Neale, Pace, & Case, 1983).

Data also revealed the individualistic nature of student teaching experiences. Phil was given total control over all aspects of curriculum, Rick planned in relative autonomy within a framework of goals provided by the cooperating teacher, and Bev was guided on a weekly basis by the cooperating teacher. Phil subsequently set short-term, mastery-oriented goals, Rick adopted the goals of the cooperating teacher, and Bev was not aware of the cooperating teacher's goals. She instead assumed that if she taught as guided by the cooperating teacher that she was meeting the expectations of her cooperating teacher.

While all three subjects encountered large numbers of pupils each week, exposure to grade/age levels of pupils varied considerably. Bev's instruction was limited to Grade 4 (216 students in eight sections). Phil's assignment included two sections each of kindergarten through Grade 2 (187 total students) until the final week, when he taught briefly in Grade 6. Rick's students represented kindergarten, primary (with the exception of Grade 1), and all intermediate und upper grade levels (208) students.

Bev and Rick assumed a manageability approach to student behavior through consideration of pupil reaction during activities. They hoped students would be able to "handle" the planned activities. In other words, students should purposefully coordinate their physical responses with the music and not produce random, uncontrolled, overt behavior. They were willing to deal with resulting behavior that was unacceptable. Phil adopted a control approach, planning activities and approaches he hoped would not require disciplinary intervention or "result in chaos."

Although all three subjects stated objectives for every lesson, the content of the objectives differed. Objectives most frequently referred to a concept and a corresponding activity and were based on perceived need for review, incorporation of specific music, and on activity implications.

> *Bev:* They could gets hands-on [experience] playing the scale on the instruments—*do, re, me, fa, sol, la*—and, um, just for fun, maybe have some rhythm ostinato—rhythm [is] going to involve more people playing instead of just a selected few.... [T]hey would also learn ostinato—the word—you know, reinforce that. They've had it before. And get some playing of the scale.
>
> *Phil:* I wanted to sing familiar songs that they already know and had been working on. Then I wanted to use simple visual aids to help understand melodic direction. Also I wanted to include the playing of an ostinato live on bells.
>
> *Rick:* In the second grade we have already gone over tempo and meter beats with this song or another, so I wanted them to clap the rhythm beats. After that, for a review of another Thanksgiving song, we would clap tempo beats to a song.

In fact, objectives functioned as a mini-overview of lesson activities (e.g., "Students will be able to clap the beat of 'Punkin.' ") Sequencing of objectives was not predetermined, nor was it based on texts or their own prior experience. The cooperating teacher did not sequence the objectives. Knowledge of objective formulation and relationship of objectives to goals was the responsibility of each subject.

None of the three subjects entered student teaching with aims or goals established. Development or adoption of goals was related to interaction with the respective cooperating teachers. Phil and Rick began to take a goal-directed approach, and they referred directly to goals in conferences with the cooperating teacher and supervisor, and kept journals:

> *Phil:* All the classes to date, with me, have touched on melodic direction, high/low sounds, loud/soft [dynamics], and a little bit on tone color. I would like to do more with tone color.
>
> *Rick:* [The cooperating teacher] game me this list that tells what each grade is to do by the end of the year, and that really helps. I look for stuff that's been left out and try to work it in.

Bev's data reveal a lack of goal awareness.

> I usually work a week at a time...and then Christmas is coming up. I don't know what'll be in there.... [The cooperating teacher and I] usually talk on Fridays to plan ahead, but there isn't any school 'cause of parent conferences. Thursday either. I'm just not sure.

Phil's goals were self-selected since the cooperating teacher provided no guidelines, and they were directed toward the time frame of student teaching. The concept goals selected had a dual purpose. First, he set goals with a mastery intent for pupil performance achievement. His second purpose was self-directed. Student goal attainment would demonstrate to him that he was a good teacher.

Rick's goals came from the cooperating teacher and, as he planned instruction, he internalized and adopted her goals as his own. He realized that these goals were not to be achieved within the time constraints of student teaching, but by viewing all goals for each grade level he was able to perceive how his instruction was part of the continuum of what had come before and what was yet to come.

The determination that goals were considered came only from conference and journal data. There was no evidence of goals or goal setting found through examination of lesson plans. Also, the fact that Bev was unaware of goals came only from conference and interview data.

Scope was purposefully limited by Phil, was gradually revealed to Bev, and was outlined for Rick when he received the cooperating teacher's goals in week five. Attention to sequence was found most within each lesson plan. Bev's sequence between lessons was most guided by the cooperating teacher. In fact, she indicated in an interview that she hadn't perceived any sequence "since I didn't go on into Grade 5." Phil's sequence was determined by his assessment of need for review and also the need to introduce and keep fresh the concepts outlined in the goals. He was the only one of the three to perceive sequence between grade levels. None of the three relied on a music basic series for sequence, scope, or objectives.

All three engaged in short-term planning. Only daily and weekly written planning was evident, but Phil's and Rick's thoughts about upcoming instruction began to project 2 to 3 weeks ahead in the last half of the student teaching experience.

> *Phil:* I needed to get to know the students, and I didn't know the students at the beginning. I didn't have a clear idea of what the cooperating teacher wanted, if anything, and there was just a certain amount of insecurity for that...as I came to know the students and have some idea...that I had free rein...I started planning long-range—more long-range certainly than I did at the start.

> *Rick:* I would do them [lesson plans] weekly instead of daily, so I would think what I wanted them to accomplish maybe by the end of the week or by the end of 2 weeks, but we'd start maybe on the first 2 days. They really hadn't accomplished that much but were building up to the main thing I wanted to do.

Bev, however, continued to plan a week at a time after receiving guidance from her cooperating teacher, as could be noted in her previous quote.

Content/concept was mostly determined by Bev's cooperating teacher. Music was selected containing the concept(s) under study. Other concepts also inherent in the music were then included by Bev. Phil determined concepts for study, searched for music with clear examples of those concepts, and then, for the majority of the 10 weeks, adopted mastery of those concepts as goals. Rick included concepts listed by the cooperating teacher. Content was most reflected in the song lyrics selected and reflected seasonal and holiday consideration for all three subjects.

Although concepts received little direct attention, each subject treated activities as concepts in action. For example, if the concept of melodic direction was identified, activities in which students exhibited physical response to melodic direction followed and were stated purely as activities. The concept/activity link became implicit in such determination as "Students will have cards with arrows and will point them up or down." The implicit sentence ending is "when they identify or recognize examples of the concept of melodic direction."

Activities were a means for students to experience musical concepts. All three subjects emphasized singing, physical movement to music, use of tonal and rhythm instruments, and response to musical notation as the basis for activities. Use of tonal instruments presented the greatest challenge for Bev, who had no music room. She maintained a prestudent teaching commitment to hands-on learning, working around the portability problems.

Phil used rhythm instruments in every class, with far less inclusion of tonal instruments, with more emphasis on movement in the final weeks. Rick's use of tonal instruments was noted during early weeks, but not in the later weeks.

All three incorporated visual aids in their teaching, but Bev also incorporated other materials, such as cutout paper shapes and yarnballs, at the suggestion of her cooperating teacher. Activities were planned for student experiences with the concept in mind and to provide a means of visual or auditory assessment of student achievement and progress.

Of the three subjects, Bev most frequently consulted but did not rely on music basic series in her planning. Phil began with a textbook emphasis, then preferred to rely on his own ideas. Rick used music basic series only twice.

As to nature-of-the-learner considerations, the three student teachers emphasized their intent that music learning should be fun and interesting, an emphasis that was present throughout the student teaching experience. All three subjects had begun to consider aspects of the learner affecting learning by the end of the experience. Potential student success in activities was considered when planning.

> *Bev:* That [game] was too competitive and not enough of the class was involved in it because they were taken out of the structure of sitting in their desks.... So the next class, I left them sitting in their desk and treated it [differently]—I was

> calling [on] the Rhythm All-Stars—people that just got [the answers] fast and
> got 'em right...and the kids like it.
>   *Phil:* I noticed after while when I got to counting, instead of them just clap-
> ping, clapping it for them, it'd be much better that way. Although I mixed those
> up [register and melodic direction], I did something to make it easier for them.
>   *Rick:* I chose to introduce a song for Thanksgiving. This one is simple,
> because I wanted them to have one song that they can sing soon.

Concern for pupil enthusiasm [or lack of it] was well documented by all three
subjects. Lack of enthusiasm sometimes led to alteration of planned instruction or
abandonment of certain musical material.

> *Bev:* One class will really be interested in something and the next one won't
> care about it at all. One time I just threw the plan out the window and went with
> what the kids wanted to do.
>   *Phil:* I've been trying to think of something to do with [the opening activity].
> It just seemed like they weren't getting anywhere and they were so bored doing
> that same thing over and over.

Phil was particularly attentive to student interests, for example, planning to incorporate songs in foreign languages when student interest was noted. Journal entries
and interview data disclosed his intent to discover student interest through probing
in class. That aspect of instruction never appeared in lesson plans.

When students responded in class, however, Phil was frequently "surprised" at all
that "such little people" were able to demonstrate and accomplish. He also noted
maturational/developmental differences between the physical responses of boys and
girls, and problems of young students when presented with tasks involving nonuni-
son responses.

Bev and Rick developed an awareness of the need to consider the steps that needed
to be taken to facilitate student learning. Rick also encountered the limitations of
younger students when they were expected to perform other than in unison, but he
noted that older students could manage the complexity of part work and more accurate, demanding, physical responses. Motivation differences among grade levels were
noted. Of the three subjects, Rick was most aware of differences in students at different age levels.

All three learned about the "nature of the learner" from their students and felt their
planning at the beginning reflected a trial-and-error approach, but became more
attuned to their students by the end of their student teaching. The student teachers
reported most satisfaction with lessons that had proceeded as anticipated and in which
their anticipations of student reactions were correct. The ability to anticipate rather
than guess about student response was one of the most noticeable changes in their
student teaching. As their ability to predict pupil responses became more accurate, at
about Week 5, the three subjects became more relaxed and confident in themselves in
their teaching.

Pupil evaluation was based on observation of and listening to student responses during activities. All three subjects noted individual student responses, but evaluation was
based on group assessment. Evaluation of one class led to adaptations in the presentation of lessons planned for presentation in more than one class. Follow-up lessons

reflected extensive consideration of evaluation. Only Bev, however, incorporated any form of written evaluation and then only at the suggestion of her cooperating teacher.

Even though subjects always included statements assessing pupil progress, they were frequently unaware that they were engaging in evaluation through observation, as indicated in the final interview through responses to the question "Did you evaluate your students?"

> *Rick:* No, I didn't given any written tests.
> *Questioner:* What about all those games they played?
> *Rick:* Oh! I guess I never thought of that as evaluation.
> *Phil:* No. I probably should've given them a quiz or something.
> *Questioner:* Did you ask them questions or watch or listen to determine if they were doing what you wanted?
> *Phil:* Oh, yeah. But I thought evaluation had to be written.
> *Bev:* Yes. I gave them a quiz over that listening lesson.
> *Questioner:* Anything else?
> *Bev:* Not that I can remember.

The three subjects evaluated themselves openly and frequently. Positive assessments were frequent but often brief. When the student teachers determined areas needing improvement or when they judged themselves negatively, elaboration was included. Bev tended to assess herself as a teacher; Rick, initially, as a musical performer, but soon as a teacher.

> *Bev:* Every time I teach a lesson it becomes better focused and the pacing improves.... Lesson was fine except the first time I taught it I had a memory lapse and did not have the students write anything down.
> *Phil:* Because I spent too much time with the first part of the lesson, it wasn't possible to complete it as planned.... I was surprised how well it went for the two grades since I didn't plan on doing this with first grade [The cooperating teacher asked him on to do it the spur of the moment], but evidently I was slowing down pretty good.
> *Rick:* But for the fact that I messed up on a simple tune, when I can sing arias without going off pitch, really upset and confused me.... I wasn't truly secure with the song—So why did I sing the wrong note?
> Everybody started moving smoother. I understand that I must always be enthused and excited about the content of the lesson.... I myself was more organized the second period. Not organized more on paper, but in mind.

Of the three, Phil expressed most satisfaction and positive assessment of his teaching and planning. Both Phil and Rick deemphasized self-evaluation as the student teaching experience progressed, but Bev maintained a more elevated level of self-evaluation throughout.

The data collected as the result of Question 2 were analyzed according to percent of data relating to each curricular category for each of the 10 weeks in order to determine the overall emphasis placed on each curricular category. Weekly data accounted for 10% of the total experience. When conference and journal data were combined, overall rank order of emphasis on curricular categories varied among the three. Category emphasis is displayed in descending order.

To determine any shifts in emphasis on curricular foci across time, line graphs were constructed to display the weekly emphasis the student teachers and significant others placed on each curricular category. Thus, comparisons could be made concerning the relative emphasis placed on each category. Those data were then analyzed for patterns of changes in emphasis within each category across time.

Bev	Phil	Rick
Activities	Nature of the learner	Nature of the learner
Self-evaluation	Activities	Activities
Pupil evaluation	Self-evaluation	Pupil evaluation
Nature of the learner	Aims/goals/objectives/ scope/sequence	Self-evaluation
Aims/goals/objectives/ scope/sequence	Pupil evaluation	Aims/goals/objectives scope/sequence
Content/concept	Content/concept	Content/concept

Bev's shifts in emphasis among and across curricular categories were found throughout the student teaching experience. These shifts in relative amounts of attention given each curricular category were the result of the interaction of planning and instruction rather than an indication of steadily increasing growth in awareness or perceived need for increased or decreased emphasis on any curricular category. Her descriptions of the nature of the learner shared in Week 10, however, contained explicit, carefully analyzed statements about her own perceptions of enriched understanding in that category.

For Phil, the category of pupil evaluation received increasing emphasis as the student teaching experienced progressed, and the category of student teacher evaluation showed declining emphasis. Other categories reflected demands of planning for ongoing instruction and response to lesson presentation. Internal fluctuations were evident but did not reveal a pattern of increasing or decreasing emphasis over time.

Overall, Rick's emphasis on nature of the learner rose steadily across the first 3 weeks and then continued to be highly emphasized. Data indicate that emphasis on the category reflect both reaction to the context of each teaching situation and increasing attention to student needs by the student teacher. There was also a decided decrease in emphasis on student teacher evaluation. Again, shifts in emphasis among categories represent student teacher response to situational demands.

In summary, two overarching schemata involved in music student teacher curricular decision making were found. One schema involved the situational considerations of all curricular categories that occurred during the context of student teaching. The second was the integrated manner in which curricular categories were considered.

Conclusions and Discussion

The conclusions listed were based on triangulation of data from journals, participant observation, structured and informal interviews, document analysis, and audiotapes. Since case-study research is limited to the study of certain individuals in specific circumstances, generalizability of these findings should be made only to those situations most like the ones described in this study.

1. The student teaching experience of elementary general music student teachers entails curricular decision making that includes attention to the curricular foci of aims/goals/objectives/scope/sequence, content/concept, activities nature of the learner, evaluation of pupils, and self-evaluation. For two of the student teachers, program evaluation was briefly addressed. Journal entries did not always include attention to all categories, but no categories were omitted when all data were considered.

2. Elementary general music student teachers organize their planning process around the Tyler rationale (1949). Each student teacher functioned within a framework of goals, included objectives for each lesson, planned activities, and evaluated pupil achievement in relation to the objectives. The thinking processes organized around the Tyler rationale were not linear (see Conclusions 3 and 4 that follow).

3. The cooperating teacher most influences the manner in which student teachers encounter or identify curricular goals. The most distinctive differences among the three student teachers arose from their frame of reference when considering goals. One student teacher assumed that the guidance she received prepared her to plan instruction leading to the goals established by the cooperating teacher; the student teacher, however, was unaware of those goals. The result was continued reliance on short-term planning and need for reinforcement from the cooperating teacher when evaluating her own performance.

   Another student teacher received no guidance from the cooperating teacher concerning upcoming instruction. He was in complete control of the curriculum for nine of the ten weeks of student teaching. His initial plans were based on the assumption that he was continuing what the cooperating teacher started that he would soon be given guidance. When no direction was forthcoming he formulated his own goals, intended for the remaining weeks of student teaching. This led to a curriculum of limited scope in which few concepts were addressed. The student planned a wealth of activities that he hoped would help students achieve his goals before the end of student teaching.

   The third student teacher began planning with an idea of activities he wanted to try. His cooperating teacher gave him a list of her yearly goals for each grade level. He subsequently began planning for students to encounter concepts outlined in the goals and to include objectives and activities leading toward the specific goals.

4. Student teachers in elementary general music do not follow a linear single-focus approach to curricular decision making. For example, although the curricular task at hand may have been the writing of objectives, their formulation of objectives involved consideration of all other categories. Therefore, student-teacher approach to curriculum decision making corresponded to integrated models described by May (1986) and Shavelson and Stern (1981).

5. Student enjoyment is a primary objective of beginning student teachers. By the conclusion of student teaching the pupil enjoyment goal was retained, but student achievement of objectives became increasingly more important.

6. Student teachers in elementary general music receive inadequate curricular information from their cooperating teachers prior to their initial planning. If integrated thinking among curricular categories is to be meaningful, student teachers need more than an introduction to the activities aspects of the ongoing curriculum before they should be expected to assume the responsibilities of planning.

7. The methods-class emphasis on creativity in teaching rather than reliance on a basal series contributed to the student teachers' lack of reliance on textbooks. All three subjects mentioned the importance placed by the methods-class professor on being able to find many ways off approaching a concept. Reliance on textbooks was not stressed in class or during the early field experience.

8. Although concepts receive little isolated attention, activities are formulated in a manner that could be described as concept in action, or the experience of concept. For example, if the concept of melodic direction were identified, activities in which students exhibited physical response to melodic direction followed and were stated purely as activities. The concept/activity link became implicit in such activity determinations as "Students will move their hands up and down." Implicit but not expressed in this sentence is the infinitive clause "to indicate melodic direction." The category of concept, although briefly addressed in pure form, is heavily emphasized in music teacher thinking embedded in activities. In fact, all instruction was based on student engagement with musical concepts.

9. Student teacher thinking about the nature of the learner is the curricular category most significantly affected and enriched by the student teaching experience. Each of the student teachers expressed marked change in their feelings of competence and confidence in themselves as teachers when they determined that their instruction became better suited to the students. They were able to discern pupil preferences in music and activities, cognitive ability levels, and psychomotor response capabilities, and began to be able to accurately predict many student responses. This change was not found through actual amount of emphasis given the category, but through qualitative changes.

10. Student teacher placements including experiences across primary, intermediate, and upper grades lead to a better understanding of the elementary music curriculum than do more limited placements. Rick was the only subject to teach pupils ranging in age from kindergarten through grade six and so participated in the implementation of most of the elementary music curriculum. His comments included reference to differences among classes, accounted for developmental differences, and indicated that he was able to plan instruction based on what he knew students had already done and also in relation to what they would be encountering as they advanced from grade to grade. In that sense, his planning by the end of student teaching was done in relation to a curricular continuum. Phil, who taught in kindergarten through second grade, and Bev, who taught only Grade 4, did not indicate their understanding of prior learning to ensuing learning as part of what they had already taught but with little or no awareness of how instruction fit into the larger elementary music curriculum.

11. Elementary general music student teachers base their evaluation of both performance and cognitive achievement on pupil psychomotor responses. Correct physical response was given more credence than were conflicting verbal responses, and only one student teacher used any form of written evaluation to assess pupil learning. Evaluation, although prevalent and consistently undertaken, was limited in scope and depth.

12. Elementary general music student teachers' preactive and postactive planning emphasizes whole group instruction, with little consideration given individual pupils. Recollections of individual pupils' behavior, verbal responses, and musical abilities were mentioned in conferences and journals, but there was no evidence that plans were made to accommodate the needs of specific students or small groups of students with varying ability levels.

13. Student teachers in elementary general music do not make explicit connections between early field experiences and student teaching. No reference to knowledge, activities, approach, pupils or any other aspect of curricular considerations encountered in early field experiences was found in any data from the three students.

14. The impact of situational and contextual demands on teacher thinking emerge only when studied *in situ* over time. When the analysis of data was undertaken to determine amount of consideration given each curricular category, it was determined that no rank ordering of categories was established between or among weeks. Study of an isolated week or sample weeks would not have provided an accurate picture of the fluctuations involved in teacher thinking.

15. The meanings and implications music education student teachers give to the curricular information available to them is more important than amount or order of consideration given each curricular category. Whether subjects addressed curricular categories briefly or at length, first or last, each of the student teachers integrated information from each curricular category in the planning of all lessons. Their ability to synthesize information and bring information from one category to bear on considerations from categories determined their complexity of thought and success in analyzing and solving problems in ways leading to improvement of further instruction.

Implications for Music Education

Students in music education courses would benefit from establishing clear relationships between the concepts and activities they plan and the scope and sequence of a music curriculum. Such connections need to be made explicitly through discussion and instruction rather than left to the assumption of implicit learning. Isolation of activity-oriented classes cannot be the only apparent focus of practice lesson plans in the methods classes.

Evaluation of the success of lesson plan presentations could be greatly enhanced if student outcomes were assessed on the basis of each curricular category in integration with the others rather than as a whole. For example, how were the activities appropriate in terms of the concept under study, in terms of what was known about the nature of the learner, and in terms of appropriateness of the curriculum? Were objectives appropriately stated and related to a long-term goal? How successful were the students for their particular point in development? Such integrated cross-checking can yield significant clues for determining weakness in a lesson and attributing success to more than happenstance or good luck.

These particular subjects were limited in their knowledge of the child voice and the known body of information about children's motor and verbal skills in music learning. A stronger research base in these areas should be included in elementary general music methods classes so that expectations will be reasonable. The subjects in this study frequently praised a lower level of musical performance than would have been acceptable to their cooperating teachers or supervisor. In contrast, their initial expectations of motor skill tended to be above the actual level.

Several implications relate to the evaluation process. Since evaluation emphasized motor performance and large-group response, a broadened base of appropriate and varied means of assessing pupil learning is advocated. Individual as well as whole-group measurement techniques, particularly observational analysis, should be part of the teaching repertoire. In addition, the distinction between psychomotor and cognitive objectives and assessment should be made clear. Also, prospective teachers should practice giving feedback of students following performance errors. Simulation of children's errors or taps of actual performance should be used instead of reliance on peer performance in microteaching episodes. An accurate basis of expectations for good singing and motor response can best be developed through broad exposure and guided observation of taped or live performance of actual children at all elementary school levels.

Student teaching placements of limited grade range should be avoided if at all possible. It seems that the practice of thinking about a total curriculum and instruction of various grade levels does not occur unless the need arises. A format for planning sequential instruction is inherently necessary as preparation for across-grade-level as well as yearly instruction.

Finally, music education students should become familiar with the curricular organization and intent of the basal series available for music instruction. Regardless of whether the music series is available for music instruction, the information contained, treatment of scope, and sequencing guidelines could serve as a most valuable guide for the beginning teacher.

REFERENCES

Biddle, B. J., &Anderson, D. S. (1986). Theory, methods, knowledge and research on teaching. In Merlin C. Wittrock (Ed.), *Handbook of research on teaching* (pp. 230–252). New York: Macmillan.

Broeckmans, J. (1986). Short-term developments in student teachers' lesson planning. *Teaching and Teacher Education, 2*(3), 215–228.

Buitink, J., & Kemme, S. (1986). Changes in student-teacher thinking. *European Journal of Teacher Education, 9*(1), 75–84.

Calderhead, J. (1983, April). *Research into teachers' and student teachers' cognitions exploring the nature of classroom practice.* Paper presented at the Annual Meeting of the American Educational Research Association, Montreal, Canada.

Carini, P. F. (1975). *Observation and description: An alternative methodology for the investigation of human phenomena.* North Dakota Study Group on Evaluation. Grand Forks: University of North Dakota Press.

Clark, C. M., & Peterson, P. L. (1986). Teachers' thought processes. In Merlin C. Wittrock (Ed.), *Handbook of research on teaching* (pp. 255–296). New York: Macmillan.

Clark, C. M., & Yinger, R. J. (1979a). *Three studies of teaching planning.* (Research Series No. 55). East Lansing: Michigan State University.

Clark, C. M., & Yinger, R. J. (1979b). Teachers' thinking. In P. L. Peterson & H. J. Walberg (Eds.), *Research on teaching* (pp. 231–263). Berkeley, CA: McCutchan.

Crocker, R. K., & Banfield, H. (1986). Factors influencing teacher decisions on school, classroom and curriculum. *Journal of Research in Science Teaching, 23*(9), 805–816.

DiNapoli, F. A. (1984). An ethnographic account of the cooperating teacher/student teaching relationship (Doctoral dissertation, University of Pittsburgh). *Dissertation Abstracts International, 45*, 3327A.

Eisner, E. W. (1976). Educational connoisseurship and criticism: Their form and functions in educational evaluation. *Journal of Aesthetic Education, 10*(3/4), 135–150.

Gay, L. R. (1987). *Educational research: Competencies for analysis and application* (3rd ed.). Columbus, OH: Merrill Publishing.

Germano, M. C., & Peterson, P. L. (1982). IGE and non-IGE teachers' use of student characteristics in making instructional decisions. *Elementary School Journal, 82*(4), 319–328.

Goetz, J. P., & LeCompte, M. D. (1984). *Ethnography and qualitative design in educational research.* Orlando, FL: Academic Press.

Grohosky, D. S. (1985). Influences on teacher decision-making in curriculum-planning (Doctoral dissertation, Pepperdine University, 1984). *Dissertation Abstracts International, 46*, 1178-A.

Guba, E. G. (1978). *Toward a methodology of naturalistic inquiry in educational evaluation.* Center for the Study of Evaluation, UCLA Graduate School of Education, University of California, Los Angeles.

Hill, J., Uinger, R. J., & Robbins, D. (1983). Instructional planning in a laboratory preschool. *Elementary School Journal, 83*(3), 182–193.

Housner, L. D., & Griffey, D. C. (1985). Teacher cognition: Differences in planning and interactive decision making between experienced and inexperienced teachers. *Research Quarterly for Exercise and Sport, 56*(1), 45–53.

Krueger, P. J. (1985). Influences of the hidden curriculum upon the perspectives of music student teachers: An ethnography (Doctoral dissertation, University of Wisconsin—Madison, 1985). *Dissertation Abstracts International, 46*, 1223A.

Malone, J. L. (1979). Decision-making behavior of kindergarten teachers. (Doctoral dissertation, Oklahoma State University, 1979). *Dissertation Abstracts International, 40*, 3104A.

May, W. T. (1986). Teaching students how to plan: The dominant model and alternatives. *The Journal of Teacher Education, 37*(6) 6–12.

McCutcheon, G. (1980). How do elementary school teachers plan? The nature of planning and influences on it. *Elementary School Journal, 81*(1), 4–23.

Meske, E. B. (1987). Learning to learn—music. *Design for Arts in Education, 89*(1), 45–48.

Miller, L. B. (1986). A description of children's musical behaviors: naturalistic. *Bulletin of the Council for Research in Music Education, 87*, 1–16.

Morine-Dershimer, G. (1978–1979). Planning in classroom reality, an in depth look. *Educational Research Quarterly, 3*(4), 83–99.

Neale, D. C., Pace, A. J., & Case, A. B. (1983, April). *The influence of training, experience and organizational environment on teachers' use of the systematic planning model.* Paper presented at the annual meeting of the American Educational Research Association, Montreal.

Oberg, A. A. (1976). *Information referents and patterns in the curriculum planning of class-room teachers.* Unpublished doctoral dissertation, University of Alberta, Canada.

Peterson, P. L., Marx, R. W., & Clark, C. M. (1978). Teacher planning, teacher behavior, and student achievement. *American Educational Research Journal, 15*, 417–432.

Rosenfeld, V. M. (1969). Possible influences of student teachers on their cooperating teachers. *Journal of Teachers' Education, 29*(1), 40–44.

Richey, M. J. (1983). A study of primary teacher planning behavior for reading instruction (Doctoral dissertation, University of Pittsburgh, 1983). *Dissertation Abstracts International, 45*, 479.

Sardo, D. (1982, October). *Teacher planning style in the middle school.* Paper presented to the Eastern Educational Research Association, Ellenville, NY.

Shavelson, R. J., & Borko, H. (1979). *Research on teachers' decisions in planning instruction.* Educational Horizons, 57(4), 183–189.

Shavelson, R. J., & Borko, H. (1979). Research on teachers' pedagogical thoughts, judgments, decisions, and behavior. *Review of Educational Research, 51*(4), 455–498.

Shulman, L. S. (1981). Disciplines of inquiry in education: An overview. *Educational Researcher, 10*(6), 5–12.

Tabachnick, B. R., & Zeichner, K. M. (1984). The impact of the student teaching experience on the development of teacher perspectives. *The Journal of Teacher Education, 35*(6), 28–36.

Taylor, P. H. (1970). *How teachers plan their courses.* Slough, Berkshire, England: National Foundation for Educational Research.

Tyler, R. (1949). *Basic principles of curriculum and instruction.* Chicago: University of Chicago Press.

Yinger, R. J. (1977). A study of teacher planning: Description and theory development using ethnographic and information processing methods (Doctoral dissertation, Michigan State University, East Lansing, 1977). *Dissertation Abstracts International, 39*, 207A.

Yinger, R. J., & Clark, C. M. (1982). *Understanding teachers' judgments about instruction: The task, the method, and the meaning.* (Research Series No. 121). East Lansing: Michigan State University, Institute for Research on Teaching.

Yinger, R. J., & Clark, C. M. (1983). *Self-reports of teacher judgment.* (Research Series No. 134). East Lansing: Michigan State University, Institute for Research on Teaching.

Zahorik, J. A. (1975). Teachers' planning models. *Educational Leadership, 33*(2), 134–139.

Zais, R. S. (1976). *Curriculum: Principles and foundations.* New York: Harper & Row.

STUDY AND DISCUSSION QUESTIONS

1. Provide an alternate title for this study by Schleuter.

2. Briefly summarize the three research questions.

3. Briefly describe ethnographic research.

4. How many subjects were there, and how were they chosen?

5. What were the data sources, and how were the data triangulated?

6. What was the quantitative measure for this study, and why was it used?

7. How did the subjects enter student teaching in regard to aims or goals?

8. To what extent did subjects plan and use "concept" teaching?

9. What role did "evaluation of students" play in the subjects' teaching?

10. Which of the subjects maintained a high level of self-evaluation?

11. Who was found to most influence the manner in which the student teachers encountered or identified curricular goals, and what does this say in regards to conclusion #6?

12. Which curricular category was found to be most significantly affected and enriched by the student teacher experience?

SUGGESTED ACTIVITIES

1. Write an abstract for Schleuter's study. It should be no more than 250 words.

2. From the insights given in Schleuter's study, state six important items you would want to share with any beginning student teacher under your direction.

3. Schleuter found that student teachers depended very little on information from basal series because they were taught to be independent of such sources in their college methods courses. How do you feel about this, and what has been your experience with basal series?

PART FIVE

Research and the Classroom

CHAPTER 15

Action Research

At one time or another all music teachers have explored an idea informally by using a quasi-research procedure (e.g., an approach to teaching sight-singing). This trial-and-error process is at the heart of what is called *action research*. The difference between an informal process and action research, however, lies in the more formal procedures used in the action approach.

Kemmis and McTaggart (1988) define action research as "trying out ideas in practice as a means of improvement and as a means of increasing knowledge about" a given topic (p. 6). They give four steps in this more formal process: (1) plan, (2) action, (3) observation, and (4) reflection. It is considered a research spiral in that once one cycle of four steps has been completed, the process is repeated in revised form(s) until the objectives of the study are met.

The "father" of action research is often cited as Kurt Lewin, who fled the Nazis and came to America during the World War II era. Lewin was a mathematician who developed an interest in the behavioral sciences, specifically in the areas of social change, social justice, and the elimination of human suffering. He was interested in research that was relevant to everyday life and worked to develop models of inquiry useful for asking and answering questions. Lewin developed a research methodology that became known later as *action research*, which he described as a multistep, collaborative, cyclical, data-driven approach to research and problem solving. He saw the process as a method for people directly affected by planned social changes to take responsibility for planning those changes and to assess the effects systematically. This process, instead of being "top-down," was intended to be "bottom-up" in the hierarchy of decision making.

ACTION RESEARCH GENRES

Three types of action research design are known: (1) technical, (2) practical, and (3) emancipatory. The second and third are commonly used by teachers in the classroom.

Technical

In the technical genre, the researcher tests a particular intervention used by a practitioner in the field. The intervention often aims at effectiveness and efficiency in performance and strives to produce change in social practice. In doing so it is used to validate and refine existing theories. In this technical format the participants often rely on the expertise of the researcher.

Practical

The second form of action research, the practical form, has the researcher and practitioner come together to identify potential problems, underlying causes, and possible solutions. Here the researcher encourages the practitioner to participate and become self-reflective, transforming the consciousness of the participants. The researcher acts as a consultant to help the participants engage in dialogue and self-reflection. This practical genre is used to help the practitioner understand practice and to solve immediate problems.

Emancipatory

The third form, emancipatory, is different, in that no hierarchy exists between the researcher and the practitioner. In this genre the expert is a process moderator who collaborates and shares equal responsibility with the participants. This increases the closeness between the problem and the theory used to explain and resolve it. It strives to make the problem very explicit and to raise participants' collective consciousness. The objective, as with all action research, is to transform the organization's social practices in which the participants are involved.

Common Characteristics

What becomes apparent in all three genres of action research is the low degree of controls exhibited in the research designs. Neither internal nor external validity are of major concern. The study involves only one group of participants, who may or may not be representative of any given population. In fact, because there is no interest in generalizing results, threats to external validity are nonexistent. Also, in that no attempt is made to follow scientific inquiry via the use of a control group, comparisons can be made only to how the group itself progresses.

The data collected in action research are mostly of the qualitative form. Observations are made in the narrative, and it is appropriate to try and validate the data through a possible triangulation process. While quantitative data can be collected, they typically are used to describe various parameters rather than to make inferences. For these reasons, action research is often viewed as the weakest form of research process in any type of research hierarchy. That is not to say that valuable information cannot be gained. The information, however, has limited use or application in the greater social or educational paradigm.

THE ACTION RESEARCH PROCESS

The process of the action research spiral is a rather simple one: plan the study, take action, collect observations in the form of data, reflect on what is happening, make adjustments, and begin the process again. While controls are necessarily weak, the design itself is not dependent on strong validity or reliability.

The Four-Part Process

1. *Plan.* Once the problem is identified, guidelines are established as to the plan of action. This plan needs to be farsighted enough to anticipate reasonably expected problems. It also needs to be flexible to accommodate unexpected changes.

2. *Action.* The plan dictates the specific activity or activities needed to implement the direction of the study. These procedures are characterized by being reflective in nature; i.e., change will be brought about by all of those involved through a well-thought-out reflective process. This process must be flexible enough to be guided by the critical reflection during the action phase.

3. *Observation.* Collection of the data occurs in whatever form the researcher and/or practitioner agree on. Most likely it will involve some type of written narrative, but it can include quantitative measures as well. The data collection must be flexible enough to allow for unintended outcomes to be observed.

4. *Reflection.* During this fourth phase the researcher and/or practitioner attempt to make sense of the data by critically reflecting on what has transpired and comparing this to what was intended. If adjustments are necessary in the plan, action, or observation phases, these are made and the cycle begins again.

Suitability to Teaching

Action research is well suited to schools, for a number of reasons: It incorporates a very democratic methodology, it shows respect for individuals, it is very inclusive by nature, it shows openness to diversity of perspective, it is a flexible approach, and it fosters grounded knowledge for changing practice (Watt, 1997, p. 1). It also brings focus to problems that can and should be explored in a more systematic way.

> When the same teacher who is responsible for implementing the change does the research, a real fit is created between the needs of the specific learner or learning community and the action taken. Action research is almost always conducted as part of a collegial enterprise. A community of practitioners with shared vision for their practice support each other as they critique and construct a more complete understanding of teaching and learning. (Watt, 1997, p. 1).

Watt also states that action research is gaining recognition by policy makers as a tool for change. However, she notes that it cannot be mandated. "To require teachers to do action research defeats the purpose and undermines its efficacy" (p. 1).

Is This "Good" Research?

The following dialogue by Shelley Gauthier-McMahon (1997) is a reflection of a practicing teacher who is struggling with the "big" question of whether or not action research is "good" research.

> I have been thinking about the "teachers as researchers" question. Again. It seems that no matter how much we discuss it, it keeps coming up over and over again. I am feeling a bit closer to calling myself a researcher. I am not quite there yet—still waiting for some stats to appear to make it official. So many years of learning that strict guidelines of "good" research makes it hard to shake that perception.
>
> Not to mention ongoing discussions at home about validity. You see, I live with a "white coat." Every aspect of the research must be clearly defined, isolated, observed, measured, compared, etc., etc. Then the whole process must be replicated by others to make sure all that work didn't somehow produce an anomaly. Validity, reliability, reproducibility, objectivity, statistical significance—all swirl around inside my head. My "white coat" partner believes that most research ever conducted by anyone, in any field (including his own), is flawed, or biased, or meaningless. Well, maybe, but certainly not good enough to really count on and definitely not proof of causality. Yet somehow he manages to get up in the morning, go to work, continue to research, live life. I struggle with all this. I try not to believe everything I hear: "Studies show that factor *x* causes factor *y*. Therefore you should blah, blah, blah, blah." I try to think critically: What do these results really mean, how have they been skewed by people who want to prove a point, was the research any good? Back to the same old questions: What is "good" research, are teachers researchers, is the work I am doing really research? I guess I feel that I am doing research. I am just not convinced it is good research.
>
> In fact, I know deep down that it is not—at least not in the strictest sense. My only indication that my assumptions and results are correct is my own sense of relief about teaching and my students' improved behavior. However, I don't think it matters very much whether I am conducting "good" research in the traditional sense. Not at this point. As long as I am learning and applying what I learn, then this process will not have been a waste. Rephrase that: It will have been worthwhile. Just as long as the research is good enough to produce positive results. No incorrect assumptions. They can lead to incorrect practice. That would be reckless and unforgivable. There will be opportunities down the road to do better research. Maybe even "good" research. (Gauthier-McMahon, 1997, p.1).

That says it all. Action research is what it is, and it should not be judged with other forms of more rigorous study unless the researcher makes the mistake of trying to generalize the results to the population. Action research focuses on one teacher and one classroom. If instruction in that classroom can be improved, why not use it?

An Action Research Example

The following is an example of action research in the music classroom. The collaborative process is apparent, because the university researcher (Colleen Conway) and the school music teacher (James Borst) have coauthored this joint study that appeared in *UPDATE: Applications of Research in Music Education*, in 2001.

Action Research in Music Education

Colleen M. Conway, *University of Michigan*
James Borst, *East Kentwood High School*
UPDATE: *Applications of Research in Music Education, 19(2), 3–8.*

Reprinted by MENC: The National Association for Music Education. Copyright © 2001 by MENC.

The music education research community works hard to reach out and connect with K–12 music educators. *UPDATE: Applications of Research in Music Education* itself is an example of this dialogue. Yet, despite these efforts, as Edwards (1992) suggests, "Research is not viewed as being in the mainstream of either music or music education. Most musicians and music teachers have little interest in what music researchers do, how they do it, or the conclusions that they reach" (p. 5). Even when music education research is presented in a practitioner-friendly way, problems arise because most research ideas and designs come from the university community. One way to make connections between research and teaching practice is through action research. When applied to music education, action research refers to studies of music teaching and learning that are designed and implemented by K–12 music teachers or in equal collaboration with them.

Colleagues in educational research currently place increased emphasis on exploring designs that involve K–12 music teachers in the process. Many teachers in general education have become involved in identifying research problems, collecting and analyzing data, and writing research reports. The field of music education has just begun to take an active interest in promoting this type of research (Bresler, 1995). Practicing music teachers, therefore, can benefit from the results of action research; this account of a recent action research study serves as an example.

Action Research in Music Education?

In relating action research to music education, Bresler (1995) states: "Action research aims at the direct improvement of teaching and curriculum within a particular class-room, gaining a more critical perspective from which the teacher/researcher can reflect and change" (p. 15). Action research refers to inquiry that is designed by teachers to make changes and affect teaching.

Altrichter, Posch, and Somekh (1993) state that "Action research is intended to support teachers, and groups of teachers, in coping with the challenges and problems of practice and carrying through innovations in a reflective way" (p. 4). Action research reports describe teachers doing research to make changes in their own classrooms (Bogdan & Biklen, 1998). Cutietta (1993) suggests that music educators may use action research to gather information for music program advocacy.

The term "collaborative action research" (Henson, 1996) refers to the collaboration among a group of teachers on a research topic or with a university researcher. Erikson (1994) suggests that the collaborative action research model may be a valuable tool for music education. It may be difficult for K–12 music teachers to find time to design and implement research. However, collaboration with the university professor, for whom research is part of job expectations, makes equal-partner action research a possibility.

As Patton (1990) states, "Action research encourages joint collaboration within a mutually acceptable ethical framework to solve organizational or community problems" (p. 129). Regelski (1994) encourages the music education profession to consider the following:

> The actions of humans are situated, contextual, and wrapped up in messy teleological issues involving the subjectivity of human wants, needs, and goals. In such a world, knowledge and practices cannot be treated as neutral, fixed, or finished, or as unconditionally objective, nor can they avoid being laden with values. (p. 60)

In order to address the "situated" and "contextual" issues to which Regelski refers, the research community must collaborate with K–12 music teachers to identify research problems and develop study designs. This collaboration may require a shift from the power structure of researcher (i.e., university professor) studying the researched (i.e., K–12 music teacher) to a collaboration between equal partners. Such studies involving real classrooms and students may also require greater use of the qualitative paradigm—which is more readily adapted to context-based inquiry (Kincheloe, 1991). Qualitative researchers in education study classrooms, schools, students, and teachers in their natural environment, They do not attempt to control for variables in a setting; instead, they examine and describe the unique characteristics of a specific teaching context.

Guidelines for Action Research

The first step for teachers interested in doing action research is to identify a problem or formulate a question regarding music teaching or learning. Because the goal of action research is to effect change, the most important consideration becomes an inquiry's usefulness in terms of the individual's own teaching. Action researchers are not concerned with generalizations outside their own context. However, in many cases, results documented by one study may be translated into other contexts. Action researchers must be careful to describe both the setting of the research and the participants involved in the study so that other music teachers can consider how findings may relate to other contexts.

Once a problem has been identified, the action researcher must begin to gather information and document issues relating to that problem. Many action researchers find it valuable to keep a diary or teaching journal to track daily incidents that may relate to the research. In some cases, videotaping a class and transcribing it may provide a form of observation data. Depending on the study, interviewing students, parents, and colleagues may also be appropriate. Existing documents, such as student grade reports, student compositions, portfolios, practice records, concert programs, audiotapes of performances, and so on, may also contain useful information. When done in collaboration with university researchers or other teachers, valuable study information may be derived from the insights of collaborative partners who observe classroom practices.

Throughout the research process, the teacher-researcher must assess when enough data have been gathered. The data-collection phase of an action research project melds together with the analysis phase so that thoughts regarding the meaning of the data begin to emerge during the process, not just after it. The action researcher must search for meaning by coding the collected data and developing categories to describe and organize themes presented in observations, diary notes, interviews, and other materials. In collaborative action research projects, teachers and university researchers may analyze data together. Such interaction adds another important dimension of reflection to the research process.

The final step for the action researcher includes making decisions regarding teaching and learning based on the results of the study. In a less systematic way, good teachers make these kinds of decisions every day. Action research provides a model for teachers in reflecting on their work. Documentation of these reflections and decisions contributes to the knowledge base of teaching. Collaboration with university researchers helps to advance this knowledge by preparing the documentation to be shared.

A Music Teacher's Personal Account

A middle and high school choral teacher in the fifteenth year of teaching, I (James Borst) have ten years of experience teaching kindergarten through twelfth-grade vocal music in the same large, suburban district. My school district includes ten elementary schools, three middle schools, one ninth-grade building, and one tenth-through twelfth-grade building. The high school choral program has seven choirs, while each middle school supports a variety of active chorus programs at all levels. I hold an applied master's degree in choral conducting and a bachelor's degree in school music, and am currently enrolled in a Ph.D. program in music education.

In the fall of 1991, I was hired to start a choral program in a new middle school. I taught sixth-, seventh-, and eighth-grade general and vocal music. After a few years, my daily schedule changed because of continued growth districtwide. In the fall of 1997, I was asked to add tenth-grade Concert Choir to my daily teaching assignments, allowing me the unique opportunity to teach former students who had graduated with three years of middle school vocal music under my direction. In this new position, I observed that many former students chose not to continue at the high school level. I had sensed this attrition before, but, after beginning the high school program, I became acutely aware of the problem and wondered why so many former middle-school students chose not to participate in high school. Where were they? This curious phenomenon disturbed me. The middle school students and I had worked very hard to establish excellence, with both girls and boys receiving a solid foundation in vocal training. Our choirs had received superior scores at district and state festivals. The students had appeared to enjoy their choral experiences, and the community had taken pride in the vocal music program. The more I pondered the situation, the more frustrated I became. Our hard work was not coming to the fruition I had expected.

This is where my research story begins. In the fall of 1998, ten of the forty-five members in the Concert Choir were graduates of my middle school program. I decided in the early stages of my inquiry to be proactive and ask these ten students: "Why did you continue vocal music from middle school to high school?" Of the ten students who studied with me for three years in the middle school, six agreed to be in the study.

Research Methods

I identified several studies concerning student perception of teacher behavior (Morgan, 1992; Schmidt, 1995; Stamar, 1995; Taylor, 1995). These studies explored choral students' responses that dealt with perceptions of their teachers. However, these projects failed to explain students' intrinsic motivation for involvement. While they helped to identify one aspect of student attraction to the choral classroom, these studies did not explain other motivations for students' continued involvement in choir from one level to another.

Mizener (1993) examined the attitudes of elementary music students toward singing and choir participation in relation to grade level, general classroom singing activities, previous and current out-of-school singing experiences, and degree of skill, both self-perceived and assessed. Her study results support previous research indicating that students generally like singing activities. Yet less than half were interested in choral singing. Other data showed that girls, younger students, those who like to sing, those who wanted to sing, and those who wanted to sing in choir responded more positively to most items on a questionnaire.

Hylton (1981) researched high school student participants' perception of the meaning and value of choral singing experiences, suggesting that meaning and value for high school students is multidimensional. Categorized as achievement, spiritualistic, musical-artistic, communicative, psychological, and integrative, these dimensions demonstrate the many possible outcomes of choral music education experiences. These categories also help to explain which factors give meaning to choral experiences and, in turn, motivate students to participate in middle school and high school choral programs.

In his investigation of elementary and secondary music students' motivation to achieve, Asmus (1986) cited reasons for success or failure in music; free responses from music students were classified according to a two-dimensional design model of attribution theory. This theory holds that beliefs students have about the causes for success and failure at a musical task will influence how the students approach the task in the future. "Teachers who encourage students with effort-related attributions are more likely to have students who adopt the view that if they try hard and apply themselves, they can achieve in music" (Asmus, 1986, p. 268).

Students attributed causes for success and failure in four major categories: ability, task difficulty, luck, and effort. Ability and task difficulty were perceived by previous research as stable causes, while luck and effort were perceived as unstable. Similarly, ability and effort were considered causes that came from within (internal) an individual, while task difficulty and luck were considered to be causes from the outside (external). Asmus (1986) suggested that 80 percent of the reasons cited for success or failure in music were internal in nature: a greater number of stable reasons were cited for success, while more external-unstable reasons were cited for failure. The current investigation received its focus from action research aimed at understanding more fully the motivations leading students to participate in or drop out of chorus in middle school and high school.

The purpose of the research involved gaining information about the relationship between personal motivation and choral involvement at multiple levels of study. The following questions were developed from reviewing research literature: (a) What personal factors exist that motivated the six vocal music students to continue their study of chorus from one school to another and from one grade to another? (b) What other nonmusical influences motivated the students to value their choir class experiences from one school to another and from one grade to another? and (c) How do these factors relate to previous research and to other teachers in the same mode of questioning?

An action research interview design was used to gather data, with an interest in collecting deep and rich description for completion of the investigation—specifically, to know *why* certain phenomena occurred. Action research fit the needs of this investigation because the information required came from a specific teacher's teaching context. Patton (1990) discussed action research as attempting to solve specific problems:

> In action research design, data collection tends to be more informal, the people in the situation are often directly involved in gathering the information and then studying themselves, and the results are used internally to attack specific problems within a program. (p. 157)

Attacking a specific problem was the precise reason for the study.

This investigation utilized three data-collection procedures to represent data triangulation. First, the six selected students were asked eight interview questions:

- As a member of your high school choral group, you are a person who sings because this experience means something to you. I am trying to find out what it is about this experience that is meaningful for you. Would you describe what this singing experience means to you and the part that singing plays in your life?
- Please describe why you stayed in the choral program throughout your middle school years. What was it about your experience that made you participate for three years?
- Can you describe the reason you chose to go on to high school choir from middle school?
- Can you describe the reasons you chose to go on to tenth-grade choir from ninth-grade choir?
- Can you think of any nonmusical reason for joining and staying in the choral program here?
- If you were to change anything about the choral program from middle school to high school, what would you change?

- Now that we have talked for a little while and you have a better idea as to what we are discussing, could you please talk again about why choir is valuable to you?
- Are you planning to continue in the choral program here? Why or why not?

Each student was asked the questions in a consistent manner. The interviews were held before and after school at the middle school or high school, whichever was most convenient for the student. The interviews lasted an average of twelve minutes and were audiotaped, transcribed, and typed into a word processing file.

Second, in order to compare responses with the earlier individual interviews, I interviewed the six students in a panel-like format during concert Choir rehearsal—peer presence might influence their responses. The six students, who were asked the same questions as in the personal interviews, sat in front of the rest of the choir during the videotaped group interview.

Third, a five-minute telephone interview with one parent of each of the six students was made during evening hours. The goal here was to enrich the information concerning why the six students continued in the vocal music program. The opening statement and question for the parent interview was as follows:

> As a parent of a student in the high school choral group, you are a person who may have insight regarding what it is about the singing experience that is meaningful for your child. I am trying to find out why your child values the choir experience. Would you describe to me how you observe this singing experience to be meaningful to your child, especially as this relates to his or her experience from middle to high school?

The parent responses also were transcribed and typed into a word processing file.

Data were analyzed through coding and categorizing of the words and concepts consistently evident from transcriptions of the audiotape, videotape, and notes taken during phone interviews. After the audiotape was transcribed on paper, each student response was placed together under the same numbered question from the interview. Words, phrases, and concepts from each question emerged through the grouping and color coding of similar responses. Anytime the word "learning" showed up, for example, it was underlined in green. The phrase "I like to sing" appeared several times and was underlined in red. Final categories were solidified by deleting and adding as coded responses were reviewed. Sometimes during the process of creating categories, multiple colors were used to underline same words or phrases because those words or phrases fit into two or more categories. Final decisions concerning categories in which words and phrases were placed were made after the coding was completed.

Seven categories emerged from analysis of data from the individual interviews:

- singing for learning's sake
- singing for self-expression
- singing for social and group reasons
- singing for enjoyment

- singing for performance
- singing to be identified with the school program
- singing for the music itself.

The audiotapes, when compared with categories in the videotape, revealed no new categories; student responses in the group interview were almost verbatim with the individual interview responses. During the panel discussion, the entire choir was invited to engage in conversation about the subject. In general, choir members were very hesitant to add their thoughts to the discussion; during this portion of the interview, the videotape contains much silence. Students appeared uncomfortable talking about this subject; possibly, they did not like being videotaped, their maturity level inhibited them, or they had never been asked to think about the issue before.

Notes from parent interviews were analyzed in the same manner as the student interviews but were not coded as specifically into categories—which did not emerge in this process as cohesively as they had in the student interviews. Parents had unique ways of responding to the questions and spoke with candor about their child's involvement in their own sincere way. Building confidence and self-esteem were the parents' most common response when asked why they thought their child continued in the choir program.

Conclusions

After I studied the results of the data, I made some conclusions. This was a challenge because I had to infer from the information what was meaningful and significant. I synthesized my documented information so that it made sense to me and yielded meaningful thoughts. Careful study and long thinking sessions helped me to do [sic] this. I organized my thoughts into concrete sentences and paragraphs and discovered several important aspects about my program and my teaching. I was pleased with the categories that emerged because they appeared to relate to previous research (Asmus, 1986; Hylton, 1981). I also determined new information that pertained to my specific school setting. The following discussion represents just a few of the implications gathered from the study—insights which helped me in my own teaching situation.

Overall, students and parents expressed positive feelings about school choral experiences. When asked if they would continue singing in the high school program after tenth grade, each student said yes; three of the six students gave strong affirmation, with expressions like "definitely," "all the way to twelfth grade," and "I really want to." The parents all spoke about the self-confidence that choir children had gained through singing experiences from middle school to high school. Most parents mentioned how much they enjoyed hearing their child sing around the house and in church as the direct result of participation in school choirs. One parent expressed appreciation for choir because it gave the child confidence in dealing with a stuttering problem. Choral experiences in this setting appeared to be a positive influence in these students' lives involving school, home, and church. These opinions argue strongly that choral music instruction, because it provides an educationally sound place for students to learn and positively influences life-long learning, needs to remain a viable course option.

Both students and parents found it difficult to articulate the value of choral music as an aesthetic outcome. The value of art for art's sake did not emerge as a significant reason for participating in choir from students or their parents. For them, choral music appears to function as something other than enjoying the craft or art of singing in a chorus for its aesthetic value; nonmusical functions of chorus may be appropriate educational outcomes, but teaching students to think broadly about the ineffable qualities of the choral art may provide a more balanced educational experience. Teaching strategies should be created to help students identify choral music as an aesthetic experience through the literature.

The findings of this study will help the overall choral program to develop a plan of action that fosters student involvement. As a means to an end, social outcomes—a prevalent response among students on the value of choir participation—might form an initial focus for teachers to create opportunities for choral students [sic] to socialize with each other from various schools. The middle school students could have mentors, or "buddies," in high school. Concerts, featuring performances by multiple levels of choirs, could include social time afterward. Recently, our school began an annual prefestival concert that includes all three middle schools in a singing showcase that capitalized on this notion and provided an appropriate venue for students to socialize. The students and parents love this concert because it shows a bigger picture and gets people together.

Teamwork, camaraderie, and working with a group were also prevalent responses as to why the students continued in choir. These factors could also become focus points for teachers. Instructional strategies that include the same vocabulary and activities should be developed to enhance these attributes of singing in a choir and should be implemented at all the schools in the same fashion. For example, teachers might talk about the importance of teamwork at all three middle schools. As a result, curriculum delivery may be more unified and validated for all students. In front of the students, the choral teaching staff must also exemplify the concept of teamwork among themselves.

Both students and parents stated that the primary reason for continuing choir from middle school to high school was the enjoyment of singing. What does that mean? What is it about singing that they enjoy? The music? The physical sensation? Further investigation might be conducted to discover what factors provide satisfaction. Students and parents hardly mentioned choral repertoire as a motivating factor for continuing in choir. Investigating this further may help to develop choral libraries and determine more specific teaching strategies.

Additional credibility may be added to this study by interviewing students who studied with me and did *not* continue from middle to high school. A comparison of their responses with those of students who continued might be revealing in light of the research questions. Also, interviewing current ninth-grade participants about the value of singing may help to solve the problem of attrition for the current school year. Ninth-grade students are closer to the middle school experience, lending more credibility to their responses. Looking back at the immediate past from a student perspective may help to look at the immediate future.

For developing the choral program, significant knowledge may be gained by looking at motivational factors that emerge from the different perspectives of boys and girls. Because more girls have tended to continue than boys, one male and five females were interviewed in the present study. Only one male chorister out of twelve in eighth-grade choir continued to tenth-grade choir. After talking with several male students who did not continue, it was learned that, because ninth-grade choir was split into separate choirs for boys and girls, these young men were disappointed in their desire to continue singing with the girls. Ironically, some males in my current Concert Choir have commented that they miss the all-male group and would rather sing in a men's choir.

Because my specific situation is typical of many similar school settings, other teachers may hopefully be challenged to think creatively about school issues by examining my study. Perhaps some teachers have asked the very same questions. However, my research does not prove anything or answer all the problems, but provides, rather, a means for interpreting phenomena. Research often answers a question by asking more questions. The cycle never ends.

By systematically investigating pertinent questions in my particular music education setting, I understood more deeply what influences my daily teaching. This study generated new ideas and stimulated dialogue with colleagues. Teachers teach students how to solve problems. By example, music educators should take up the same challenge and ask, "Why conduct action research in the music classroom?" Do it for your profession, for your students, and for the music program.

REFERENCES

Altrichter, J., Posch, P., & Somekh, B. (1993). *Teachers investigate their work: An introduction to the methods of action research.* New York: Routledge.

Asmus, E. (1986). Student beliefs about the causes of success and failure in music. *Journal of Research in Music Education, 34*, 262–78.

Bogdan, R. C., & Biden, S. K. (1998). *Qualitative research for education* (3rd ed.). Boston: Allyn and Bacon.

Bresler, L. (1995). Ethnography, phenomenology and action research in music education. *The Quarterly Journal of Music Teaching and Learning, 6*(3), 4–16.

Burnaford, G., Fischer, J., & Hobson, D. (1996). *Teachers doing research: Practical possibilities.* Mahwah, NJ: Lawrence Erlbaum Publishers.

Cutietta, R. (1993). Action research for advocacy. *Teaching Music, 1*(1), 40–41.

Edwards, R. H. (1992). Research: Going from incredible to credible. *The Quarterly Journal of Music Teaching and Learning, 3*(1), 5.

Erikson, F. (1994). Where the action is: On collaborative action research in education. *The Bulletin of the Council for Research in Music Education, 123*, 10–26.

Henson, K. T. (1996). Teachers as researchers. In J. Sikula (Ed.), *Handbook of research on teacher education* (2nd ed.), 53–64.

Hylton, J. B. (1981). Dimensionality in high school participants' perceptions of the meaning of choral singing experience. *Journal of Research in Music Education, 29*, 287–303.

Kincheloe, J. L. (1991). *Teaching as researchers: Qualitative inquiry as a path to empowerment.* London: Falmer Press.

Morgan, R. (1992). A study of a director's behaviors and his students' perceptions in a high school choral ensemble. *Dissertation Abstracts International, 53*, 06A. (University Microfilm No. AAG92-29967).

Patton, M. Q. (1990). *Qualitative evaluation and research methods*. Thousands Oaks, CA: Sage Publications.

Regelski, T. A. (1994). Action research and critical theory: empowering music teachers to professionalize praxis. *Bulletin of the Council for Research in Music Education, 43*, 313–329.

Schmidt, C. (1995). Attributions of success, grade level, and gender as factors in choral students' perceptions of teacher feedback. *Journal of Research in Music Education, 43*, 313–329.

Stamar, R. (1995). Choral student perceptions of effective motivation strategies based on Madeline Hunter's motivation variables. *Dissertation Abstracts International, 56*, 08A. (University Microfilms No. AAI95-44375).

Taylor, O. (1995). Student interpretations of teacher verbal praise in selected seventh- and eighth-grade choral classes. *Dissertation Abstracts International, 56*, 12A. (University Microfilm No. AA196-12629).

STUDY AND DISCUSSION QUESTIONS

1. How is action research described?

2. How and when did action research evolve?

3. What are the three basic types of action research, and how do these differ?

4. Is action research weak or strong in external validity? Why?

5. In what form is most action research data collected?

6. What is the four-part process of action research?

7. Why is the process of action research a spiral procedure?

8. Action research is often carried out in a collaborative process by whom?

9. Should teachers be required to do action research? Why or why not?

10. Is action research "good" research? Explain your answer.

11. What is the mistake that action researchers should not make?

12. Why does Regelski believe that action research is good for educators?

13. When do "thoughts regarding the meaning of the data" emerge in action research?

14. What role does "reflection" play in action research?

15. What was the problem Borst identified in his action research study?

16. Asmus (1986) concluded that about 80% of the reasons students cited for success or failure in music was what?

17. How did Borst triangulate the data in his study?

18. How did Borst analyze the data from his study?

19. What did Borst find regarding the importance of the aesthetic experience for being in choir?

20. What was the primary reason by both students and parents for continuing choir from middle school to high school?

21. What did Borst say his study proved?

SUGGESTED ACTIVITIES

1. Consider what types of action research studies you might think interesting to explore in your own classroom environment.
2. Take one idea from your list in Activity 1 and make a brief outline of the (1) plan, (2) action, and (3) observation.

CHAPTER 16

Integrating Research and Teaching

It is sad but true that most of what is taught in schools is not the product of well-defined research. Fads in curricula come and go, and rarely do these fads have a research base. Phonics was all but abandoned at the end of the twentieth century for a whole-language approach. Then it was found that students' reading scores were plummeting because they had no tools for deciphering new words. The legislature of the State of California reacted to students' low reading scores by mandating that phonics again be taught in all elementary schools. It is educators, not politicians, who need to be making curricular decisions.

TEACHING BASED ON RESEARCH

Slavin (1984) states: "The primary antidote to educational change (or failure to change) based on the passions of the moment is well-designed, unbiased research" (p. 3). Unfortunately, research as to how students learn best is hampered by many problems: time, access to students, difficulty in implementing a true-experimental design, and the public's general suspicion of research. "But only research can provide the kind of objective information needed to intelligently make educational decisions on which so much depends" (p. 3).

Appendices A and B of this text present topics that have been researched in music education through the end of the twentieth century, as exemplified in the tables of contents of two major handbooks of research. While a wealth of information exists in those handbooks' contents (most of it unknown to school music teachers), an in-depth observation reveals more questions than answers. For example, would you not think that by the twentieth-first century music educators would know how best to teach music reading? No, not really. While many claims are made by differing "camps" (e.g., Orff, Kodály, Dalcroze, Gordon), the paucity of research in music literacy is appalling. Why is this the case? Because it is very difficult to design experiments in which the subjects are not already contaminated by some knowledge of music reading. In addition, how is it possible to assign students randomly to treatment and control groups using intact classrooms? It is a huge challenge to researchers outside the regular school system.

The research base for children's singing is one of the more developed areas of the music curriculum. Research (Phillips, 1992) indicates that inaccurate singing among older students stems more from motor-coordination problems than from lack of aural acuity. However, problems in aural acuity seem to be more prevalent among primary-age children. These findings are basic information for all elementary music teachers, and yet many still operate on the old notion that singing is something you either can or cannot do. It takes a long time for research findings to "trickle down" to classroom practitioners.

The development of creativity among students is one of the nine National Standards, and yet, most teachers would admit that they don't know how to teach or assess creativity. In fact, we are not sure what constitutes the creative process. Theories abound, but definitive research has yet to explain why one person is highly creative and another is not and whether all people can learn to be creative. Yet one of our National Standards states that the development of creativity is an important part of every child's music education.

How do people process music information? That is an important question and theories abound, but little concrete information is known. In fact, how people process information in general is a subject about which we know little. Is it not interesting that the very people who are in charge of students' education know so little about how children learn? If we knew more about the process of learning, schools might be more successful in what they try to do—develop independent learners.

The truth is, most of what and how we teach is based on decades of trial-and-error procedures; some of it works and a lot of it does not. The lowly state of education in America today is a testimony to the fact that we go through the motions, but students benefit only minimally. The Bush administration seeks to solve this problem through standardized testing. "No Child Left Behind" is forcing teachers to teach for the test, the most common complaint heard from educators. But in some parts of the country test scores are on the rise. What is going on? We aren't sure, but we do know this— there is no research evidence that shows standardized testing helps students to learn. The belief that testing fosters learning is an assumption on which billions of dollars are being spent. If it is found it doesn't work, then what? Who knows, but one thing is certain: whatever it is will be as unlikely to be based on research as on the adoption of standardized testing. Slavin (1984) states:

> It is only natural to expect that what goes on in schools is of critical interest to the nation as a whole, and it is true that few issues of local government are more hotly debated than education. Yet much of the constant debate about how best to educate students, both within the education community and in society, is based on passion rather than facts, ideology rather than data. (p. 3)

We are an educated people who do not know how to educate. Billions of dollars are spent on education each year and we have so little to show for it. Moreover the arts continue to be relegated to "service" roles in the curriculum. Where is the research that demonstrates the value of an arts education in the lives of our children?

TEACHERS AS RESEARCHERS

The people who have the greatest access to students are teachers. Why don't teachers take advantage of this situation and involve themselves in research? Is it no time, no interest, or no knowledge of how to go about it?

What if every classroom became a lab for finding out what really works best for student learning? It could change the course of education in this country. "Impossible," you say. Probably so, but what if even a few teachers took the challenge to be actively engaged in research in their own classrooms? I suggest the impact would be the advancement of learning, even music learning.

The discussion of action research in Chapter 15 presents the starting point for a discussion about teachers becoming researchers in their own classrooms. Can you imagine yourself defining a problem, making a plan of action, observing and collecting data, analyzing and reflecting on the changes being observed? Probably not. Who has the time? But what if it became a collaborative process where those trained as researchers joined with you in the process? That is what Ursula Casanova (1989) asks you to consider in the following article.

Research and Practice: We Can Integrate Them

Ursula Casanova, *Arizona State University*
NEA Today, 7(6), 44–49.

Reprinted by permission of the NEA: National Education Association.
Copyright © 1989 by the NEA.

There seems to be general agreement about the desirability of improving schools and instruction. There is less agreement about the best way to achieve that worthy goal. Within the education community, the role of educational research is often central to the arguments.

Some say that an existing body of knowledge, generated in the last 20 or so years by educational researchers, could contribute significantly to school improvement if only teachers would use it. Others argue that the research available is useless because it fails to take into account the realities of schools and classrooms and so does not address teachers. And some, particularly school administrators at various levels, have actually tried to apply research findings to the school improvement efforts. These attempts have usually met with only minimal success.

Clearly, difficulties stand in the way of integrating educational research and educational practice. Practicing educators and researchers bring different perspectives to the problem. These differences must be recognized and deliberately addressed in any efforts at integrating research and practice in education.

The Theory/Practice Split

Education is a highly stratified field. Differences in status distinguish those working at various levels, such as elementary or higher education. Status distinctions also exist among different roles. We have teachers and professors, special teachers, administrators, paraprofessionals, and—oh, yes—educational researchers. Among all these, those who "only teach" are accorded one of the lowest places in the hierarchy. Conversely, those who engage in educational research tend to be placed at one of the highest levels.

Why should this be so? Why should those who handle the thousand daily problems of instruction be accorded a lower status than those who handle only one of those problems at a time? The answer can be found in the traditional value placed on two types of endeavor: practice and theory. Teachers—as practitioners—engage in *praxis*, while the researchers' work is in *theoria*, theorizing.

Praxis and *theoria* are ancient Greek terms that we have inherited along with the values they symbolize. Traditionally, those who engage in thinking have been accorded a higher status than those who engage in doing, not only in education but throughout the professions. The same status differences can be found, for example, between the physicians who daily interact with patients and those who engage in laboratory research.

In education, the dichotomy between theory and practice has been particularly harmful, contributing to the opening of a wide gulf between teachers and researchers. Teachers tend to disparage educational researchers. They get impatient with researchers' unwillingness to provide solutions for their problems. They find research writing unintelligible and irrelevant to their daily concerns. And the explicit status differences between theoria and praxis don't improve the relationships. Teachers tend, perhaps unconsciously, to feel that they hold a lower status than researchers. This perception often inhibits them from expressing their own opinions when confronting research findings and contributes to their avoidance of articles that appear difficult and incomprehensible.

Researchers, on the other hand, strive to build theories. They study specific occurrences and isolate them in order to understand them better. They find the world of the classroom too cluttered, so they choose to work with well-defined segments of education. Even when researchers conduct their studies in the classroom, as many do now, they limit themselves to a particular problem, or to the behavior of specific children. They get impatient with teachers who seek answers and solutions to their messy practical problems.

Researchers, even the best-intended ones, also cannot avoid contamination with the existing social values that assign them a higher status than teachers. This perception, even when unconscious, may lead them to discredit teachers' legitimate concerns and to undervalue teachers' capacity for participating as equal partners in research activities.

It is not surprising, then, that teachers and researchers eye each other with suspicion. Their behavior recalls Prof. Higgins' plaintive demand in *My Fair Lady*: "Why can't a woman be more like a man?" Teachers would like researchers to be more like them, to address real problems. Researchers, for their part, would like practitioners to emulate them by taking a detached, scientific approach to their plans and problems.

But there is hope. After decades of keeping their distance, many researchers have entered the schools and classrooms during the last 20 years. Their experience has given them a greater respect for teachers and a better understanding of the difficulties teachers face. In the best situations, teachers and researchers have begun to collaborate as equals, in the process gaining a better understanding of each other. Theory and practice are becoming more comfortable together. Unfortunately, positive effects of this trend have been counteracted by another trend: an increased tendency for state and local administrators to misapply research to school improvement efforts.

School Improvement and Misuse of Research

School improvement, like motherhood and apple pie, is an unassailable concept. The movement is strengthened by its ostensible reliance on "research." But what appears to guide most of these efforts is the selective use of research findings to support administrative decisions. Such findings become the framework for policies that are then imposed from above.

As researchers will quickly admit, their findings are meant to inform, not to become policies. Research reports are carefully preceded by caveats that limit their applicability to situations similar to those studied. These caveats are often ignored by policymakers eager to satisfy public demands. Thus we find bizarre uses of instruments designed for specific purposes. For example, observers in one southeastern state found school personnel using an instrument specifically designed for monitoring teacher/student interaction in primary classrooms during reading lessons—to monitor teacher/student interaction during a junior high drama class.

Efforts to use research findings to improve education are also hampered by the complexities inherent in the educational process. The need to develop simple, straightforward, and easily understood policies often results in simplistic interpretations of research findings. The complex interaction of time and classroom activities that resulted in the concept of Academic Learning Time (ALT), for example, has been translated far too often into the simple time-on-task concept. Reducing ALT to time-on-task ignores important differences between allocated and engaged time. The two concepts also require different relationships between the difficulty of the task and student ability, and between the curriculum and the outcome measures. This reduction and simplification of the original concept has led many districts to increase time-on-task by extending the school day or the school year. It is not surprising that, by themselves, such policies have only minimal impact on student achievement.

In some cases administrators go beyond simplification to outright distortion of research findings in their eagerness to improve their school's performance. A principal, for instance, was overheard reviewing with her staff the six characteristics of an effective school proposed by the late Ron Edmonds. To Edmonds' original five, she had added one more: "to obey the principal."

Classroom and Academy: Demands in Conflict

These misuses of research have not endeared researchers to teachers. Instead, teachers will often see research as a tool used by administrators to limit their autonomy. Administrators' tendency to preselect research topics and findings that are to their liking, freely interpret them, and impose them on teachers is one reason teachers resent researchers and their findings.

In addition teachers who have an interest in research lack time to delve into libraries in search of articles. When they do, and actually locate the information they want, they find they're unfamiliar with the prose conventions of research reports.

Teachers also lack opportunities to discuss and digest the pros and cons of a given idea in an open, nonjudgmental atmosphere. Finally, the effort seems unnecessary, since they usually find that policymakers do not value their opinions.

Researchers operate under their own set of pressures. While the teacher is under pressure to be efficient and effective, the academic researcher is under pressure to discover new theories and to produce publishable articles. The kind of research teachers want and the questions they would like answered may be of interest to the researcher, but they may also be tainted in academic circles as too "applied" and, therefore, may not lead to academic advancement. In addition, academically valued writing must be "scholarly"—that is, it must be written in the specialized jargon of the researcher and carefully stated, with appropriate caveats, in order to escape criticism. This jargon is unfamiliar to teachers, and the carefully stated conclusions seem designed to confuse rather than clarify.

Lastly, research results must be published in the "right" journals if they are to count in obtaining desirable academic rewards. Publication in the magazines most teachers read is not highly valued in the academy.

There are also methodological problems connected with classroom or school-based research. The positivist approach has dominated the research enterprise for many years. Positivist research tends to remain distant from the site and the subjects being researched. Its findings are understood within a statistical framework based on generalizations that don't easily translate to the daily problems of instruction.

Emphasis has recently shifted to qualitative research based on observation and description. This genre is more compatible with school and classroom realities, and the findings from such research tend to be more applicable to classroom problems. But researchers who engage in this type of study have to deal with their own set of problems. For example, they may have to secure administrators' permission to conduct research in the schools, but they are also ethically responsible to protect participants in the study from their supervisors. Thus they must balance pressures from administrators against pressures from participants. In their conclusions they must weigh the personal relationships that inevitably develop between researchers and participants against the need for honesty and candor in their reports.

Approaching Integration

What I am describing, then, is a situation where people who share similar goals differ in their values, methods, and perspectives. Both teachers and researchers consider themselves educators, but their different roles subject them to unique sets of pressures that they do not mutually understand.

It is also evident, however, that in the best of circumstances teachers and researchers can and do learn from each other. For example, Shirley Brice Heath in *Ways with Words* describes the cooperative relationship she established with teachers while conducting the study she's reporting. The teachers' "why" questions were answered by a researcher who had learned how to bridge the gap between the classroom and the students' homes. The teachers contributed to the research, and findings of the study were applied to the problems they faced in their classrooms.

When this happens, the combined knowledge of teacher and researcher can be beneficial to the students they both care about. How then can we facilitate this relationship? How can we bridge the gap?

Closing the Gap

The recognition of the need for bridges between research and practice is not new. Much has been written, and some steps have been taken, to give teachers better access to research. The Ohio State University publication *Theory in Practice* and the twin monthly column, "Putting Research to Work," by Berliner and Casanova in *Instructor* magazine are two examples of this effort. Other projects have sought to promote joint efforts of teachers and researchers to solve educational problems. Less has been done, however, to encourage analysis and evaluation of ideas, and to promote collegial relationships, among teachers.

Researchers also need to accept their responsibility to achieve an integrated view of educational theory and practice. This is a matter not only of bringing the research to bear on the practice, but also of bringing the practice to bear on the research. The researchers need to recognize teachers' needs and problems, listen to their questions, and assume a more respectful attitude toward teachers and praxis.

Powerful precedents must be overcome for integration to happen. Teachers are not accustomed to "owning" educational research. Through the years they have deferred to the power of universities, politicians, and administrators who have expected them to implement ideas initiated by others. "Teacher-proof" materials are just one example. Limited to the delivery of instruction, teachers naturally would rather discuss activities and techniques than pedagogical theory. Educational researchers have moved into the vacuum to do the theoretical work. But they carry on their task in paths parallel to those of the teachers, so their impact on practice remains minimal, although their efforts are rewarded by academic favors.

The initiative for change is arising from both sides. Many researchers, frustrated about their inability to affect school practice, are increasingly aware of the distance that separates them from the practitioners. Many have moved their research into the classroom; some work closely with teachers. Rather than regard themselves as "the experts," they see themselves as contributing one kind of expertise while teachers contribute another. That is, they assume a reciprocal rather than a hierarchal relationship. This is the model Shirley Brice Heath describes.

Many teachers have also become aware of the potential that research may hold for them. Beyond seeking out the literature generated by educational researchers, they have initiated research activities they conduct either by themselves or with colleagues or academicians. In the process, these teachers have learned that they can actually muster the time, information, and resources to conduct research. Ultimately, they learn, too, that increase knowledge of their professional literature and increased control over that knowledge base can build feelings of competence and professional empowerment.

Responding to the Challenge

The challenge is to extend these initiatives and make the integration of research and practice the norm rather than the exception. Accomplishing this goal will require, first, attention to the attitudes already described. But attitude changes are slow. They must be encouraged through specific activities that increase teachers' reflection, familiarity with knowledge base, participation in inquiry, and collegiality.

Reflection. Teachers are seldom included in philosophical discussions—or in making the subsequent decisions—that determine the content or process of schooling. They work in isolation from their peers. They are almost always expected to implement what others have developed.

One way teachers can combat these pressures for unreflective action is to keep journals—and, in one way or another, share their thoughts. Teachers may choose to retain the privacy of their thoughts and use journals only as a way to understand their own behavior or identify concerns to be discussed or ideas to share with colleagues. Other teachers may choose to exchange journals with their colleagues or perhaps with researchers who are willing to assume a reciprocal relationship with them.

Such was the case, for example, in Dee Ann Spender's study of women teachers. Participating teachers conversed with her through their journals. They found that keeping a journal provided a useful catharsis as well a vehicle for gaining valuable insights into their professional (and personal) lives. By capturing thoughts and incidents that might otherwise be forgotten, they found, journals provide valuable data for later reflection.

Knowledge. To become familiar with the existing knowledge base, teachers need to approach the task not as students fulfilling an assignment, but as professionals expanding their own expertise. They must identify a real problem before turning to the literature to further their understanding.

Teachers will then need help in overcoming their aversion to research studies through materials that bridge the gap between researcher and practitioner. Annotated primary source material, packaged around a theme, can do much to help teachers gain confidence in their ability to read, analyze, and critique the research. (Predigested materials, in contrast, tend to leave out caveats and limitations that are an integral part of competent research.)

Teachers should be encouraged to discuss and analyze the primary research findings, then judge the applicability of a given finding to a specific situation. This process gives them the knowledge and expertise they will need in order to evaluate research findings when they seek solutions to instructional problems, or to publicly challenge the inappropriate use of research findings. This process is also what is expected of other professionals, from oncologists to computer programmers.

Inquiry.   Teachers also need to expand their perception of themselves to include the role of inquiring professionals. Educational inquiry springs from two sources. What researcher Garth Boomer calls "Big-R" research has dominated the field. "Big-R" research originates outside the classroom among people who are detached from the daily problems of instruction. "Action research," in contrast, is conducted by a group or individual engaged in instruction and is, as well, a solution-oriented investigation. But all research begins with a question.

Teachers, always full of questions and always seeking answers for them, already have what they need to begin the process of inquiry.

The difference between professional researchers and professional teachers lies in the point of origin of the question. Teachers-as-researchers originate their own questions and take them seriously enough to seek their own answers. They may do this individually or collectively, through methods that are compatible with their work, such as the qualitative methods mentioned above. Or they may choose to do so in collaboration with researchers who are willing to meld their own expertise with that of teachers.

Collegiality.   Inherent in all these ideas is the need for teachers to develop collegial relationships at the workplace and beyond. Teachers in collegial groups can reflect upon their profession, gain increased knowledge about their field, and engage in inquiry. No teacher can do this alone, and no teacher alone can challenge existing norms.

Teacher preparation, unlike preparation for other professional roles, provides little opportunity to learn from the profession's practicing experts or from peers. Medical doctors and lawyers provide internship experiences designed to enhance the specialness of the group of aspiring professionals. Aspiring doctors do their rounds in groups led by an expert; junior lawyers participate as assistants to their more experienced peers and are mentored through that process.

In contrast, aspiring teachers complete a short internship in one classroom, isolated from their peers. Professional isolation continues when they are expected to "sink or swim" on their own. Teachers normally focus their attention on the daily problems of running the classroom, because they have little time or support to do otherwise. Like other professionals, teachers need to discuss their problems in neutral settings and to learn from one another as well as from educators engaged in other aspects of schooling, such as educational researchers.

Educational researchers Stan Aronowitz and Henry Giroux suggest alliances between teachers and academics to pursue projects designed to expand understanding of the critical role educators play at all levels of schooling. In the course of these projects, educators of all persuasions can grapple together with the seldom-addressed larger questions of schooling. These writers call for a redefinition of the traditional theory–practice relationship within the context of these alliances. Collegial groups can provide opportunities for such activities within and outside the school.

A Shared Responsibility

Researchers.   The alliances proposed above, and a new relationship between theory and practice, cannot be established by teachers alone. Educational researchers need to change long-standing attitudes that give them the advantage of presumed expertise and isolate them from the battleground. Those who are established need to contribute to changes in the academy that reduce that isolation.

Russell Jacoby has recently decried the academy's absorption of intellectual energy since the early 1940s. He argues that the demands of university careers have helped erode the power of the intellectual elite to influence social change. Professors gathering at their annual conferences to compare notes, Jacoby contends, constitute their own universe. Educational researchers need to keep that assertion in mind. If they're as concerned as they claim to be with the condition of education, it is not enough to stand on the sidelines. They have a responsibility to act in concert with those who practice the profession.

Teacher-Training Institutions.   Teacher-training institutions also practice the profession, and they also have a responsibility here: to prepare potential teachers for an expanded role. Norms of reflection, inquiry, and collegiality must be set during teachers' preparation. Teacher preparation programs must begin a socialization process that leads to professional empowerment. The process and content of courses must be designed with that goal in mind. And professional empowerment should lead teachers to assume a leadership role—not only in educational circles, but in the society at large.

School Administrators.   Finally, school administrators need to expand their perceptions of the teacher's role. They must understand that the desire for teacher competence is incompatible with a top-down approach to management. Control over professional growth is a vital part of professionalism. Teachers, alone among those with extensive professional preparation, lack full control over their professional development.

The difference may be due to the characteristics of the teaching force during the early years of the profession, when most teachers were inexperienced and very young women. These young teachers often worked by themselves in isolated areas where supervision was intermittently provided by older, sometimes more experienced men. It is likely this situation that led to the development of materials and structures that could be easily implemented and evaluated, as well as to a patriarchal model of supervision.

But times have changed. Most teachers are now experienced men and women who have at least as good an understanding of instruction as their supervisors or the researchers do. These teachers may not use the same jargon. They may not be able to confidently provide numbers to back up their intuitions. But their intuitions are usually distilled out of experience and must be taken into account.

Teachers as Partners

Teachers are smart. Much has been said lately about the low academic qualifications of the undergraduates who enter teacher preparation programs. We forget that as, say, juniors in an undergraduate program they are already part of an academically elite group: Only 74% of all U.S. citizens in 1985 had completed high school. Once teachers earn their bachelor's degrees, they join an even more select group; only

19% of our total population had achieved that goal. If, as is usually the case, these individuals pursue additional academic degrees, they join an even smaller percentage of our citizenry. Academic degrees may not be the only measure of intelligence, but they are a fair yardstick for determining whether individuals are capable of full emancipation in their profession.

Unfortunately, demands for school improvement have not taken into account the intelligence, judgment, and experience teachers can contribute. A recent study the by Carnegie Foundation suggests that most teachers have little to say about school policy in areas other than textbook selection or curricular content.

Ernest Boyer, a former U.S. commissioner of education and current president of the Carnegie Foundation for the Advancement of Teaching, notes that failure to give teachers more authority will make it difficult to attract outstanding young people to the profession. Most of the mandates for reform, he points out, have been imposed from the top down.

Boyer provides a strong argument that teachers should be full partners in the educational endeavor. Participation in school improvement activities is easy to mandate, but desired change is difficult to force. A culture does not change unless the inhabitants of that culture feel the need for change. In consequence, the field of education is littered with the bodies of aborted innovations that someone tried to impose on teachers.

Possibilities for school improvement are among the benefits of truly integrating research and practice. Those benefits are many, perhaps exceeded only by the difficulties that stand in the way. It is time to honestly acknowledge those difficulties and to coordinate our efforts across various educational interest groups to ensure that this integration takes place for the benefit of all—particularly our children.

For Further Reading

Education Under Siege: The Conservative, Liberal, and Radical Debate over Schooling. S. Aronowitz and H. Giroux. Bergin & Garvey, 1985. The authors explore an alternative vision for the schools that places pedagogy in the service of creating citizens who are able to exercise power over their own lives. This is exciting and challenging reading that provokes thinking and suggests action.

Great Readings in Educational Research. U. Casanova, D. C. Berliner, and P. Placier. Unpublished manuscripts. These are a set of packaged research articles accompanied by introductory and explanatory text. They are meant to provide teachers with guided reading of educational research in a topic of their own selection. Reading is to be followed by discussion and analysis in the company of colleagues. Individual components have been successfully piloted by teachers at several sites.

Reclaiming the Classroom: Teacher Research as an Agency for Change. D. Goswami and P. D. Stillman, eds. Boynto/Cook, 1987. A book of readings that argue persuasively for teacher participation in research activities. These authors see such participation as a necessary component of educational change.

Ways with Words. S. B. Heath. Cambridge University Press, 1983. An outstanding exemplar of the ideas proposed in this article. Heath managed to write a scholarly book that is both accessible and useful for teachers. The research narrative captures and sustains the reader's interest. It is followed by a description of Heath's collaborate relationship with teachers.

Working Together: A Guide for Teachers. M. M. Mohr and M. S. Maclean. National Council for Teachers of English, 1987. A "how-to" manual for teachers interested in expanding their role to include inquiry. Although directed at teachers of English, the ideas can be adapted by teachers in other disciplines.

STUDY AND DISCUSSION QUESTIONS

1. What is the answer to educational change based on the "passion of the moment"?
2. What are the major research content areas in the two handbooks for music education?
3. Why does it take so long for research to "trickle down" to classroom teachers?
4. Why is so much emphasis placed on standardized testing in education?
5. Why are most teachers not involved in doing classroom research?
6. Do all parts of the population want to see education improved?
7. Why is the collaboration agenda between researcher and teacher so difficult?
8. What has worked against the collaborative effort?
9. What does Casanova mean by research "caveats" being ignored?
10. Is the distortion of research results ever helpful?
11. According to Casanova, what may be the "real" reason teachers don't do research?
12. What drives the demand for research to be scholarly and in the "right" journals?
13. What are some ways the gap between researcher and teacher can be closed?
14. What powerful precedent must be overcome for teachers to become researchers?
15. What does Casanova recommend to foster reflection among teachers?
16. What is the main difference between "Big-R" and action research?
17. Why is collegiality important in the workplace and beyond?
18. What is Jacoby's view of "scholarly" research?
19. Why are teachers often viewed by the public as not being a very smart group?
20. Do you think Boyer's thoughts about the role of teachers in schools will happen?

SUGGESTED ACTIVITIES

1. Based on what you have learned from this text about research and its role in improving education, how important do you think research is or should be in governing educational reform?
2. What immediate steps can you take to make research a more useful tool in your teaching?

3. If, as Slavin states, research is the only thing that will keep the field of education from jumping on one bandwagon after another, how can you be part of a change in attitude toward research in your teaching environment?

EPILOGUE

Hopefully the reading of this text has reduced some of your confusion and suspicion regarding research. While a thorough understanding of the research process is not possible without actually have done some research, this text will have met its primary objective if you have gained an understanding of the value that research can have in the fields of music education and music therapy. This understanding may even lead to your desire to do research, an added bonus.

To be sure, a lot of research is not worth reading. However, the articles chosen for this text were included not only because each represents a certain research genre, but also because each has something worthwhile to say to music teachers and/or therapists. This text only skims the surface in offering valuable research information for practitioners in the field. The challenge is for you to keep looking for research articles that can provide added insights to your already-growing knowledge base.

While lack of time may be an oft-cited reason for not reading research, people tend to make priorities of those things they value. If you have come to value research, you will make time to read it. The payoff is that you will become better at what you do.

APPENDIX A

Contents of the *Handbook of Research on Music Teaching and Learning*

(Richard Colwell, ed.), Schirmer Books, 1992.

SECTION A: CONCEPTUAL FRAMEWORK

- Philosophical Foundations (Eleanor V. Stubley)
- Toward a Philosophical Foundation of Music Education Research (Bennett Reimer)
- Model Building (Roger H. Edwards)
- A History of Music Education Research (Michael L. Mark)
- Sources of Theory for Research in School Music (Henry L. Cady)

SECTION B: RESEARCH MODES AND TECHNIQUES

- Qualitative Research Methodology in Music Education (Liora Bresler and Robert E. Stake)
- On Philosophical Method (Estelle R. Jorgensen)
- Historical Research (George N. Heller and Bruce D. Wilson)
- Descriptive Research: Techniques and Procedures (Donald E. Casey)
- Experimental Research Methodology (John Christian Busch and James W. Sherborn)
- Experimental Research Methodology (Edward P. Asmus and Rudolf E. Radocy)
- Regression-Based Research Designs (Randi L'Hommedieu)
- Curriculum and Its Study (Lizabeth Bradford Wing)
- Toward a Rational Critical Process (Carroll Gonzo)
- A Guide to Interpreting Research in Music Education (Hal Abeles)

SECTION C: EVALUATION

- Evaluation of Music Ability (J. David Boyle)
- Research on Creative Thinking in Music: The Assessment Literature (Peter R. Webster)
- Curriculum and Program Evaluation (Paul R. Lehman)
- The Measurement of Attitudes and Preferences in Music Education (Robert A. Cutietta)
- The Evaluation of Music Teachers and Teaching (Donald K. Taebel)

SECTION D: PERCEPTION AND COGNITION

- Aural Perception (Lola L. Cuddy and Rena Upitis)
- Auditory-Visual Perception and Musical Behavior (Robert Walker)
- Structure of Cognition and Music Decision-Making (Harold Fiske)
- Developmental Theories of Music Learning (David J. Hargreaves and Marilyn P. Zimmerman)
- Surveying the Coordinate of Cognitive Skills in Music (Lyle Davidson and Larry Scripp)
- Affective Response (Nancy G. Thomas)
- Motivation (Nancy G. Thomas)
- The Transfer of Music Learning (Thomas W. Tunks)

SECTION E: TEACHING AND LEARNING STRATEGIES

- The Acquisition of Music Listening Skills (Paul Haack)
- The Acquisition of Music Reading Skills (Donald Hodges)
- The Role of Mental Presents in Skill Acquisition (Roger R. Rideout)
- Technology (William Higgins)
- Methodologies in Music (Peter Costanza and Timothy Russell)
- The Study of Biomechanical and Physiological Processes in Relation to Music Performance (Frank R. Wilson and Franz L. Roehmann)
- Teaching Strategies and Styles (Malcolm J. Tait)
- Sequencing for Efficient Learning (Darrel L. Walters)
- Critical Thinking and Music Education (Carol P. Richardson and Nancy L. Whitaker)

SECTION F: THE TEACHING OF SPECIFIC MUSICAL SKILLS AND KNOWLEDGE IN DIFFERENT INSTRUCTIONAL SETTINGS

- Issues and Characteristics Common to Research on Teaching in Instructional Settings (Hildegard C. Froehlich)
- Research on the Teaching of Singing (Kenneth H. Phillips)

- Research on the Teaching of Instrumental Music (Richard Weerts)
- Research on the Teaching of Keyboard Music (Marienne Uszler)
- Research on the Teaching of Elementary General Music (Betty W. Atterbury)
- Research on Teaching Junior High and Middle School General Music (Patricia E. Sink)

SECTION G: SCHOOLS/CURRICULUM

- Research Regarding Students with Disabilities (Kate Gfeller)
- Research on Music in Early Childhood (Carol Scott-Kassner)
- Research on Music Ensembles (Jere T. Humphreys, William V. May, and David J. Nelson)
- Student Outcomes of Teaching Systems for General Music, Grades K–8 (Steven K. Hedden and David G. Woods)
- Music Teacher Education (Ralph Verrastro and Mary Leglar)
- General Music Curriculum (Maria Runfola and Joanne Rutkowski)

SECTION H: SOCIAL AND INSTITUTIONAL CONTEXTS

- Sociology and Music Education (Charles R. Hoffer)
- Professional Organizations and Influences (Samuel Hope)
- Multicultural Music Education in a Pluralistic Society (Joyce Jordan)
- Trends and Issues in Policy-Making for Arts Education (Ralph A Smith)
- The Nature of Policy and Music Education (Anthony L. Barresi and Gerald Olson)
- Research Methods in International and Comparative Music Education (Anthony Kemp and Laurence Lepherd)

Contents of *The New Handbook of Research on Music Teaching and Learning*

(Richard Colwell and Carol Richardson, eds.),

Oxford University Press, 2002

PART I: POLICY AND PHILOSOPHY
(John W. Richmond, Editor)

- Introduction (John W. Richmond)
- Policy Frameworks, Research, and K–12 Schooling (Samuel Hope)
- MENC: A Case in Point (John J. Mahlmann)
- Recent Trends and Issues in Policy Making (Ralph A. Smith)
- Law Research in Music Education (John W. Richmond)
- Philosophical Issues in Curriculum (Estelle R. Jorgensen)
- Educating Musically (Wayne Bowman)
- Philosophical Perspectives on Research (David J. Elliott)

PART II: EDUCATIONAL CONTEXT AND THE CURRICULUM
(Peter Webster and Nancy Whitaker, Editors)

- Introduction Toward an Understanding of the "Aims" of Music Education (Ian Westbury)
- Contemporary Curriculum Practices and Their Theoretical Bases (Betty Hanley and Janet Montgomery)
- Theory, Research, and the Improvement of Music Education (Ian Westbury)
- Critical Thinking (Betty Ann Younger

- Improvisation (Christopher D. Azzara)
- Improvisation and Curriculum Reform (Edward Sarath)
- Adult Education (Don D. Coffman)
- Music and Early Childhood Education (Joyce Jordan-DeCarbo and Jo Ann Nelson)
- Systematic Research in Studio Instruction in Music (Richard Kennell)
- Distance Learning and Collaboration in Music Education (Fred J. Rees)

PART III: MUSIC DEVELOPMENT AND LEARNING
(Hildegard Froehlich, Editor)

- Introduction Looking Multiple Ways in Research (Rosamund Shuter-Dyson)
- Learning Theories as Roots of Current Musical Practice and Research (Laurie Taetle and Robert Cutietta)
- Systematic Instruction (Barak Rosenshine, Hildegard Froelich, and Inshad Fakhouri)
- Behavioral Research on Direct Music Instruction (Patricia K. Sink)
- Self-Regulation of Music Learning: A Social Cognitive Perspective (Gary E. McPherson and Barry J. Zimmerman)
- Motivation and Achievement (Martin L. Maehr, Paul R. Pintrich, and Elizabeth A. Linnenbrink)
- Developmental Characteristics of Music Learners (Maria Runfola and Keith Swanwick)
- Creativity Research in Music, Visual Art, Theater, and Dance (Maud Hickey)
- Computer-Based Technology and Music Teaching and Learning (Peter R. Webster)

PART IV: MUSICAL COGNITION AND DEVELOPMENT
(Andreas Lehmann, Editor)

- Introduction Music Perception and Cognition (Andreas C. Lehmann)
- The Neurobiology of Music Cognition and Learning (Wilfred Gruhn and Frances Rauscher)
- Cognitive Constraints on Music Listening (William Forde Thompson and E. Glenn Schellenberg)
- The Development of Music Abililties (Heiner Gembris)
- A Comparative Review of Human Ability Theory: Context, Structure, and Development (Bruce Torff)
- Making Music and Making Sense Through Music: Expressive Performance and Communication (Reinhard Kopiez)

PART V: SOCIAL AND CULTURAL CONTEXTS
(Marie McCarthy, Editor)

- Introduction: Social and Cultural Contexts of Music Teaching and Learning (Marie McCarthy)
- The Sociology of Education and Connections to Music Education Research (Stephen J. Paul and Jeanne H. Ballantine)
- Perspectives from the Sociology of Music (Renate Mueller)
- Social Psychology and Music Education (Adrian C. North, David J. Hargreaves, and Mark Tarrant)
- Music, Culture, Curriculum, and Instruction (Barbara Reeder Lundquist)
- Feminism, Feminist Research, and Gender Research in Music Education: A Selective Review (Roberta Lamb, Lori-Anne Dolloff, and Sondra Wieland Howe)
- The Social Construction of Music Teacher Identity in Undergraduate Music Education Majors (Paul G. Woodford)
- Transforming Research in Music Education History (Gordon Cox)
- Music Transmission and Learning: A Conspectus of Ethnographic Research in Ethnomusicology and Music Education (C. K. Szego)
- Community Music: Toward an International Overview (Kari Veblen and Bengt Olsson)

PART VI: MUSIC TEACHER EDUCATION
(Liz Wing and Janet R. Barrett, Editors)

- Introduction: Fuzzy Teacher Education (James Raths)
- Reform-Minded Music Teachers: A More Comprehensive Image of Teaching for Music Teacher Education (Dennis Thiessen and Janet R. Barrett)
- Teaching as a Profession: Two Variations on a Theme (Randall Pembrook and Cheryl Craig)
- Changing Concepts of Teacher Education (Glenn E. Nierman, Ken Zeicher, and Nikola Hobbel)
- Strengthening the Teaching of Music Educators in Higher Education (Susan Wilcox and Rena Upitis)
- Research by Teachers on Teacher Education (Mary Leglar and Michelle Collay)
- Research in Music Student Teaching (Roger Rideout and Allan Feldman)
- Professional Development (Mary Ross Hookey)

PART VII: MUSIC EDUCATION CONNECTIONS
(David Myers, Editor)

- Introduction: The Growth Impact of Partnerships: A Reason for Research (Richard J. Deasy)

- The Evaluation of Arts Partnerships and Learning in and Through the Arts (Hal Abeles, Mary Hafeli, Robert Horowitz, and Judith Burton)
- The "Use and Abuse" of Arts Advocacy and Its Consequences for Music Education (Constance Bumgarner Gee)
- Research in Visual Arts Education: Implications for Music (Lynn Galbraith)
- A Review of Research in Theater, Dance, and Other Performing Arts Education: Implications for Music (Kent Seidel)

PART VIII: NEUROSCIENCE, MEDICINE, AND MUSIC
(John W. Flohr, Editor)

- Music and Neuroscience (John W. Flohr and Donald A. Hodges)
- Performing Arts Medicine (Alice G. Brandfonbrener and Richard J. Lederman)
- Musicians' Health (Kris Chesky, George Kondraske, Miriam Henoch, John Hipple, and Bernard Rubin)

PART IX: OUTCOMES IN GENERAL EDUCATION
(Michael L. Mark, Editor)

- Nonmusical Outcomes of Music Education: Historical Considerations (Michael L. Mark)
- Teaching Other Subjects Through Music (Merryl Goldberg and Carol Scott-Kassner)
- Research: A Foundation for Arts Education Advocacy (Liora Bresler)

PART X: RESEARCH DESIGN, CRITICISM, AND ASSESSMENT
IN MUSIC EDUCATION (Jack J. Heller and Nicholas
DeCarbo, Editors)

- Introduction: Scholarly Inquiry and the Research Process (Jack J. Heller and Nicholas DeCarbo)
- Maintaining Quality in Research and Reporting (Jack J. Heller and Edward J. P. O'Connor)
- Trends in Data Acquisition and Knowledge Development (Lee R. Bartel and Rudolf E. Radocy)
- Assessment's Potential in Music Education (Richard Colwell)
- Contemporary Issues in Qualitative Research and Music Education (David J. Flinders and Carol P. Richardson)

An Annotated Listing of Research Journals in Music Education and Music Therapy[1]

NATIONAL AND INTERNATIONAL RESEARCH JOURNALS

- *Australian Journal of Music Therapy* (AJMT): Publishes articles that represent diverse viewpoints among music therapists and health and education professionals. Subscribe through: Australian Journal of Music Therapy, P.O. Box 79, Turramurra, NSW, Australia 2074.

- *Boletin de Investigacion Educativo-Musical* (BIE-M): Includes the following: editorials, special collaborations (invited papers), research in Argentina, international research, student papers, special publications, and news. Subscribe: Republica Dominicana 3492 (1425), Buenos Aires, Argentina.

- *British Journal of Music Education* (BJME): Publication of Cambridge University Press. Includes research worldwide and current book reviews. Strives to strengthen professional development and improve practice within the field of music education. A refereed journal is also available online. Order by phone (800–872–7423) or on the web.

- *British Journal of Music Therapy* (BJMT): Publication of the Association of Professional Music Therapists and the British Society of Music Therapy. Focuses on the fields of health, social sciences, and education. Subscribe: BSMT, 25 Rosslyn Ave., East Barnet, Herts EN4 8DH, UK.

- *Bulletin of the Council for Research in Music Education* (BCRME): Publication of the School of Music, University of Illinois at Urbana-Champaign. Recognized as second in rank only to the JRME in music education. Publishes thematic issues of various symposia, research articles, and dissertation reviews. A refereed journal. Subscribe: School of Music, University of Illinois at Urbana-Champaign, 1114 West Nevada St., Urbana, IL 61801.

---

[1] Partially based on Price, H. E. and Chang, C. (2000). An annotated bibliography of music education research journals. *Update: Applications of Research in Music Education*, *18*(2), 19–26.

- *Canadian Music Educator: Research Edition* (CMERE): The research edition appears as the last issue of each volume of the CME. Covers the broad range of specialties in school music. Subscribe: Faculty of Education, Memorial University of Newfoundland St. John's NF, Canada A1B3X8.

- *Choral Journal* (CJ): Publication of the American Choral Directors Association. Not a "journal" in the strictest sense. Contains many "news" items for the membership, and many of the articles are "how to do" types. The research articles are predominantly historical/analytical summaries of dissertations. Published monthly. Subscribe online at ACDA.org.

- *International Choral Bulletin* (ICB): A quarterly publication of the International Federation for Choral Music, "a forum for choral leaders to discuss the importance of choral music in their respective countries." Subscribe: Ms. Jutta Tagger, editor, 13 rue Parmentier, F 92200, Neuilly-sur-Seine, France. E-mail: jtagger@ifcm.net.

- *Jazz Education Journal* (JEJ): Publication of the International Association of Jazz Educators. Publishes articles all related to jazz education. A refereed journal appearing six times a year. Subscribe: JEJ, P.O. Box 52, St. Bonaventure University, St. Bonaventure, NY 14778.

- *Journal of Band Research* (JBR): Publication of the American Bandmasters Association. All articles relate to band issues and band literature. A refereed journal published twice a year. Subscribe: Journal of Band Research, Managing Editor, Troy State University, Troy, AL 36082. Online at: americanbandmassters.org/JBR.HTM.

- *Journal of Historical Research in Music Education* (JHRME) (Formerly the *Bulletin of Historical Research in Music Education*): Publication of the School of Music, Ithaca College. One of the only journals to focus exclusively on historical studies. A refereed journal, it is published two times a year. Subscribe: JHRME, James J. Whalen Center for Music, 953 Danby Rd., Ithaca College, Ithaca, NY 14850; e-mail: jrhme@Ithaca.edu.

- *Journal of Music Therapy* (JMT): Publication of the American Music Therapy Association. This is the premiere journal of research in music therapy. It is refereed, and its standards are very high. Subscribe: JMT, Center for Music Research, The Florida State University, Tallahassee, Florida 32306.

- *Journal of Research in Music Education* (JRME): Publication of the Society for Research in Music Education/MENC. This is the premiere journal of research in music education. Standards are very high; refereed and difficult to be accepted for publication. Emphasis in the past on quantitative research. Subscribe through yearly membership application to MENC, 1806 Robert Fulton Dr., Reston VA 20191.

- *Journal of String Research* (JSR): Publishes articles on the philosophical, historical, and scientific bases of teaching and learning string instruments. Subscribe: University of Arizona, School of Music and Dance, Tucson AZ 85721.

- *Music Education Research* (MER): Publishes traditional and less orthodox articles. Particularly interested in encouraging new researchers. Subscribe: Music Education Research, Carfax Publishing Ltd., P.O. Box 25, Abingdon, Oxfordshire OX14 3UE, UK.

- *Music Therapy Perspectives* (MTP): Publishes research relevant to the clinical practice of music therapy. Subscribe: AMTA, Inc., 8455 Colesville Rd., Silver Spring, MD 20910.

- *Philosophy of Music Education Review* (PMER): Publication of the Indiana University Press, Bloomington. The only journal to focus exclusively on philosophical inquiry in music education. A refereed journal published twice a year. Subscribe at: Indiana University Press Journals, 601 N. Morton St., Bloomington, IN 47404, or email: iuporder@Indiana.edu.

- *Psychology of Music* (PM): Published in association with the Society for Education, Music, and Psychology Research. Premiere journal in the field of music cognition. Refereed and published biannually. Subscribe: Sage Publications, 2455 Teller Road, Thousand Oaks, CA 91320, or e-mail: www.sagepub.com.

- *Psychomusicology*: Publication of the Center for Music Research, Florida State University, Tallahassee, Fl 32306. Founded in 1981 to offer a high-quality, refereed publishing resource for researchers in music cognition. Abstracts of articles are available online. Subscribe at address just given or via email: taylor@cmr.fsu.edu.

- *The Quarterly Journal of Music Teaching and Learning* (Quarterly): Extinct publication of the University of Northern Colorado, School of Music. Copies of this journal remain on library shelves, but publication ceased in 1996–97. This was unfortunate because it was fast becoming a major research source in the field. Citations to it can be found throughout the research literature.

- *Wychowanie Muzyczne w Szkole: Czasopismo dla nauczycieli* (WMS) (Musical Education in Schools: Journal of Teachers) Subscribe: Wychowanie Muzyczne w Szkole, plac Dqbrowskiego 8, 00–950 Warszawa, Poland.

STATE AND REGIONAL JOURNALS

- *Center Review*: Publication of the Center for Educational Excellence, College of Education at Northeastern State University, Tahlequah, OK, 74464. Publishes at least once annually articles on research findings, opinions, book reviews, and position papers. The major focus is on teacher preparation and continuing education.

- *Contributions to Music Education* (Contributions): Publication of the Ohio Music Education Association. This is a refereed journal that is published four times a year. Features both quantitative and qualitative research. Subscribe at *Contributions*, Dr. Wm. Bauer, Ed., Case Western Reserve University, Dept. of Music, 306 Haydn Hall, Cleveland, OH 44106.

- *Missouri Journal of Research in Music Education* (MJRME): Publishes research in music education, including studies by university students. Subscribe: University of Missouri—Columbia, 2112 Townsend Hall, Columbia, MO 65211.

- *PMEA Bulletin of Research in Music Education* (PBRME): An annual publication of the Pennsylvania Music Educators Association. Publishes a wide variety of articles. Subscribe: School of Music, Penn State University, University Park, PA 16802.

- *Research Perspectives in Music Education* (RPME): Publication of the School of Music, University of South Florida. This research bulletin is distributed annually to all members of the Florida Music Educators Association. A refereed journal addressing all topics in music education. Subscribe: Florida Music Educators Association, 207 Office Plaza Drive, Tallahassee, FL 32301.

- *Southern Music Education Journal* (SMEJ): Publication of the Department of Music, The University of Mississippi. A new journal (2004), it is refereed and published two times a year. Features articles from mostly regional authors. Subscribe: SMJE, c/o Alan Spurgeon, 162 Scruggs Hall, University of Mississippi, University, MS 38677.

- *Southeastern Journal of Music Education* (SJME): Publication by the University of Georgia School of Music and the Georgia Center for Continuing Education. Content is based on presentations given at the annual Southeastern Music Education Symposium. Subscribe: SJME, Room 179, Georgia Center for Continuing Education, University of Georgia, Athens, GA 30602.

- *Texas Music Education Research* (TMER): Publishes presentations/reports presented at the annual conference of the TMEA. Subscribe: TMEA, P.O. Box 49469, Austin, TX 78765.

ONLINE JOURNALS

- *Journal of Research in Music Education* (see earlier listing): Available online to members who subscribe through MENC.

- *International Journal of Research in Choral Singing* (IJRCS): Publication of the University of Kansas. A refereed journal published annually. Began in 2003 and is free online. Nonelectronic mail may be addressed to: 311 Bailey Hall, University of Kansas, Lawrence, KS 66045.

- *UPDATE: Applications of Research in Music Education* (UPDATE): Publication of the National Association of Music Education (MENC). Available only online at MENC.org and free to all MENC members. Content covers all curricular areas, and writing style requires some knowledge of research jargon. Published twice a year.

- *Journal of Music Teacher Education* (JMTE): Publication of the Society for Music Teacher Education/MENC. Available only online at MENC.org and free to all MENC members. Content aimed at those interested in music teacher preparation. Nontechnical writing style. Published twice a year.

- *Research and Issues in Music Education* (RIME): Publication of the University of St. Thomas, St. Paul. One of the newest online journals, includes both traditional and nontraditional research. A free, peer- reviewed journal published annually. Contact: www.stthomas.edu/rimeonline.

- *Research Studies in Music Education* (RSME): Publication of the Callaway International Resource Centre for Music Education, School of Music, University of Western Australia. Formerly available only in hard copy, now available online at: www.rsme.callaway.uwa.edu.au.

Glossary

ABA design. An experimental design in which a baseline behavior (A) is established, a treatment is introduced (B), and the treatment is removed (A). Also known as a *reversal design*.

abstract. A comprehensive summary of the contents of a research investigation that commonly appears at the beginning of a research article.

action research. A genre of qualitative or mixed-methods research used to study events without the constraints of formal research design.

alpha error. *See* Type I error.

alpha level. A level set in advance of an experiment to indicate the probability at which the researcher is willing to reject the null hypothesis (e.g., $p = .05$).

analysis of covariance (ANCOVA). A statistical procedure that compares two or more group means after adjusting for a control variable or covariate such as a pretest.

analysis of variance. A statistical procedure that compares two or more group means for significant difference(s); typically reported as an F statistic.

analytic proposition. A statement used in the argument of a philosophical study that is straight-forward and requires little or no explanation.

APA style. The writing style of the American Psychological Association, commonly used in quantitative research.

argument. The section of a philosophical research article in which the "data" are presented in a logical and sequential process and from which the conclusions are expected to be drawn. The argument involves individually three styles of statements: propositional, dialectical, and critical.

attribute variable. An independent variable used in factorial analysis that represents some attribute of the subjects, such as grade level, occupation, or SES.

beta error. *See* Type II error.

case study. A genre of qualitative research used to study a single event, activity, or process over an extended time period.

causal comparative research. A genre of quantitative, experimental, referential, *post hoc* research used to determine cause after the fact.

ceiling effect. A characteristic of a population when the distribution of scores is skewed, with many scores near the maximum possible value.

chi square (X^2). A nonparametric statistical test used with frequency counts (nominal data) to assess the relationship between two or more categorical variables.

clinical research. Investigations that take place in more of a laboratory setting where one or a small group of subjects are tested under highly controlled conditions.

concurrent research. A genre of mixed-methods research in which quantitative and qualitative data are collected at the same time and integrated.

control group. In an experimental study, those subjects who receive some type of placebo factor in place of the treatment.

correlation. The degree to which two variables are related positively or negatively.

correlational research. A genre of quantitative, nonexperimental, nonreferential research that describes relationships.

correlation coefficient. A statistic (r) that indicates the degree to which two variables are correlated.

correlation matrix. A table of correlation coefficients that shows all possible paired correlations between a set of variables.

covariate. A control variable used in analysis of covariance to correct for unequal pretest variance between groups, e.g., a pretest or IQ.

critical argument. A style of argument used in philosophical research in which practices, objectives, or views are evaluated and revised.

critical theory. A type of qualitative research that is concerned with empowering human beings to transcend the constraints placed on them by race, class, or gender.

data. Information collected in empirical research by some type of observation or measurement; the plural of the singular *datum*.

degrees of freedom. A statistic (*df*) used with a parametric test that represents two numbers (between groups and within groups) to find, in a table, values of *t* and *F* that are statistically significant at various probability levels, e.g., .05.

dependent variable. An outcome variable or measure that is hypothesized to be affected by the independent or treatment variable.

descriptive research. A genre of quantitative, nonexperimental, nonreferential research that describes "what is" at the time of data collection.

dialectical argument. A style of argument used in philosophical research that considers both or opposite sides of an issue in a dialogue format.

dissertation. A major research investigation that typically concludes doctoral studies.

distribution. A pattern of scores for a population, e.g., a bell-shaped curve.

empirical. Research based on observation or experience rather than on theory or logic.

ethnography. A genre of qualitative research used to study intact cultural groups in natural settings.

experimental group. A group of subjects who receive the treatment in an experimental study.

external criticism. The process whereby data for a historical study are verified as truthful.

external validity. The degree to which the results of a study can be generalized from a sample to a population.

F-test. A parametric test used to determine the difference between two or more means for statistical significance.

factor. A variable in factorial design (i.e., independent variable) that is hypothesized to affect the dependent variable (measure).

factorial analysis of variance. Analysis of variance (or covariance) employing two or more factors (variables) as independent variables, e.g., 2×2; 2×3; $3 \times 3 \times 3$.

factorial design. A research design in which two or more factors are employed as independent variables.

false-negative error. Incorrectly accepting the null hypothesis in an experimental study.

false-positive error. Incorrectly rejecting the null hypothesis in an experimental study.

floor effect. A distribution in which many of the scores are near the minimum or lowest possible value, making improvement almost certain on a posttest.

generalization. A concept in experimental research where the results from a sample are extrapolated to the larger population.

grounded theory. A genre of qualitative research used to study theories grounded in the view of the participants.

Hawthorne effect. The tendency of subjects in an experimental study to work harder when they are aware they are in a study.

historical research. A genre of research inquiry that investigates the "elusive truth about the past" through historical documentation and primary sources.

history. A threat to internal validity in which specific events occurring between the first and second testings may affect the outcome of a study.

homogeneity of variance. The variances of two or more samples can be considered equal when there is homogeneity.

hypothesis. A declarative statement reflecting a "hunch" about the relationship of variables in a study.

independent variable. In experimental research, the treatment that is hypothesized to produce a change in the dependent variable.

instrumentation. A threat to internal validity in which changes in the calibration of an instrument or changes in the observers may produce changes in the measurement.

interaction. The combined effect of two or more independent variables on a dependent variable, which may cancel or confound a main effect.

internal criticism. The process whereby data for a historical study are determined to be valid.

internal validity. The degree to which the results of a study can be attributed to the treatment or independent variable and not to other confounding effects, such as maturation and history.

interpretive study. A type of qualitative research in which the investigator collects a detailed description of context, participants, actions, and perceptions that serve as the basis for an understanding of what is happening or how things work.

interval scale. A level of measurement in which any two adjacent values are the same distance apart but in which there is no meaningful zero.

IRB. Institutional Review Board that considers human beings as subjects or participants in a study.

John Henry effect. Subjects in a control group of an experimental study work harder because they know they are in the control group.

kurtosis. The degree to which the shape of a distribution departs from the normal bell-shaped curve.

main effect. The simple effect of an independent variable on a dependent variable, which answers one of the main research questions in an experimental study.

maturation. A threat to internal validity of an experimental study in which the passage of time may affect the outcome of the study.

mean. A measure of central tendency, it is the average of a set of numbers.

median. A measure of central tendency, it is the middle number in a set of ranked scores.

meta-analysis. A genre of quantitative research that implies cause-and-effect relationships through the combining of results of numerous studies.

mixed methods. A research genre that involves the collection and analysis of both quantitative and qualitative data.

mode. A measure of central tendency, it is the most frequent score in a set of scores.

mortality. A threat to internal validity when loss of subjects from an experimental study may imbalance groups and/or affect normalcy.

multivariate analysis of variance (or covariance). A statistical procedure that compares two or more groups for significant difference(s) on two or more combined dependent variables considered as a set.

narrative. A genre of qualitative research used to study peoples' lives through their stories.

nominal scale. A scale of measurement that uses numbers to classify categories and frequencies within categories, i.e., counted data.

nonexperimental research. Quantitative research in which subjects or factors are described or correlated.

nonparametric statistics. Statistics used in analysis that involve data of the nominal or ordinal scale.

normal distribution. The distribution of scores in a sample or population cluster around the mean in a bell-shaped curve.

null hypothesis. A hypothesis used in experimental research and stated in the negative form that two or more variables or groups are *not* related.

one-tailed test. A test of significance for which the results of the hypothesis can only be in one direction.

one-way analysis of variance. Analysis of variance (or covariance) involving only one factor or independent variable.

ordinal scale. A level of nonparametric measurement in which numbers indicate rank but differences between ranks may not be equal.

organismic variable. An independent variable used in factorial analysis that represents some physical characteristic of the subjects, such as height, age, or gender.

parameter. Any statistic that describes a distribution of scores.

parametric statistics. Statistics that are used with interval or ratio data and that approximate a normal distribution of scores.

participants. The persons participating in a qualitative research study from whom data are collected.

Pearson's *r*. The Pearson product-moment correlation is the most common parametric test for determining the relationship between two observations.

phenomenology. A genre of qualitative research used to study the essence of human relationships.

philosophical research. A genre of research inquiry that investigates concepts of truth through theoretical or logical reasoning.

pilot study. A preliminary study used to investigate procedures before a main study is conducted.

population. A larger group of people (*N*) to which the results of a sample (*n*) are to be generalized.

posttest. A test or measure given to subjects following the application of a treatment in experimental research.

pretest. A test or measure given to subjects before the treatment is applied in experimental research.

primary source. A firsthand or original source of data in the historical research genre.

proposition. A statement used in the argument of philosophical research that reflects a belief or opinion about an issue. Propositions are either analytic or synthetic.

qualitative research. A form of holistic study in which participants are observed in natural settings for their reactions to various experiences. Data are collected typically in the narrative, and analysis often involves triangulation of data.

quartile deviation. A measure of variability in which 25% of the scores fall into the bottom, or first, quartile, another 25% into the second quartile, etc. The quartile deviation is the computed difference between scores in the second and third quartiles.

quasi-experimental research. A genre of quantitative, experimental, referential research that implies cause-and-effect relationships; it typically involves intact groups to which subject have not been randomized.

random assignment. Assigning subjects randomly to either the treatment or the control group in an experimental study.

range. A measure of variance that represents the difference between the highest and lowest scores in a distribution.

ratio scale. A level of parametric measurement in which any two adjacent scores or values are the same distance apart and a true zero level is possible.

reactivity. Subjects may react differently from normal behaviors when they know they are in a study.

reliability. The consistency of a measure to produce the same results over time.

reliability coefficient. A statistic (r) that represents the consistency of a measure to produce the same results over time.

replication. The repetition of a research investigation in another setting with a different group of subjects or participants.

research. The search for solutions to problems via a systematic process of data collection and interpretation.

sample. A smaller group (n) chosen from and representative of a larger population used as the subjects in an experimental study.

sampling. The process of choosing a sample from a population for a study.

scientific method. A method of investigation in which the suspected cause of a certain phenomenon is isolated and tested under highly controlled conditions.

selection. A threat to internal validity when students are selected for a study who do not represent the normal comparison group.

sequential research. A genre of mixed-methods research in which data are collected in a fixed or sequential order.

standard deviation. A statistic (SD) indicating the average dispersion for a set of scores.

standard deviation unit. A unit (z-score) from -4 to $+4$ that represents the place of a score within a normal distribution as reflected in the bell curve.

standard error of the mean. A statistic indicating the degree of potential error with which a sample mean might estimate a population mean.

statistic. A number that describes some characteristic of a variable such as the mean or standard deviation.

statistical regression. A threat to internal validity when students who score extremely low or high on the pretest may naturally regress toward the mean on the posttest.

statistical significance. Results of a means-difference analysis in which one group is found to be more different from the other than would be expected by chance.

subjects. The persons (Ss) participating in a quantitative research study from whom data are collected.

synthetic proposition. A statement used in the argument of philosophical research that hides the truth through its choice of words or use of unclear logic; requires further explanation.

***t*-test.** A parametric test used to determine the statistical difference between two means.

testing. A threat to internal validity in which the taking of a pretest may affect or sensitize subjects to the posttest.

thesis. The research investigation that sometimes concludes masters study and that leads to the awarding of the masters degree (MA, MMEd, etc.).

three-way analysis of variance. Analysis of variance (or covariance) involving three factors or independent variables.

transformative research. A genre of mixed-methods research that uses a lens technique as a framework for topics of interest.

treatment. In an experimental study, a systematic set of instructions or conditions applied to the experimental or treatment group.

triangulation. A technique used in qualitative research involving three concurrent data analyses of the same data for validation purposes.

true-experimental research. A genre of quantitative, experimental, referential research that implies cause-and-effect relationships; it requires randomization of subjects and homogeneity of variance.

two-tailed test. A test of significance for which the results of the hypothesis can be found in either direction.

two-way analysis of variance. Analysis of variance (or covariance) involving two factors or independent variables.

Type I error. An error resulting in the incorrect rejecting of the null hypothesis.

Type II error. An error resulting in the incorrect accepting of the null hypothesis.

validity. The degree to which a test or survey actually measures what it is supposed to measure.

variable. Anything that can take on more than one value, e.g., dependent measures.

variance. A statistic that indicates the degree of dispersion of a set of scores.

References

Asmus, E. P., & Radocy, R. E. (2006). Quantitative analysis. In R. Colwell (Ed.), *MENC handbook of research methodologies*. New York: Oxford University Press, 95–175.

Asmussen, K. J., & Creswell, J. W. (1995). Campus response to a student gunman. *Journal of Higher Education, 66*, 575–591.

Birge, E. B. (1928). *History of public school music in the United States*. Washington, DC: MENC.

Bogdan, R. C., & Biklen, S. K. (2003). *Qualitative research for education, an introduction to theories and methods*. New York: Allyn & Bacon, 107–108.

Brand, M. (2002). An ethnographic study of Hong Kong and American music education students. *Contributions to Music Education, 29*(2), 47–65.

Brandfonbrener, A. G., & Lederman, R. J. (2002). Performing arts medicine. In R. Colwell & C. Richardson (Eds.), *The new handbook of research on music teaching and learning*, New York: Oxford University Press, 1009–1022.

Bresler, L., & Stake, R. E. (2006). Qualitative research methodology in music education. In R. Colwell (Ed.), *MENC handbook of research methodologies*. New York: Oxford University Press, 270–311.

Busch, J. C., & Sherborn, J. W. (1992). Experimental research methodology. In R. Colwell (Ed.), *Handbook of research on music teaching and learning*. New York: Schirmer Books, 124–140.

Campbell, D. T. & Stanley, J. C. (1963). *Experimental and quasi-experimental designs for research*. Boston: Houghton Mifflin Co.

Casanova, U. (1989). Research and practice: We can integrate them. *NEA Today, 7*(6), 44–49.

Colwell, R. (Ed.). (1992). *Handbook of research on music teaching and learning*. New York: Schirmer Books.

Colwell, R., & Richardson, C. (Eds.). (2002). *The new handbook of research on music teaching and learning*. New York: Oxford University Press.

Conway, C. M., & Borst, J. (2001). Action research in music education. *UPDATE: Applications of Research in Music Education, 19*(2), 3–8.

Creswell, J. W. (2003). *Research design: Qualitative, quantitative, and mixed methods approaches* (2nd ed.). Thousand Oaks, CA: Sage Publications. (Citations in this book reprinted by permission of Sage Publications, Inc.)

Creswell, J. W., & Brown, M. L. (1992). How chairpersons enhance faculty research: A grounded theory study. *The Review of Higher Education, 16*(1), 41–62.

Davis, G. L. (1990). A study of factors related to career choices of high school senior honor band students in Nebraska. (Doctoral dissertation, The University of Iowa). *Dissertations Abstracts International*, 52/03-A, 838.

Ebie, B. D. (2002). Characteristics of 50 years of research samples found in the *Journal of Research in Music Education*, 1953–2002. *Journal of Research in Music Education, 50*(4), 280–291.

Engen, R. L. (2005). The singer's breath: Implications for treatment of persons with emphysema. *Journal of Music Therapy, 42*(1), 20–48.

Fay, B. (1987). *Critical social science*. Ithaca, NY: Cornell University Press.

Flohr, J. W., & Hodges, D. A. (2002). Music and neuroscience. In R. Colwell & C. Richardson (Eds.), *The new handbook of music teaching and learning*. New York: Oxford University Press, 991–1008.

Gaston, E. T. (Ed.). (1968). *Music in therapy*. New York: Macmillan.

Gauthier-McMahon, S. (1997). *Is this "good" research?* Retrieved February 16, 1999, from http://educ.queensu.ca/-ar/oerc97/goodrshr.htm

Gfeller, K., Hedden, S. K., & Darrow, A. (1990). Perceived effectiveness of mainstreaming in Iowa and Kansas schools. *Journal of Research in Music Education, 38*(2), 90–101.

Gleason, B. P. (1995/1996). The effects of beginning band instruction using a comprehensive, multicultural, interdisciplinary method on the knowledge, skills, attitudes, and retention of sixth-grade students. (Doctoral dissertation, The University of Iowa, 1995). *Dissertation Abstracts International*, A 57/01.

Goetze, M. (1986). Factors affecting accuracy in children's singing (Doctoral dissertation, University of Colorado, 1985). *Dissertation Abstracts International, 46*(10), 2955A.

Gordon, E. E. (1989). *Learning sequences in music*. Chicago: G.I.A. Publications.

Heller, J. J., & O'Connor, E. J. P. (2006). Maintaining quality in research and reporting. In R. Colwell (Ed.), *MENC handbook of research methodologies*. New York: Oxford University Press, 38–72.

History and definition of action research (n.d.). Retrieved September 9, 1998, from http://excelencia.uat.mx/desarrollo/content2.htm

Hooper, M. (1969). *Major concerns of music education: Content analysis of the Music Educators Journal, 1957–1967*. Unpublished Doctoral dissertation, University of Southern California.

Huck, S. W., Cormier, W. H., & Bounds, Jr., W. G. (1981). *Readings statistics and research*. New York: Harper & Row.

Humphreys, J. (1998). Membership of the Music Educators National Conference from 1912–1938: A demographic and economic analysis. *Bulletin of the Council for Research in Music Education, 137*, 16–31.

Isaac, S., & Michael, W. B. (1981). *Handbook in research and evaluation* (2nd ed.). San Diego, CA: Edits.

Jellison, J. A. (2002). On-task participation of typical students close to and away from classmates with disabilities in an elementary music classroom. *Journal of Research in Music Education, 50*(4), 343–355.

Johnson, R. E. (1981). E. Thayer Gaston: Leader in scientific thought on music in therapy and education. *Journal of Research in Music Education, 29*(4), 279–286.

Jorgensen, E. R. (2002). Philosophical issues in curriculum. In R. Colwell & C. Richardson (Eds.), *The new handbook of research on music teaching and Learning*. New York: Oxford University Press, 48–62.

Jorgensen, E. R. (2003). *In search of music education: Transforming music education*. Bloomington, IN: Indiana University Press.

Jorgensen, E. R. (2006a). On philosophical method. In R. Colwell (Ed.), *MENC handbook of research methodologies*. New York: Oxford University Press, 176–198.

Jorgensen, E. R. (2006b). Reflections on futures for music education philosophy. *Philosophy of Music Education Review, 14*(1), 15–21.

Kemmis, S., & McTaggart, R (Eds.). (1988). *The action reader* (3rd ed.). Deakin: Deakin University Press (Australia).

Lind, V. R. (2001). Adapting choral rehearsals for students with learning disabilities. *Choral Journal, 41*(7), 27–30.

Locke, L. F., Silverman, S. J., & Spirduso, W. W. (2004). *Reading and understanding research* (2nd ed.). Thousand Oaks, CA: Sage Publications. (Citations in this book reprinted by permission of Sage Publications, Inc.)

Madsen, C. K., & Kelly, S. N. (2002). First remembrances of wanting to become a music teacher. *Journal of Research in Music Education, 50*(4), 523–532.

Mark, M. L. (1999). The public policy roots of music education history. *Journal of Research in Historical Music Education, 20*(2), 103–114.

Mark, M. L. (2002). Nonmusical outcomes of music education: Historical considerations. In R. Colwell & C. Richardson (Eds.), *The new handbook of research on music teaching and learning.* New York: Oxford University Press, 1045–1052.

Martin, R. (2000). *Beethoven's hair.* New York: Broadway Books.

McCullough, D. (2005). *1776.* New York: Simon & Schuster.

Mertens, D. M. (2003). Mixed methods and the politics of human research: The Transformative-emancipatory perspective. In A. Tashakkori & C. Teddlie (Eds.), *Handbook of mixed methods in the social and behavioral sciences.* Thousand Oaks, CA: Sage.

Pearson, B. (1993). *Standard of excellence.* San Diego, CA: Neil A. Kjos Music Co.

Pemberton, C. (1985). *Lowell Mason: His life and times.* Ann Arbor, MI: UMI Research Press.

Phelps, R. P. (1980). *A guide to research in music education* (2nd ed.). Metuchen, NJ: The Scarecrow Press.

Phillips, K. H. (1985). The effects of group breath control training on the singing ability of elementary students. *Journal of Research in Music Education, 33*(3), 179–191.

Phillips, K. H. (1992). *Teaching kids to sing.* New York: Schirmer Books.

Phillips, K. H. (1993). A stronger rationale for music education. *Music Educators Journal, 84*(5), 10.

Phillips, K. H., & Aitchison, R. E. (1999). Second-year results of a longitudinal study of the relationship of singing instruction, pitch accuracy, and gender to aural acuity, vocal achievement, musical knowledge, and attitude towards singing among general among students. *Contributions to Music Education, 26*(1), 67–85.

Phillips, K. H., & Emge, S. W. (1994). Vocal registration as it affects vocal range for seventh- and eighth-grade boys. *Journal of Research in Singing and Applied Vocal Pedagogy, 18*(1), 1–19.

Phillips, S. L. (2003). *Contributing factors to music attitude in sixth-, seventh-, and eighth-grade students.* Unpublished Doctoral dissertation, The University of Iowa.

Price, H. E., & Chang, C. (2000). An annotated bibliography of music education research journals. *Update: Applications of Research in Music Education, 18*(2), 19–26

Publication Manual of the American Psychological Society (5th ed., 2001). Washington, DC: American Psychological Society.

Rainbow, E. L., & Froehlich, H. C. (1987). *Research in music education: An introduction to systematic inquiry.* New York: Schirmer Books.

Raines, A. (2005). Celebrating fifty years of choral artistry: An interview with Don Neuen. *Choral Journal, 45*(10), 30–35.

Riley, M. C. (1990). Portrait of a nineteenth-century school music program. *Journal of Research in Music Education, 38*(2), 79–89.

Roske, M. (1987). The professionalism of private music teaching in the 19th century: A study with social statistics. *Bulletin of the Council for Research in Music Education, 91*, 145–148.

Rossman, G. B., & Rallis, S. F. (1998). *Learning in the field: An introduction to qualitative research.* Thousand Oaks, CA: Sage Publications.

Scheffler, I. (1973). *Reason and teaching.* Indianapolis, IN: Bobbs-Merrill.

Scheib, J. W. (2003). Role stress in the professional life of the school music teacher: A collective study. *Journal of Research in Music Education, 51*(2), 124–136.

Schleuter, L. (1991). Student teachers' preactive and postactive curricular thinking. *Journal of Research in Music Education, 39*(1), 46–63.

Schleuter, L. (1994/1995). Qualitative study of dialogue: A thought process. *Bulletin of the Council for Research in Music Education. 123*, 58–62.

Schwadron, A. A. (1973). Philosophy in music education: State of research. *Council for Research in Music Education, 34,* 41–53.

Schwadron, A. A. (1984). Philosophy and aesthetics in music education: A critique of the research. *Bulletin of the Council for Research in Music Education, 79,* 11–32.

Seashore, C. E. (1919/1960). *Seashore measures of musical talent.* New York: Psychological Corp.

Seashore, C. E. (1938). *Psychology of music.* New York: McGraw-Hill.

Sehmann, K. H. (2000). The effects of breath management instruction on the performance of elementary brass players. *Journal of Research in Music Education, 48*(2), 136–150.

Sims, W. L., & Nolker, B. D. (2000). Individual differences in music listening responses of Kindergarten children. *Journal of Research in Music Education, 50*(4), 292–300.

Slavin, R. E. (1984). *Research methods in education: A practical guide.* Boston: Allyn & Bacon.

Southern, E. (1971). *The music of black Americans: A history.* New York: W. W. Norton.

Stauffer, S. (2002). Life experiences of young composers and their compositions. *Journal of Research in Music Education, 50*(4), 301–322.

Steele, D. (1988). *An investigation into the background and implications of the Yale Seminar on music education.* Unpublished Doctoral dissertation, University of Cincinnati.

Tashakkori, A., & Teddlie, C. (Eds.). (2003). *Handbook of mixed methods in the social and behavioral sciences.* Thousand Oaks, CA: Sage.

Tesch, R. (1990). *Qualitative research: Analysis types and software tools.* New York: Falmer.

Tilly, C. (1990). How (and what) are historians doing? *American Behavioral Scientist, 33* (July/August), 698–706.

Turner, C., Gantz, B., Lowder, M., & Gfeller, K. (2005). Benefits seen in acoustic hearing + electric stimulation in same ear. *The Hearing Journal, 58*(11), 53–55.

Volk, T. M. (1993). Factors influencing music educators in the "rote-note" controversy, 1965–1900. *Bulletin of Historical Research in Music Education, 15*(1), 31–43.

Volk, T. M. (2003). Looking back in time: On being a music education historian. *Journal of Historical Research in Music Education, 25*(1), 49–59.

Watt, M. L. (1997). *Action research: Evolving professional practice through collaborative inquiry.* Retrieved April 6, 1999, from http://info.csd.org/WWW/resources/arc/essay1.html

Wheeler, B. L. (2002). Experiences and concerns of students during music therapy practica. *Journal of Music Therapy, 39*(4), 274–304.

Wolcott, H. T. (1994). *Transforming qualitative data: Description, analysis, and interpretation.* Thousand Oaks, CA: Sage Publications.

Yarbrough, C., & Price, H. E. (1989). Sequential patterns of instruction in music. *Journal of Research in Music Education, 37*(3), 179–187.

York, J., & Tundidor, J. (1995). Issues raised in the name of inclusion: Perspectives of education, parents, and students. *Journal of the Association for Persons with Severe Handicaps, 20,* 31–44.

Index